THE SELECTED LETTERS OF VOLTAIRE

THE SELECTED LETTERS
OF VOLTAIRE

Edited and
Translated by

RICHARD A. BROOKS

New York: NEW YORK UNIVERSITY PRESS   1973

CONTENTS

PREFACE

Voltaire was a man of his age and ours. He epitomizes in many ways the concerns of the Enlightenment and the profound belief of our own contemporary culture in the political and social commitment of the man of letters. To a greater degree and more consistently, perhaps, than any other important French literary figure of the eighteenth century, he worked in almost every one of the major genres of the period for purposes that seemed of immediate relevancy to the European Enlightenment. The expression of Voltaire's beliefs and concerns found many formats and many occasions as his art encompassed the theater, poetry, dialogue, narrative prose, history, philosophical treatises, the epic, dictionary and encyclopedia articles, literary criticism, and scientific discourses. But the most persistent of all the genres he practiced was the epistolary.

Voltaire's deep concern for the issues of his times is one source of his attraction for the modern reader. By following his life and work over the years of his long career, which lasted for well over three quarters of a century from the declining years of the Age of Louis XIV until the dawn of the French Revolution, one may have a perception of the entire gamut of eighteenth-century culture—its political and social life, the evolution of its history, the transformation of its religious and philosophic ideals, and the literary, theatrical and artistic life of the period. Yet, it is also precisely Voltaire's identification with the issues of his time and the use of his powerful pen for polemic and propaganda that have made a good part of his literary output—fifty-two volumes in the last complete edition of his works published at the end of the nineteenth-century —somewhat transitory and ephemeral. As the author of *Candide*, the *Philosophical Letters* and the *Age of Louis XIV* Voltaire has unquestionably achieved his immortality, but one ought not neglect the fact that he was also the creator of countless propagandistic plays and tracts that have long been forgotten by all but specialists of the period.

Certainly to Voltaire's desire to participate critically in the events and institutions of his time we owe a good part of his correspondence, a magnificent masterpiece of the epistolary art only recently published in the original French in an accurate and faithful edition of 107 volumes. These letters are not only a monument of eighteenth-century culture but of world literature as well. Voltaire wrote some twenty thousand letters over a period of sixty-seven years and about half of these have been preserved or have so far been recovered for posterity. This no doubt constitutes one of the most extensive and significant collections of letters by any important writer in world literature.

The history of the publication of these letters in successive censored editions in the eighteenth and nineteenth centuries reveals much about taste and editorial criteria during these periods. Understandably much of Voltaire's correspondence was unpublished in his lifetime and what did see the light of day was frequently bowdlerized so as not to offend living individuals. But even well into the nineteenth century, Voltaire was hardly looked upon as a neutral figure in French culture. During the return of the Bourbons to power after the French Revolution, for example, critical references to monarchy in his correspondence were excised from published editions, and later in the nineteenth century some of his letters were considered too scabrous or even obscene according to contemporary standards of taste to reach the public unexpurgated. French editors in the nineteenth century did not hesitate to edit his correspondence by omitting passages or by amalgamating a number of letters written at various times "to enhance their interest." Only during the last twenty years has a faithful edition of Voltaire's letters, based on high standards of editorial and scholarly criteria, been published in Switzerland through the efforts of Theodore Besterman as Director of the Voltaire Museum and Institute in Geneva. The new Voltaire to emerge from this unexpurgated edition is a livelier, more variegated, more forthright figure, and a more full-blooded human being.

Voltaire's correspondents numbered approximately twelve hundred. To be sure, these included a host of prominent and varied writers and intellectual figures of the age. There were, to cite some of the luminaries of this correspondence, the two principal editors of the *Encyclopédie*, D'Alembert and Diderot, his literary and philosophical *bête noire*, Jean-Jacques Rousseau, the playwrights Beaumarchais and Sedaine, the novelist and journalist Prévost, the scientific popularizer and academician Fontenelle, the naturalist Buffon, the philosophers Helvétius and Condorcet, the British writers Pope, Swift, Boswell and Walpole, the German playwright and essayist Lessing, the scientists Spallanzani, Bernoulli, Haller, Maupertuis, La Condamine and Mairan, the Italian writers Algarotti, Goldoni and Maffei, and the Russian dramatist and poet Sumarokov. Among the more secondary French writers there were Jean-Baptiste Rousseau, Destouches, Marmontel, Duclos, the anti-Encyclopedist Palissot, the critic La Harpe, etc.

From the time of his early adult years, Voltaire enjoyed the society of French aristocracy; he combined work and pleasure in various chateaux of the countryside and participated in the social life of Fontainebleau. He curried the favor and influence of men and women in power, and characteristically, in later life, he sought to use his connections for the public good in campaigning for freedom of the press, for international peace, for the correction of acts of judicial injustice or for other enterprises that might improve social, intellectual or religious conditions. Understandably, then, among Voltaire's correspondents are to be found many persons of influence in contemporary European political, social or religious life.

Among these were a number of the reigning princes of the period including Frederick II of Prussia to whom he wrote off and on over a period of some forty years, Catherine II of Russia who eventually acquired his library and a considerable portion of his personal archives, the kings of England and France, the queens of Prussia and France, Ulrica of Sweden and Christian VII of Denmark, and Stanislas Leszczynski and Stanislas Poniatowski, Kings of Poland. Important but lesser members of the nobility included Wilhelmina, Margravine of Bayreuth, Louise Dorothea, Duchess of Saxe-Gotha who sheltered Voltaire for a time after his falling out with Frederick of Prussia, the cosmopolitan Prince de

Ligne, adviser to Emperor Joseph II, and Dukes Charles Eugene and Louis Eugene of Württemberg with whom Voltaire had financial dealings.

Within France, Voltaire was in contact with many of his country's powerful statesmen. These included the foreign ministers Amelot de Chaillou and Choiseul, the D'Argenson brothers, the one foreign minister and the other minister of war, Cardinal de Bernis, the French ambassador to Vienna and secretary of state for foreign affairs, the prime ministers Cardinal Fleury and Cardinal Dubois, the libertine general and marshal of France, the Duc de Richelieu, and the physiocratic controller general of finances, Turgot. And outside of France, there were Kaunitz, the Austrian minister in control of foreign policy, the British statesmen Bolingbroke and Wilkes, Podewils, the Prussian secretary of state and foreign minister, Cocceji, the German jurist and chancellor of Prussia, the Hungarian Janos Fekete, chamberlain at the court of Vienna, the Russians Shuvalov, counsellor to Empress Elizabeth, Dmitry Alekseevich Galitzin and Dmitry Mikhailovich Galitzin, ambassadors to Paris and Vienna respectively, and Aleksandr Vorontsov, ambassador to The Hague, and the Danish foreign minister and later prime minister Bernstorff.

Despite his hostility to organized religion, Voltaire maintained a correspondence with some of the powerful ecclesiastical figures of the period when he found it necessary or to his advantage. These included Popes Benedict XIV and Clement XIII, many cardinals and bishops including Tencin, Passionei and Quirini, and influential Jesuits like Father Tournemine, editor of the important *Journal de Trévoux*, whom Voltaire had known from his student days under the Jesuits at the Lycée Louis-le-Grand.

Many of the social figures of the period with whom Voltaire corresponded were, of course, women, and his intimate exchange of letters with the important women in his life is among the more fascinating and revealing aspects of his correspondence. Naturally, he had never intended that most of these would reach the public eye and they expose, therefore, sides to his character that are most human and personal. Among the numerous ladies with whom he maintained an epistolary exchange were the Duchesse d'Aiguillon, whose son was an important figure at the court of Louis XV, Countess Bentinck, wife of the first earl of Portland and probably mistress of Voltaire during his Prussian sojourn, the Marquise de Bernières, wife of the president of the parlement of Rouen, Mme. Du Châtelet, Voltaire's mistress for many years and a fascinating woman of letters in her own right, the Duchesse de Choiseul, wife of the French foreign minister, Mme. Denis, Voltaire's niece and lover, Mme. Dupin, wife of the farmer-general and owner of the chateau at Chenonceaux, Mme. Du Deffand, one of the prominent social figures of Paris and a woman of letters, the Duchesse du Maine who was married to the son of Louis XIV and Mme. de Montespan, Mme. Necker, wife of the financier and leader of one of the principal salons in Paris, and the Marquise de Pompadour, mistress of Louis XV.

As a literary form, the letter was in great vogue in the eighteenth century. In the realm of fiction, it was the basis of one of the popular genres of the period, the epistolary novel. Important examples include Jean-Jacques Rousseau's *Nouvelle Héloïse* and Laclos's *Liaisons Dangereuses* in France and Richardson's *Clarissa* and *Pamela* in England. The epistolary novel could be practiced with extreme sophistication; it allowed for the introduction of sentiment, emphasis on individual personality, psychological analysis and realism during a period when authors were still largely committed to the theoretical principles of seventeenth-century classical aesthetics. Perhaps no work better than the *Liaisons Dangereuses* illustrates the capacity of the epistolary novel to be used with subtlety for the investigation of the human heart, for the achievement of psychological realism and for the destruction of personal illusion. The use of letters to depict a multifaceted reality is one of the brilliant accomplishments of Laclos's novel.

The popularity of the letter as a literary genre is also indicated by the wide use made of it in the dissemination of critical ideas. Two of the major works in the first part of the eighteenth century that were instrumental in the popularization and diffusion of liberal ideas in France were Montesquieu's *Persian Letters* (1721) and Voltaire's own *Philosophical Letters* (1734). The genre offered a number of advantages. It could treat a large variety of different topics through many individual letters; it could popularize important ideas by creating the illusion of personal communication; it allowed for flexibility since the letter was not hindered by the formalities of a classical aesthetic that still governed the major genres. The *Persian Letters* used the guise of a novelistic plot as a link between a series of letters whose principal purpose was a critique of contemporary France. In the *Philosophical Letters,* Voltaire refined the process by eliminating any fictional pretense and the use of the customary addressee and signature, and thereby broadened the concept of the term "letter." The *Philosophical Letters* were serious and witty at the same time. They were intended to reach a large popular audience who, under ordinary circumstances, would have been unaffected by or disinterested in a formal philosophical treatise, and these letters were extremely critical of the existing state of affairs in French intellectual, religious, political and social life. As Gustave Lanson put it, Voltaire's *Philosophical Letters* were the first bomb hurled against the *ancien régime.* Thus, as a purely personal form of communication, as a polemical device addressed to the public at large, as a novelistic form, and as a popular substitute for formal philosophical or political treatises, the letter played an extremely important role in eighteenth-century literary and intellectual life.

The more traditional type of public letter, addressed to patrons or friends, in which an author outlined aesthetic principles governing his craft, explained his purposes in writing a literary work, defended himself from critical attacks, praised the person to whom the work was dedicated or solicited something from him also had wide currency. Many of Voltaire's plays, like *Brutus, Alzire, Sémiramis, Tancrède* and *Irène,* contain such public letters which were often simply literary prefaces or dedicatory pieces. However, Voltaire had other and more frequent uses for the public letter. He wrote open letters to periodicals outlining his ideas on a great variety of subjects, like his letter of May 1764 to the *Gazette littéraire de l'Europe,* included in this volume, which sets forth his views on the writing of ancient history. He also exchanged letters with public figures that he knew would ultimately find their way into the public domain. A celebrated example is his literary and philosophical quarrel with Jean-Jacques Rousseau which was carried on in part by an exchange of letters that included the communication of August 30, 1755 to Rousseau criticizing the *Discourse on the Origin of Inequality* which began unforgettably: "I have received your new book against the human race. I thank you for it." On a more subtle level, Voltaire was also aware that certain of his private letters, like those to Mme. Du Deffand and some of his Encyclopedist friends, might be read by others in addition to their designated recipients.

Voltaire's correspondence may be usefully considered in three categories. (1) There were letters that were highly confidential and intended strictly for their addressees or a limited group of acquaintances. These might include his passionate love letters to his niece, Mme. Denis, or certain letters to philosopher friends like D'Alembert or Diderot or to his publisher which, if published or disseminated widely, might have placed either party in jeopardy. Voltaire's business letters may also be included here. (2) A second grouping comprises letters that were less personal and which could be passed around among friends frequenting his social milieu. These would include letters to Mme. Du Deffand read to guests at her Parisian salon, letters to persons in public life, and letters to antagonists in which Voltaire defended himself or friends, and letters to philosophical and literary friends that would not have compromised him with the authorities. (3) A third grouping includes the manifestly public letters discussed above. Clearly, these three categories are not mutually exclusive since the distinction between the private and public aspects of Voltaire's career was frequently confused by one who was so involved in public affairs and who was also surely among the most social human beings of his time. Yet this private-public distinction can be useful since this characteristic of Voltaire's letters had a profound effect on their composition, their language and style, and their publication.

Among the interesting aspects of the letter as a genre is its flexibility with respect to content, language, style, purpose, publication and, to some degree, form. While Voltaire practiced a good many of the accepted literary forms of his time and possessed an infinitely subtle command of the French language, perhaps in no other genre did he make use of so great a variety of styles and incorporate such diverse subject matter as in his letters. Voltaire was capable of being obsequious, correct, cold, merely didactic, ironic, insulting, familiar, intimate, pathetic, passionate, ribald or obscene depending upon the occasion, and this stylistic variety makes for much of the literary and human interest of his letters.

Something of the range of Voltaire's epistolary styles and purposes may be suggested by two letters he wrote in the 1740s, both in the Italian language. The first is dated January 9, 1746 from Versailles and was addressed to the papal nuncio Cardinal Domenico Passionei. Around this time, Voltaire had been engaged in a campaign to gain entrance to the conservative Académie Française. Apparently, despite his scorn for the Church and his liberal religious attitudes, he did not think it unworthy of himself to solicit the support of the Vatican as a guarantee for the propriety of his religious opinions and hence fitness to be elected to the Académie. The laudatory and flattering style of the following letter to the Vatican official indicates much about Voltaire's sense of pragmatism:

> Your Eminence's pupil has the audacity to write in Italian to one who is his master in French. Truly I am not astonished that Your Eminence is one who belongs to all countries. He was appreciated and held in esteem by everyone in Holland at the time of the Peace of Utrecht; he later gained the affection of Louis XIV; he obtained the friendship and admiration of the entire imperial court in Vienna, and he is presently profiting from all of these favorable feelings in the world's capital where he has been its principal embellishment.
>
> . . . And while abandoning hope of being able to place myself under Your Eminence's protection in Rome, I will derive some advantage in Paris at least from such great kindness of yours. . . . In the meantime, I humbly kiss the border of Your Eminence's sacred purple robe. With deep obeisance, I remain Your Eminence's very humble, very devoted and very indebted servant.

If this letter was written by one of the severest critics of the Roman Catholic Church and its hierarchy in the eighteenth century, it should also be pointed out that Voltaire was elected to the Académie Française on April 25, 1746.

The second communication is one of a series of passionate love letters in Italian that Voltaire wrote to his niece Mme. Denis. Here, apparently, the use of a foreign language was for the purpose of greater intimacy, candor and liberty of expression; clearly also the psychological effect of a letter written in a language foreign to both the writer and the recipient was quite different from one composed in their native French. Curiously, by making use of Italian Voltaire was able to express himself with greater permissiveness and directness than if he had written this letter in French. Composed in September 1747, the letter reveals a number of interesting sides to Voltaire's personality: his sensitivity to the variations of his physical health, his sentimentality, his unabashed sensuality, and his social grace.

> I fell sick at Anet, my dearest, but I hope to recover my health with you. As soon as I arrive, I will rush to you to restore my strength. So today is the day I will see you; today I will rediscover the only consolation that can sweeten the bitterness. Nature, which granted me the tenderest of hearts, forgot to give me a stomach. I am incapable of digesting, but I am capable of love. I love you; I will love you until the day I die. I embrace you a thousand times, my dear virtuoso. You write Italian better than I do. You deserve to be admitted to the Academy della Crusca. My heart and my phallus send you the most affectionate compliments. Tonight I will see you for sure.

The traditional myth of a totally rational and intellectual Voltaire, with no deep emotions or compassion, is certainly belied by his correspondence.

Voltaire's letters will be of interest to a diversity of readers. For the student of literature, they are an outstanding example of a significant genre whose traditions go back to antiquity. They are the creations of a man for whom style and form were of the utmost importance, and in them one may observe a master craftsman exercising total control over his instrument of expression. At the same time, they record the life of a fascinating human being in his public disguises and private passions. They are varied, many-sided, and stimulating as a revelation of humanity and inspiring as an example of human potentiality and artistry. These letters are also, to be sure, an important literary document by one of the great writers of the eighteenth century: a document about himself as a creative writer and thinker, about contemporary and past writers, and about literary taste, judgment and criticism.

The historian may use Voltaire's letters to advantage as a primary source for information about life in the eighteenth century. The social, political, military, religious, intellectual and cultural life of the period is reflected in thousands of letters written over a period of almost seventy years that includes the Regency, the regime of Louis XV and the initial years of Louis XVI. Marie Leszczynska, Louis XV, Frederick the Great, Pope Benedict XIV, Mme. de Pompadour, Catherine the Great and Turgot, among the luminaries of the period, all figure in one way or another in this vast correspondence. The professional historian also has the opportunity through this correspondence to observe at close range one of the great historical writers of the Enlightenment—the author of the *Age of Louis XIV*, the *History of Charles XII* and the *Essay on Customs*—at work reflecting over the problems of historiography both ancient and modern: the criteria of historical evidence, the role of censorship, questions of access to source materials, the ethics of sponsored history and the elaboration of the fundamentally new concept of cultural history.

For the philosopher and the student of the history of ideas, the letters will clarify Voltaire's contributions in the dissemination of liberal ideas and in changing the intellectual climate of his period from one in which Cartesian metaphysics and established Christianity were accepted as part of the order of the day to one in which they were replaced by Newtonian physics, Lockean epistemology and the principles of deism. The letters can be extremely useful in illuminating the background to and the shaping influences on Voltaire's way of thinking. Voltaire's great admiration for freedom of thought in eighteenth-century England, his faith in the value of the natural sciences and his proselytizing on behalf of Newton and Locke, and the background to the publication of one of the most important intellectual documents of the period, his *Philosophical Letters*, are described in fascinating detail in his letters. One may observe Voltaire in the process of philosophizing with his former Jesuit masters, arguing ideas with the Royal Prince of Prussia, and arriving at his essential conviction about the futility of metaphysics and the limited profit to be derived from abstract philosophical speculation. Voltaire frequently reacted very personally and emotionally to the philosophical issues of the day, and this is demonstrated in his letters time and again; we may note his developing antipathy for Leibnizian metaphysics and philosophical optimism, the catalytic effect on his moral and religious outlook caused by the Lisbon earthquake of 1755 and the anguish he experienced for the human condition after that event, and his pathetic expression of a need for a "God who speaks to the human race." His consistent rejection of atheism, his unrelenting critique of established religions, his work on behalf of religious toleration, and his criticism of religious suppression, whether in Catholic Paris or Calvinist Geneva, are among the religious issues discussed in clarifying detail in this vast correspondence. Voltaire's belief in the capacity of the *philosophes* and the Encyclopedists to bring about a transformation of the intellectual climate of the *ancien régime* and, more pragmatically, his tactics in effecting meaningful change with the assistance of men of influence and power in the framework of a rather conservative political stance are frequently illustrated in his daily exchange of letters. His speculations on economic theory with the physiocrats are an interesting feature of the closing years of his correspondence. In general, the historian of ideas will find that most of Voltaire's major concerns as a thinker and as an activist make their way into this rich epistolary exchange.

In fact, the wealth of information about life in the eighteenth century to be garnered from Voltaire's letters is almost endless. The subjects that form the basis of his letters are often unpredictable since the rhythm and content of his correspondence follow the vagaries of his life and thought, obviously without the predetermined plan of more formal literary works. A seemingly unimportant letter that Voltaire wrote in December 1723 may be used to illustrate this point. The addressee was the Baron de Preuilly, the father of Mme. Du Châtelet, Voltaire's mistress during the Cirey period of the 1730s and 1740s, and the occasion was Voltaire's stay at the Chateau of Maisons during which both he and his host, the young Président de Maisons, contracted smallpox. The letter provides an invaluable description of smallpox as it was popularly understood in the eighteenth century and indicates various contemporary theories for curing it. The seriousness of the disease in Voltaire's time is suggested by some of his reactions on learning of his affliction: he took confession, drew up his last will and testament, and calmly proceeded to await his death. His treatment consisted of several emetics, two hundred pints of lemonade (but none of the stimulants usually given to such patients in the eighteenth century) and bleeding. Voltaire's rationale for the bleeding and the terminology he uses in the letter are rather informative about the state of medical knowledge in the eighteenth century:

When it [smallpox] is accompanied by a high fever, when the increased volume of blood in the vessels is about to burst them, when the deposit is ready to form in the brain and the body is filled with bile and foreign matter whose fermentation excites mortal destruction in the machine, then reason itself should teach us that bleeding is indispensable. It will purify the blood; it will relax the vessels; it will make their resiliency easier and more supple; it will relieve the skin glands and favor the breaking out of rashes. Then, medicines will remove the source of the illness by means of large evacuations and in carrying away a part of the smallpox leaven with them will freely allow what remains to develop more completely and prevent the smallpox from being confluent. Finally, it is evident that lemon syrup in refreshing infusion relaxes the acrimony of the blood, pacifies its ardor, flows with it through the miliary glands up to the pimples, opposes the corrosion of the leaven, and even prevents the marks which the pustules usually make on the face.

The letter alludes to various contemporary remedies like the powder of Countess Kent, the balm of Vauseguer and the remedy of M. Agnan—stimulants designed to separate coagulating blood—and, to be sure, we hear the author's complaints about the medical charlatans overrunning Paris.

The same letter also reveals interesting details about an apparently unrelated subject—eighteenth-century architecture. After Voltaire had recovered from his bout with smallpox and just as he was leaving Maisons, the castle caught fire and apparatus had to be called in from Paris to help quench the flames. The source of the conflagration was discovered to be a faulty construction beam situated beneath a fireplace. Evidently the heat generated from the fireplace built up very gradually and caused the beam to ignite after a period of two days, just at the moment of Voltaire's departure. This type of architectural defect was subsequently corrected in new construction, Voltaire informs us, but only after numerous lawsuits occasioned by similar accidents.

If one reads through this vast correspondence widely enough, then, it will yield unexpected and fascinating firsthand information about almost every aspect of eighteenth-century life ranging from architecture, medicine and science to literature, politics, society and history.

Among Voltaire's great qualities as a letter writer was his ability to observe the contemporary scene and to communicate to his correspondents some of the special moments of his existence. An interesting example is his description of the marriage of Louis XV which he sent to the Marquise de Bernières on September 17, 1725. The letter is a rather telling commentary on French society in the early part of the eighteenth century; in a few pages one discovers the true relationship of the ordinary citizen to royalty, one learns about the rights of succession to government offices, and one becomes aware of the paramount importance of amusing the Queen. Voltaire's pen roams from speculating about the King's wedding night and His Majesty's boasts about his sexual prowess on that occasion to describing the Queen's physical and moral characteristics, the public and private amusements of the wedding celebration, the form and the substance of a royal marriage and inevitably to Voltaire's own courting of the Queen in his search for literary patronage.

As I have suggested, one of the revelations of the correspondence is the peculiarly emotional and sensitive side of this man. With it the stereotype of a totally cerebral Voltaire evaporates as the reader accompanies him through his personal crises. We witness him weeping at the death of his sister, concluding that his experience of life is "but a dream full of starts of folly, and of fancied and true miseries." We observe him complaining to correspondent after correspondent over the years of poor health and physical suffering and sometimes expressing doubts about his ability to carry on with the affairs of life. "My life is merely the journal of a sick man," he wrote characteristically to his niece Mme. Denis in 1748, predicting the possibility of his imminent death some thirty years before the actual event. We feel his grief at the death of his mistress Mme. Du Châtelet and as he seeks consolation for his anguish in the company of Mme. Denis and Mme. Du Deffand. "The sensitivity of your heart is my refuge in my despair," he wrote to the latter as he asked for permission to weep at her feet. To be sure, we also witness his experiences of personal joy and of deep emotional satisfaction with life on other occasions. We learn of his pleasure in gardens and beautiful residences, of his desire for personal comfort and of his deep need for independence. Curiously, but characteristically, the same man who thought he had been at death's door ten years earlier wrote in 1758 to his friend Formont from Geneva: "I know of no condition preferable to mine. It would be madness to want to change it."

The variability of Voltaire's emotional state, evident in these letters, is perhaps the most important factor in explaining otherwise apparently contradictory mutations in his philosophical attitudes. This is particularly true of his evolution from the optimism of the Cirey period, based in large part on personal feelings of physical and emotional well being, to repeated expressions of despair and anxiety over the human condition in works of the Ferney period like the *Poem on the Lisbon Earthquake* and *Candide*. The process of aging and the physical disrepair accompanying it that also surely took their toll on Voltaire's outlook are reflected in this correspondence. As he wrote in a letter to Mme. Du Deffand at the age of seventy: "Rarely is the final period of life very pleasant. We have always hoped vainly that we would enjoy life, and in the end all we can do is endure it."

Among the most moving letters of this emotional man of reason were those written in Paris during the last four months of his life, from February to May 1778, to his doctor, Theodore Tronchin, describing in detail his agonizing final illness. Always sensitive to pain and to any diminution of his health, Voltaire already considered himself a dead man on his arrival in Paris in February after long years of exile, but the process of dying actually took about ten weeks. These last letters are all the more remarkable since despite great physical pain and his pleas for pity from his physician, the hand of the great stylist of the French language remains very much in evidence. His very last letter dated May 26, 1778, just four days before his death at the age of eighty-four, is a worthy finale to his career as *auteur engagé*. Among the various campaigns against injustice in which Voltaire had involved himself was his attempt to rehabilitate the memory of the Comte de Lally, a French officer who had conceived the idea of reconquering India from the English but who was ultimately obliged to surrender to the British military forces at Pondichéry. Judged responsible for the French defeat there, Lally was condemned to death by his compatriots in 1766 as punishment for this ignominy. Voltaire's campaign for his rehabilitation began in 1773, but proved to be successful only after five years of struggle. This is the subject of his last letter addressed to Lally's son and which contains but four short sentences:

> The dying man was restored to life when he learned of this great piece of news. He embraces M. de Lally very affectionately. He sees that the king is the defender of justice. He will die content.

To the very end, Voltaire's commitment to the struggle against injustice and intolerance was not a purely cerebral and disinterested affair but one that was totally personal and passionate. Nowhere is the character of this commitment more in evidence than in the most personal of his writings—his letters.

In preparing this English translation of the selected letters of Voltaire, I wish to make available to American readers a representative cross section of this vast correspondence. The limitations of such an enterprise are obvious. I have attempted to select "representative" letters covering a wide variety of topics and from the various periods of Voltaire's long career. While it is likely that any selection from a storehouse of many thousands of letters published in a single volume will reflect the prejudices and tastes of an editor, it is, nevertheless, hoped that the reader's comprehension of eighteenth-century culture will be broadened and that his appetite will have been whetted to read more of Voltaire's work.

Translation should ideally serve as a bridge between cultures. In rendering these letters into English, I have attempted to reconcile the goal of reproducing in English as accurately as possible what Voltaire wrote in French (and other languages) with that of conveying the tone of voice and rhythm of the original. When the two occasionally came into conflict, verbal accuracy was considered secondary to recreating a literate text that might be appreciated by an English-speaking reader. Nevertheless, every effort has been made to reproduce these letters in a manner as faithful to the original as possible, and no additions, excisions or alterations of any kind have been made in the texts. Modern usage has been observed, however, in the spelling of proper nouns and in punctuation, except in the case of Voltaire's English letters which are reproduced as he wrote them.

A brief chronology of Voltaire's life follows this introduction. In addition, biographical notes are provided throughout to help the reader situate the letters in the context of Voltaire's career. Editorial notes have been provided at the conclusion of each chapter to clarify references or occasional difficult points in the letters. Finally, an index of proper names, prepared with the assistance of Carmen Coll, is provided for the entire volume.

The editor wishes to express his debt to Theodore Besterman's monumental edition of Voltaire's *Correspondence* published in Geneva in 107 volumes from 1953 to 1965. It is a pleasure to thank my colleagues Professor J. Robert Loy of the City University of New York and Professor John Pappas of Fordham University for reading the manuscript of this volume and for making a number of useful suggestions and corrections. My debt to my wife Eva who helped nurture this project and who read the manuscript with both a critical eye and tender loving care is not to be expressed in words.

CHRONOLOGY OF IMPORTANT DATES
IN VOLTAIRE'S CAREER

1694	November 21	Birth of Françoise-Marie Arouet in Paris.
1701	July 13	Death of Voltaire's mother.
1704	October	Voltaire enrolls in the celebrated Jesuit school, the Collège Louis-le-Grand.
1711	August 5	Voltaire leaves Louis-le-Grand and becomes a law student.
1713	September	Voltaire joins the Marquis de Châteauneuf, the French ambassador to The Hague, as his secretary. He becomes enamored of "Pimpette" to the consternation of her mother.
	December 24	Voltaire is dismissed by the ambassador and returns to Paris. His father wishes to exile him to America.
1714		Voltaire resumes his law studies. He meets Thieriot who will become one of his most intimate friends for many years. He frequents the freethinking Society of the Temple.
1715	September 1	Death of Louis IV. Voltaire is at work on his tragedy *Oedipus* and his epic poem *The Henriade*.
1717	May 16	Voltaire is imprisoned in the Bastille for eleven months.

1718	November 18	The premiere performance of *Oedipus* is a tremendous success. The author assumes the name Voltaire.
1719	Summer	Voltaire leads a worldly existence visiting chateaux in the French countryside.
1720		Visits the Duc de Richelieu at his chateau and the exiled Lord Bolingbroke at the Chateau de La Source near Orleans.
1721	November	Voltaire offers the manuscript of *The Henriade* to the Regent. He profits from the speculative collapse of Law's System.
1722	January 1	Death of Voltaire's father.
	July-October	Travels to Cambrai, Brussels and The Hague in the company of Mme. de Rupelmonde. Quarrels with the poet Jean-Baptiste Rousseau. Composes his deistic poem, *The Epistle to Urania*.
1723	November	Voltaire catches smallpox at Maisons.
1725	September 5	Voltaire attends the marriage of Louis XV on which occasion three of his plays are performed.
	October 6	He send *The Henriade* to George I of England.
1726	April 17	After attempting to provoke the Chevalier de Rohan to a duel, Voltaire is sent to the Bastille.
	May 5	Voltaire is in Calais on his way to exile in England.
	September	Death of Voltaire's sister, Mme. Mignot.
1727	January	Presented to King George I.
	April 8	Newton is buried at Westminster Abbey during Voltaire's stay in London.

	December	Voltaire publishes two treatises in English: *The Essay on Civil Wars* and *The Essay on Epick Poetry.*
1728	March	Dedicates *The Henriade* to the Queen of England.
	November	Voltaire returns to France and is allowed to live in Paris the following April.
1729	May	At the court of Lorraine.
1730	March 15	Voltaire is present at the death of the celebrated actress Adrienne Lecouvreur. Her body is cast in the garbage dump after being denied burial by the clergy. Voltaire's indignation is aroused and he writes his poem on *The Death of Mademoiselle Lecouvreur.*
	December 11	Premiere performance of his tragedy *Brutus,* a great success.
1731		Voltaire's *History of Charles XII* is published.
1732	August 13	Tremendous success of his play *Zaïre.*
1733	June	The beginning of his long affair with Madame du Châtelet.
1734	May 6	Voltaire flees to Lorraine following the publication of his *Philosophical Letters* and the issuance of a warrant for his arrest.
	July	Voltaire settles at Mme. du Châtelet's castle in Cirey.
1735	March 2	He receives permission to return to Paris.
1736	August 8	Frederick, Crown Prince of Prussia, begins a correspondence with Voltaire.
	December 9	Voltaire flees to the Netherlands following the circulation of numerous copies of his poem *Le Mondain* [*The Worldling*].

1737	March	Return to Cirey.
	October	Voltaire's brother, Armand Arouet, is arrested for Jansenist activities.
1738		Publication of Voltaire's *Elements of the Philosophy of Newton.*
	May 2	Voltaire and Mme. du Châtelet compete separately and unsuccessfully for the prize of the Academy of Science awarded for a treatise on the nature of fire.
1740	September 11	First meeting of Voltaire and Frederick, who had become King of Prussia.
	November	Voltaire is in Remusberg and Berlin.
1741	April	Successful presentation of his tragedy *Mohammed* in Lille.
		The war of the Austrian Succession. Voltaire has a financial interest in the supplying of meat and munitions.
1742	August 19	Premiere performance of *Mohammed* in Paris. Performance of the play is prohibited following religious protest.
	September 2-7	Voltaire meets Frederick II at Aix-la-Chapelle. He is authorized semi-officially by the French government to persuade Frederick to join its side in the war.
1743	September-October	Another diplomatic mission to Berlin and Bayreuth. Frederick tries to persuade Voltaire to settle in Prussia to the chagrin of Mme. du Châtelet who fears she will be abandoned.
	November 3	Voltaire is elected to the Royal Society of London.
1744	November 28	Voltaire's old schoolmate, the Marquis d'Argenson, becomes Minister of Foreign Affairs.

1745	January	At Versailles to direct rehearsals of his play *The Princess of Navarre,* which is to be performed at court in honor of the dauphin's marriage.
	February 18	Voltaire's brother Armand dies.
	March 27	Voltaire is named Royal Historiographer.
	August	Correspondence with the Pope.
	September	Beginning of Voltaire's affair with his niece, Mme. Denis.
1746	April 25	Elected to the French Academy.
	November	Named Gentleman Ordinary of the King's Chamber.
1747	June	The first version of Voltaire's tale *Zadig* is printed in Holland.
1748	February-April	Voltaire visits Nancy, Lunéville and Commercy and stays at the court of Stanislas Lesaczinski, father-in-law of Louis XV.
	October	Voltaire discovers Mme. du Châtelet in the arms of her lover, Saint-Lambert.
1749	January	Mme. du Châtelet is pregnant, and M. du Châtelet is told he is to become a father.
	September 10	Death of Mme. du Châtelet in childbirth.
	October	Voltaire returns to Paris and the house he occupied with Mme. du Châtelet.
1750		Mme. Denis joins Voltaire and lives with him in Paris.
	June	Voltaire is named Chamberlain by Frederick II and he leaves for his court. Voltaire will return to Paris only twenty-eight years later, shortly before his death.
	November-December	Growing disenchantment between Voltaire and Frederick.

1751	September 2	Frederick comments on Voltaire: "We squeeze the orange and throw away the rind."
1752		Publication of the *conte Micromégas.*
	December 24	Frederick publicly burns in Berlin *The Diatribe of Doctor Akakia,* a work in which Voltaire ridiculed an important official of the Prussian government, Maupertuis, Director of the Berlin Academy.
1753	March 27	Having quarreled with Frederick, Voltaire leaves Berlin.
	April-May	Voltaire stays with the Duchess of Saxe-Gotha.
	May 31-July 7	Arrest and detention of Voltaire in Frankfurt on orders from Frederick.
	October 2-November 11	Voltaire settles in Colmar having been forbidden by Louis XV from coming to Paris.
1754	December	Voltaire is in Geneva.
1755	February	Voltaire purchases his property in Geneva and calls it *Les Délices.*
	July	The Consistory of Geneva complains of the theatrical performances given at Les Délices.
	November 24	Voltaire learns of the earthquake at Lisbon and begins his *Poem on the Disaster at Lisbon.*
	December	Beginning of his collaboration on the *Encyclopédie.*
1756	May 18	Beginning of the Seven Years War.
	August	D'Alembert comes to Les Délices. Preparation of the article "Geneva" for the *Encyclopédie.*

	December	Voltaire intervenes unsuccessfully on behalf of the British admiral Byng who is sentenced to death on charges of treason.
		Publication of Voltaire's *Essay on Customs*.
1757	December	The publication of the article "Geneva" causes a scandal in Geneva, and Voltaire is accused of having inspired its composition. In Paris a campaign is launched against the *philosophes*.
1758	January	D'Alembert resign from the *Encyclopédie*.
	July-August	Voltaire is at Schwetzingen with the Palatine Elector. He works on *Candide*.
	October-December	Voltaire wants to acquire property outside of Geneva and purchases Ferney and Tournay.
1759	January	Publication of *Candide*.
	February 6	The Parlement of Paris condemns the *Encyclopédie*, Voltaire's *Poem on Natural Law*, and Helvétius's *De l'Esprit*.
	May 2	Palissot's comedy ridiculing the *philosophes* is published.
	Fall	Voltaire is used as an intermediary in secret peace negotiations between France and Prussia.
1760	October	Frequent theatrical performances at Ferney and Les Délices cause renewed complaints from religious authorities.
	December	Voltaire adopts Marie-Françoise Corneille, a descendant of the playwright.
1761		Voltaire at work on his edition of Corneille to provide a dowry for Mlle. Corneille.

	September	The Parlement of Paris orders an examination of the Jesuit Constitutions, a device that will eventually lead to the expulsion of the Jesuits from France.
1762	April 4	Voltaire begins his campaign on behalf of Jean Calas who had been executed in Toulouse on March 10.
	June 19	Condemnation of Rousseau's *Emile* and the *Social Contract* in Geneva.
1763	December	Publication of Voltaire's *Treatise on Tolerance*.
1764	March	Voltaire proposes the establishment of a colony of French Protestants in Guyana.
	June	First edition of the *Philosophical Dictionary*.
1765	March 9	Final rehabilitation of Calas.
		The printing of Voltaire's *Philosophy of History* in Holland.
1766	May	*The Ignorant Philosopher.*
	July	The Chevalier de La Barre is executed, and Voltaire's *Philosophical Dictionary* is burned with his body. *The Account of the Chevalier de La Barre* by Voltaire.
		Voltaire proposes that the *philosophes* leave France and settle in Cleves on Prussian soil.
1767		Publication of his *conte*, *The Ingénu*, and of his burlesque poem on *The Civil War of Geneva*.
1768	March	Voltaire quarrels with Mme. Denis and orders her to leave Ferney.
		The Princess of Babylon, a *conte*.
1769	October	Mme. Denis returns to Ferney.

1770	January	Voltaire begins a two-year project: the nine volumes of his *Questions Concerning the Encyclopédie*.
	August	Voltaire composes a refutation of D'Holbach's atheistic treatise *The System of Nature*.
1771	November 25	Final acquittal of Sirven on whose behalf Voltaire had been working.
1772	November 23	Death of Voltaire's friend Thieriot.
1773	February-March	Voltaire is seriously ill with strangury, a disease that will eventually kill him.
1774		*The White Bull*, a *conte*.
	May 10	Death of Louis XV.
1775	December	Turgot issues his edict separating the territory of Gex from the *fermes générales,* an act sought by Voltaire.
		Voltaire expresses his admiration for Turgot's economic policies.
1776	April	Publication of Voltaire's *The Bible Finally Explained*.
1778	February 10	Voltaire returns to Paris and is publicly acclaimed.
	May 30	Voltaire dies in Paris in his eighty-fourth year.
		Clandestine burial of Voltaire in the Abbey of Seillières at five o'clock in the morning.

I

YOUNG VOLTAIRE

(1694-1734)

YOUNG VOLTAIRE

[François-Marie Arouet, the future Voltaire, was born on November 21, 1694 in the parish of Saint-André-des-Arts in Paris, the son of François, an influential notary, and of Marguerite d'Aumard. At the age of ten, he lost his mother and began a Jesuit education at the Collège Louis-le-Grand. In 1711, the seventeen-year old François-Marie Arouet became associated with the Templars, noted for their impiety and libertinism, concluded his studies at Louis-le-Grand, and became a law student. Dissatisfied with his son's libertine life, Arouet's father, in an effort to get him to settle down, sent him off to the French embassy at The Hague as a secretary. In Holland he became amorously involved with young Olympe Du Noyer (nicknamed Pimpette), a French Protestant girl who had fled to Holland with her mother to escape religious persecution in France. The girl's mother opposed the relationship and complained to the French ambassador.]

1. *"Our love is based on virtue."*

To Catherine-Olympe Du Noyer. c. November 28, 1713.

I am a prisoner here in the name of the king. But it is within their power to take my life away and not my love for you. Yes, my adorable mistress, I will see you tonight even if it means the scaffold. In the name of God, do not speak to me in terms as fatal as those you use to write me. Live and be prudent. Be on your guard with your mother as you might with your most cruel enemy. What am I saying? Be on your guard with everyone; trust no one. Be ready as soon as the moon is out. I will leave *incognito;* I will get a carriage or a chaise; we will be off to Scheveningen like the wind! I will bring paper and ink; we will compose our letters. But if you love me, console yourself; heed all your virtue and presence of mind. Restrain yourself with your mother. Try to get your portrait, and you may believe that the preparation of the greatest tortures will not prevent me from serving you. No, nothing can keep us apart. Our love is based on virtue; it will last as long as we live. Order your bootmaker to get a chaise; no, I do not want you to confide in him. Be ready at four. I will wait for you near your street. Farewell. There is nothing to which I would not expose myself for you. You deserve much more. Farewell, my dear heart.

A ***

2. *"I only know that I love you."*

To Catherine-Olympe Du Noyer. Thursday morning, December 28, 1713.

I left The Hague with M. de M. . . last Monday at eight o'clock in the morning; we embarked at Rotterdam where it was absolutely impossible for me to write you. I instructed Le Fèvre to inform you of my departure. Instead of taking the road to Antwerp where I was expecting one of your letters, we took the road to Gand; consequently I mailed a letter for you at Gand in care of Mme. Santoc de Maisan. I arrived in Paris on Christmas eve. The first thing I did was to see Father Tournemine.[1] This Jesuit had written me at The Hague the day I left. He is having your relative, the Bishop of Evreux, act in your behalf. I handed your three letters over to him, and they are now preparing your father to see you again soon. That is what I have done for you. Here is my present fate. I had hardly arrived in Paris when I learned that M. L. . . had written a scathing letter against me to my father, that he had sent him the letters your mother had written him, and, finally, that my father has a *lettre de cachet* to have me locked up. I dare not show my face. I have had people speak to my father; the most they could get him to concede to was

4

to ship me out to the islands.[2] But they were unable to get him to change his mind about his will in which he disinherits me. That is not all. For more than three weeks, I have had no news from you. I do not know whether you are alive and living really miserably. I fear you wrote me in care of my father and that your letter has been opened by him. In such cruel circumstances, I must not present myself to your family. They will all be unaware that you are returning to France by my doing, and that Father Tournemine is now completely charged with your affair. You see that I am now in the depths of unhappiness and that, unless I were abandoned by you, it would absolutely be impossible to be more wretched. You see, on the other hand, that your happiness depends on you alone. You have only one additional step to take. Leave as soon as you receive your father's orders. You will be at the Parisian convent with Mme. C. . . .[3] You will easily endear yourself to your entire family, completely gain the friendship of your father, and make a happy lot for yourself in Paris. You love me, my dear. . . . You know how much I love you. Certainly my affection deserves to be reciprocated. I have done everything I could to restore your well-being. To make you happy, I have steeped myself in the greatest of misfortunes; you can make me the happiest of all men. To do that, come back to France; make yourself happy; then I will consider myself well rewarded. In a day, I can restore myself completely in the good graces of my father, and we can freely enjoy the pleasure of seeing each other. I picture these happy moments as the end of all our sorrows and as the beginning of a sweet and pleasant life, such as you should lead in Paris. If you are cruel enough to make me lose the fruit of all my misfortunes and to persist in remaining in Holland, I promise you most assuredly that I will kill myself as soon as I hear such news. In the sad state I find myself, you alone can make me love life. But, alas, I speak here of my ills while you, perhaps, are unhappier than I. I have all sorts of fears for your health; I have all sorts of fears about your mother. Horrible ideas come to my mind about these things. In the name of God, enlighten me. But, alas, I even fear that you will not receive my letter. Ah, how unhappy I am, my dear heart, and how my heart is given over to a deep and just sadness. Perhaps you wrote to me in Antwerp or Brussels. Perhaps you wrote to me in Paris. But, in fact, for three weeks I have had no news

5

from you. As soon as you can, write me everything in care of M. Du Tilly, rue Maubuë, at the Red Rose. Write me a really long letter, giving me reliable news about your situation. We are both very unhappy, but we love each other. Mutual affection is very sweet consolation. Never has love been equal to mine because no one ever deserves to be loved more than you. If my sincere affection can console you, I myself am consoled. A host of thoughts come to mind. I cannot put them on paper. Sadness, fear, and love are stirring me violently, but I keep repeating to myself secretly that I have done nothing that could offend an upright man, and that helps me considerably in bearing my sorrow. I have made it a real point of duty to love you; I will fulfill this duty all my life. You will never be cruel enough to abandon me, my dear. . . . My beautiful mistress, my dear heart, write me soon, or better yet immediately. As soon as I have seen your letter, I will inform you of my fate. I do not know yet what will become of me. I am horribly uncertain about everything. I only know that I love you. Ah! When will I be able to embrace you, my dear heart?

A ✻✻✻

[Back in Paris, Arouet returned to his law studies. At the age of twenty, he competed unsuccessfully for the poetry prize of the Académie Française. In 1716, he wrote his first tragedy, Oedipus, triumphantly presented on the Parisian stage two years later. He formed a new liaison with Suzanne de Livry, a young lady Arouet brought back with him to Paris from his stay at the country estate of the Duc de Sully. For Suzanne, he had the famous portrait of himself executed by Largillière. Arouet was accused of writing a satirical poem critical of the Duc d'Orléans, Regent of France, and on May 17, 1717 he was sent to the Bastille where he remained until April 11 of the following year. It was around this time that he assumed the name Voltaire.]

3. *"I believe I have profited from my misfortunes."*

To Louis-Charles de Machaut.[4] Chatenay. Holy Wednesday, April 15, 1718.

Sir,
Let the first use of my freedom be to thank you for procuring it. I will be able to indicate my gratitude to you only by making myself worthy, through my conduct, of this grace and of your protection. I believe I have profited from my misfortunes, and I dare assure you that I have no less obligation to Monseigneur, the Regent, for my imprisonment than for my freedom. I have committed many faults, but I beseech you, sir, to assure His Royal Highness that I am neither so wicked nor so half-witted as to have written against him. I have never spoken of this prince except in admiration of his genius, and I would have said the same about him even if he had had the good fortune of being a private person. I have always revered him all the more deeply since I know that he detests being praised as much as he deserves it. Although you resemble him in that respect, I cannot keep from expressing my satisfaction at being in your hands and from telling you that your integrity assures me of my life's good fortune.
I am, with much respect and gratitude, sir, your very humble and very obedient servant.

Arouet

4. *The Liberty of Asking Three Favors*

To Philippe II, Duc d'Orléans, Regent of France.
November 1718(?)

Monseigneur,
Will poor Voltaire be compelled to be in your debt only because you punished him with a year in the Bastille? He felt sure that after placing him in purgatory you would remember him when you opened the gates of paradise to all. He takes the liberty of asking three favors of you: the first to allow him the honor of dedicating to you the tragedy he has just composed,[5] the second

7

to be willing one day to hear selections of an epic poem about that ancestor of yours whom you resemble the most,[6] and the third to consider that I have the honor of writing you a letter in which the word subscription does not appear. I am with deep respect, Monseigneur, Your Royal Highness's very humble and very poor secretary of foolishness.

Voltaire

[In 1721 Voltaire offered the manuscript of his epic poem, La Henriade, to the Regent. In the same year, he profited from the financial bubble of Law's System. On New Year's Day, 1722, Voltaire's father died. Later that year, he travelled to Brussels and The Hague in the company of Mme. de Rupelmonde.

He led a worldly existence and travelled from chateau to chateau in the French countryside, staying at La Rivière-Bourdet, Sully, La Source, Ussé and Richelieu. Of his many peregrinations, his stay at La Source near Orléans was perhaps most notable. There he met Henry St. John, Viscount Bolingbroke, British statesman and writer, and from this meeting we have a first indication of Voltaire's sympathy for England and English culture.

In 1723, he took up with Mme. de Bernières, wife of the president of the Parlement of Rouen. In November and December of that year, Voltaire came down with smallpox and was cared for by the actress Adrienne Lecouvreur, and by his friend, Thieriot. On March 6, 1724, his play Mariamne was first presented in its original form, with a revised version performed the following year. The premiere of his play, L'Indiscret, took place on August 18, 1725, and that fall Voltaire sent a copy of La Henriade to George I of England with a note expressing his desire to visit that country. In 1726, Voltaire quarrelled with the Chevalier de Rohan and, as a result, was sent to the Bastille for two weeks. Obliged to go into exile, Voltaire left for England.]

5. *"I have observed this city with respect."*

To Marguerite-Madeleine Du Moutier, Marquise de Bernières.
The Hague. October 7, 1722.

Your letter added new pleasure to my life at The Hague. Of all the world's delights, I know of none more flattering than to be able to count on the friendship of a lady as estimable as you. I will remain in The Hague a few days to make all the necessary arrangements for the printing of my poem,[7] and I will leave once the fine weather disappears. There is nothing more pleasant than The Hague when the sun condescends to shine. Here one sees nothing but prairies, canals, and green trees. From The Hague to Amsterdam it is a terrestrial paradise. I have observed this city, which is the storehouse of the universe, with respect. There were more than a thousand vessels in port. Of the five hundred thousand men living in Amsterdam, not one is an idler, a poor person, a fop, or an insolent man. We came across the stadholder walking among the people without footmen. One does not observe persons obliged to pay their court; people do not line up to see a passing prince. Work and modesty alone have their currency here. More magnificence and society exist in The Hague through the gathering of the ambassadors. I spend my life here between work and pleasure, and so I live in the Dutch as well as in the French manner. There is an abominable opera house but, on the other hand, I see Calvinist ministers, Arminians, Socinians, rabbis, and Anabaptists all speaking marvelously and, in truth, with reason. I am becoming quite accustomed to do without Paris, but not to do without you. Once again I respect my pledge to come and see you at La Rivière [8] if you are still there in November. Do not stay because of me, but allow me only to keep you company if you are inclined to remain in the country for awhile. Permit me to present my respects to M. de Bernières and to everyone in your household. I am always, with very respectful devotion, your very humble and obedient servant.

Volt.

6. *Lord Bolingbroke.*

To Nicolas-Claude Thieriot.[9] Blois. Thursday morning, December 4, 1722.

I must communicate to you my delight with my trip to Lord Bolingbroke and Madame de Villette [10] at La Source. In that illustrious Englishman, I have found all the erudition of his country and all the polish of ours. I have never heard our language spoken with more energy and exactness. This man, who has given himself up to pleasure and business all his life, has nevertheless found a way to learn and remember everything. He knows the history of the ancient Egyptians like that of England; he possesses Virgil like Milton; he likes English, French and Italian poetry but differently because he discerns their different geniuses perfectly. After my depiction of Lord Bolingbroke, it will perhaps suit me ill to tell you that Madame de Villette and he were infinitely satisfied with my poem. In the enthusiasm of their approval, they considered it superior to all the works of poetry that have appeared in France. But I know how much of this exaggerated praise must be discounted. I am going to spend three months deserving a part of it. It seems to me that by dint of correction, the work is finally taking on a reasonable form. I will show it to you when I return, and we will examine it at our leisure. At the present time, M. de Canillac [11] is reading it and forming a judgment of me. I write you awaiting that judgment. Tomorrow I will be at Ussé [12] where I expect a letter from you. I am very sick but have become accustomed to the ills of the body and those of the soul. I am beginning to suffer them with patience, and in your friendship and my philosophy I am finding resources against many things. Farewell.

7. *A Faithful Account of Smallpox.*

To Louis-Nicolas Le Tonnelier de Breteuil, Baron de Preuilly.[13]
c. Dec. 5, 1723.

I am going to obey you, sir, by giving you a faithful account of the smallpox from which I have recovered, of the astonishing way I was treated, and, finally, of the accident at Maisons [14] which will long prevent me from considering my return to life as a blessing.

President de Maisons [15] and I were indisposed last November 4, but fortunately all of the danger befell me. We had ourselves bled the same day. He felt fine, but I came down with smallpox. This malady appeared after two days of fever and became evident through a slight rash. I took it on myself to be bled a second time in spite of popular prejudice. The following day, M. de Maisons was good enough to send for M. de Gervasi, the physician of Cardinal de Rohan, who came only reluctantly. He was afraid of becoming uselessly involved treating, in a delicate and weak body, a smallpox that had already reached the second day of its rash and whose consequences had only been warded off by two excessively mild bleedings without any purgatives.

Nevertheless, he came and found me with a high fever. At first, he had an extremely poor opinion of my sickness; the servants who were beside me noticed this and did not let me remain unaware of it. It was announced to me at the same time that the curé de Maisons, who was interested in my health and not afraid of smallpox, asked if he could see me without causing me any inconvenience. I had him shown in immediately. I confessed and made my will which, as you might well believe, was not a long one. After that, I awaited death calmly enough not, however, without regretting that I had not put the last touch to my poem and to *Mariamne,* nor without being a little sorry for taking leave of my friends so early. However, M. de Gervasi did not leave me out of his sight for a moment; attentively he studied all the movements of nature in me; he gave me nothing to take without telling me why; he let me have an idea of the danger and showed me the remedy clearly. His reasoning carried conviction and confidence in my mind, a method indeed necessary for a doctor with his patients since the

11

hope of being cured is already half the cure. He was obliged to have me take an emetic eight times. And instead of the stimulants that are ordinarily given in this sickness, he had me drink two hundred pints of lemonade. This procedure, which will seem extraordinary to you, was the only one which could save my life. Any other course would have led to my death without a doubt, and I am persuaded that most of those who have died from this fearful malady would still be alive if they had been treated like me.

Popular prejudice abhors bleeding and medicines in smallpox. People only want stimulants; they give wine to the patient; they even make him eat small amounts of soup, and the error has taken hold by the fact that several persons have been cured through this diet. People do not bear in mind that the only cases of smallpox treated successfully in this way are those accompanied by no fatal mishap and which are in no way dangerous. Smallpox by itself, divorced of all foreign circumstances, is only a cleansing of the blood favorable to nature which, by cleaning the body of its impurities, prepares it for vigorous health. Whether such smallpox is treated with stimulants or not, whether one uses the purge or not, one is cured of it with certainty.

When no essential part of the body has been injured, the most serious wounds close easily whether sucked, whether fomented with wine and oil, whether Rabel's [16] water is used, whether ordinary plasters are applied, or whether, in the end, nothing is applied. But when the very energy of life has been attacked, the assistance of all of these small recipes becomes useless, and all the artistry of the cleverest surgeons will scarcely do. This is also true for smallpox.

When it is accompanied by a high fever, when the increased volume of blood in the vessels is about to burst them, when the deposit is ready to form in the brain and the body is filled with bile and foreign matter whose fermentation excites mortal destruction in the machine, then reason itself should teach us that bleeding is indispensable. It will purify the blood; it will relax the vessels; it will make their resiliency easier and more supple; it will relieve the skin glands and favor the breaking out of rashes. Then, medicines will remove the source of the illness by means of large evacuations and in carrying away a part of the smallpox leaven with them will freely allow what remains to develop more completely and prevent the smallpox from being confluent. Finally, it is evident that lemon syrup in a refreshing infusion relaxes the acrimony of the blood, pacifies its ardor, flows with it through the miliary glands up to the pimples, opposes the corrosion of the leaven, and even prevents the marks which the pustules usually make on the face.

There is one case when even the most powerful stimulants are absolutely necessary: when sluggish blood, further slackened by the leaven encumbering all its fibers, is not strong enough to eject the poison with which it is burdened. Then the powder of Countess Kent,[17] the balm of Vauseguer, the remedy of M. Agnan,[18] etc., breaking up the parts of this nearly coagulated blood, cause it to flow more rapidly by separating the foreign matter and opening the perspiration passages to the venom seeking escape.

But, in the state that I found myself, these stimulants would have been fatal. This shows conclusively that all those charlatans overrunning Paris who give the same remedy (I do not say for all maladies, but always for the same one) are poisoners who ought to be punished.

I constantly hear people reason rather erroneously and fatally. "This man," they say, "was cured by such a means; I have the same illness as he. Therefore, I must take the same remedy." How many people have died for reasoning this way? They cannot see that the illnesses afflicting us are as different as the features on our faces, and as the great Corneille says (for you will allow me to cite the poets):

That often one is doomed where another is saved
And by what one perishes another is preserved.[19]

But this is overplaying the part of the doctor. I am like those persons who, after winning an important suit through the help of a skilful lawyer, continue to speak the language of the bar for a time.

What consoled me the most during my sickness, however, was the interest you took in it, the attention of my friends and the inexpressible kindness with which Mme. and M. de Maisons honored me. In addition, I enjoyed the sweetness of having beside me a friend, I mean a man who must be included among the very small number of virtuous men who alone are familiar with that friendship which the rest of the world knows only by name. He is M. Thieriot who, on rumor of my sickness, came forty leagues by post chaise to watch over me and who has not left me for a moment since. On the 15th, I was absolutely out of danger, and on the 16th I was writing verse in spite of my extreme weakness, which still persists, caused by the sickness and the remedies.

I impatiently awaited the moment I could escape their solicitude for me at Maisons and put an end to the inconvenience I was creating there. The more people were solicitous of me, the more I hastened not to take advantage of the situation for long. Finally, I was in a state to be moved to Paris on December 1. That, sir, was a very fatal moment. I was barely two hundred steps from the chateau when a part of the floor of the room I had occupied caved in completely in flames; the neighboring rooms, the apartments below, the precious furniture with which they were decorated, everything was consumed by the fire. The loss has amounted to almost a hundred thousand pounds, and without the assistance of the fire apparatus which was sent for in Paris, one of the most beautiful buildings in the kingdom would have been entirely destroyed. This strange piece of news was concealed from me on my arrival; I learned of it when I awoke. You cannot imagine my despair. You know of M. de Maisons's generous solicitude toward me; I had been treated in his home like a brother, and the reward for so much kindness was the fire in his chateau. I could not understand how the fire could have caught hold so suddenly in my room where I had only left one half-burnt log that was almost extinguished. I learned that the cause of this conflagration was a beam which passed precisely beneath the fireplace. This is a defect that has been corrected in the structure of buildings today, and indeed the frequent accidents that occurred made recourse to the law necessary in order to prohibit this dangerous method of construction. The beam I am talking about had caught fire little by little from the heat of the fireplace which was directly above it and (through a singular destiny whose good fortune I certainly did not savor) the fire, which had been seething for two days,

14

only broke out a moment after my departure. I was not the cause of this accident but its unfortunate occasion. I grieved over it just as if the guilt had been mine. My fever took hold again immediately, and I assure you that at that moment I was not grateful to M. de Gervasi for saving my life.

Madame and M. de Maisons received the news more calmly than I; their generosity was as great as their loss and my grief. M. de Maisons crowned his kindness by informing me himself in letters that show his heart to be as excellent as his mind. He solicitously took it upon himself to console me, and it seemed as if I were the one whose chateau he had burned. But his generosity only makes me feel the loss I have caused him even more acutely, and I shall preserve my grief as well as my admiration for him for the rest of my life, etc. . . .

I am, etc.

8. *"The King of Spain has just locked up his wife."*

To Marguerite-Madeleine du Moutier, Marquise de Bernières.
Paris. July 20, 1724.

I really wished you had no knowledge of the news from Spain. I would have the pleasure of informing you that the King of Spain [20] has just locked up his wife, the daughter of the late Duke of Orleans, who, despite her pointed nose and long face, did not fail to follow the great examples of her sisters. I have been assured that she occasionally amused herself by stripping completely naked with her prettiest maids of honor and in that outfit invited the comeliest gentlemen of the kingdom. Her whole household has been dismissed, and only an old prudish maid of honor has been left with her in the chateau where she is locked up. We are assured that when the poor queen found herself closeted with this duenna, she resolved courageously to throw her out of the window and would have succeeded if help had not arrived. I believe that this adventure may rather serve to bring about the dismissal of our little infanta.[21] You see I am becoming shrewd with the ambassadors.[22] Up to now, I have confined all my political activity to not going to Vienna and arranging to see you again at La Rivière. The waters have had an unexpectedly good effect on me. I am beginning to breathe and experience good health. Up until now, I have only been half alive. May it please God that this small ray of hope not soon disappear. It seems to me that I will love my friends much more when I no longer suffer. My sole preoccupation henceforth will be to give them pleasure whereas in the past I thought only of my ills. Allow me to present my respects to Madame de Leseau,[23] your nephew and those who are with you. Let me know if they have begun to plant your forests and dig your canals. I am interested in La Rivière as in my homeland.

9. *"I am serving both God and the devil rather acceptably."*

To Marguerite-Madeleine du Moutier, Marquise de Bernières.
Paris, at the Comédie. August 20, 1725.

For the entire month, I have been surrounded by attorneys, charlatans, printers, and actors. Every day, I wanted to write to you, and still have not found the moment. I am presently taking refuge in an actress's dressing room to surrender myself to the pleasure of conversing with you while they play *Mariamne* and *L'Indiscret* for the second time. The latter play was presented here the day before yesterday, Saturday, with considerable success. But it seemed to me that the boxes were even more pleased than the parterre. Dancourt and Legrand [24] have accustomed the parterre to low comedy and vulgarity, and imperceptibly the public has acquired the prejudice that little one-act plays must be farces full of filth and not noble comedies that respect morality. The common people are not satisfied when one only makes the mind laugh. You must make them laugh out loud, and it is difficult to bring them to prefer subtle jokes to insipid puns and Versailles to the rue Saint Denis. *Mariamne* has finally been printed in my own way after the appearance of three surreptitious editions one after the other. I am sending you a package of *Mariamnes* by messenger. One of them, which I ask you to put in your library, is bound. I beg you to give the others, which I have not had time to have bound, to Messrs. de Cideville and de Brevedent despite their predilection for the verse of M. Houdar.[25] You will give the others, in my name, to those persons whose good will toward me you will want to assure. As I believe M. and Mme. de Leseau to be in the country, I am also including in the messenger's package a copy of *Mariamne* for them or rather for your nephew. It is addressed in your care; please have it picked up. If I could only come and offer you *Mariamne* myself! I must have really been cursed by God to have lived with you only when I had scabies and you the gout, and to be far from you when we are both in good health. My illnesses and health have certainly come at the wrong times.

Moreover do not think that I am confining myself in Paris to the presentation of tragedies and comedies. I am serving both God and the devil rather acceptably at the same time. In society, I have a slight veneer of devoutness which the miracle of the *faubourg St. Antoine* gave me. The lady of the miracle [26] came to my room this morning. Do you see what honor I do your house and what a scent of holiness will cover us? Cardinal de Noailles [27] composed a beautiful pastoral letter on the occasion of the miracle and as a crowning (either of honor or of ridiculousness) I am cited in this letter. I have been formally invited to attend the *te deum* which will be sung to Our Lady as a thanksgiving for the cure of Mme. La Fosse. The Abbé Couet, grand vicar of his Eminence, sent me the letter today. I sent him a copy of *Mariamne* with the following verses:

> You send me a pastoral letter:
> Receive a tragedy,
> So that to one another
> We present a spectacle.

Ah, my dear *présidente*, with all of this I am sometimes in bad humor because I find myself alone in my room and feel you are thirty leagues away. You must be in the land of milk and honey. The Abbé d'Amfreville, with his prelate's belly and cherubic face, does not have a poor likeness to the king of the land of milk and honey.[28] I imagine you are having some charming dinner parties, that the lively and fertile imagination of Mme. Du Deffand [29] and the Abbé d'Amfreville will endow our friend Thieriot with some, and that, finally, all your moments are delightful. Is the Chevalier des Alleurs [30] still with you? He told me he would stay as long as he enjoyed himself. I think that he will stay a long while. A thousand respects, I pray you, to the master of the house. I do not have the time to write to Thieriot, but since he has no lawsuits to defend, actors to direct, or plays to correct, *he* must write me. Let him send me news of himself; let him be your secretary; let him tell me how his plans are progressing. Farewell, my dear queen. Always keep much affection for me. I am leaving instantly for Fontainebleau. If I find a place to lay my head down there, I will pay my court to the Queen. If I have no lodgings, I will go to La Rivière Bourdet. My only preference to you is Marie Leszczynska.[31] Farewell, farewell.

10. *The Marriage of Louis XV.*

To Marguerite-Madeleine du Moutier, Marquise de Bernières.
Fontainebleau. Monday, September 17, 1725.

While Louis XV and Marie-Sophie-Félicité [32] of Poland are together with the entire court at the Comédie Italienne,[33] I am closeting myself in my room to send you some idle gossip of this locality which you will perhaps be somewhat curious to learn. I have no liking whatsoever for those foreign pantaloons and love you with all my heart. First, Monsieur de La Vrillière just died last night at Fontainebleau, and the Maréchal de Grammont died in Paris at the same hour. Certainly, both of them did not choose their time advantageously for, in the midst of all the hubbub over the marriage of the King, their deaths will not make the slightest impression. A few days ago the carriage of the Prince de Conti knocked down poor Martinot, the King's clockmaker, as it passed; he was crushed under the wheels and died instantly. No more attention will be paid to the deaths of Messrs. de La Vrillière and Grammont than to that of Martinot unless someone dares to make a request for the positions of Secretary of State and Colonel of the Guards in spite of the right of succession to these offices. However, everything possible is being done here to amuse the Queen. The King is going about that task very well. He boasted that he gave her seven sacraments for the first night, but I do not believe a word of it. Kings always deceive their peoples. The Queen is looking well even though she is not pretty at all. Everyone here is delighted with her virtue and her politeness; the first thing she did was to distribute to the princesses and to the ladies of the palace all of those magnificent trifles called her wedding presents. They consisted of jewels of every kind, with the exception of diamonds. When she saw the case in which they were all laid out, she said, "This is the first time in my life I have been able to give presents." She wore a bit of rouge on her marriage day, enough not to make her look pale. She swooned for a brief moment in the chapel, but only for form. There were theatrical presentations the same day. I had prepared a small amusement which M. de Mortemart did not allow them to produce. Instead *Amphytrion* and the *Doctor in Spite of Himself*,[34] which did not seem too appropriate, were performed. After the supper, there were fireworks with many rockets but very little originality and variety after which the King prepared himself to produce a dauphin. Moreover the place is a din, a fracas, a rush, and a frightful tumult. During these first days of confusion, I shall be very careful not to have myself presented to the Queen. I shall wait for the crowds to disappear and for Her Majesty to recover a little from the giddiness which all of this witches' sabbath must be inducing in her. Then I shall try to have *Oedipe* and *Mariamne* performed in her presence. I shall dedicate them both to her. She has already informed me that she would be very pleased if I took that liberty. The King and Queen of Poland, for we no longer recognize King Augustus here, have requested my poem on Henry IV about which the Queen has already heard commendable things. But here one must not be hasty about anything. The Queen will tire very soon of the harangues of the sovereign companies; both prose and verse at the same time would be too much. I prefer Her Majesty to be bored by the *parlement* and *Chambre des Comptes*[35] than by me. I pray you, the Queen of La Rivière, to inform me whether you are still really content in your kingdom. I assure you that in my heart I much prefer your court to this one, especially since yours has Mme. Du Deffand and the Abbé d'Amfreville as ornaments. Unfortunately I left for Fontainebleau on the same day the Chevalier des Alleurs returned to Paris. I thought I would find him in this part of the country but he has gone off elsewhere with his philosophy. I am really sorry about this for I intended to speak to him about you. My regards, I pray you, to Thieriot. I love you dearly. I embrace you. A thousand times farewell.

11. *A Request for Royal Patronage.*

To King George I of England. Fontainebleau. October 6, 1725 (New Style).

Sire,
For a long time, I have considered myself one of Your Majesty's subjects. I make bold to implore your protection for one of my works. It is an epic poem whose subject is Henry IV, the best of our kings. The resemblance he bears you by virtue of his title of father of his peoples authorizes me to address Your Majesty.

I was compelled to speak of the politics of Rome and of the intrigues of the monks. I have respected Reformed religion; I have praised the illustrious Elizabeth of England. I have spoken in my work with freedom and truth. You are the protector of both, sire, and I dare flatter myself that you will grant me your royal protection to have a work, which must be of concern to you since it is a panegyric of virtue, printed in your states.

To learn how to better portray virtue, I eagerly seek the honor of coming to London to present to you the deep respect and gratitude with which I have the honor of being, sire, Your Majesty's very humble, very obedient and very grateful servant.

Voltaire

12. *"The Catholics do not forgive me for not having said enough."*

To Isaac Cambiague. c. December 1725.

The kindness with which you honor me has found its way to me more than once. Let me take this opportunity to indicate my very humble gratitude. To present you with my *Mariamne* will perhaps diminish your good opinion of me. Pay no consideration to the homage but rather to the zeal with which I offer it, and may the desire to please you stand me in stead of merit. I should like the honor of sending you immediately a more important work, a feeble sketch of which has appeared and already found favor with you. It is the poem on Henry the Great. You will find it quite different from the sample which has been circulated against my wishes. The poem is in ten cantos, and more than a thousand verses differ from those you have seen.

I have had engravings made which equal the finest works of our best masters and ought to embellish the edition I am readying, but I am still quite uncertain as to where I will have it published. The only thing I am certain of is that it will not be in France. I have recommended a spirit of peace and tolerance in religious matters much too much in my poem; I have told the court of Rome too many home truths; I have spread much too little venom against the Reformed to hope that I might be permitted to print this poem, written in praise of the greatest king my country has ever had, in my homeland.

It is a very strange thing that my work, which at heart is a eulogy of the Catholic religion, cannot be printed in the states of the very Christian king, of the grandson of Henry IV, and that those whom we here call *heretics* allow it to be printed in their country. I have spoken ill of them, and they forgive me for it. But the Catholics do not forgive me for not having said enough. I do not know whether my edition will be produced in London, Amsterdam, or Geneva. My admiration for the wisdom of the government of this last city, especially for the manner in which the Reformation was established there, makes me lean in that direction. I will have a poem printed in that locality that was composed for a hero who left Geneva against his wishes but always loved it. How delighted I would be to be able to spend some time there with you and profit from your conversation!

I am respectfully your very humble and very obedient servant.

A. de Voltaire

13. *"I ask for permission to go to England immediately."*

To Jean-Frédéric Phélypeaux, Comte de Maurepas.[36] c. April 20, 1726.

Monseigneur,

I point out again very humbly that I was thrashed by the good Chevalier de Rohan with the help of six ruffians behind whom he was boldly stationed. From that moment, I have continually sought to repair not *my* honor but *his* which was too difficult a thing to accomplish.

If I have come to Versailles, it is absolutely not true that I either asked or had someone else ask for the Chevalier de Rohan Chabot at Cardinal de Rohan's residence. It is very easy for me to prove the contrary, and I will consent to remain in the Bastille for the rest of my life if I am being deceptive.

I ask to be allowed to eat with the governor of the Bastille and see some people. I ask even more earnestly for permission to go to England immediately. If there is any doubt about my leaving, a police officer can be sent to accompany me to Calais.

These two favors, which I consider very great ones in my present horrible state, are a trifle compared to a greater one that I ask of you: to continue your protection and kindness which I have always merited by the respectful devotion and sincere esteem with which I am, Monseigneur, your very humble and obedient servant.

Voltaire

14. *"This is a country where people think freely and nobly."*

To Nicolas-Claude Thieriot. August 12, 1726.

My dear Thieriot,

I received a letter from you dated last May 1 rather tardily. You saw me in Paris quite unhappy; the same fate has pursued me everywhere. If the character of the heroes in my poem is as sustained as my bad luck, my poem will assuredly succeed better than I. You give me such touching assurances of your friendship through your letter that I rightly reply to it by taking you in my confidence. So I will confess to you, dear Thieriot, that I took a small trip to Paris recently.[37] Since I did not see you, you will easily conclude that I saw no one. I sought only one man whose cowardice instinctively concealed him from me as if he suspected that I was on his track. In the end, the fear of being discovered made me leave more hastily than I had come. That is over with, dear Thieriot. It seems very likely that I shall never see you again. I am still very uncertain as to whether I shall retire to London. I know that this is a country where all the arts are honored and rewarded, where there is a difference among conditions but no other among men except that of merit. This is a country where people think freely and nobly without being held back by servile fear. If I followed my inclination, I would settle there with the idea of simply learning how to think. But I do not know if my small fortune, which is in quite a disarray because of so many trips, my poor health which has worsened more than ever, and my predilection for the deepest retirement will allow me to interject myself into the hubbub of Whitehall and London. I have received very good recommendations in that country and I am awaited with kindly enough feelings, but I cannot answer you that I will take the trip. There are only two things left for me to do in the course of my life: risk it with honor as soon as I can and end it in the obscurity of a retirement suitable to my way of thinking, my misfortunes, and my knowledge of men. I willingly abandon my pensions from the King and Queen; my only regret is that I was unsuccessful in having you share in them. It would console me in my solitude to think that once in my life I might have been of some use to you. But I am fated for every kind of misfortune. The greatest pleasure the just man can experience—to please his friends —has been denied me. I do not know what Mme. de Bernières thinks of me.

> Would she take care to reassure my heart
> Against the suspicion connected with misfortune? [38]

I shall always respect her friendship for me, and I shall preserve mine for her. I wish her better health, a steady fortune, much pleasure, and friends like you. Speak to her about me occasionally. If I still have some friends who utter my name before you, speak to them soberly about me and keep my memory alive so that they speak of me willingly. As for you, write me occasionally without scrutinizing the punctuality of my replies. Rely on my heart more than on my letters. Give me the pleasure of writing via M. du Noquet [39] at Calais. Wherever I may live in this world, that will be my only address, and letters will be delivered to me without fail. Farewell, dear Thieriot. Love me despite absence and ill fortune.

[In England, Voltaire was presented to King George I, attended Newton's funeral in Westminster in 1727, and in December of that year published two English essays: the Essay on Civil Wars and the Essay on Epick Poetry. Among his British acquaintances were Swift, Pope, Congreve and Gay. The following year, at the age of thirty-four, he published an edition of La Henriade in London through subscription and dedicated the work to the Queen of England.

In November 1728, he returned to France, and the following April was given permission to re-enter Paris. The year 1729 was a significant one for Voltaire's literary career. He was actively at work on three important works: the History of Charles XII, the tragedy Brutus, and most importantly the radical critique of eighteenth-century French culture known as the English Letters or Philosophical Letters. In January 1731, his Charles XII was seized by the police, and from that date forward Voltaire's writings became freer and inevitably involved him in difficulties with the authorities. In 1732, Voltaire first set to work on his major historical masterpiece, The Age of Louis XIV, to be published only some twenty years later. The year 1732 also marked another triumphal stage success with the presentation of his tragedy Zaïre.

The following June, he began his liaison with Mme. Du Châtelet, one of the most influential persons in his career. This affair lasted sixteen years and ended only with her death in childbirth in 1749, the result of her relationship with the Marquis de Saint-Lambert. Voltaire continued his influential relationships; in

March 1734, for example, he was a witness to the marriage of the Duc de Richelieu and Mlle. de Guise. On June 10, his English Letters, which had been published in France against his wishes and better judgment, were condemned by the Parlement of Paris to be pilloried and burned. A lettre de cachet was issued against the author, but he had taken flight and gone into exile once again, this time in Mme. Du Châtelet's chateau at Cirey in Champagne. The year 1734 may be said to mark the end of the early phase of Voltaire's career. He was now forty years of age.]

15. "... by god English wisdom and English Honesty is above yours."

To Nicolas-Claude Thieriot. October 26, 1726.[40]

... I intend to send you two or three poems of Mr. Pope, the best poet of England, and at present, of all the world. I hope you are acquainted enough with the English tongue, to be sensible of all the charms of his works. For my part i look on his poem call'd the essay upon criticism as superior to the art of poetry of Horace; and his rape of the lock, la boucle de cheveux, (that is a comical one) is in my opinion above the lutrin of Despréaux.[41]. I never saw so amiable an imagination, so gentle graces, so great varyety, so much wit, and so refined knowledge of the world, as in this little performance.

Now my dear Tiriot after having fully answered to what you asked about English books, let me acquaint you with an account of my for ever cursed fortune. I came again into England in the latter end of July very much dissatisfied with my secret voiage into France both unsuccessfull and expensive. I had about me onely some bills of exchange upon a Jew called Medina for the sum of about eight or nine thousand French livres, rekoning all. At my coming to London i found my damned Jew was broken. I was without a penny, sick to death of a violent ague, a stranger, alone, helpless, in the midst of a city, wherein i was known to no body. My lord and my lady Bolingbroke were in the country. I could not make bold to see our ambassadour in so wretched a condition. I had never undergone such distress; but i am born to run through

25

all the misfortunes of life. In these circumstances, my star, that among all its direful influence pours allways on me some kind refreshment, sent to me an English gentleman unknown to me, who forced me to receive some money that i wanted. An other London citizen that i had seen but once at Paris,[42] carried me to his own country house, wherein i lead an obscure and charming life since that time, without going to London, and quite given over to the pleasures of indolence and of friendship. The true and generous affection of this man who sooths the bitterness of my life brings me to love you more and more. All the instances of friendship indear my friend Tiriot to me. I have seen often mylord and mylady Bolinbroke. I have found their affection still the same, even increased in proportion to my unhappiness. They offered me all, their money, their house; but i refused all, because they are lords, and i have accepted all from m^r Faulknear, because he is a single gentleman.

I had a mind at first to print our Poor Henry at my own expenses in London, but the loss of my money is a sad stop to me design: i question if i shall try the way of subscriptions by the favour of the court. I am weary of courts my Thiriot. All that is King, or belongs to a King, frights my republican philosophy, i won't drink the least draught of slavery in the land of liberty.

I have written freely to the abbot Desfontaines [43] it is true, and i will allwais do so, having no reason to lay myself under any restraint. I fear, i hope nothing from your country. All that i wish for, is to see you one day in London. I am entertaining myself with this pleasant hope. If it is but a dream, let me enjoy it, don't undeceive me, let me believe i shall have the pleasure to see you in London, (drawing up) the strong spirit of this unaccountable nation. You will translate their thoughts better, when you live among em. You will see a nation fond of their liberty, learned, witty, despising life and death, a nation of philosophers, not but that there are some fools in England, every country has its madmen. It may be, French folly is pleasanter, than English madness, but by god English wisdom and English Honesty is above yours. One day i will acquaint you with the character of this strange people, but tis time to put an end to my English talkativeness. I fear, you will take this long epistle for one of these tedious English books that i have advised you not to translate. Before i make up my letter, i must acquaint you with the reason of receiving yours so late. T'is the fault of my correspondent at Calais, master Dunoquet. So you must write to me afterwards, at my lord Bolingbroke's house, London. This way is shorter and surer. Tell all who will write to me that they ought to make use of this superscription.

I have written so much about the death of my sister [44] to those who had writ to me on this account, that i had almost forgotten so speak to you of her. I have nothing to tell you on that accident but that you know my heart and my way of thinking. I have wept for her death, and i would be with her. Life is but a dream full of starts of folly, and of fancied, and true miseries. Death awakes us from this painful dream, and gives us, either a better existence or no existence at all. Farewell. Write often to me. Depend upon my exactness in answering you when i shall be fixed in London.

Write me some lines in English to show your improvement in your learning.

I have received the letter of the marquess of Willars, [45] and that which came from Turky by Marseille.

I have forgot the romance which you speak of. I don't remember i have ever made verses upon this subject. Forget it, forget all those deliriums of my youth. For my part i have drunk of the River Lethe. I remember nothing but my friends.

16. *A Letter to Jonathan Swift.*

To Jonathan Swift. In London, Maiden lane, at the White perruke, Conventgarden. December 25, 1727. [46]

Sir,

You will be surprised in receiving an English essay from a french traveller. [47] Pray forgive an admirer of you, who ows to y^r writings, the love he bears to y^r language, which has betray'd him into the rash attempt of writing in english.

You will see by the advertisement that i have some designs upon you, and that i must mention you for the honour of y^r

27

country, and for the improvement of mine. Do not forbid me to grace my relation with y^r name. Let me indulge the satisfaction of talking of you as posterity will do.

In the mean time can i make bold to intreat you to make some use of y^r interest in Ireland, about some subscriptions for the Henriade, which is almost ready and does not come out yet for want of little help.[48] The subscriptions will be but one guinea in hand.

I am with the highest esteem and the utmost gratitude,
Sir,

y^r most humble and most obedient servant

Voltaire

17. *The English Letters.*

To Jean-Baptiste Nicolas de Formont.[49] Paris, Saturday, December 6, 1732 (?)

It has been a thousand years, my dear Formont, since I have written you. I am sorrier about this than you are. You spoke to me in your last letter of *Zaïre* [50] and gave me some very good advice. I am a total ingrate. I have let two months go by without thanking you and without taking sufficient advantage of this time. I should have used part of my time writing you and the rest correcting *Zaïre*. But I wasted it completely in Fontainebleau creating squabbles among the actresses over starring roles and between the Queen and princesses over the performance of comedies, causing great disputes about trifles and creating dissension in the entire court over trivia. In the intervals left me by this important nonsense, I amused myself reading Newton instead of making corrections on our *Zaïre*. I am finally determined to have these English letters [51] appear, and to that end I had to reread Newton since I cannot speak of such a great man without having some familiarity with him. I have completely reshaped those letters in which I discussed him, and I make bold to give a small précis of his entire philosophy. I am writing his history and that of Descartes. I briefly touch upon the fine discoveries and innumerable errors of

28

our René; I am bold enough to support the system of Isaac which seems to me to have been proven correct. All this will make up four or five letters that I am attempting to make lively and as interesting as the material will allow. I am also compelled to change everything I had written about Mr. Locke since, in the end, I want to live in France and I cannot be as philosophical as an Englishman. In Paris I must veil what I can say only too strongly in London. This unfortunate but necessary caution makes me eliminate more than one rather amusing passage about the Quakers and Presbyterians. My heart is sick over it. Thieriot will suffer.[52] You and I will miss these passages, but

> Non me fata meis patiuntur scribere nugas
> auspiciis, et sponte meâ componere cartas.[53]

I read two letters about the Quakers to Cardinal de Fleury [54] from which I very prudently eliminated anything that might excite his devout and wise eminence. He found what still remained quite amusing, but the poor man does not know what he lost. I intend to send you my manuscript as soon as I have tried to explain Newton and obfuscate Locke. You also seem to want certain light-hearted literary pieces about which the Abbé de Sade [55] spoke to you. I want to send both you and M. de Cideville my entire stock as a New Year's gift. But I do not want to give away something for nothing. You scoundrel, I know that you wrote Mlle. de Launay one of those charming letters in which you combine reason and the graces and in which you cover your philosopher's cap with roses. If you made us privy to those sweet nothings, you would really be doing the right thing and I would consider myself repaid excessively for the stock of goods I have in mind for you. Our baroness sends you her compliments. Everybody yearns for you here. You really ought to come and take back your old apartment with Messrs. des Alleurs and spend your winter in Paris. You would also perhaps induce me to compose another new tragedy. Farewell. I beseech M. de Cideville to tell you how much I hold you in affection, and I pray M. de Formont to assure dear Cideville of my affectionate friendship. Farewell. I will consider myself happy only when I can spend my life with the two of you. A thousand regards to Messrs. de Bourgtroulde and Brevedent.

18. *"I would be fond of Calvin if he had not had Servetus burned."*

To Jacob Vernet.[56] Paris. September 14, 1733.

Sir,

Conversing with you has given me an extreme desire to be in continuous communication with you. I observe with extreme satisfaction that you are not one of those travelers who visit men of letters in passing as one goes and observes statues and paintings to satisfy a momentary curiosity. You make me aware of the entire value of your correspondence, and without flattering you, I tell you right now that you have a friend in me. For what can friendship be based on if not esteem and the harmony of tastes and feelings? You impressed me as a philosopher who thinks freely and speaks wisely. Moreover you scorn that effeminate style, full of affectation and devoid of substance, with which the frivolous authors of our Académie Française have weakened our language. You are a lover of truth and of the masculine style which is alone relevant to truth. After all this, can I not hold you in affection? There must be no indulgence for the impertinent style with which France is inundated today because men are brought back to their good senses with these trifles. But in matters of religion, I believe we are both tolerant because men are never persuaded on this matter. Provided men do not persecute, I will forgive them for anything. I would be fond of Calvin if he had not had Servetus[57] burned. I would be the servant of the Council of Constance without John Huss's bundle of firewood.

These English letters you speak to me about are written in that spirit of freedom which will perhaps bring persecution upon me in France but entitle me to your esteem. Thus far they have only appeared in English, and I have done everything possible to have the French edition suspended. I do not know if I will be successful, but you must appreciate the difference that exists between the English and the French. These letters merely struck readers in London as philosophical, and in Paris people are already calling them impious without having seen them. A man considered tolerant here will soon be considered an atheist. Devout persons and frivolous minds, some of them deceitful and others misled, shout impiety against anyone who dares think humanely, and because a man has spoken in jest against the Quakers our Catholics conclude that they do not believe in God.

With respect to the Quakers, you ask my opinion in your letter about the words *you* and *thou*. I shall tell you as boldly what I think about this trifle as I will be timid with you on an important question. I believe that in ordinary discourse *you* is necessary because it is customary, and we must speak to men in the language instituted by them. But in those movements of eloquence when one must rise above the common language as when one speaks to God or causes the passions to speak, I believe that *thou* has added strength when it is distinct from *you* because *thou* is the language of truth and *you* the language of flattery.

I am not astonished that you have been unable to read the tragedy *Gustave*.[58] Every writer of verse must compose beautiful verse or he will not be read. Poets are only successful through the beauty of detail. Otherwise Virgil and Chapelain, Racine and Campistron, Milton and Ogilby, and Tasso and Rolli would be equals.

I would be obliged if you would recommend to me the book dealer you spoke about. I would be even further obliged if you would consent to write me occasionally. You have made me fond of your person and of your letters. Make me your correspondent here.

I am, etc.

Voltaire

19. "I committed a great blunder by writing an opera."

To M. Berger.[59] c. Feb. 1, 1734.

I received three letters from you at the same time. I am only too pleased to have a friend like you. Others content themselves with saying: "That is too bad," but you are filled with the most obliging concern and I shall always consider correspondence with you as the most flattering consolation for your absence.

I committed a great blunder by writing an opera, but the desire to work for a man like M. Rameau [60] carried me away. I thought only of his genius and did not understand that mine (if indeed I have any) is not at all suited for the lyric genre. Therefore I informed him some time ago that I would rather have written an epic poem than fill in someone else's outlines. I certainly do not scorn that sort of work. None of it is despicable, but this is a talent which I believe I lack entirely. Perhaps with tranquillity of mind, care, and the advice of my friends, I may succeed in achieving something less unworthy of the talents of our Orpheus. But I predict that the production of this opera will have to be postponed until next winter. It will only be improved and be more sought after by the public. Our great musician, who doubtless has enemies in proportion to his merit, must not feel sorry that his rivals are getting ahead of him. The point is not to be performed soon, but to be successful. It is better to be applauded late than to be hissed at early. It is only the pleasure of seeing you that I can postpone no longer. I cherish the hope of embracing you this winter. The day I see you will be my first consolation, and my readiness to obey you with respect to M. de Richelieu will be my second. I pray you to write me often and send me the affection of dear Desforges. [61]

20. *"The pious and stupid clamorings of superstitious imbeciles."*

To René Hérault. [62] Montjeu par Autun. May 6, 1734.

I am surprised and grieved to see that the backbiting of my unworthy enemies has deceived a man as enlightened as you. Must you listen to the pious and stupid clamorings of superstitious imbeciles, infected with the poison of Jansenism, who maintain that one attacks God and the state when one makes sport of the shaking of the Quakers? I make bold to write not to the police magistrate, but to a man of wit and consummate knowledge. Do not listen to the foolish multitude of those who are *sicut equus et mulus quibus non est intellectus.* [63] For a whole week they mumble without knowing why and then remain forever silent about things beyond their understanding. Please consult a M. de Mauper-tuis, a M. de Mairan, a M. Boindin, a M. de Fontenelle, a M. Du Fay, or a M. de La Condamine [64] about my book. These are reasoning men whose opinions will sooner or later become those of the public because, in the long run, the common man is always led by a small number of superior minds. This is as true of literature as it is of politics.

My book has been translated into English and German and has found more persons in Europe who approve than unworthy critics in France.

Again I have had no part in the publication. Please use all your authority with Jore, Bauche, the Pissot woman,[65] and with whoever is under suspicion.

As for myself, I earnestly ask you either to speak to Cardinal de Fleury again of my innocence or to be good enough to inform me or have M. d'Argental [66] write whether I must look abroad for the rest and consideration at least due me in my homeland. I shall live honorably anywhere, never complain, regret nothing save a few friends, and never forget your kindness. I pray you, do not consider me a part of the crowd that harasses you because you are a magistrate, and like me please heed only that which a superior mind like yours owes to humanity. My gratitude will match my fondness and the loving and respectful zeal with which you know that I shall always be your very humble and obedient servant.

Voltaire

21. *"I thank you in the name of all the adherents of Locke and Newton."*

To Anne-Charlotte de Crussol-Florensac, Duchesse d'Aiguillon. c. May 23, 1734.

Madam,

If you are still in Paris, allow me to have recourse to the French language which you employ so well rather than to the old Gascon dialect [67] which, I think, would be of little use to me at present with the Keeper of the Seals.[68] I am full of gratitude, and I thank you in the name of all the adherents of Locke and

Newton for the kindness you have shown in getting the Princesse de Conti to side with the *philosophes* despite the outcries of the devout.[69] I am informed in my retreat that the *parlement* wants to condemn me and deal with me in the manner of a pastoral letter. Why not? There have been many decrees against antimony and in favor of Aristotle's substantial forms.

People say that I must issue a retraction. Very willingly. I will declare that Pascal is always correct, that *fatal laurel, beautiful heavenly body* [70] is good poetry, that if Saint Luke and Saint Mark contradict each other, it is a proof of the truth of religion for those who know how to take these things into consideration the right way, and that one of the beautiful proofs of religion is still its unintelligibility. I will confess that all priests are unbiased and that monks are not proud, scheming or foul-smelling. I will say anything people want provided they leave me in peace and do not spend all their energy persecuting a man who never did anybody any harm, who lives in retirement, and who had no other ambition than to court you.

Moreover, it is quite certain that the work was published against my wishes, that many things were added, and that I have done what I humanly could to discover the author.

Let me express my gratitude and prayers once again. The favor I am asking of the ministry is not to deprive me of the honor of seeing you. This is a favor for which one could not become too persistent.

I have the honor of being, with deep respect,

. . . V.

May I greet the Duc d'Aiguillon, present him my respects, thank him, and exhort him to read the *Philosophical Letters* without being shocked? They are frightfully printed and full of absurd mistakes. That is what makes me despair.

Notes

1. A Jesuit and one of Arouet's teachers at Louis-le-Grand.
2. i.e., the Antilles.

3. Probably Mme. Constantin, Olympe's elder sister.

4. Head of the Paris police and the magistrate charged with referring petitions to the Council of State.

5. *Oedipe.*

6. *La Henriade,* an epic poem about Henry IV, King of France from 1589 to 1610.

7. *La Henriade.*

8. The country estate of the De Bernières near Rouen.

9. Thieriot (1696-1792) was a man of letters, one of Voltaire's closest friends, and a frequent correspondent.

10. Henry Saint John, Viscount Bolingbroke (1678-1751), former British Minister of War, had fled to France in 1715 where he formed a liaison with Mme. de Villette whom he subsequently married.

11. Philippe de Montboissier-Beaufort, Marquis de Canillac, was a friend of the Regent recently exiled to Blois.

12. A beautiful sixteenth-century chateau in the valley of the Loire owned by Voltaire's friend, Louis-Sébastien Bernin de Valentiné, Marquis d'Ussé.

13. The father of Mme. Du Châtelet, a future mistress of Voltaire.

14. Maisons, known today as Maisons-Lafitte, is a masterpiece of the architect François Mansart and one of the most beautiful residences near Paris.

15. Jean-René de Longueil, Marquis de Maisons, at the age of twenty-four had already been President of the Parlement of Paris for seven years.

16. Rabel was a celebrated physician.

17. Elizabeth Grey, Countess Kent, a seventeenth-century English writer, published *A Choice Manuall of Rare and Select Secrets in Physick and Chyrurgery* in 1653.

18. i.e., François Aignan, a physician and monk, who published *L'Ancienne Médecine à la mode [The Old Medicine in Fashion]* in 1693.

19. *Cinna,* Act I, scene 1.

20. i.e., Luis who ruled briefly in 1724-1725 during the temporary abdication of his father Philip V. He had married Louise-Elisabeth, daughter of the French Regent.

21. Maria-Anna-Vittoria, the six-year old daughter of Philip

V, who had been brought to Paris two years earlier to be engaged to Louis XV.

22. Voltaire's friend, the Duc de Richelieu, a great nephew of the cardinal, had been named ambassador extraordinary to Vienna.

23. The wife of a friend of Voltaire's in Rouen. Her son Ango was Mme. de Bernières's nephew.

24. Florent Carton Dancourt and Marc-Antoine Le Grand were dramatic authors of the period.

25. Pierre-Robert Le Cornier de Cideville was a friend of Voltaire's from his school days, a frequent correspondent, and a counsellor in the Parlement of Rouen. Brevedent was another friend. Antoine Lamotte-Houdar, or Houdar de La Motte (1672-1731), was a contemporary poet and playwright.

26. The reference is to one Anne Charlier La Fosse who had had a "miraculous cure" for which the Jansenists received credit.

27. The Archbishop of Paris.

28. Most likely a reference to Le Grand's Play *The King of the Land of Milk and Honey [Le Roi de Cocagne]*.

29. The Marquise Du Deffand (1697-1780) was to conduct one of the great salons of the eighteenth century and to be a frequent correspondent of Voltaire.

30. Rolland Puchot, Chevalier des Alleurs, later French ambassador to Constantinople.

31. Queen of France and daughter of Stanislas, the exiled King of Poland.

32. Catherine, Sophie, Félicité, and Marie were the Christian names of the Queen of France.

33. Name given to various Italian theatrical groups performing in Paris in the seventeenth and eighteenth centuries before their merging with the Opéra-Comique in 1762.

34. Two comedies of Molière.

35. The *Chambre des Comptes* was an institution of royal government going back to the Middle Ages. Its duties included, among other things, a verification of the accounts of all the financial agents of the King as well as of the expenses of the sovereign and members of his family. The *Chambre des Comptes* was abolished in 1790.

36. As Secretary of State for the King's household, Maurepas's

office included the department of Paris and the Police (from March 1718 to 1749) and later the Navy and Colonies (1723-1749).

37. In violation of his exile which was to be at least fifty leagues away from Paris.

38. A reminiscence of Racine's *Mithridate* (Act II, scene 4, verses 574-578).

39. Louise-Antoine Leveux du Noquet was administrator of the port of Calais.

40. One of a number of letters written in English by Voltaire included in this collection.

41. Alexander Pope's *The Rape of the Lock* was modelled on Nicolas Boileau-Despréaux's *Le Lutrin* (1672-1683), a mock-epic account of an ecclesiastical dispute regarding the placing of a lectern. Boileau has been considered the founder of the critical doctrine of French literary classicism.

42. Everard Fawkener, a merchant who later became British ambassador in Constantinople and Minister of Postal Services.

43. Pierre-François Guyot, Abbé Desfontaines (1685-1745), a Jesuit man of letters. Voltaire had helped secure his release from prison in 1724, but the two became enemies. Desfontaines later composed a violent attack on Voltaire entitled *La Voltairomanie*.

44. Marie-Marguerite Mignot.

45. i.e., Claude-Louis-Hector, Marquis and later Duc de Villars and Maréchal de France (1653-1734), a friend of Voltaire.

46. This letter to Swift was written in English.

47. The reference is to Voltaire's *Essay upon the civil wars of France . . . and also upon the epick poetry of the European nations from Homer down to Milton* (London, 1727).

48. Swift acquiesced to Voltaire's request. He also possibly composed a preface for the 1760 edition of the *Essays* which appeared in Dublin.

49. A poet and friend of Voltaire.

50. Voltaire's famous tragedy had its premiere performance on August 13, 1732.

51. On Voltaire's *English Letters* or *Philosophical Letters*, which appeared in 1734, see the preface to this edition.

52. Thieriot had been promised the profits from the sale of the work.

53. "The Fates have not suffered me to compose trifles to my

liking and to write books as I please." Adapted from Virgil, *The Aeneid,* Book IV, verses 340-341: "Me si fata meis paterentur ducere vitam/ auspiciis et sponte mea componere curas. . . ." ("If the Fates had suffered me to shape my life after my own pleasure and resolve my cares at my own will. . . .")

54. André-Hercule de Fleury (1653-1743), a cardinal and prime minister of France (without the title) from 1726 to 1743.

55. Jean-François-Paul-Aldonce, abbé de Sade (1701-1767), a man of letters and uncle of the marquis de Sade.

56. A Swiss Protestant clergyman (1698-1789).

57. Michael Servetus (1511-1553) was a Spanish physician and theologian burned at the stake in Geneva at the behest of Calvin.

58. A play by Alexis Piron first performed in 1733.

59. Secretary to the Prince de Carignan and director of the Paris Opera.

60. The composer Jean-Philippe Rameau (1683-1764) with whom Voltaire collaborated on the opera *Samson.*

61. Secretary to the Parlement of Rouen.

62. A high Paris police official.

63. Like a horse and an ass by whom it is not understood.

64. Pierre-Louis-Moreau de Maupertuis (1698-1759) was a geometer and mathematician instrumental in the spreading of Newtonianism in France. Jean-Jacques Dortous de Mairan (1678-1771) was a geometer, mathematician, and future perpetual secretary of the Académie des Sciences. Nicolas Boindin (1676-1751) was a playwright. Bernard Le Bovier de Fontenelle (1657-1757) was a philosopher and popularizer of science. Charles-François de Cisternay Du Fay (1698-1739) was a chemist. Charles-Marie de La Condamine (1701-1774) was an astronomer, traveller and author of *Voyage into the Interior of South America* (1745).

65. Claude-François Jore was a Rouen printer involved in the clandestine publication of Voltaire's *English Letters* contrary to the author's wishes. The book was condemned and ordered burned by the Parlement of Paris. Bauche was a Parisian printer, and Mme. Pissot was the widow of another of Voltaire's publishers.

66. Charles-Augustin Feriol, Comte d'Argental (1700-1788) was councillor in the Parlement of Paris, a friend of Voltaire and one of his most frequent correspondents.

67. Aiguillon is located in Gascony.

68. i.e., the Minister of Justice.

69. Voltaire propagandized on behalf of Locke and Newton in his *Philosophical Letters*. The Contis were one of the great noble families of France; the title of Prince de Conti, assumed by a younger branch of the house of Condé, goes back to the sixteenth century.

70. In his "Letter on the *Pensées* of M. Pascal" with which he concludes his *Philosophical Letters*, Voltaire criticized, among other things, Pascal's sense of poetic beauty using this example.

II

CIREY

(1734-1749)

CIREY

[Voltaire's years at Cirey and his numerous trips with Mme. Du Châtelet to Brussels, Lunéville, Paris, Sceaux and Versailles were important to his intellectual and literary development. He continued to delve into philosophical problems, and according to Ira Wade (Voltaire and Madame Du Châtelet), *he was concerned most particularly at this time with the question of happiness and "the four traditional problems of the Paduan School: the proofs of the existence of God, the nature and immortality of the soul, free-will, and the origin of evil." With the Marquise Du Châtelet's encouragement, Voltaire's writing and research extended themselves as well to scientific areas.*

While at Cirey, he began the composition of the highly unorthodox and burlesque satire of Joan of Arc called The Maid, *but was restrained by Mme. Du Châtelet from publishing it. In March of 1735 he was once again given permission to return to Paris, and in May he took a trip to Lunéville to visit the Court of Lorraine. The year 1736 marked the premieres of his plays* Alzire *or the* Americans *and the* Prodigal Child, *the beginning of his long and noteworthy correspondence with Frederick, Crown Prince of Prussia, and his brief flight to Holland for a few weeks to escape possible repercussions from the circulation of his poem,* Le Mondain [The Worldling], *which presented a rather unholy portrait of Biblical Paradise and expressed the author's preference for the luxuries of eighteenth-century Paris.]*

22. *"I want to go from an experiment in physics to an opera or comedy."*

To Pierre-Robert Le Cornier de Cideville. April 16, 1735.

My dear friend,

Truly, I have not yet thanked you for that agreeable collection you gave me. I have just reread it with added pleasure. How I love the simplicity of your descriptions! How cheerful and fertile your imagination is! And what makes all of this so inexpressibly charming is that it all comes from the heart. Love or friendship is your constant inspiration. Merely to write you in prose after your fine example is a sort of desecration on my part. But, my dear friend, *carmina secessum, scribentis et otia quaerunt.*[1] My mind is not at ease; I have been living a dissipated life since coming to Paris. *Tendunt extorquere poemata.*[2] My poetic ideas take flight from me; business and duty have dulled my imagination. I will have to take a trip to Rouen to become reinvigorated. Poetry is hardly fashionable any more in Paris. Everybody is beginning to play at being a geometrician and a physicist. People are dabbling with reason; feeling, imagination, and the graces have been done away with. Someone from the age of Louis XIV who came back to this world would no longer recognize the French. He would think the Germans had taken this country over. Literature is clearly in decline. Not that I am sorry about the cultivation of philosophy, but I would not want it to become tyrannical to the exclusion of all the rest.

Philosophy is merely a fashion in France coming after a number of others and which will give way in turn. But no art, no science ought to be fashionable. They must all go hand in hand and be constantly nurtured. I have no desire to pay tribute to fashion; I want to go from an experiment in physics to an opera or comedy and not ever have my sense of taste dulled by study. Your sense of taste, dear Cideville, will always sustain my own. But I ought to see you; I ought to spend a few months with you. And our destiny keeps us apart when everything ought to bring us together.

I saw Jore at your behest. He is a big scatter brain. He brought the whole difficulty about with his ridiculous behavior.

Nothing can be done for Linant either through the *présidente* or at the theater.[3] He will have to give some thought to becoming a tutor. I am getting him to learn to write. Then he will have to learn Latin if he wants to teach it. Do not spoil him if you hold him in affection. Vale.

V.

23. *A Friendly Letter of Reproach.*

To Nicolas-Claude Thieriot. Lunéville. June 12, 1735.

Yes, I will be abusive to you until I have cured you of your laziness. I do not reproach you for dining every evening with M. de la Popelinière;[4] I do reproach you for confining all your thoughts and hopes to that. You live as if man had been created solely to go to dinner parties, and your entire existence is from ten in the evening until two in the morning. No man dines and goes to bed later than you, nor is there a prude who rises later. You stay in your little room until theater time to clear away the vapors of yesterday's supper party. As a result, you do not have a moment to think of yourself and your friends. So writing a letter becomes a burden, and it takes you a month to answer. And you still indulge yourself with delusions, imagining yourself capable of employment and of making your fortune. You who cannot even pursue a steady occupation in your own study and have never been able to assume the responsibility of writing your friends regularly, even concerning affairs of mutual interest! You talk twaddle to me about "the most titled lords and ladies"; what does this mean? You have spent your youth; you will soon be old and infirm. That is what you must give thought to. You must prepare yourself for a late season of calm, happiness, and independence. What will become of you when you are sick and forsaken? Will it be any consolation to say: I drank champagne in good company in the old days! Remember that the bottle you celebrated with, when it was full of Barbados water,[5] is thrown into some corner as soon as it is broken and remains smashed to pieces in the dust. Remember this is what happens to all those who had merely thought of being accepted at a few supper parties and that the final years of an old, infirm, and useless person are rather pitiful. If that does not give you a little courage and impel you to shake off the lethargy into which you have let your soul drift, nothing will cure you. If I held you in less affection, I would joke about your laziness. But I am fond of you and scold you a great deal.

Such being the case, think of yourself and then of your friends. Drink champagne in pleasant company, but do something that will someday enable you to drink wine of your own. Do not forget your friends and spend entire months without writing a word. The point is not to write letters that you have carefully meditated and reflected over and which may infringe a little on your idle moments. It is simply a matter of two or three friendly words, some news about literature or human follies, all quickly set down on paper without effort or care. To do this, you have merely to face your writing desk for ten minutes or so. Is that really such a painful effort? My desire to be in regular correspondence with you is all the greater since your letter pleased me extremely. I may ask you from time to time for anecdotes concerning the age of Louis XIV. Remember this may be useful to you one day, and that work would earn for you as much as twenty volumes of *Philosophical Letters*.[6]

I have read the book on Turenne.[7] The fellow has copied entire pages out of Cardinal de Retz and sentences out of Fénelon.[8] I forgive him; he is an old hand at that. But he has not made his hero at all interesting. He calls him *great*, but does not make him so. He praises him like a rhetorician. He pillages the funeral orations of Mascaron and Fléchier,[9] and then has them reprinted among the proofs. What fine historical proof a funeral oration makes!

I am surprised neither by your judgment of the Abbé Le Blanc's play nor by its success.[10] It is quite possible for the plays to be both hateful and applauded.

Write me and always keep your affection for a true man who has never changed his ways.

P.S. What is this four-page portrait of me that has made the rounds? Who is the scribbler? Send me that misshapen portrait.[11]

Remember me to the Froulays, to the Des Alleurs, to the Pont-de-Veyles, to the Du Deffands,[12] *et totam hanc suavissimam gentem*.[13]

24. A *Philosophical Discussion with a Jesuit Father.*

To René-Joseph Tournemine. c. August 1735.

My dear and reverend Father,

The unalterable friendship you honor me with is indeed worthy of a heart such as yours. I will cherish it all my days. I beg you to receive new assurances of my own and to assure Father Porée [14] as well of my everlasting gratitude to him. You have both taught me to love virtue, truth, and letters. Please be good enough also to assure Reverend Father Brumoy [15] of my sincere esteem. I am not acquainted with Father Moloni nor with Father Rouillé whom you mention, but if they are friends of yours, they are worthy men.

I read the Latin poem you sent me with considerable pleasure, and I am always sorry that those who write so well in a foreign and almost useless tongue do not apply themselves to enriching our own. I send the author my compliments and hope, for the honor of the nation, that he will accomplish in a spoken language what he has done in one that no longer is. One of your merits, dear Father, is to speak our language with nobility and purity. A man who thinks and speaks like you ought to make the funeral oration for the late Maréchal de Villars; the panegyrist is worthy of the hero. I have always been very attached to you both, and I earnestly beseech you to please send me that composition.

You take pity on my present state. I am only to be pitied for my poor health, but I patiently bear the real injuries inflicted on me by nature. Those brought upon me by fortune are fanciful ills. I am far from being unfortunate, so much so that I refused a position three weeks ago with a German sovereign that would have provided a stipend equivalent to ten thousand pounds. I only refused that position to live in France with a few friends, not suspecting there would be persons so barbaric as to persecute me. If such were to be the case, I would live elsewhere in happiness and tranquillity.

With respect to the answers to my philosophical questions which you were good enough to formulate, I confess that they astonished me considerably and that I was expecting something quite different.

1. I did not ask you whether a principle of attraction and gravitation exists in matter, but whether scholars in your order were beginning to generally familiarize themselves with this principle and whether those who still reject it raise plausible objections.

You reply "that a body weighs on another when it pushes another, etc.," which makes me conclude that neither you nor those to whom you showed these replies have, as yet, been willing to apply yourselves to reading Mr. Newton's principles. For the question is not one of a body being pushed. The point is to know whether there is a reciprocal tendency, gravitation, or attraction from the center of each body, however great the distances between these bodies may be. This property of matter, discovered and demonstrated by Sir Isaac Newton, is as true as it is astonishing, and half of the Academy of Sciences, i.e., those who thought it not unworthy of their reason to learn what they were ignorant of, has started to recognize this truth which is beginning to be taught in all of England, the country of philosophers. As for our university, it is still unaware of who Newton was. It is deplorable that a good book has never come out of French universities and that even an adequate introduction to astronomy is unavailable in them, while Cambridge produces admirable books of this sort every day. It is, therefore, not without reason that astute foreigners look upon France as simply superficial.

I would hope that the Jesuits, who were the first to introduce mathematics into the education of the young, would also be the first to teach such sublime truths which, one day indeed, they will be forced to when there will no longer be any honor attached to being aware of them but only shame in being uninformed.

What you say about motion (which is certainly not essential to matter) really proves once more that neither you nor your friends have been willing to read or do not now remember the truths taught by this great philosopher. For, once again, the question here is not one of the ordinary motion of bodies but of the principle inherent in matter which causes each particle of matter to be attracted and to attract in direct ratio to its mass and in a ratio that is twice the inverse of its distance. Neither Mr. Newton nor any man worthy of the title of philosopher has said that this principle is essential to matter. They consider it only a property

48

given by God to that existence we know so little about and call *matter*. Your statement that motion is one of the proofs of the existence of God again has no bearing on the subject, unless you harbor a secret suspicion that those who have demonstrated God's existence most effectively are his unworthy and abominable enemies. (They really are his most respectable interpreters.) But I do not suspect you of an idea so unjust and cruel. You are so unlike those who accuse anyone not agreeing with them of atheism. Now please come back to this question: "Can God communicate the gift of thought to matter as he communicates attraction and movement to it?" The answer is boldly stated that this is impossible for God to do, the reason being that anyone who forms a judgment perceives an object indivisibly. Therefore thought is indivisible, etc. And this is called a proof. It is, however, nothing but a very obvious fallacy which assumes the thing in doubt.

The question is to know whether God can give an organism the power to perceive a piece of bread and have the sensation of appetite as he sees it. You say: "No. God is incapable of this since the organism would have to perceive all of the bread. Now part A of the bread only strikes part A of the brain, part B only part B, and no part of the brain can receive the entire object."

This is something you will certainly never be able to prove, and you will find no principle from which you will be able to derive the conclusion that God was incapable of giving an organism the faculty of simultaneously receiving the impression of a complete object. You see a thousand rays of light come and depict an object in the eye. But how can you reasonably guarantee that God is unable to impart to the brain the ability to sense that which is perceptible in light?

It is useless for you to say that matter is divisible. Neither divisibility nor extension enables it to think. But thought can be imparted to it by God just as God provided it with movement and attraction, which are not essential to it and which have nothing in common with divisibility. I do know that a thought is neither square, octagonal, red, nor blue, and that it cannot be divided into quarters or halves. But movement and gravitation are none of these things and nevertheless exist. It is, therefore, no more difficult for God to add thought to matter than movement and gravitation.

I confess that the more I consider this question, the more I

49

am astonished by the temerity of those who dare limit the power of the creator this way through a syllogism.

You think that the words *I* and *me* and those things constituting personality are another proof of the immateriality of the soul. Isn't that still assuming the thing in question? For who will prevent a thinking organism from saying *I* and *me*? Wouldn't it always be a person distinct from another body whether that body be thinking or non-thinking?

You ask where a totally material being would obtain the idea of immateriality. My answer is from the same source that a finite being receives the concept of the infinite. After that, you speak about Aristotle and a child reasoning about his doll. The two comparisons are only too suitable. In matters of sound philosophy, Aristotle was only a child. Can you possibly cite as an example a man who always substituted words for things? With respect to the child and his doll, what possible connection can that have with the question at hand? I said that one would have to be thoroughly familiar with matter to dare decide that God cannot impart thought to it. It is quite true that we do not know what matter and mind are, and then you tell me that free thinkers reply that they have no conception of matter, mind, virtue or vice in order to escape from their predicament.

I pray you, how are virtues and vices relevant here? Will God be any less of a lawgiver to men when he has enabled their bodies to think? Will a son owe his father any less respect? Will we have to be less just, less gentle, or less indulgent? Will the soul be any less immortal? Will God find it more difficult to preserve forever the small particles to which he imparted feeling and thought? What difference does it make what your soul is made of if it puts the freedom God had deigned to grant it to good use? This question has so little relevance to religion that some church fathers used to conceive of God and the angels as corporeal. But they do not guarantee the materiality of the soul. They only affirm that it is quite possible for God to have constituted it that way, and I do not see that the contrary can ever be proved.

In order to tell what it really is we can only proceed by probabilities, and sound philosophy requires that in those questions where we can only hope for probable answers, we not delude ourselves into thinking we have proofs.

50

People then say: "It is very likely that animals have feelings and no spiritual soul such as is attributed to man." We all have organs, food, propagation, needs, desires, wakefulness, rest, feeling, simple ideas, and memory in common with animals. So there are some common principles that bring this about in us and in them for *frustra fit per plura, quod potest fieri per pauciora.*[16]

Why would our superiority not consist of our ability to have and combine ideas that are much further developed than in animals, and especially of the immortality which God has bestowed on man and not animals?

Is this superiority not sufficient? And must pride still prevent us from recognizing all that we have in common with them? On this matter, I implore people to read the chapter on the extent of human knowledge in the last edition of the *Essay on Human Understanding* by Mr. Locke. If what this wise and moderate philosopher has said is not satisfactory, nothing will be.

Once you have explained the reasons in support of your opinion and carefully read those of your adversary, if you do not change your opinion, you must at least always remain prepared to yield to new reasons when you recognize their force.

My very dear Father, this, I swear to you, is the way I conduct myself. For a very long time, I thought the existence of God could only be proved by *a posteriori* reasons because I had not yet applied my mind to the few metaphysical truths that can be demonstrated.

Reading Dr. Clarke's [17] excellent book showed me my error, and I found in his demonstrations a clarification I had been unable to obtain elsewhere. He is the only one to provide me with clear notions about man's freedom. All other writers have merely confused the matter. If ever I find someone who can similarly prove to me the spirituality and immortality of the soul by reason, I will be in his eternal debt, etc.

51

25. *Congratulating a New Ambassador.*

To Sir Everard Fawkener. Cirey. September 18, 1735 (n.s.).[18]

My dear friend: your new title, will change neither my sentiments, nor my expressions, my dear Fawkener.[19] Friendship is full of talk, but it must be discreet. In the hurry of business you are in, remembering only, i talk'd to you about seven years ago, of that very same *ambassy.* Remember i am the first man, who did forestall the honour you enjoy. Believe then, no man is more pleas'd with in than i am. I have my share in y^r happiness. If you pass through France i advise you, i am but twenty leagues from Calais, almost in the road to Paris, in Champaine; the castle is call'd, Cirey, four milles from Vassy, on s^t Disiers road, and eight miles from s^t Dizier. the post goes thither. There lives a young lady, call'd the *marquise du Chatelet,* whom i have taught english, and who burns to see you. You will lye here, if you remember y^r friend Voltaire.

At Cirey by Vassy in Champagne, this September 18, 1735 (new style).

I only learned that you were named ambassador by a gazette which accidentally fell into my hands.

26. *On M. Rameau and M. de Marivaux.*

To M. Berger. Cirey. c. February 2, 1736.

The success of my *Americans*[20] is all the more flattering, my dear sir, since it justifies your friendship for my person and your predilection for my works. I dare say that the virtuous feelings in this play come from my heart and that is what makes me rely much more on the friendship of a person like you who knows me than on the suffrage of an ever capricious public that takes pleasure in raising idols in order to destroy them and that, for a long time now, has been spending one half of the year praising me and the other half slandering me. I would hope that the indulgence with which this work has just been received might encourage our great composer Rameau to place renewed confidence in me and complete his opera on Samson along the lines I have always had in mind. My work was solely for him. I departed from the ordinary road in the poem only because he does the same in music. I thought it time to open opera to a new career. Since the beauties of Quinault and Lully have become commonplaces on the tragic stage, few persons will be bold enough to advise M. Rameau to create music for an opera in which love is absent from the first two acts. But he must have the courage to set himself above prejudice. He must have confidence in me and in himself in this matter. He may be sure that the role of Samson, played by Chassé,[21] will be at least as effective as that of Zamore played by du Fresne.[22] Try and convince that semiquaver head of this. Let his self-interest and pride give him courage; let him promise to act entirely in concert with me; let him especially not wear his music out by having it played from house to house; let him adorn the pieces I have written for him with new beauties. I will send him the play when he wishes; M. de Fontenelle will be the examiner. I feel sure that the Prince de Carignan [23] will be its patron and that, in the end, of all the works by this great musician it will unquestionably bring him the greatest honor.

As for M. de Marivaux, I would be very sorry to include a man of his character, whose mind and integrity I hold in esteem, among my enemies. In his works, there is above all a character of philosophy, of humanity, and of independence in which I have discovered, with pleasure, my own feelings. It is true that I sometimes wish he had a style that was less mannered and subjects that were more noble. But I had no desire, far from it, to point to him when I spoke about metaphysical comedies. By this term, I simply mean comedies in which characters not to be found in nature are introduced, allegorical characters suitable at best for an epic poem but very much out of place on the stage where everything must be depicted according to nature. This is not, it seems to me, M. de Marivaux's defect. On the contrary, I will twit him for writing of the passions in excessive detail and for occasionally missing the path of the heart by taking roads that are a bit too roundabout. I cherish his wit all the more since I would pray him to be less lavish with it! A comic character should never think of being witty; he must be amusing in spite of himself and unconsciously. Comedy and simple dialogue ought to differ in this way. This is my way of thinking, my dear sir; I submit it to your judgment.

I made a loan to the late M. de la Clède but with no promissory note. I would have preferred to lose ten times that amount and have him still alive. I beg you to write me everything you hear about my *Americans*. I embrace you affectionately.

What has become of the Abbé Desfontaines? [24] In what cage have they put that dog who used to be in the habit of biting his masters? Alas! I would still give him some bread as mad as he is. I am not writing you in my own hand because I am slightly ill. Farewell.

27. *"The Marquise Du Châtelet did me the honor of reading Descartes's* Dioptrics *with me several days ago."*

To Henri Pitot.[25] Cirey par Vassy, Champagne. August 31, 1736.

I was unable to read M. de Mairan's memoir on driving forces in Paris, and several pursuits foreign to mathematics further delayed the pleasure of reading his work in my retreat. I finally did read it, and it seems to me, as it does to you, a masterpiece of reason with this difference: you have read it as an authority and I as a schoolboy taking lessons. M. de Mairan, one of the fairest, most discriminating and most exact of minds, has very effectively proved, in more than one way, that the quantity of motion is, at bottom, never anything but the product of velocity and mass.

It seems that the discovery of the acceleration of falling bodies by Galileo was the basis of the error of Messrs. Leibniz and Bernoulli. It all comes down then to proving that in this very acceleration the force is really always the same since it acts uniformly from one moment to the next. The distance travelled is, in truth, proportional to the square of the time or the velocity, but each infinitely small part of this distance is only proportional to the velocity and time. Consequently, the strongest point against the old mechanics, which only allows the product of velocity and mass in the quantity of motion, is adequately refuted.

M. de Mairan has considered the matter from all aspects *sapiens et victor ubique*.[26] In Paris he was kind enough to lend me his memoir which I was unable to study at the time. I instructed a young man named M. de la Marre to return it to him. I beg you, please ask M. de Mairan about this and assure him of my respectful esteem.

Let me speak to you here of the new relationship you found between the surfaces of bodies: that their magnitudes are in inverse ratio to the areas of their corresponding sides. From this, you especially derive a very useful observation: that if twelve horses were required to draw a boat twenty-five feet wide, five times twelve horses would be required to draw five boats five feet wide. It seems that you always strive to relate mathematics to man's use.

Since I am already wound up, I must bother you again about a small problem. The Marquise Du Châtelet did me the honor of reading Descartes's *Dioptrics*[27] with me several days ago. We both admired the proportion that he says he found between the sine of the angle of incidence and the sine of the angle of refraction. But, at the same time, we were quite astonished that he said these angles are not proportional while the sines are. I do not understand this at all; I do not understand how the measurement of an angle is proportional and the angle is not. May I make bold and beseech you to clear up my ignorance on this?

My health is rather feeble to apply myself to mathematics. I cannot work one hour a day without great suffering.

Inquire, I pray you, whether it is true that Snellius[28] found the proportion of sines of refraction before Descartes and whether Father Grimaldi[29] found the proportions of sounds with the diffractions of the seven primary rays before Newton. I highly doubt this last allegation. There are storytellers in Paris who will give you the full information. I am with infinite esteem, sir, your very humble and very obedient servant. Voltaire.

28. *In Praise of an Enlightened Prince.*

To the Royal Prince of Prussia.[30] c. September 1, 1736.

Your Royal Highness,

One would have to be unfeeling not to be infinitely moved by the letter with which Your Royal Highness has deigned to honor me. My pride has been flattered by it excessively, but the love for humanity which I have always felt in my heart, and which, I dare say, accounts for my character, provided me with pleasure a thousand times more pure when I learned that there is in this world a prince who thinks as a man, a philosopher prince who will make men happy.

Suffer me to tell you that there is not a man on earth who ought not give thanks for the care you take, through sound philosophy, to cultivate a soul born to command. Believe me that there have never been truly good kings apart from those who began, as you did, by educating themselves, by coming to know men, by loving truth, and by detesting persecution and superstition. If he shared these ideas, there is not a prince who could not bring back the golden age to his states. Why do so few kings seek out that advantage? You suspect the reason, Your Royal Highness, because almost all of them think of royalty more than of humanity. You do precisely the opposite. You may be certain that one day, if the hurly-burly of affairs and the wickedness of men do not spoil so divine a character, you will be worshipped by your people and cherished the world over. Philosophers worthy of the name will flock to your states, and as famous craftsmen come in droves to the country most favorable to their craft, thinking men will come and congregate about your throne.

The illustrious Queen Christina [31] left her kingdom in search of the arts; rule, Your Royal Highness, and let the arts come in search of you.

May you never hold knowledge in disgust because of quarrels among scholars. From the things you deign inform me of, Your Royal Highness, you realize that these are men who are, for the most part, like courtiers. They are sometimes as greedy, as intriguing, as false, and as cruel, and the entire difference between

56

a wretch at court and a wretch at school is that the latter is more absurd.

It is very sad for humanity that those who consider themselves proclaimers of heavenly commandments, the interpreters of the Divinity, in a word, theologians, are sometimes the most dangerous of all; that there are some who are as pernicious in society as they are obscure in their ideas, and that their souls are swelled with venom and pride in proportion to their being devoid of truth. They would disturb the world's tranquillity for a sophism and lead all kings to avenge, with the sword or with firearms, the honor of an argument *in ferio* or *in barbara*.[32]

Any thinking person who does not agree with them is an atheist, and any king who does not favor them will be damned. You know, Your Royal Highness, that the best that can be done is to abandon these supposed preceptors and real enemies of humanity to themselves. Their words, when neglected, vanish into the air like the wind. But if the weight of authority becomes involved, that wind takes on a force that may sometimes overthrow the throne.

Your Royal Highness, I observe with the joy of a heart filled with love for the public good the great distinction you set between men who peacefully seek truth and those who would make war over words they do not understand. I see that the Newtons, the Leibnizes, the Bayles, the Lockes, those souls so elevated, so enlightened, and so gentle, are the ones that nourish your mind and that you cast aside other so-called sustenance which you would find poisonous or insubstantial.

I could not thank Your Royal Highness enough for your kindness in sending me the little book about Mr. Wolff.[33] I consider his metaphysical ideas to do honor to the human mind. They are flashes of light in the deep of night; that is all that can be expected, I believe, of metaphysics. There is no likelihood that the first principles of things will ever be well understood. Mice, occupying a few little holes in an enormous house, do not know whether that building is eternal, who the architect is, nor why that architect built the house. They struggle to go on living, to populate their holes, and to flee harmful animals pursuing them. We are the mice, and the divine architect who built this universe has not, as far as I know, told his secret to any of us. If there is anyone who can claim to speculate justly, it is Mr. Wolff. One may engage him in combat, but one has to hold him in esteem. His philosophy is far from pernicious. Is there anything finer and truer than to say, as he does, that men must be just even if they be atheists?

The protection it seems you give to that learned man, Your Royal Highness, is a proof of your right-mindedness and of the humanity of your feelings.

You are kind enough, Your Royal Highness, to promise to send to me the *Treatise on God, the Soul and the World*. What a gift, Your Royal Highness, and what a correspondence! From his inner palace the heir to a monarchy deigns to send instructions to a recluse! Do condescend to make me this gift, Your Royal Highness; my extreme love of truth alone makes me worthy of it. Most princes are afraid of hearing the truth, but you will be its propagator.

With regard to the verses you speak of, your views on this art are as sensible as on all others. Verse that does not teach men new and inspiring truths is hardly worth reading. You are aware that there would be nothing more reprehensible than spending one's life rhyming worn-out commonplaces that do not deserve being called ideas. If there is anything more vile, it is to be merely a satirical poet, writing only to disparage others. These poets are to Parnassus what those doctors, whose knowledge consists only of words and who intrigue against those who write of real things, are to schools of learning.

If it was possible for the *Henriade* not to displease Your Royal Highness, I must thank that love of truth, that horror which my poem inspires in the sedition-minded, in persecutors, in the superstitious, in tyrants and in rebels. It is the work of a civilized man; it was bound to find grace before a philosopher prince.

You order me to send you my other works. I will obey you, Your Royal Highness; you will be my judge and a substitute for my public. I will submit my philosophical exercises; your intelligence will be my reward. It is a prize few sovereigns are capable of giving. I am certain of your discretion; you must be as virtuous as you are wise.

I will consider my coming to pay court to Your Royal Highness a most precious joy. We travel to Rome to see churches, paintings, ruins and bas-reliefs. A prince like you is far more worthy of a journey; he is a more marvelous rarity. But friendship, which keeps me in my present retreat, prevents me from leaving. No doubt, you think as Julian,[34] that great man so maligned, who said that friends must always be preferred to kings.

In whatever corner of the world I end my days, you may be sure, Your Royal Highness, that I will continually wish you well, that is, wish for the happiness of an entire people. My heart will be among your subjects; your glory will always be dear to me. I will always want you to be as you are and other kings to resemble you.

I am, with deep respect for Your Royal Highness, the very humble, etc.

29. *An Unorthodox View of Paradise.*

To Nicolas-Claude Thieriot. Cirey. Saturday, November 24, 1736.

I have been informed that *Le Mondain*[35] was found in the home of M. de Luçon,[36] and that President Du Puis[37] distributed many copies of the work. A completely disfigured copy was sent to me. It is sad to be thought of as heterodox and to still see oneself truncated, maimed and mutilated like an ancient author. I find that people are quite right to become enraged with the dangerous author of that abominable work in which it is daringly stated that Adam never shaved his beard, that his fingernails were a little too long, and that he had a swarthy complexion. This would make one think straightaway that there were no scissors, razors, or soap in earthly paradise, which would be as shocking a heresy as ever existed. Besides, it is taken for granted in that pernicious lampoon that Adam caressed his wife in paradise, and in the anecdotes concerning the life of Adam found in the archives of the ark on Mount Ararat by Saint Cyprian[38] it is expressly stated that the fellow never had an erection and only had one after being chased out whence, according to what all the rabbis say, the expression to *have an erection of woe*. Such indeed is the insolent absurdity worthy of the folly of the age of gold and of the cruelty of the age of iron. The arrogance and stupidity with which a certain individual spoke to one of our friends would have made me extremely indignant if it had not caused me to burst out laughing.

My going to Prussia is still not certain. Tell your brother to send the philosopher prince's package by coach. Your M. Chambrier [39] is a strange man. I sent him a large package for our prince. I asked him to please acknowledge its receipt. No news. These irregular procedures are not those of a minister. I pray you to speak to him about this. I suppose he has received the packages although I did not know his address. *In Paris* is the address, the street, the house of every minister. He surely received my packages, but inquire about it.

Find out if your prince has some French actors at his court. If so, we would send him the *Prodigal* [40] as an amusement.

I suppose the Ministry finds this little literary exchange very good.

In this package (about which there is no news), I sent to Berlin *Le Mondain,* the *Ode to Emilie,* the *Newtonic* and a letter on Locke [41] in order to pay him my court *in omni genere.*[42]

Now who is the author of that beautiful didactic poem? M. de La Chaussée [43] probably. I expect such masterpieces only from him. Let me know if my conjecture is correct.

Go to the two brothers. Tell them *par amabile fratrum cum pace vostra* [44] that I must see the lesson of the prodigal son that was sent to you almost a month ago. Then my Father Mersenne [45] will read that lesson, and he will decide whether it is not much better written, much more discriminating, much more amusing, in sum much less boring than what is now being performed.

Here is a more exact copy of the *Newtonic.* You may circulate it, but you should begin with those persons who are a little philosophical and poetic. *Pauci quos aequus amavit Jupiter.*[46] My copyist, who is neither a poet nor a philosopher, wrote, instead of "the period of 26,000 years," "six hundred entire centuries beyond twenty thousand years." That made eighty thousand years instead of six thousand.[47] A trifle.

A thousand regards to you and your Parnassus. If you see the good philosopher Mairan, tell him to think of me, to give you his letter, and tell him that I am going to Berlin. Henceforth only write to Madame Faveroles at Bar sur Aube.[48] Remember. A reply on every item. Hold me in affection. Farewell, Mersenne.

30. *A Heartbreaking Separation.*

To Charles-Augustin Feriol, Count d'Argental. 4 a.m., Sunday, December 9, 1736.

Your friend [49] was quite astonished, at first, when she discovered that a work as innocent as *Le Mondain* was used as a pretext by some of my enemies. But her astonishment turned into the utmost bewilderment and the most intense revulsion when she learned that they wanted to persecute me on that miserable pretext. Her righteous grief overcame her determination to spend her life with me. She could not endure my staying any longer in a country that treats me so inhumanly. We have just left Cirey. It is now four o'clock in the morning at Vassy where I am to get some post horses. But, my true, my dear and respectable friend, as I see the moment approach when I will have to be separated forever from one who has done everything for me, who gave up Paris, all her friends and all of life's luxuries for me, one I adore and ought to, you can certainly sense what I am going through. It is an awful state. I would leave with joy beyond words. I would visit the Prince of Prussia who writes me frequently asking me to come to his court. I would keep envy at a sufficient distance so as not to be troubled by it any further. I would live abroad like a Frenchman who will always respect his country. I would be free and not abuse my freedom. I would be the happiest of men. But your friend is before me melting into tears. My heart is broken. Must I let her return alone to a chateau she built only for me and deprive myself of life because I have enemies in Paris? In my despair, I am momentarily disregarding my determination. I will still wait until you tell me of the extremes of rage that may be vented against me.

To threaten me because of such a work would, most assuredly, be combining the absurdity of the golden age with the barbarity of the iron age. The work must have been tampered with. In the end, I do not know what to believe. All I know is that I would like to remain totally unknown, except to you and your friend. At nine o'clock in the evening, she was determined to let me leave. But now at four in the morning, we are in agreement, and I tell you, do whatever you think is suitable. If you think the tempest is too strong, let us know at the usual address, and I will complete my journey. If you think it has really settled down, I will stay. But what a horrible life! Eternally racked by the fear of losing one's freedom on the slightest report without any form of trial! I would prefer death. In the end, I am relying on you. You determine what I must do. I am worn out with fatigue, overwhelmed by despair and sickness. Farewell. I embrace you and your good brother a thousand times.

Why does Mademoiselle Quinault [50] not like me enough to be willing to accept a trinket from me?

[*Voltaire continued his active correspondence with Frederick of Prussia through 1737 and 1738. One of the dominating themes of this exchange of letters was Voltaire's conviction that the study of metaphysics was largely futile and that philosophers would do well to concentrate on ethics and social justice. By the end of 1737 Voltaire had finished the composition of his play* Mérope *which was not to be presented on the stage until 1743. 1738 saw him at work on his* Discours sur l'homme [Discourses on Man] *and occupied with historical writing, particularly the* Age of Louis XIV. *At the same time, he was conducting scientific experiments with Mme. Du Châtelet at Cirey, and he published his* Eléments de la Philosophie de Newton, *a work important for the popularization of Newton's scientific principles in France. The correspondence for the year 1738 ended with an interesting letter to Father Tournemine, his teacher at Louis-le-Grand who had become editor of the* Mémoires de Trévoux, *one of the leading Jesuit journals of the period. He attempted to reassure the old Jesuit that his belief in the philosophical principles of Locke and Newton did not have "dangerous consequences" for religion.*]

31. *"What will I gain from knowing the path of light and the gravitation of Saturn?"*

To Pierre-Robert Le Cornier de Cideville. February 18, 1737.

My dear Cideville,

I have received your letters in which you bring your heart to speak with such great wit. Forgive me, my dear friend, if I have been so tardy in replying. I am really going to hate philosophy which has deprived me of the punctuality of friendship. What will I gain from knowing the path of light and the gravitation of Saturn? These are sterile truths. One feeling is a thousand times more important. You may be sure that while it has held my attention for a while, this study has nevertheless not made my heart insensitive. You may be sure that the compass has not made me abandon our gay rustic verses. It would be much sweeter to sing with you *lentus in umbra, formosam resonare docens Amarillidas silvas* [51] than to travel in the land of scientific demonstrations. But, my dear friend, we must give our soul all possible forms. It is a flame God has confided to us; we must nourish it with those things we find most precious. We must bring all imaginable modes into our being, open all the doors of our soul to all sciences and all feelings. Provided all these things do not come in pell-mell, there is room for everyone. I want to improve my mind and hold you in affection; I want you to be a Newtonian and understand that philosophy just as you are capable of love. A thousand affectionate regards to M. de Formont whom you see or write.

I do not know what people in Rouen and Paris are thinking, and I am unaware of why you speak to me of Rousseau. [52] He is a man I scorn infinitely as a man and whom I have never held in much esteem as a poet. All he is capable of is rhyme. There is nothing great or affectionate about him. His only genius is for detail; he is a craftsman, and I seek a genius. You must have been mistaken when you advised me to praise him and even flatter a few persons for whose approval you think one ought to beg. I shall never praise what I scorn, and I shall never court anyone. Have more elevated and honorable feelings for humanity. Besides do not think France is the only place one can live. It is a country made for young women and sensual men, the country of madrigals and powder puffs. But elsewhere are to be found reason, talent, etc. Bayle could only live in a free country;[53] the vigor of that happily transplanted tree would have been stifled in his homeland. I know that jealousy pursues the arts everywhere; I am familiar with that rust that clings to our metals. Rousseau's poison has been hurled against me even here. He wrote that I had a dispute concerning atheism with 'S-Gravesande.[54] His slander was brought to naught, and so, sooner or later, will all the slander with which I have been defamed. I fear no one; I shall ask a favor of no one; and I shall never dishonor with flattery the little talent given me by nature. A man with such ideas deserves your friendship; otherwise I would be unworthy. This friendship alone will make me come back to France if I do come back.

Farewell. I embrace you with all my heart.

I have read Rousseau's poor *Ode on Peace*. It is almost as bad as all of his latest works.

32. *On Human Justice.*

To the Royal Prince of Prussia. Cirey. c. October 15, 1737.

Your Royal Highness,

I have received the last letter, dated September 27, with which Your Royal Highness honored me. I am very anxious to know whether my last package and that intended for Mr. de Keyserling[55] reached their address. These packages were sent at the beginning of August.

Your Royal Highness, you ordered me to give you an account of my metaphysical doubts. I am taking the liberty of sending you an extract from a chapter on freedom. Your Royal Highness will at least see good faith in it even if he finds ignorance. And would to heaven that all who are ignorant were at least sincere!

Humanity, which is the principle of all my thought, has perhaps led me astray in this work. Perhaps my idea that there would be no vice or virtue, that neither punishment nor reward would be necessary, that especially among philosophers society would be an exchange of wickedness and hypocrisy if man did not have full and absolute freedom—I say, perhaps this opinion has carried me too far. But if you find any errors in my thought, make allowances for them by reason of the principle that gave rise to them.

As far as possible, I always reduce my metaphysics to ethics. With all the care I am capable of, I have sincerely examined whether I may have any notions about the human soul, and I have observed that ignorance is the fruit of all my research. I find the same to be more or less true of this thinking, free and active principle as of God himself. Reason tells me that God exists, but this same reason also tells me I cannot know what He is. In truth, how could we know the nature of our soul, we who are incapable of a single idea about light if we have the misfortune to be born blind? Therefore, I observe sadly that nothing ever written about the soul can teach us the slightest truth.

After groping about to ascertain the nature of this soul, my principal aim is at least to try and govern it. It is the spring in our clock. All of Descartes's fine ideas on elasticity do not teach me anything about the nature of this spring; I am still ignorant of the cause of elasticity. Nevertheless I wind my clock, and it goes after a fashion.

Man is the object of my study. However he may be constituted, we must determine whether there is in reality any vice and virtue. This is the important point with respect to man. I do not say with respect to a specific society living under specific laws, but for the entire human species, for you, Your Royal Highness, who must rule, for the woodsman in our forests, for the Chinese doctor, and for the American savage. While justifiably attacking innate ideas, Locke, the wisest metaphysician I know of, seems to think that there is no universal moral principle. I venture to oppose or rather clarify the idea of this great man on this point. I agree with him that there really are no innate ideas. It follows obviously that there are no innate moral propositions in our soul. But from the fact that we were not born with beards does it follow that we inhabitants of this continent were not born to be bearded at a certain age? We were not born with the ability to walk, but whoever is born with two feet will walk some day. Thus no one carries with him at birth the idea that we must be just, but God has shaped men's organs in such a way that all men, at a certain age, are agreed on this truth.

It seems evident to me that just as he gave the bees an instinct and instruments suited for the making of honey, God wanted us to live in society. Since our society is unable to endure without ideas of justice and injustice, he therefore gave us the wherewithal to acquire them. Our different customs, it is true, will never allow us to apply the same idea of justice to identical notions. A crime in Europe will be a virtue in Asia, just as certain German stews will not find favor with gourmands in France. But God has formed the Germans and the French in such a way that they will all like good cooking. All societies, therefore, will not have the same laws, but no society will be without any laws. Thus the good of society is certainly established by all men, from Peking to Ireland, as the immutable virtue: that which is useful to society will therefore be good in every country. That one idea reconciles at once all of the apparent contradictions in human morality. Thievery was permitted in Lacedaemon. Why? Because wealth was held in common there, and stealing from a miser who kept for himself what legally belonged to the public was a service to society.

It is said that there are savages who eat men and think they are doing the right thing. My answer is that these savages have the same ideas we do of justice and injustice. They wage war as we do out of rage and passion. One sees the same crimes being committed everywhere; eating one's enemies is only one additional ceremony. The evil is not in putting them on the spit; it is in killing them. And I venture to assure you that there is not one savage who thinks he is acting properly by cutting his friend's throat. I observed four savages from Louisiana who were brought to France in 1723. Among them there was a woman of very gentle humor. I asked her through an interpreter if she had occasionally eaten the flesh of her enemies and if she had found it to her taste. She answered yes. I asked her whether she would have willingly killed or had one of her compatriots killed for the purpose of eating him. She answered me trembling and evidently horrified at the thought of this crime. I defy the most determined liar among those who travel to dare state that there exists a small tribe or a family where one is allowed to go back on his word. I am quite justified in believing that since God created certain animals to graze in common, others to see each other only very rarely and in pairs, and spiders to spin webs, each species has the instruments necessary for the work it must do. Just as man has received a stomach for digestion, eyes for sight, and a soul for judgment, he has received all that is necessary to live in society.

Place two men on earth. They will call only what is good for both of them good, virtuous, and just. Place four of them there. Only what is suitable for all four will be virtuous, and if one of the four eats his companion's supper or beats him or kills him, he will surely provoke the others. What I say about these four men should be said about the entire universe. Your Royal Highness, this is more or less the plan on which I wrote that moral metaphysics, but when the subject is virtue should I be the one to treat it in your presence?

Virtues are attributes
That you received from above;
The throne of your ancestors
Beside these precious gifts
Is truly a feeble advantage.
It is the man within you, the wise man
Who subjects me to his law.
Ah! If you were simply king
You would not have my homage.[56]

Be a judge of my ideas, great prince, for your soul is the tribunal with jurisdiction over my opinions. May Your Royal Highness provide me with the desire to live and one day see the Solomon of the North with my own eyes! But I am really afraid I will not be as fortunate as good old Simeon.[57] We do not pass by your portrait without reciting our song of praise which begins:

Let us hope for the world's happiness.

I await your decision concerning the *History of Louis XIV* and the *Elements of the Philosophy of Newton.* If my tribute has been kindly received, I hope I will be rewarded with instructions.

I make bold to beseech Your Royal Highness to please send

me by a safe passage (and I believe that of M. Thieriot to be safe) the memoirs about the czar which you were good enough to promise me. However, I am not giving up poetry. My love for it is greater than ever since you are writing some, Your Royal Highness. I hope to send something shortly that can be presented in the theater of Remusberg. I am indignant that they could present Your Royal Highness with the miserable manuscript of the *Prodigal Son* now in your hands. It has as much resemblance to my play as a monkey does to a man. I know of no other course to take than to publish it to vindicate myself.

There are no words by which I can thank Your Royal Highness for his kindness. With what generosity, I thought I was going to say with what affection, he condescends to take interest in me! You write me what Horace told Maecenas, but you are both Maecenas and Horace.[58] The Marquise Du Châtelet, who shares my admiration for your person and whose respects you allow her to add to my own, makes use of that liberty. I am with the deepest respect and the most affectionate gratitude, etc.

33. *On the Writing of History.*

To Jean-Baptiste Dubos.[59] Cirey. October 30, 1738.

Sir,
I have already been devoted to you with the greatest esteem for a long time. Now I am going to be devoted to you out of gratitude. I will not repeat here that your books ought to be the breviary of men of letters, that you are the most useful and judicious writer I know. I am so delighted to find you the most obliging of writers that I am completely taken with this last idea.

A long time ago, I gathered materials to write the history of the age of Louis XIV. It is not simply the life of that prince that I am writing, and not the annals of his reign. It is rather the history of the human spirit derived from the most glorious age of the human spirit.

This work is divided into chapters. There are about twenty devoted to general history; these are twenty tableaux of the great events of the age. The main characters are in the foreground of the canvass, the masses in the background. The devil with the details! Posterity pays no attention to them at all; they are a vermin that destroys all great works. That which characterizes the age, caused revolutions, and will be important a hundred years from now—that is what I want to write about now.

There is a chapter on the private life of Louis XIV; two on the great changes brought about in the government of the kingdom, in commerce and in finance; two on ecclesiastical government in which the revocation of the Edict of Nantes and the affair of the *régale* are included; [60] five or six on the history of the arts beginning with Descartes and ending with Rameau.

For the general history I have no additional memoirs except for some two hundred printed volumes with which everyone is familiar. The aim is simply to shape a well proportioned body out of all those scattered parts and to depict with true colors but one stroke of the brush what Larrey, Limiers, Lamberty, Rousset,[61] etc. falsify and expatiate upon in volumes.

For the private life of Louis XIV I have the memoirs of M. Dangeau [62] in forty volumes from which I have extracted forty pages. I have things I have heard from old courtiers, valets, great lords and others, and I relate those facts on which they agree; the rest I leave to fabricators of conversations and anecdotes. I have an extract from the famous letter of the King about M. Barbézieux,[63] all of whose defects he indicates and forgives as a favor for his father's services, which characterizes Louis XIV much better than the flattery of Pellisson.[64]

I am rather well informed about the adventure of the man with the iron mask who died in the Bastille. I have spoken to people who served him.

There is a sort of memoir written in the hand of Louis XIV which should be in Louis XV's study. M. Hardion [65] is doubtlessly acquainted with it, but I do not dare ask to have it sent to me.

On church affairs I have the whole mishmash of partisan insults, and I will try to extract an ounce of honey from the absinthe of the Jurieus, the Quesnels, the Doucins,[66] etc.

For the internal affairs of the kingdom I am examining the memoirs of the intendants and the good books on this subject. The Abbé de Saint-Pierre [67] has compiled a political journal on Louis

XIV which I would like him to confide to me. I do not know whether he will do that charitable act to reach paradise.

With respect to the arts and sciences, it is only a matter, I believe, of tracing the course of the human spirit in philosophy, eloquence, poetry and criticism; of indicating the progress in painting, sculpture, music, the goldsmith's craft, and the making of tapestries, mirrors, golden fabrics and clocks. In the process I only want to portray those geniuses who have excelled in these areas. May God save me from using three hundred pages for the history of Gassendi! [68] Life is too short, time too precious to say useless things.

In a word, you see my plan better than I could draw it for you. I am in no hurry to erect my structure. *Pendent opera interrupta, minaeque murorum ingentes.*[69] If you condescend to give me guidance, I will then be able to say: *aequataque machina coelo.*[70] See what you can do for me, for truth, and for an age that includes you among its ornaments.

To whom will you deign to communicate your knowledge if not to a man who loves both his homeland and truth, and who seeks to write history neither as a flatterer, a panegyrist or a gazeteer but as a philosopher? The historian who cleared up the confusion about the origin of the French so well will doubtlessly help me shed light on France's finest days. Remember that you will be rendering a service to your disciple and admirer.

My gratitude to you will always be as great as my esteem, etc.

Voltaire

I pray you, tell me whether the book by La Hode [71] merits my purchasing it and who this La Hode is.

34. *"Metaphysics . . . an immense abyss where everyone is blind."*

To Rolland Puchot des Alleurs. Cirey. November 26, 1738.

If you had not signed the ingenious and substantial letter with which you honored me, I would have easily surmised it was you. I know that you are the only man of your sort capable of doing

70

philosophy such honor. I recognized the soul of Bayle whom the heavens have rewarded by allowing it to lodge in your body. It is appropriate for a genius, cultured as yours is, to be skeptical. Many lightweight and careless minds bedeck their ignorance with an air of pyrrhonism, but the sole reason for your great doubt is that you think very much.

I will walk under your banners a good part of the way, and I will ask you to give me your hand for the rest of the day's march. I believe that in metaphysics you will scarcely find me outside the ranks you will have indicated. There are two points to this metaphysics: the first is composed of three or four little glimmerings of light that everyone perceives equally well; the second is an immense abyss in which everyone is blind. When we agree, for example, that a thought is neither round nor square, that sensations are only in us and not in objects, that our ideas all come to us through the senses (despite what Descartes and Malebranche may say on the subject), that the soul and. . . . If we want to go a step further, then we are in the vast realm of possibility.

From the eloquent Plato to the profound Leibniz, all metaphysicians are, in my judgment, like curious travellers who may have entered the anterooms of the seraglio of the Grand Turk and who, having seen a eunuch passing from afar, would then venture to conjecture how many times his highness caressed his odalisque that night. One traveller says three, another says four, etc. The fact is that the great sultan slept the entire night.

You are certainly quite right to be indignant with Descartes's decisive manner in producing his bad fairy tales. But, I pray you, do not reproach him for his algebra and geometric calculus. He has forsaken them only too much in all his works; he built his magic castle without condescending even to take the slightest measurement. He was one of the greatest geometricians of his time, but he abandoned his geometry and even his geometric spirit for the spirit of contrivance, of systematization and of fiction. That should have discredited him, but, to our shame, is what is responsible for his success. We must admit that his entire physics is only a tissue of errors: erroneous laws of motion, imaginary vortices demonstrated to be impossible in his system and uselessly reconciled by Huyghens,[72] false notions on anatomy, an erroneous theory of light, impossible corrugated magnet matter, three elements to be placed among the thousand and one nights, no observation of nature, no discovery. Yet this is Descartes.

In his time, there was a Galileo, a true inventor, who fought against Aristotle with geometry and experimentation while Descartes only set new chimeras and old figments of the imagination in conflict. But Galileo did not presume to create a universe like Descartes; he was satisfied to investigate it. This did not imply deceiving ordinary men, whether they were important or insignificant. Descartes was a lucky charlatan and Galileo a great philosopher.

How I agree with you about Gassendi! As you vigorously say, he slackens the force of all his reasoning. But a still greater misfortune is his lack of reason. He guessed at many things that were subsequently proven.

For example, it is not enough to contest the plenum with plausible arguments. By examining the trajectory of comets, someone like Newton had to demonstrate by what amount they necessarily rise more rapidly to the height of our planets and consequently are unable to be carried by an ostensible vortex of matter which cannot both go slowly with a planet and rapidly with a comet in the same stratum. Mr. Bradley [73] had to discover the progression of light and demonstrate that it is not delayed in its path from a star to us and that consequently there is no matter there. That is what is meant by being a physicist. Gassendi [74] is a man who tells you roughly that somewhere there is a gold mine, and the others bring you the gold which they have excavated, purified and worked over.

So I shall not be a complete sceptic in physics, for how can one doubt what experience discovers and geometry confirms? Because Anaxagoras, Leucippus, Aristotle and all the babbling Greeks uttered absurdities at great length, does that prevent Galileo, Cassini [75] and Huyghens from discovering new skies? Will the theory of moving forces be any less true as a result? We have the longitude and latitude of two thousand stars whose existence the ancients did not even suspect, and we have discovered more physical truths on earth than the number of stars included in Flamsteed's [76] catalogue.

All of this is insignificant in relation to the immensity of nature, I agree. But it is considerable in relation to man's feebleness.

The little that we know really stretches the powers of the soul; the mind finds as many pleasures in it as the body experiences in other delights not to be scorned.

In all of this, I am relying on you. If the gift of thought makes one happy, I consider you the most fortunate of men. You know how to enjoy things, how to exercise doubt, and how to affirm something when necessary.

Very politely, you gave me a rather wise piece of advice: to look as if I doubt those things about which I wish to be persuasive and to present those things which have been proven as probable.

> Così alegro franciull' porgiamo aspersi
> di soave licor gli orti del vaso.[77]

My answer is that certainly if I had made some discovery and thought it irrefutable, I would present it under the modest guise of doubt. Surely one ought to be a little ashamed when serving local wines. But let me apologize if I have overly praised Newton a little. I was intoxicated with my God. I do not give myself over to enthusiasms, at least not in prose. You know that when I wrote the *History of Charles XII* I merely discovered a man where others saw a hero. But Newton seemed to me altogether another sort. Everything he said seemed so true that I did not dare be too finicky. Besides you know the French. Speak suspiciously about what you give them, and they take you at your word.

In the end, caution will not induce posterity to accept counterfeit currency for the real thing, and if Newton has discovered the truth, both he and it deserve to be confidently presented to his century.

I pass on to a part of your letter which is not the least remarkable, where you demonstrate a refinement of taste. You want only those adornments proper to philosophy assigned to it, and you would not have us take on the role of a wag or man of good cheer when the issue is only one of method and clarity.

> Ornari res ipsa negat, contenta doceri.[78]

It was fine for M. de Fontenelle to make his *Worlds* [79] lively. That cheerful subject could allow flowers and powder puffs, but truths investigated in greater depth belong to those masculine beauties for which the draperies of Poussin are required. You strike me as one of the best creators of drapery I have ever seen. Madame Du Châtelet agrees with you entirely. Hers is a mind which, as La Fontaine says of Madame de La Sablière: [80]

Has the beauty of man with the graces of woman.

She has read and reread your letter with a kind of pleasure she rarely experiences. She was already pleased by an argument you won in favor of Bayle at the expense of de Crousaz. She would like to see one of your gags placed in the chattering mouth of that dogmatic professor.

Continue demonstrating that persons of a certain rank in France do not spend their lives grovelling before ministers or lingering wearily from house to house. Prevent the use of barbaric directives and do honor to France.

Allow me to present my very humble compliments to another worldly philosopher [81] who, they say, is much chubbier than you today. He reads less of Bayle and Cicero than you, but he resides with you and that is certainly worth a few good books. Madame Du Châtelet will be as delighted as I am if you communicate your ideas to her. She is much worthier of them although I appreciate all their value.

I am and. . . .

35. *Some Philosophical and Religious Reassurance to a Jesuit Father.*

To René-Joseph Tournemine. c. December 31, 1738.

My very dear and very reverend Father,

Is it true that my *Mérope* gave you pleasure? Did you recognize some of those generous feelings with which you inspired me

74

during my childhood? *Si placet tuum est* [82] is what I always say when I speak about you and Father Porée. I wish you a good year and a life as long as you deserve. Continue to hold me in affection a little in spite of my predilection for Locke and Newton. It is not a fanatical predilection obstinately opposed to the truth.

Nullius addictus jurare in verba magistri.[83]

I confess that Locke had really charmed me with the idea that God can join, at will, the most sublime gift of thought to the most apparently unformed matter. It seemed to me that the omnipotence of the creator could not be extended too far. Who are we, I said, to limit it? Its apparently marvelous conformity with the immortality of our soul confirmed this feeling for me. Since matter is imperishable, who could prevent divine omnipotence from preserving the eternal gift of thought for a portion of matter to which it might give eternal duration? I did not understand the incompatibility, and here I was probably mistaken. My assiduous readings of Plato, Descartes, Malebranche, Leibniz, Wolff and the modest Locke have all only served to show how incomprehensible the nature of my soul was to me, to what extent we must admire the wisdom of that supreme being who has given us so many gifts which we enjoy unconsciously, and who has deigned to even add the faculty of daring to discuss him. I have always held to the limits to which Locke confines himself, making no assurances about our soul while believing that God is capable of anything. If this opinion has dangerous consequences, however, I will renounce it forever most willingly.

You know whether the poem *La Henriade,* a very amended edition of which I hope to present you with soon, shows evidence of anything but affection for the laws and obedience to the sovereign. When you come down to it, it is a poem about the conversion of a Protestant king to the Catholic religion. If there are propositions one might complain about in works that slipped from my pen in my youth (that period of misconduct) and which were not intended for the public, which have been truncated and falsified, and to which I have never given my approval, my answer is quite brief: I am prepared to eliminate mercilessly anything that may scandalize, however innocent it may truly be. I lose nothing by correcting myself. I am still correcting my *Henriade;* I am retouching all my tragedies; I am recasting the *History of Charles XII.* When I go to so much trouble to correct words, why would I not take pains to correct essential things when a stroke of the pen is all that is necessary.

What I shall never have to correct are the feelings in my heart for you and for those who raised me. I have kept all the same friends I had in your school. My respectful affection for my masters is the same. Farewell, reverend Father. I remain forever, etc.

[The years 1739 to 1741 are marked by Voltaire's peregrinations from Cirey to Paris, Holland, Belgium, and Prussia. His letters of the period describe the hustle and bustle and dissipation of Parisian life and reflect his continuing relationship with Mme. Du Châtelet whom, as he says, he had come to look upon "as a great man and as a most solid and respectable friend."

In 1740, he met Frederick, who had recently ascended the Prussian throne, for the first time. He devoted considerable time and energy getting Frederick's Anti-Machiavelli *through the press, and his letters express his admiration for him both as a person and as a monarch.*

Voltaire's correspondence for the period bespeaks his diversity of interests; to the Russian envoy in Paris he writes about Russian history and culture; he is in touch with the British ambassador to Constantinople; to the actress Quinault he writes of the state of the French theater and of his new play Mahomet *(on the subject of religious fanaticism) which had its premiere in 1741; to John Hervey, the British lord privy seal, he defends his thesis in the* Age of Louis XIV, *a work that was to be published only more than a decade later, that the Sun King had contributed gloriously to civilization by making his age one of history's supreme cultural periods; and to the young French philosopher Helvétius he emphasized the importance of style in communication. His continuing interest in science is expressed in the correspondence of the period, and his old conviction that metaphysical speculation was a vain*

pastime is the subject of a letter to the Dutch physicist and philoso-
pher 'S-Gravesande. His particular displeasure with Leibnizian
metaphysics, which was to loom large in later years, is vented in
letters to the physicist Mairan and to the mathematician Mauper-
tuis.]

36. *Some Thoughts on Russia.*

To Antiochus Cantemirŭ.[84] Cirey en Champagne. March 13,
1739.

Monseigneur,
I am indebted to Your Highness for many reasons. He has
condescended to acquaint me with more than one truth on which
I had been misinformed, and his method of instruction is filled
with kindness which is as valuable as the truth itself. I am presently
reading the *Ottoman History* of the late Prince Cantemir, your
father, which I shall have the honor of returning to you forthwith
and for which I cannot overly thank Your Highness. Please forgive
me for having been mistaken about your origins. The many talents
of your father, the Prince, and of your family led me to believe
that you were probably descended from the ancient Greeks, and
I would have suspected you to be of the race of Pericles rather
than of Tamerlane. However that may be, having always made
it a practice to honor personal merit rather than birth, I am taking
the liberty of sending you a copy of the material I am including
about your illustrious father in my *History of Charles XII* which
is presently being reprinted. I will send it to Holland only when
I have been informed by one of your secretaries that I have your
permission.
In the *Ottoman History* written by Prince Demetrius Cantemir,
I find, to my sorrow, what I find in all histories. They are the
annals of the crimes of the human race. I confess to you especially
that the Turkish government seems to me absurd and horrible. I
congratulate your house for leaving those barbarians in favor of
Peter the Great who, at least, sought to eradicate barbarity, and
I hope that those of your kinsmen who are in Muscovy will help
the arts (which seem to be cultivated by your entire house) to

flourish. Doubtless you have not made an insignificant contribution by introducing the civility that is taking root among these peoples, and you have done them more good than you have received. Would it not be an excessive abuse of your kindness, monseigneur, to dare and take the liberty of asking you a few questions about that vast empire which is now playing such a beautiful role in Europe and whose glory you add to in our midst?

I am informed that Russia is thirty times less populous than it was seven or eight hundred years ago. Someone has written me that there are only about 500,000 gentlemen, 10,000,000 paying head taxes if you include women and children and about 150,000 ecclesiastics; on this last point Russia differs from many other European countries where there are more priests than noblemen. I have been assured that the Cossacks of the Ukraine, of the Don, etc., with their families, only amount to 800,000 and that when all is said and done there are not more than 14,000,000 inhabitants in those vast countries subject to the Russian emperor. This underpopulation seems strange to me for, in the end, I do not see that the Russians have been ravaged by war more than the French, Germans, or English, and I observe that France alone has about 19,000,000 inhabitants. This disproportion is astonishing. A physician has written me that this dearth of the human species had to be ascribed to syphillis which has caused more ravage there than elsewhere and that its scurvy renders one incurable. Under the circumstances, the inhabitants of the earth are indeed unfortunate. Must Russia be unpopulated because a citizen of Genoa took it into his head to discover America two hundred years ago?

I have heard it said, moreover, that all the great ideas of Czar Peter are followed by the present government and that, among its projects, that of showing kindness to foreigners, was a principal one. I flatter myself, sire, that you will imitate him and forgive all these questions that a foreigner dares address to you. There are few princes who are asked such favors, and you are among the very small number of those capable of instructing other men.

I am with deep respect, monseigneur, the very humble and very obedient servant of Your Highness.

Voltaire

37. *The Bustle of Parisian Life.*

To Mme. de Champbonin.[85] Paris. c. Sept. 28, 1739.

My dear friend,

Paris is an abyss in which the repose and self-communion of the soul, without which life is only unwelcome confusion, are lost. I am leading no life at all. I am being carried, being swept far away in a whirlwind. I come and go; I have supper at one end of town and the following day at the other end. One must fly from the company of three or four intimate friends to the Opera, to the Comédie, to see curiosities the way a foreigner would, to embrace a hundred persons in a day, to make and receive a hundred declarations of friendship; not a moment for oneself, no time to write, to think or to sleep. I am like that ancient who died overwhelmed by the flowers that had been thrown at him. From this continuous tempest, from these whirling visits, from this brilliant chaos, I was still on my way to Richelieu with Mme. Du Châtelet. I was leaving by post or almost, and we were coming back the same way to end all this dissipation in Brussels. The Duchesse de Richelieu [86] took it upon herself to have a miscarriage, and now that is one long trip less to take. We will probably leave at the beginning of October to plead our case sadly after having been bustled about here rather gaily but too vigorously. It is like having the gout after jumping. This is our life, my dear fat cat. And you, peaceful in your gutter, make sport of our misbehavior. I miss those sweet moments when we enjoyed both our friends and ourselves in Cirey. What is this package of books that has arrived in Cirey? Is it a packet of works against me? I will tell you in passing that the horrors of the Abbé Desfontaines are of no greater consequence here than if he had never existed. That wretch can no more intrude upon the well-bred people of Paris than Rousseau can in Brussels. These are spiders one does not come across in houses that are well maintained. My dear fat cat, I kiss your velvet paws a thousand times.

38. *"She understands Newton, she despises superstition, in short she makes me happy."*

To Sir Everard Fawkener. Brussels, rue de la Grosse Tour. March 2, 1740 (n.s.).[87]

Dear s[r],

I take the liberty to send you my old follies having no wise things to present you with. I am now at Bruxelles with the same lady Duchastelet who hinder'd me some years ago from paying a visit to you at Constantinople and whom i shall lives with in all probability the greatest part of my life, since these ten years i have not departed from her. She is now at the trouble of a Damn'd suit in law that she pursues at Bruxelles. We have abandon'd the most agreable retirement in the country, to bawl here in the grotte of the flemish chicane; the high dutch baron who takes upon himself to present you with this packet of french *reveries,* is one of the noble players whom the emperor sends into Turquy to represent the majesty of the Roman empire before the highness of the musulman power. I am persuaded you are become nowadais a perfect turk; you speak their language very well, and you keep to be sure a pretty harem. Yet i am affraid you want two provisions which i think necessary, to make that nauseous draught of life go down, i mean books, and friends. Should you be happy enough to have met at Pera,[88] with men whose conversation agrees with y[r] way of thinking? If so, you want for nothing, for you enjoy health, honours, and fortune. Healt, and places i have not, i regret the former, i am satisfied without the other. As to fortune i enjoy a very competent one, and i have a friend besides. Thus i compt my self happy, tho i am as sickly as you saw me at Wandsworth.

I hope ill return to Paris with my lady Duchastelet, in two years time. If about that season you return to y[r] dear England by the way of Paris, i hope ill have the pleasure to see y[r] dear excellency at her house which is without doubt the finest of Paris, and situated in a position worthy of Constantinople; for, it looks upon the river; and a long tract of lands interspers'd with pretty houses is to be seen from every window. Upon my word i would with all that, prefer the visto of the sea of Marmara [89] before that of the Seine, and i would pass some months at Constantinople with you, if i could live without that Lady; whom i look as a great man, and as a most solid and respectable friend. She understands Newton, she despises superstition, in short she makes me happy. I have receiv'd this week two summons from a frenchman who intends to travel to Constantinople, he would fain intice me to that pleasant journey. But since, you could not, no body can. Farewell my dear friend! whom i will love and honour all my life's time, farewell. Tell me whow you fare, tell me you are happy. I am so if you continue to be so.

Y^r for ever.

Voltaire

39. *The Age of Louis XIV.*

To John Hervey, Baron Hervey d'Ickworth.[90] c. June 1, 1740.

I compliment your nation, milord, on the capture of Portobello [91] and on your position as keeper of the seals. Now you are settled in England; that is reason enough for me to take another trip there. I guarantee you that if a certain lawsuit is successful, you will see the arrival in London of a small select company of Newtonians whom the power of your attraction and that of milady Hervey will induce to cross the sea. I pray you, do not judge my essay on the age of Louis XIV by the two chapters that were printed in Holland with so many mistakes that they make my work unrecognizable and unintelligible. If the English translation has been based on this misshapen copy, the translator would be worthy of doing a version of the Apocalypse. But, above all, do not be cross with me for calling the last century the age of Louis XIV. I am certainly aware that Louis XIV did not have the honor of either being the master or benefactor of a Bayle, a Newton, a Halley, an Addison or a Dryden. But in the century called the age of Leo X did Pope Leo X [92] do everything? Were there no other princes who contributed to the civilization and enlightenment of mankind? The name of Leo X prevailed nevertheless because he encouraged the arts more than any other person. Now what king has done more service to humanity in this domain than Louis XIV? What king distributed more benefits, showed evidence of more taste, and distinguished himself by more beautiful establishments? He did not accomplish everything he could doubtless because he was a man, but he did accomplish more than any other person because he was a great man. My strongest reason for holding him in great esteem is that despite his well known faults his reputation is greater than that of any of his contemporaries; in spite of a million men of whom he deprived France and who were all intent on denouncing him, all of Europe holds him in esteem and places him in the ranks of the greatest and best of monarchs.

Now tell me the name of a sovereign who attracted more resourceful foreigners and fostered greater merit among his subjects. Sixty European scholars, amazed that he knew of them, were rewarded by him. Under his reign, the Corneilles, Racines, Quinaults, Lullys, Molières, La Fontaines, Le Sueurs, Lebruns, Jouvenets, Mansards, Perraults, Girardons, Pugets and Coysevox [93] flourished. One also saw a Bossuet, a Fénelon, a Fléchier, a Mascaron, a Bourdaloue and a Massillon [94] introducing men to new forms of eloquence! All the arts were perfected and rewarded at the time. Paris made Rome and Athens look insignificant. Mind you that while this great prince was waging war against more than half of Europe, he was sending geometers and physicists to the heart of Africa and America in search of new knowledge. Remember, milord, that without the voyage and the experiments of those he sent to Cayenne in 1672,[95] I shall add, without the measures of M. Picard,[96] Newton would not have made his discoveries on gravitation. I pray you, take note of a Cassini and a Huyghens who both forsook their country, which they respected, to come and enjoy the esteem and benefaction of Louis XIV. And do you think the English themselves are not indebted to him? Tell me, I pray you, from what court did Charles II acquire so much civility and taste? Weren't the good authors of Louis XIV your models? Didn't your wise Addison, the most discerning of your countrymen, often derive his excellent critiques from them? Do you think the author of Cato was not indebted to the Corneilles and Racines for his method and wisdom? Tell me whether the good books of that age were not useful in the education of all the princes of the empire? What German court does not have a French theater? What prince has not tried to imitate Louis XIV? What people did not hold him in esteem? What nation did not follow French styles at the time? Milord, you counter with the example of Czar Peter the Great who was responsible for the birth of the arts in his country and created a new nation. You tell me, however, that his century in Europe will not be called the age of Czar Peter. Hence you conclude that we ought not to call the last century the age of Louis XIV. It seems to me there is an obvious difference. Czar Peter received his education from other peoples. He brought their arts back home whereas Louis XIV gave instruction to other nations. He was, so to speak, the soul of European princes. Everything, including his very faults, was useful to them. The Protestants who left his states even brought you an industry responsible for the wealth of France. Do you consider so many silk and crystal factories unimportant? The latter especially were improved in your land by our refugees, and our loss was your gain. Finally the French language has become almost universal. To whom are we indebted for that? Was it as widespread in the time of Henry IV? No, without a doubt, Italian and Spanish were the only languages people knew. Our excellent writers brought about this change. But who protected, employed, and encouraged these excellent writers? Do not look upon Louis XIV simply as a fortunate man who had no part in the glory of his reign. He alone reformed the taste of his court in more than one genre. He chose Lully as his composer and took Lambert's prerogatives away because Lambert was a mediocrity and Lully a man of excellence.[97] He was capable of distinguishing wit from genius. He gave Quinault the subject of his operas; he directed the paintings of Lebrun; he supported Corneille and Racine against their enemies; he encouraged the practical arts as he did the fine arts, always advisedly; he lent money to Van Robais to establish factories; he advanced millions to the East India Company he had formed; he gave pensions to scholars and brave officers. Not only were great things accomplished under his reign, but he was the one that accomplished them. Allow me then, milord, to attempt to raise a monument to his glory which I dedicate even more to the service of the human race. I not ony revere Louis XIV because he benefited the French but because he benefited mankind. I am writing as a man and not as a judge. I want to depict the past century and not merely one prince. I am tired of histories that consider merely the adventures of a king as if he existed alone or as if nothing existed except in relation to him. In a word, I am writing the history of a greater age rather than that of a greater king. I think you will find some of your own sentiments in this work. The more I think like you, the more I will have the right to hope for public acceptance.

40. *The Marcus Aurelius of the North.*

To Jean-Baptiste de Boyer, Marquis d'Argens.[98] The Hague. October 2, 1740.

My dear friend whose imagination and integrity do honor to letters, you did indeed warn me. I was going to write and tell you how sorry I was not to find you here. I had been assured you were staying with the man you made rich.[99] I rushed there; they said you were in Stuttgart. Why can't I go there? I am deluged with business matters; I can get there only in another four or five days. Besides I will have to return to Brussels immediately. But you, why go to Switzerland? What! The world has a King of Prussia! What! The most amiable of men is on the throne! The Algarottis, Wolfs, Maupertuis and all of the arts are rushing there in droves, and you would go to Switzerland! No, believe me. Settle in Berlin. Reason, the mind and virtue will have a new birth there. It is the native land of every thinking man; it is a beautiful city and a healthy climate; it has a public library which the wisest of kings will make worthy of himself. Where else will you find the same overall assistance? Do you know that everyone is eager to live under the Marcus Aurelius of the North? Today I saw a gentleman with an income of fifty thousand pounds who said to me: "I will have no homeland except Berlin. I am renouncing my own and will settle there; there will be no other king for me." I know a very great lord of the Empire who would leave His Holy Majesty for the humanity of the King of Prussia. My dear friend, enter the temple he is erecting for the arts. Alas! I will not be able to follow you; a sacred duty draws me elsewhere. I cannot leave Madame Du Châtelet to whom I have dedicated my life for any prince, not even for this one. But I will be consoled if you make a pleasant life for yourself in the only country where I would want

to be were I not with her. Paupie has apprised me of your arrangements; I send you my most affectionate compliments on them.
Why can I not have the honor of embracing you? Farewell, my
dear Isaac. Live a contented and happy life.

If you have anything to inform me of regarding your destiny,
write to me in Brussels. Farewell, my good and charming friend.

41. *Against Machiavelli.*

To Charles-Jean-François Hénault.[100] The Hague. October 31,
1740.

Sir,

If the King of Prussia had come to Paris, he would in no way
have belied the charms you find in the letters that have been
shown to you. He speaks as he writes. I do not know yet quite
specifically whether there have been greater kings, but there have
scarcely been more amiable men. It is a miracle of nature that the
son of a royal ogre, who was raised among animals, had an inkling
in his wasteland of all the subtlety and natural graces which are
shared in Paris by only a small number of persons who, nevertheless, are responsible for the city's reputation. I think I have already
said that his dominant passions are to be just and to please. He is
as suited for society as he is for the throne. When I had the honor
of seeing him, he asked me for news about those chosen few who
deserved a visit from him to France. I placed you at their head. If
he can ever come to France, you will see that you are known to
him and you will observe a slight difference between his suppers
and those you occasionally attended with princes in France. You
are quite right to be surprised by his letters; you will be even
more so by his *Anti-Machiavelli.*[101] I do not favor kings becoming authors, but you will admit that if there is a subject worthy
of being treated by a king it is this one. In my opinion it is a fine
thing for a hand bearing the sceptre to create the antidote for the
poison which an Italian scoundrel had been feeding sovereigns for
two centuries. This may do humanity a little good and certainly
bring considerable honor to royalty. I was almost alone in believing

that this unique work ought to be printed since prejudice never sways me. I was very pleased that through my good offices a king took such an oath to the universe to be good and just.

I detest and scorn base and infamous superstitition which brings dishonor to so many states as much as I adore true virtue. I think I have found true virtue both in this prince and in his book.

If this king ever betrays such great commitments, if he is ever unworthy of himself, if he is not at all times a Marcus Aurelius, a Trajan and a Titus, I will weep and cherish him no more.

M. d'Argenson [102] must have received a copy of the *Anti-Machiavelli* for you. I am going to turn it into a beautiful edition. I was forced to do this one hastily in order to head off all the defective ones that are being circulated and to quash them. I should like to be able to send copies to everyone, but how can I do this through the mails? It remains to be seen whether the censors will give their approval to this book and whether it will be signed Passart or Charrier.[103]

I would have already decided to spend the rest of my life with that kind prince and in his court forget the unworthy manner I have been treated in a country that was supposed to be a refuge for the arts. But the person [104] who showed you the letters has more influence over their writer, and although I may be indebted to this king for being (until now) a model of kings, my debt to friendship is a hundred fold greater. Let me always include you among those who preserve my affection for my homeland, and let Mme. Du Deffand not think that the desire to please her and have her approval will ever leave my heart. Is M. de Formont in Paris? He is, as you know, among the chosen few. My respects to *quelli pochissimi signori* [105] and especially to you, sir, who have always held me in affection only fleetingly and to whom I am devoted forever.

I hope that Dumolard [106] won't be bad and that he will be indebted to you for the rest of his life.

42. *On the Retirement of a Noted Actress*

To Jeanne-Françoise Quinault. Brussels. April 1, 1741.

Mademoiselle,

I have been informed of two items of news in which everyone ought to take equal interest: that you are ill and that you are abandoning the theater. For my part, I am more interested in your health than in the pleasures of Paris, and whatever your talents may be, I think you are even more needed by society than the theater.

People say that your brother has also left out of disgust. Only barbarians are capable of discouraging persons of talent. I pity both the theater and Paris. It seems to me that the arts are not getting favorably treated there. Your loss and your brother's will at least be felt. This is how they deal with persons of great talent. They are neglected or persecuted when they serve; they are missed when they are gone.

I see that *Mahomet* is no longer an issue and that I will have to abandon forever an art with which you reconciled me. Everything in France is tending toward the total extinction of good taste which will survive, however, as long as you are alive. Send me, I pray you, news of your health. You may be sure that you will never have a servant more truly devoted to you than I.

V.

43. *Rules for the Study of Nature*

To Claude-Nicolas Le Cat.[107] April 15, 1741.

Sir,

If you wish to apply yourself seriously to the study of nature, let me inform you that necessarily the way to begin is by constructing no systems. One must proceed like Boyle, Galileo, and Newton. Examine, weigh, calculate, and measure, but never speculate. Mr. Newton never constructed a system; he saw and demonstrated but never substituted his imagination for the truth. What our eyes and mathematics demonstrate to us we must hold to be true. For all the rest we can only say: "I do not know."

It is undeniable that the tides follow the course of the sun and the moon exactly. It has been mathematically demonstrated that these two stars weigh upon our globe and to what degree, whence Newton not only calculated the action of the sun and moon on the earth's tides but also the action of the earth and sun on the moon's waters (assuming some to exist). In truth, it is strange that a man was able to make such discoveries. But that man used the torch of mathematics which is the great light of mankind.

So be careful not to let yourself be beguiled by imagination. Imagination must be relegated to poetry and banished from physics. To imagine a central fire in order to explain the flow of the sea is like solving a problem with a madrigal.

That there is fire in every body is a truth that cannot be doubted. There is some even in ice, and experiment proves it. But the existence of a furnace precisely in the earth's center is something no one can know and which, consequently, cannot be admitted in physics.

Even if this fire were to exist, it would neither explain the high tides, nor the tides of full moons, nor why the tides lag with the moon of equinoxes and solstices, nor why the seas which do not communicate with the ocean have no tide, etc. Consequently there would not be the slightest reason to admit this so-called hearth as a cause for the swelling of the waters.

You ask what becomes of the waters of rivers that are carried to the sea? Are you unaware that a calculation has been made to within one degree of heat in a specific amount of time of the extent to which the action of the sun causes the water to rise and then dissolves it into rain with the help of the winds?

You say that you find the assertion by several authors that snow and rain are sufficient for the formation of rivers a very poor notion. You may be sure that the notion is neither good nor bad but a truth recognized by computation. You may consult Mariotte and the *Transactions* [108] of England on this.

And in a word, if I may reply to the honor of your letter with some advice, read the good authors whose only guides are experience and computation and think of all the rest simply as fiction not worth the time of anyone desirous of improving his mind. I have the honor of being, etc.

44. *"Frankly Leibniz only came to put science into confusion."*

To Jean-Jacques Dortous de Mairan.[109] Brussels. May 5, 1741.

My dear sir,

I have received your certificate,[110] but I see that the Academy is neutral and does not dare judge a dispute which, it seems to me all the same, you have clarified adequately.

I think the Royal Society would be bolder and not hesitate to state that in equal amounts of time two makes two and four makes four since, in truth, after taking everything into consideration that is what the question comes down to.

Frankly Leibniz's only contribution was to put science into confusion. His insufficient reason, his continuity, his plenum, his monads, etc. are seeds of confusion with which Mr. Wolff [111] has methodically caused fifteen in-quarto volumes to blossom and which will turn German heads more than ever to reading much and understanding little. I find more from which to profit in one of your memoirs than in all of this verbiage which is given us *more geometrico*. You speak *more geometrico et humano.*[112]

This Koenig,[113] a student of Bernoulli who brought us the religion of the monads to Cirey, made me shiver several years ago with his long demonstration that a double force communicates a quadruple force in a single amount of time. This sleight of hand is one of Bernoulli's and very easily explained.

I am sorry that my friends let themselves be caught in this trap, even more so because of the dispute that has arisen. But we must not try our friends in their profession of faith, and I, who only preach toleration, cannot damn the heretics. I look upon the monads in vain with their perception and apperception as an absurdity; I am accustoming myself to them in the same way that I would let my wife go to a Protestant sermon if she was a Protestant.

Peace is preferable even to truth. I have scarcely known either in this world but what I do know very well is the esteem and friendship with which I shall always be, my very dear philosopher, your etc.

The first time a midbrain is dissected, my respects to the soul that is housed in it.

45. *On the Importance of Style.*

To Claude-Adrien Helvétius.[114] Brussels. June 20, 1741.

My dear and kind friend,

I certainly disapprove of my laziness but I have been so shamefully occupied with prose for a month that I hardly dared speak to you of verse. My imagination has been weighed down by studies which bear the same relation to poetry as dark and dusty warehouses to a well-lighted ballroom. I must shake the dust off to answer you. You wrote me a letter, my charming friend, in which I recognize your genius. You do not think that Boileau measures up at all; there is nothing sublime in him, his imagination has no brilliance. I agree with you. This is the reason, it seems to me, that he does not have the reputation of a sublime poet. But what he could and wanted to do, he did well. He set reason in harmonious verses; he is clear, consistent, easy and successful in his transitions. He does not rise to heights, but he also scarcely stumbles. His subjects do not allow that loftiness possible for those you treat. You have been conscious of your talent just as he was of his. You are a philosopher; you see everything full size; your brush is strong and bold. I tell you this with the greatest sincerity: nature has made you far superior to Despréaux in all these respects. But these talents, however great, will be meaningless without his. You require his precision all the more since the magnitude of your ideas can make less allowance for constraint and servitude. Thinking is no effort at all for you, but writing is an infinite one. Therefore, I will always extol to you that art of writing which Despréaux knew and taught so well, that respect for language, that interconnection and continuity of ideas, that facile appearance with which he guides his reader, that naturalness which is the result of art and that appearance of ease which is only the product of work. A word out of place spoils the most beautiful thought. The ideas of

90

Boileau are, I admit again, never great but they are never disfigured. In a word, to be superior to him one must begin by writing as clearly and as correctly as he did.

Your lofty dance cannot allow a false step; he takes none in his little minuets. Your brilliance is that of gems; his dress is simple but well made. Your diamonds must be set in good order or else you would seem ill at ease with a diadem on your head. Now send me something so well worked over as to befit the nobility of your imagination, my dear friend. Do not sneer at being both the owner of the mine and the worker of the gold it produces. Since I speak to you in this way, you know how interested I am in the splendor of your reputation and in that of the arts. My friendship for you increased even further during your last trip. I certainly give the impression of not writing verse any more. From now on, I want to admire yours alone. Madame Du Châtelet, who has written you, sends you a thousand regards. Farewell. I will be attached to you for the rest of my days.

46. *Vanitas vanitatum et metaphisica vanitas.*

To Willem Jacob 'S-Gravesande.[115] Brussels. August 1, 1741.

I thank you for the diagram you were kind enough to send me of the machine you use to fix the sun's image. I will order one made on your design and will be rid of a great obstacle since, being quite inept, I am having the greatest difficulty with the mirrors in my dark room. As the sun moves on, the colors disappear and resemble the affairs of this world which are never alike for two consecutive moments. I call your machine a *Sta sol.*[116] Since Joshua's time, no one before you has stopped the sun.

In the same package, I received the work I requested in which my opponent takes about three hundred pages to discuss some of Pascal's thoughts which I had examined in less than one page.[117] I still hold to what I have said: the fault with most books is they are too long. With reason on one's side, one would be brief, but little reason and much invective have produced three hundred pages.

I have always thought that Pascal only set his ideas down on paper to review and reject part of them. This critic disagrees completely. He maintains that Pascal cherished all his ideas and would not have eliminated any of them. But if he knew that the publishers themselves eliminated half of them, he would be quite surprised.

He has merely to consult those written in Pascal's own hand which Father Desmolets recovered a few years ago.[118] He will be even more surprised. They are printed in the *Recueil de littérature*. Here are a few:

"If according to natural reason there is a God, he has neither parts nor limits. He has no relation to us. We are, therefore, incapable of knowing what he is or if he exists."

Do you really believe that Pascal would have preserved "if he exists." Apparently Father Hardouin [119] had seen this *pensée* when he included Pascal in his absurd list of modern atheists.

"I would not feel capable of finding anything in nature with which to convince atheists."

But Clarke, Locke, Wolff and so many others could and surely Pascal would have.

"Every time a proposition is inconceivable, one must not deny it but examine its opposite, and if it is clearly false one may assert the contrary however incomprehensible."

Pascal had forgotten his geometry when he reasoned so strangely. Two squares make a cube and two cubes make a square. These are two contrary propositions, both equally absurd, etc.

"I want to show you an infinite and indivisible thing: a point is moving it everywhere with infinite speed for it is everywhere and complete."

This is very anti-mathematical; there are as many mistakes in it as there are words. Certainly such ideas were not meant to be implemented. My critic would change his mind a little if he were tutored by you.

We must not blindly believe everything Pascal said, far from it. He was a believer; in his last year, he believed that he was constantly looking at an abyss next to his chair. Should we therefore imagine the same? For my part, I also see an abyss, but it is in the things he thought he was explaining.

You will find in the miscellanea of Leibniz that melancholy

finally led Pascal's reason astray. He even makes the statement a bit harshly. After all, it is not astonishing that a man with as mournful an imagination as Pascal finally deranged his mental organs through a poor diet. This malady is neither more astonishing nor more humiliating than a fever or a migraine. If the great Pascal was afflicted by it, it was like Samson losing his strength. I do not know with what malady the doctor who argues so bitterly against me was afflicted. But he has been misled on every point and especially on the state of the question.

The substance of my little notes on Pascal's *Pensées* is that one must doubtlessly believe in original sin since faith commands it, and one must believe in it all the more since reason is absolutely powerless to teach us that human nature has fallen from grace. Revelation alone can teach us this. Plato came a cropper over this matter a long time ago. How could he know that men had at one time been more handsome, taller and stronger, that they had had beautiful wings, and that they had produced children without women?

All who have used physics to prove the decline of this little globe of ours have had no better luck than Plato. "Do you see these ugly mountains?" they said, "these seas that come into land? These lakes with no outlet? They are the debris of a cursed globe." But when these mountains were examined more closely, people saw that they were necessary to provide us with rivers and mines, and that they are the perfections of a blessed world.

Similarly, my castigator assures us that our life is very short compared to that of ravens and deer. He heard his governess tell him that deer live three hundred years and ravens nine hundred. Hesiod's governess had apparently told him the same tale. But my philosopher should simply question any hunter, and he will discover that deer live to be twenty. His inquiring will be of no avail. Of all the animals, man is the one to whom God gave the longest life, and when my critic shows me a raven a hundred and two years old M. de St. Aulaire [120] and Mme. de Chanclos [121] he will delight me.

Some gentlemen are strangely mad in their desire that we be absolutely miserable. I detest a charlatan who would delude me into believing that I am sick in order to sell me his pills. Keep your drugs, my friend, and leave me to my health. Now why do you curse me because I am healthy and do not want any of your quack medicine?

This man tells me coarse stories in line with the laudable habit of persons whose humor no one shares. He ferreted out of a nondescript journal some letters or others on the nature of the soul, which I never wrote and which a publisher has persisted in printing under my name at small cost, as well as many other things I do not read.[122] But since this man does read them, it ought to be evident to him that these letters on the nature of the soul were not written by me and that entire pages were copied word for word from material I wrote some time ago on Locke. Clearly they were written by some plagiarist. I do not perpetrate such plagiarisms however indigent I might become.

My learned man goes to no ends to prove that the soul is spiritual. I want to believe that his is, but in truth his reasoning really shows very little spirit. He wants to rebuke Locke by using me because Locke said that God was powerful enough to cause an element of matter to think. Locke neither says nor knows of what the human understanding consists. He confines the direction of his undertaking to showing us our weaknesses and to believing that God knows more about them than we do.

The more I reread Locke, the more I wish these gentlemen would study him. It seems to me that he has acted like Augustus who gave an edict *do coercendo intra fines imperio*.[123] Locke consolidated the authority of science to strengthen it. What is the soul? I know nothing about this. What is matter? I know nothing about this. Joseph Leibniz discovered that matter is a collection of monads. So be it. I do not understand it nor does he. Well, my soul will be a monad! Now I am well informed, aren't I? "I am going to prove that you are immortal," my learned man says to me. But he will really delight me; my desire for immortality is as great as his. I wrote the *Henriade* for that reason alone. But my man thinks he is more certain of gaining immortality by his arguments than I am by my *Henriade*.

Vanitas vanitatum et metaphisica vanitas.[124]

94

Measure, weigh and calculate. That is what Newton did; that is what you are doing with Mr. Musschenbroek.[125] But as for the first principles of things, we do not know any more about them than Epistemon and master Editue.[126] Philosophers who form systems on the secret construction of the universe are like our travellers who go to Constantinople and speak of the seraglio. They have only seen the outside and claim to know what the sultan is doing with his favorite ladies. Farewell. If anyone has any understanding at all, it is you. But I consider my critic blind. I also have the honor of being blind. But I am a blindman from Paris, and he is a blindman from the provinces. However, I am not so blind as not to see all your qualities, and you will discover how appreciative my heart is of your friendship.

47. On Leibniz and Wolff.

To Pierre-Louis Moreau de Maupertuis. Brussels. August 10, 1741.

My dear flattener of planets and of Cassinis,[127] I will not place such quatrains beneath the portrait of Christian Volffius.[128] For a long time, I have considered with a monad's stupor what dimensions that Germanic chatter-box assigns the inhabitants of Jupiter. He judged them by the size of our eyes and the earth's distance from the sun. But the honor of inventing that stupidity does not belong to him since Volffius compiles the inventions of others in thirty volumes and has no time of his own for inventing. That man has brought all the horrors of scholasticism back to Germany encumbered with sufficient reasons, monads, indiscernibles and all the scientific absurdities which Leibniz brought into the world out of vanity and which the Germans study because they are Germans. It is very deplorable that a French woman like Mme. Du Châtelet used her mind to embroider such cobwebs. You are the guilty party for furnishing her with that fanatic Koenig[129] from whom she derived the heresies which she makes so charming. If you were generous enough to send me your cosmology, I would surely swear to you by Newton and yourself not to make a copy and to return it after I had read it. You must not place "the candle under the bushel" [130] as is nobly said by you know who, and, in truth, a man who is unfortunate enough to have read Christianus Volffius's cosmology needs yours to subdue his anger.

Is it true Euler [131] is in Berlin? Is the purpose of his visit to form an Academy of Sciences at discount prices? Has Count Algarotti [132] written you? I imagine that the same charitable soul who pestered me about your very vigorous philosophy also pestered me about his politics.

The king still writes to me in his ordinary manner and in the same style. Keyserlingk [133] is still sick in Berlin where I think he is bored, and where your boredom will probably end. They say you are going to a much more delightful place and to a lady superior to any king you have seen. She is not likely to become a Wolffian disciple.

The more one reads, the more one discovers that these metaphysicians do not know what they are talking about, and all their works increase my esteem for Locke. There is not a word of truth, for example, in all the figments of Malebranche's imagination. Not even his system on the apparent size of stars on the horizon is factual. Mr. Smith has lately shown that this is a very natural effect of the rules of optics. Your old Academy will be quite angry once again because of this new truth discovered in England. However, Privat de Molière, [134] who is not the equal of Poquelin de Molière, is still investigating vortices, and university professors teach these fantasies, so prone are professors of every kind to deceive men.

Good night. Madame Du Châtelet, who deep in her heart really feels you are superior to Wolff, sends you regards that are more sincere than her Leibnizian ideas. I am forever yours.

V.

48. *". . . my dear friend, how I would like to see you again in Paris during our Ramadan!"*

To Pierre-Robert Le Cornier de Cideville. Grai en Franche-Comté. January 19, 1742.

The most ambulatory, the most literary of your friends, and the one who writes the least throws himself at the foot of the altar of friendship and confesses his wretched laziness with a contrite heart. I ought to have written you from Paris and Cirey, my good Cideville. Did I have to wait until my arrival in Franche Comté? We are leaving here in a week, are returning to Cirey to spend a few days, and from there we are taking a small trip to Paris. In Paris, we will stay in the home of the Countess d'Autray, near the Royal Palace, which belongs to the lady of the City of Grai where we presently find ourselves. I do not know if Mme. Du Châtelet gave you all these details in her letter, but I owe you this full account of my movements in order to have a letter from you for sure on my arrival in Paris.

Won't you spend a part of the holy period of Lent in that great capital of frivolity? Didn't I hear that the philosopher Formont is to be there? My dear friend, it would be very sweet for us to assemble a small number of the elect, servants of Apollo and of pleasure. I am not too well informed as to how the theater is thriving. That is what interests me, since as far as the spectacle of Europe, the armies of Germany and the comedy in Frankfurt [135] are concerned, I have only a passing interest in them. I pay my tithe to stand in the orchestra for a moment and then think no more about it. But the interesting thing is we need actors at the Comédie Française. My need to see a replacement for Dufresne is greater than that of seeing Maximilian of Bavaria on the throne of Charles VI. A great German actor named the King of Prussia has informed me that he will have La Noue.[136] On the other hand, we flattered ourselves that we would have him in Paris, and I should like La Noue to follow me and abandon kings for his friends. I will have *Mahomet* staged if he joins the company on condition, of course, that you are satisfied with the famous rascal whom I have reshaped, recut, refiled, planed down, and re-embroidered all to please you because we must start with you

97

and then I will be sure of the public. I will still have time to wait for the departure of the Turkish ambassador for, in truth, it would not be right to denigrate the prophet while we feed the ambassador and make sport of his chapel in our theater. We Frenchmen respect the law of nations, especially with the Turks.

My goodness, my dear friend, how I would like to see you again in Paris during our Ramadan! [137] For whether I get my rascal to perform or not, I won't stay long. I have to go to Brussels again to drain the cup of sorrow of my quarrels and to vegetate for two years in the land of insipidity. A few sparks of your imagination and a few days of your presence would be an antidote for me. I run a great risk of staying for at least another two years among the barbarians. Can I not have the consolation of seeing you for two days? Farewell, my dear friend to whom my heart is joined for life. I embrace you very affectionately.

V.

49. *"He fidles and fights as well as any man in christendom. . . ."*

To Sir Everard Fawkener. c. June, 1742.[138]

If i have forgot the scraps of english i had once gathered, i'll never forget my dear ambassador. I am now at Paris, and with the same she philosopher i live with these tuevlve years. Was i not so constant in my bargains for life, i would certainly come to see you in y^r kiosk, in y^r quiet and y^r glory.

You will know the new victory of my good friend the king of Prussia, who wrote so uvell against Machiavel, and acted immediately like the heroes of Machiavel. He fidles and fights as well as any man in christendom; he routs austrian forces, and loves but very little y^r king, his dear neigbour of Hanover. I have seen him twice since he is free from his father's tyranny. He would retain me at his court, and liv'd whith me in one of his country houses just with the same freedom and the same goodness of manners you did at Wanshorth. But he could not prevail against the marquise du Chastellet. My only reason for being in France is that i am a friend. You must know my prussian king, when he was but a man, lov'd passionatley y^r englhish gouvernment, but the king has altered the man, and now he relishes despotik pouver, as much as a Mustapha, a Selim, or a Solyman.

News came yesterday at our court the king of Sardinia [139] would not at all hearken to borbonian propositions. This shrubb will not suffer the french tree to extend his branches over all Italy. I would be affraid of an universal war, but i hope much from the white pate of our good cardinal, who desires peace and quiet, and will give it to christendom if he can.

I have seen here our ottoman minister, Sayd bacha; i have drank wine with his chaplain and reason'd with Laria, his interpreter, a man of sense who knows much, and speaks well. He has told me he was very attached to you. He loves you, as all the world does. I have charg'd him to pay to you my respects, and i hope the bearer of these will tell you with what tenderness i'll be for ever y^r humble and faithful servant.

Voltaire.

[*For the next four years, from 1742 to 1745, Voltaire continued travelling, to Franche-Comté, Aix-la-Chapelle, Berlin, Paris, Holland, etc. He had come to realize the duplicity of Frederick II, "my good friend the King of Prussia who wrote so well against Machiavel and acted immediately like the heroes of Machiavel." He convinced the French government to let him go to Frederick in 1743 on a diplomatic mission to discover the king's political and military intentions. Voltaire's correspondence for the period includes a number of dispatches, some of which are in code, to Amelot de Chaillou, the new French foreign minister.*

In the same year, Voltaire sought membersehip in the elite Académie Française, but his efforts failed. He did succeed, however, in being elected to the Royal Society of London, and he wrote expressing his deep satisfaction: "the title of brother you honor me with is the dearest to me of all titles."

In April 1744, the husband of his niece Mme. Denis died, and Voltaire wrote her offering sincere condolence and consolation. He had, however, already begun a passionate love affair with her, and his correspondence includes a goodly number of letters written in Italian that express his feelings for his new mistress. Also in Italian was his correspondence with Pope Benedict XIV to whom he had dedicated his play Mahomet *as part of a campaign to convince members of the French Academy of his "orthodoxy" in a further attempt to gain membership in that body. He was finally successful on April 25, 1746.*

His letters from this period include an interesting exposition of his innovative conception of history as a discipline devoted to "customs, science, laws, usage, and superstition." His work on the Essai sur les moeurs [Essay on Customs] *continued, and he shared his thoughts on the writing of history with, among others, the Swiss Protestant minister Jacob Vernet.]*

50. A Candidate for the French Academy.

To Odet-Joseph de Vaux de Giry.[140] February 1743.

I have the honor of sending you the first sheets of a second edition of the *Elements of Newton* in which I have provided an abstract of his metaphysics. You will see that of all philosophers Newton was most persuaded of the existence of a God and that I was correct in stating that a catechist announces God to children whereas a Newton demonstrates Him to the wise.

I look forward to the honor of presenting you in time with the complete edition, now being undertaken, of the few works truly written by me. Throughout this edition, you will behold the character of a good citizen. That is the only reason I merit your suffrage, and all the rest I submit to your enlightened criticism.

I heard you say with great consolation that I had dared depict religion in its proper complexion in the *Henriade*, and that I had even had the good fortune of exhibiting as much propriety in my interpretation of dogma as I had sensibility in my eulogy of virtue. You even condescended to approve my daring transposition of Christian heroism on the profane stage following our great masters.[141] In sum, you will discover whether there is anything in this edition with which a man who does as much honor as you to the world and the Church cannot be content. You will see how vilified I have been by slander. My works, which all describe my inner feelings, will be my apologists.

I have written against fanaticism which spreads so much bitterness in society and arouses so much discord in the political state. But the more I oppose this spirit of factionalism, fanaticism, and rebellion, the more I revere a religion whose morality makes a family of mankind and whose practices are based on indulgence and charity. Having always celebrated it, why could I not cherish it? You, in whom I find that religion so attractive, could alone endear it to me. Stoicism only gave us one Epictetus while Christian philosophy forms thousands of unknowing Epictetuses in whom virtue is so developed that they are even unaware of it. Christian philosophy sustains us especially in misfortune, in oppression, and in the forlornness that follows. It is perhaps the only consolation for which I must beg after thirty years of tribulations and slander, the rewards of thirty years of work.

I confess that it is not this true respect for Christianity which motivated me never to write against decency. That must be attributed to the natural antipathy I have had since childhood for the rhymed nonsense and indecencies which give pleasure, because of their subject matter, to an unbridled youth. At the age of nineteen, I did an adaptation of a tragedy of Sophocles in which love does not even play a role.[142] At twenty, I began an epic poem whose subject is the triumph of virtue over mankind and which I offer to God.[143] I have spent my time in obscurity studying a little physics and collecting memoirs for the history of the human spirit, especially that of an age when the human spirit reached perfection. [144] I worked on it every day, if not successfully at least with an assiduousness which love for my country has inspired in me.

Perhaps that is what may have enticed some of your colleagues into showing me courtesies which could have encouraged me to request the honor of admission to a body that is responsible for the glory of that very age whose history I am writing.

I was flattered that the Academy would even find nobility in replacing a cardinal who for a time was the arbiter of Europe with a simple citizen whose only merits are his studies and his zeal.

My true feelings on matters of possible concern to the state and religion, however unprofitable they may be, were well known in the end to the late Cardinal de Fleury. During the last period of his life, he did me the honor of writing me twenty letters which prove well enough that my true feelings did not displease him.

101

He even deigned to impart to the king himself a little of the kindness with which he honored me. These reasons would be my excuse if I dared ask for this wise minister's place in the republic of letters.

The desire to give just praise to the father of religion and of the state might perhaps have closed my eyes to my incapacity.

I would have at least shown the extent of my affection for that religion which he supported and of my zeal for the king he educated. That would be my reply to the cruel accusations I have suffered. That would be my defense, a solemn homage to truths I revere and an assurance of my obedience to the feelings of those who are preparing the Dauphin [145] to be a prince worthy of his father.

51. *On Corneille, Racine and Other Literary Figures.*

To Luc de Clapiers, Marquis de Vauvenargues.[146] Paris. April 15, 1743.

I had the honor of telling the Duc de Duras [147] yesterday that I had just received a letter from a very intelligent philosopher who also happened to be a captain in the king's regiment. He immediately surmised it was M. de Vauvenargues. It would really be difficult for two persons to be capable of writing such a letter, and ever since I have heard the subject of taste being discussed, I have seen nothing as fine and as searching as that which you did me the honor of writing.

In the last century, there were not four men who would dare admit to themselves that Corneille was often no more than a declaimer. You sense and express this truth like a man with truly just and clear ideas. I am not at all astonished that so sagacious and fine a mind would give preference to the art of Racine, to that wisdom which is always eloquent, always master of the heart, which brings it to say only what is necessary and in the manner necessary. But I am also persuaded that the same discernment which made you so keenly aware of the superiority of Racine's art causes you to admire the genius of Corneille, the creator of tragedy in a barbaric age. Creators are rightfully in the forefront of the memory of mankind. Certainly Newton knew much more than Archimedes, but Archimedes' *Equiponderants* will always be a work worthy of admiration. The beautiful scene of Horace and Curiace,[148] the two charming scenes of the *Cid*, a large part of *Cinna*, the role of Sévère,[149] almost all of Pauline's [149] and half of the last act of *Rodogune* would hold their own against *Athalie* [150] even if these passages were written today. How then should we judge them when we think of the times during which Corneille wrote! I have always said: *Multae sunt mansiones in domo patris mei*.[151] Molière has not prevented me from prizing *Le Glorieux* of M. Destouches; [152] *Rhadamiste* [153] has moved me even after *Phèdre*. A man like you ought to have preferences but not make exclusions.

You are quite correct, I think, to condemn the wise Despréaux for having compared Voiture [154] to Horace. The reputation of Voiture had to decline because he is almost never natural and the few charms he does possess are of a most petty and frivolous sort. But there are such sublime things in Corneille amidst his cold reasoning, and even things that are so moving that he ought to be respected despite his defects. They are like Da Vinci paintings that we still like to look at alongside those of Veronese and Titian. I know that the public is not yet sufficiently informed about all of Corneille's defects; there are some which are still mistakenly confused with the small number of his rare beautiful qualities.

Only time can fix the value of each thing; the public is always dazzled at first. To begin with they went mad over the *Persian Letters* which you mention; they disregarded the small book on *The Decline of the Romans* by the same author.[155] However, I notice that all solid minds prize the great intelligence governing that good book which was at first scorned, and now set very little worth on the frivolous imagination of the *Persian Letters* whose boldness in certain passages constitutes its greatest merit. In the long run, the vast majority of critics come to their decision by following the opinions of the enlightened few. You seem to me suited to lead these few. I am sorry that the military profession which you have undertaken keeps you away from a city where I could be edified by your intelligence. But that same spirit of exactness which makes you prefer the art of Racine to the intemperance of Corneille and the wisdom of Locke to the profusion of

Bayle will serve you in your profession. Exactness is always useful. I imagine that M. de Catinat [156] would have thought as you do.

I have taken the liberty of placing on the coach to Nancy a copy that I found of one of the less imperfect editions of my feeble works. The desire to offer you this small testimony of my esteem has prevailed over the fear aroused in me by your sense of taste. With all the sentiments you merit, sir, I have the honor of being your etc.

52. A Diplomatic Mission.

To Jean-Jacques Amelot de Chaillou.[157] The Hague. August 2, 1743.

Monseigneur,
Yesterday after my letter had gone off, I received one from
876 31 49 350 221 19 0701 94 110 343 0842 34 20 847 45
the King of Pruusia at the camp at Husfeldt in Silesia where he is
0713 22 0631 789 0542 350 526 96 254 37 370 108 987 233 13 276 25
going to build a city while fortifying his frontiers. On the 14th
74 946 107 283 924 480 317 917 851 249 29 330 770 794 60 329 275
he will be in Berlin, and on the 18th or the 20th he will be in Spa
51 213 14 99 641 89 221 18 807 231 311 107 281 141 154 96 666 161
and not Aix-la-Chapelle. You probably received with some delay my
0691 48 31 490 398 74 324 87 0811 8 66 900 445 847 0713 73 431 88
letter of the 21st which was brought to Lille by mail-boat after a
33 343 0302 790 55 35 22 21 0712 81 369 83 282 383 353 99 86 0162
long journey.
231 463 317 911 312946154350 572 42 708 889 0851 635 52 682 24
I am still as hopeful about the small favor being rendered
0642. 929 121 727 25 74 804 033 510 221 808 707 420 566 10 0631
by the King of Prussia, but I fear the consequences of this step
538 853 0853 13 410 969 322 177 013 461 171 0702 95 0523 196 380
will not be important enough if this prince holds to the ideas he
121 725 987 18 103 56 45 55 226 228 607 128 80 585 091 513 0673 96
indicated to me. All of his correspondents have persuaded him that
770 409 0331 0852 601 0373 344 219 625 43 889 923 586 492 83 289
France was presently too debilitated to cast a great weight in the

0663 819 081 15 27 0713 196 891 25 74 532 60 13 38 0653 702 804
balance. I have been unable to prevent an intimate friend of mine
910 129 317 0332 969 707 572 10 106 959 19 268 383 348 708 678 998
here from writing him things which ought to make him disgusted
0601 538 898 682 110 0562 42 850 62 345 0731 0732 513 177 0332
with your alliance. This friend is, however, completely committed
830 031 651 0510 0501 211 25 775 051 369 0631 292 0701 14 383 215
to your interests, and the King of Prussia is perfectly aware that at
89 54 769 336 327 345 825 381 219 987 108 841 9 537 64 0853 177
heart your cause and his are common ones. But this friend cannot
0332 720 0881 383 348 56, 0762 27 110 808 346 95 159 62 215 375,
write otherwise out of fear of being contradicted by other corre-
463 228 0762 409 0331 369 0631 720 73 99 102 863 112 597 322 178
spondents, and the King of Prussia can now only form unfavorable
607 380 678 909 0721 152 770 52 851 206 141 282 3800 642 929 121
ideas on so many reports. I must tell you that in his last letter he
932 66 0622 0543 708 10 226 890 947 0842, 329 45 496 071 572 25
spoke most severely about the conduct of things in the past, but
228 850 677 681 48 789 883 52 219 546 143 0232 281 83 0493 107 482
he appears to be so distressed about this that he speaks violently
108 292 839 451 377 923 0293 382 150 29 20 463 221 0752 774.
of the subject.
    You may be sure that ever since 1741 he has foreseen every-
        553 371 64 70 0373 10 206 46 374 0351 701 0473 132 41 329
thing that has occurred. At present, he thinks that if His Majesty
154 140 558 0673 112 0601 830 0742 60 107 0693 383 99 102 322 987
sent or led one to believe that he was sending a large contingent
890 761 0813 104 807 406 772 109 708 80 791 0713 755 749 692 564
toward the Meuse, this well contrived measure would create great
45 219 585 397 281 177 0131 0771 572 461 915 83 386 808 708 0231
disunity between the English party prevailing in Holland and the
0713 70 196 210 687 174 0671 0812 231 199 113, 0601 49 648 939
party of peace which ought not, however, be called the French
841 20 0371, 161 231 199 147 344 471 720 538 031 0232 0402 808
party.
0301 682 0701 701 526 466 01 435 512 0466 60 54.
    It is not for me to have an opinion on these matters. Here
        329 841 373 0402 463 201 94 0232 377 445 317 980 191 174
I leave these things to the judgment of the Ambassador and M. de

0671 52 0783 971 60 98 108 234 213 0841 27 959 154 0871 383 237
la Ville [158] whose insights are too superior to my feeble conjectures.
369 99 459 110 219 917 250 228 516 89 86 496 808 429 20 18 9 889
0383 8 217 760 56 96 81 677 793 999 45 0361 730 0642 01 0662.

My only advantage is that I am able to get the different parties
435 513 13 461 371 33 821 909 0721 344 023 19 0863 681 199
and foreign ministers to speak freely to me. I confine myself now
128 495 0331 369 233 137 697 154 282 83 35 110 585 0701 0301 0293
and will continue to confine myself to providing you with a simple
0271 215 513 929 572 489 41 720 369 585 489 88 0682 490 727 154
and faithful overall account.
0622 853 0713 0791 372 55, 0602 0141 0282 350 213 0663 0486 60
730.

But as it seems necessary for the King of Prussia to have a
435 01 0853 0791 107 482 504 322 0631 0653 370 317 386 191
very favorable opinion of France's forces and vigorous resolutions,
174 319 70 909 823 0143 275 210 89 678 481 150 0521 1 0562 346
I venture to implore you to send me some materials that might en-
0821 770 19 74 625 0462 281 8 0383 139 26 110 396 791 88 811 17 265
able me to present a striking picture of the situation when I pay
36 228 946 343 0801 154 45 666. 161 929 8 20 071 83 377 451 48 10
him my court at Spa, and I beseech you to do so all the more since
13 121 0121 515, 231 431 999 24 0852 427 98 51 242 60 74 625 43
I am certain that that presentation will give him great pleasure.
317 960 281 80 154 0601 391 55 383, 0493 29 0653 572 381 29 636
France is a mistress he has forsaken but one he loves and passion-
143 0702 987 389 720 211 110 597, 617 186 185 86 0293 685
ately hopes to see more beautiful.

Mr. Trevor [159] asked me today if I believed that the House
123 343 158 85 20 863 0282 454 18 987 13 109 938 10 219 609
of Lorraine had a large following in Lorraine.
571 0821 370 0713 196 199 108 571 512 0446 513 60.

I am with very profound respect, Monseigneur, your very
humble and obedient servant.

53. *On the War of the Austrian Succession*

To Louis-François Armand du Plessis, Duc de Richelieu. The Hague. August 8, 1743.

Monseigneur,

I have received the letter you honored me with by way of Frankfurt, but there is no longer any way of writing you via Germany without letting the Austrian hussars know how fond I am of you. Please give me your orders then in the packets you send to Mme. Du Châtelet.

The Dutch troops will certainly be able to join the Allies only on the 15th or 16th of September. It appears, however, that the English government is beginning to think that the entire burden of the war will fall back on it and it is destroying itself with the fanciful idea of compensating the Queen of Hungary at the expense of France. Half of the United Provinces still have peaceful inclinations, and I would not like to wager that the troops of the republic will not soon be ordered to hold back if France only shows signs of energy and good direction. Most likely they will profit greatly from our past mistakes. Dunkirk may be reconstructed never to be destroyed again, and in the space of two or three months France can become more respectable than ever. It appears that we are not very much wanted in foreign countries. When I say we, I mean our power because individuals are held in affection while France is detested. They treat us as we treat the Jesuits; they talk against the body and are quite content to live with its members. They invite us to supper and curse our Ministry. By permission of the magistrate, there are public performances of a comedy entitled *The Punished Presumption* [160] in which the Queen of Hungary is presented under the name of Mimi and Cardinal de Fleury [161] under that of an old impotent bailiff who, unable to sleep with Mimi, wants to deprive her of her father's entire inheritance. Prince Charles, under the name of Charlie, dismisses the bailiff and his associates, and that is the punished presumption. People travel ten leagues to see this poor buffoonery performed in Amsterdam. I still prefer this farce to the tragedy of Dettingen. [162] It is not earthshaking; there are no heads or arms broken. Keep your head, monseigneur, and permit me to offer good wishes on behalf of a very kind person who is greatly indebted to you for help. Please let me ask you to remember me to the Duc de Duras [163] *in quo bene complacuisti*.[164] If you can send me some good news, if you will be good enough to present me with a truly brilliant picture of your situation, you may be sure you will please me greatly. You know with what affectionate respect I am devoted to you for life.

54. *Voltaire's Election to the Royal Society of London.*

To Martin Ffolkes.[165] Paris. November 25, n.s. 1743.

S^r,

One of my strongest desires was to be naturaliz'd in England; the royal society, prompted be you vouchsafes to honour me with the best letters of naturalisation. My first masters in y^r free and learned country, were Shakespear, Adisson, Dryden, Pope; i made some steps afterwards in the temple of philosophy towards the altar of Newton. I was even so bold as to introduce into France some of his discoveries; but i was not only a confessor to his faith, i became a martir. I could never obtain the privilege of saying in print, that light comes from the sun and stars, and is not waiting in the air for the sun's impulsion; that vortices cannot be intirely reconcil'd with mathematics; that there is an evident attraction between the heavenly bodies, and such trash.

But the liberty of the press was fully granted to all the witty gentlemen who teach'd us that attraction is a chimera, and vortices are demonstrated, vho printed that a mobile lanch'd out from on high describes a parabola because of the resistance from the air below, that t'is false and impious to sai, light comes from the sun. Even some of them printed, *col la licenza dei superiori*,[166] that Newton ridiculously mistook, when he learn'd from experience the smaller are the pores of transparent bodies, the more pellucid they are; they alleg'd very wisely that the widest windows give the greatest admittance to light in a bed chamber. These things i have seen in our booksellers shops, and at their shops only.

You reward me sir for my sufferings. The tittle of brother you honour me with is the dearest to me of all titles. I want now to cross the sea to return you my hearthy thanks, and to show my gratitude and my veneration for the illustrious society of which you are the chief member.

Be pleas'd sir to be so Kind as to present y^r worthy bretheren with my most humble respects. I hope you will sai to mylord duke of Richemont, to m^r Jurin, m^r Turner [167] etc. how deeply i am sensible of their favours.

I am with the greatest esteem, and the most sincere respect s^r

y^r most humble and faithfull servant, i dare not say brother.

Voltaire

55. *"When you have also proved, in verse or otherwise, why so many men slaughter one another in the best of possible worlds, I will be very much in your debt."*

To Ludwig Martin Kahle.[168] March 1744 (?)

Mr. Dean,

I am pleased to inform the public that you have written a little book against me.[169] You have honored me greatly. On page 17, you reject the proof of the existence of God based on final causes. If you had reasoned the same way in Rome, the Jacobin reverend father, master of the sacred palace, would have subjected you to the Inquisition; if you had written against a theologian in Paris, he would have had your proposition censured by the sacred faculty; if against a fanatic, he would have cursed you, etc. etc. But I have neither the honor of being a Jacobin, a theologian, nor a fanatic. I leave you to your opinion and hold to mine. I will always be convinced that a clock proves the existence of a clockmaker and that the universe proves a God. I hope that you yourself understand what you say about space and duration, the necessity of matter, the monads, and preestablished harmony, and I refer you to what I have said about these things lately in this new edition where I should like to have understood what I was doing which is no mean proposition in metaphysics.

With reference to space and the infinite, you quote Seneca's *Medea*, Cicero's *Philippics*, Ovid's *Metamorphoses*, verses of the

109

Duke of Buckingham, of Gombaud, Régnier, Rapin, etc.[170] I must tell you that I know as much poetry as you, that my fondness for it is as great as yours, and that if the issue were poetry we would see a fair game. But I believe poetry not very suitable for clarifying a metaphysical question, even the poetry of Lucretius or of Cardinal de Polignac.[171] Besides if you ever understand anything about monads, about preestablished harmony, and to cite some poetry

> If the dean can ever conceive a notion
> Of how it all being a plenum, it could all be set in motion,[172]

if you also discover how despite everything being determined man is free, you will please me by letting me know. When you have also proved, in verse or otherwise, why so many men slaughter one another in the best of possible worlds, I will be very much in your debt.

I await your reasoning, your verse, and your invectives, and I protest to you most sincerely that neither you nor I know anything about this question. I beg to remain, moreover, etc.

56. *A Letter of Condolence to his Niece.*

To Marie-Louise Denis. Cirey par Bar sur Aube. April 18, 1744.

My dear niece,

I write to you on paper that is moistened with my tears. If my deplorable health permitted me to do so and if I could immediately leave by carriage, I would certainly come and weep with you. Des Aunais [173] was here with the Marquis Du Châtelet when we received the crushing news.[174] The poor boy is as distressed as I am. He cannot go to you because he must go to Nevers to join his regiment which has changed colonels. The Marquis de Castries,[175] not the Duc de Nivernais,[176] has the Limousin regiment now. If I could only come with him to console you, to be of service to you, and to show you all my affection. But this is only very feeble consolation for such great and unexpected misfortune. My dear child, this is one of those cruel occasions when we need all our courage, yet of how little consequence this courage is! How I pity you, how I share in all your grief, and how I fear for your health! Tend to that at least, and let me continue to be consoled. Think of your pursuits, think of life. Write me, I implore you, about what is happening to you and what decisions you are making. Is your brother-in-law [177] with you? Leave Lille as soon as you can. What could you do there except consume yourself with grief? Go live in Paris where I hope to embrace you in October. One of my misfortunes is not to spend all of the remaining days of my life with you. But I want to see you as much as possible. I absolutely want to know everything you will be doing. Give us this comfort in our distress. Fortunately you have a brother-in-law who is a good man and will not add to the grief of your loss that suffered in discussions of inheritance. Apparently you have a decent bequest with marital property rights. Of course, this is not what preoccupies you, but you must try to give it some thought. Monsieur and Madame Du Châtelet share your misfortune keenly. They ask me to assure you of this. Des Aunais is writing you. Farewell. Courage, philosophy. Life is a dream and a sad dream, but live for your friends and for me. I love you tenderly.

V.

57. *On the Writing of History and Getting a Good Publisher.*

To Jacob Vernet.[178] Cirey en Champagne. June 1, 1744.

Sir,

One of the great advantages of literature is to receive letters like yours. I am in receipt of the letter with which you have honored me; we spoke of you with Father Jacquier,[179] whom you saw in Geneva, and I certainly envied him for that satisfaction. I take no sides between Geneva and Rome as you know, but I would like to see them both and especially your Academy which has so many illustrious men and you as its ornament.

The friendship which has made me refuse all the considerable

111

establishments with which the King of Prussia has wished to honor me at his court retains me in France. It prevents me from satisfying the disposition I have always had to visit your republic. It makes Cirey my kingdom and academy.

I am flattered that my little reflections on history have not displeased you. I have tried to put these ideas in practice in an essay on universal history since the time of Charlemagne on which I have made satisfactory progress.[180] It seems to me that history, until now, has scarcely been looked upon as more than chronological compilations. Those who have engaged in writing it have done so neither as citizens nor as philosophers. What does it matter if I know for sure that Adaloaldus was the successor of King Agilulf [181] in 616, and of what importance are the anecdotes concerning their court? These names ought to be recorded once in the dusty registers of the times so that we may perhaps consult them once in a lifetime. But what misery to make a study out of things that can neither instruct, please, nor bring improvement! I have applied myself, as far as possible, to writing the history of customs, science, laws, usage, and superstitions. I see almost nothing but histories of kings; I seek that of men. Let me submit what I say in the foreword to my essay.

This is how I express myself: "I consider chronology and the successions of kings to be my guides and not the aim of my work. This work would be thankless indeed were I to confine myself to trying to determine in what year one unworthy prince succeeded another barbaric prince. When I read histories, I have the impression that the world was created merely for a few sovereigns and for those who have served their passions. Almost everything else is neglected. In this respect, historians are like some tyrants they discuss: they sacrifice the human race for a single man."

I should like to be able to consult with you on the essay I have written in this spirit. Perhaps one day I shall have it printed in your city. As for my other literary works, every collection of them that has been published is very imperfect and incorrect. I have always hoped that a good edition might be published, and since you are willing to discuss the matter, I will tell you that if some book dealer in your city [182] wanted to publish a complete edition, I would give him all the facilities and encouragement at my disposal. I would even assure him of a sale of three or four hundred copies for which I would pay at cost plus a profit we would agree upon. I would deliver the money for it to him (which would remain in the hands of a banker and released to him upon delivery of the three or four hundred copies). I am extremely dissatisfied with the booksellers of Amsterdam, and perhaps yours will serve me better. But this is an enterprise that I should like to be kept very secret in light of the precautions that I must observe in France. Your book dealers could be certain they would be the sole depositaries of the works I would confide to them and that their edition would surely cause all others to be unsuccessful. The proposition I am offering them would in itself be a good guarantee. So if you find some book dealer whom this enterprise might suit, I would be indebted to you for finally seeing myself in print in proper fashion.

Your reflections on the *Postquam nos Amaryllis* [183] and the Kings of Naples seem to me those of a man very well acquainted with books and the world.

You may be certain that I am, with the sincerest esteem, etc.

Voltaire

58. *On Literary Taste.*

To Luc de Clapiers, Marquis de Vauvenargues. Versailles. January 7, 1745.

The last work [184] you were kind enough to send me is added proof of your great sense of taste in an age when everything seems to me a trifle petty and genius has been replaced by specious wit. I believe that if the term *instinct* has been used to characterize La Fontaine, the word meant genius. The character of this good man was so simple that in conversation he was scarcely superior to the animals to whom he gave a voice, but as a poet he had a divine instinct. This was particularly true since instinct was his only talent. The bee is admirable but in its hive; outside its hive it becomes a mere fly.

I would have many things to tell you about Boileau and Molière. I would doubtlessly agree that Molière's verse is uneven, but I would not agree that his choice of characters and subjects

113

was too base. The delicate, glib, ridiculous characters you mention are only amusing to a small number of nimble minds. The public requires more conspicuous traits. Besides such delicate, ridiculous individuals can scarcely be the basis for dramatic characters. A defect that is almost imperceptible is scarcely amusing. We need characters who are ridiculous in the extreme, irrelevancies that are violent, and which are suitable to the plot. We need a gambler, a miser, a jealous man, etc. I have been struck by this truth even more since I am presently concerned with a festivity for the dauphin's marriage in which there is a comedy, and more than ever I notice that this delicacy, nimbleness and subtlety which are charming in conversation are scarcely suitable to the theater. That festivity is what prevents me from going into greater detail and from submitting my ideas to you, but nothing prevents me from experiencing the pleasure afforded by your ideas.

I will not lend anyone the last manuscript you were kind enough to confide to me. I could not keep the first manuscript from someone worthy of being stirred by it. While creating admirers, the striking singularity of that work necessarily led some persons to be indiscreet. The work has been circulated. It has fallen into the hands of M. de La Bruère [185] who, unaware of its author, people say, wanted to enrich his *Mercure* [186] with it. This M. de La Bruère is a man of merit and taste; you will have to forgive him. He will not always have such gifts for the public. I tried to prevent its publication but was told it was too late. I pray you, stomach this little misgiving if you detest pride. The more I see the products of so true, so natural, so easy, and sometimes so sublime a mind like yours, the more I am moved by your situation. May it serve to console you as it will serve to charm me. Keep your friendship for me which is due to that which you have inspired in me. Farewell. I embrace you affectionately.

V.

59. *"I am getting along quite splendidly with His Holiness."*

To Paul-Frédéric-Charles, Abbé de Valory.[187] Paris. May 3, 1745.

The favors of kings and popes are not equal to those of friendship. You know how dear your friendship is to me. I received your
letter and your brother's almost on the same day. I feel quite proud
not to be forgotten by two men to whom I have vowed such great
devotion, but you will admit that I must be held in somewhat
greater affection since the Holy Father has given me benedictions.
His Holiness shared your opinion of *Mahomet* because he has not
been led astray by religious fanatics. We suffer injustices in our
homeland, but foreigners judge dispassionately and a pope is above
passions. I am getting along quite splendidly with His Holiness.
Now the devout ought to ask for my protection both in this world
and the next.

You are going to see great company in Lille. The King will
free the Dutch from the painful chore of guarding the border positions. It is also claimed that he will free the former Bishop of
Mirepoix[188] of the temptation he finds himself in daily of making poor choices among the servants of God, and that he will complete the work of his sanctification in his abbey at Corbie.[189] He
will have the monks there do penance. He is a man suited ior
heaven according to what people say, since he is supremely disliked
in this world.

I answered your kind letter somewhat later, but it was delivered to me very late. That was in Chalons[190] where I had
joined Mme. Du Châtelet who was caring for her son afflicted with
smallpox. The prejudices of this world, which never do anything but
harm, prevent me from seeing your friend, M. d'Argenson.[191] In
Lille, you will probably have the pleasure I regret. May he return
very quickly with the olive branch! Never has there been less reason
on all sides to wage war. Everyone needs peace, and yet we fight. I
should like the historiographer[192] to be able to say: The Princes
were wise in 1745.

On granting me this post, you know that the King condescended to promise me the first vacant position of gentleman
dinary. I am overwhelmed by his kindness. Farewell. Mme. **Du**

Châtelet sends you a thousand regards. My most affectionate respects to you and your entire family.

Voltaire

60. *A Letter to the Pope.*

To Pope Benedict XIV.[193] Paris. August 17, 1745.

Most blessed father,
Your Holiness will forgive the audacity of one of His most humble faithful but also of one of the greatest admirers of virtue for submitting this work, directed against the founder of a false and barbaric sect, to the head of the true religion.[194]

To whom might I most opportunely refer the cruelty and errors of a false prophet if not to the vicar and imitator of a God of truth and gentleness? Your Holiness will then allow me the possibility of placing both this small book and its author at his feet, and to humbly ask him his protection for the one and his blessings for the other.

In such deep obeisance I shall kiss your sacred feet.

Voltaire

61. *A Love Letter to His Niece.*

To Marie-Louise Denis.[195] Monday, December 27, 1745.

You wrote me an enrapturing letter which I kissed. I am not astonished that you write Italian so well. That you are a connoisseur of the language of love is very appropriate and proper. Of course, I cannot believe you when you tell me you have no lovers. How do you manage that? Indeed, how can such charms be idly concealed? *You* not make love? Oh, you offend your God, my dear. You tell me that my letter even brought you sensual delight. My senses are like yours; I could not read your caressing expressions without feeling excitement deep in my heart. I have paid your letter the tribute I should have wanted to pay your entire person. Sensual pleasure passes and flies away in an instant, but the friendship that joins us, the mutual confidence, the pleasures of the heart, and the voluptuousness of the soul are not destroyed and lost in the same way. I will love you until death. You will find the four tickets for *Armide* [196] here in my room. I should like to come and place them at your feet, and then take the trip from Paris to Versailles with my dear Denis. Farewell. I kiss you a thousand times.

Do you know that Madame de P.'s mother [197] died? I am very much in the daughter's debt, but not a word.

62. *A Letter of Recommendation and Love.*

To Marie-Louise Denis.[198] December 1745.

Here is a letter for M. Vallier, my dear. I send it to you because I do not know where he lives. A young man who is very wise, learned, well brought up, and talented is introducing himself and placing himself under your protection so that he may be received by Mme. Pagnon [199] as a preceptor for her son. His name is Marmontel; [200] he is from Toulouse. He will have the honor of coming to your quarters; I beg you with all my heart to help him. I do not yet know when my affairs will allow me to leave a country that I detest. The court, society and the great bore me. I will only be happy when I can live with you. Your company and better health would make me happy. I embrace you a thousand times. My soul embraces yours; my phallus and my heart are enamored of you. I kiss your pretty ass and all of your adorable body.

[The years 1746 to 1749 mark the end of Voltaire's Cirey period. His lengthy relationship with Mme. Du Châtelet was terminated by her death on September 10, 1749 after she gave birth to the child of another lover, the Marquis de Saint-Lambert. As he wrote to his mistress and niece, Mme. Denis, he was filled with anguish, though he had for a long time no longer looked upon Mme. Du Châtelet as a woman.

By mid-century, Voltaire was well into middle age having

117

*reached his fifty-sixth year. And with middle age, his correspond-
ents repeatedly heard complaints of his poor health: "My life is
merely the journal of a sick man." He was not too ill, however, to
continue his passionate affair with Mme. Denis whom he considered his only consolation in his spiritual anguish and physical
suffering.*

*Except for the presentation of two new plays, Sémiramis
(1748) and Nanine (1749) and the composition of Memnon
(1747), a first version of his celebrated tale Zadig, Voltaire produced little of literary significance in the last years of the decade.
He was, however, finally elected to the French Academy on April
25, 1746, and in December, he met for the first time Jean Le Rond
d'Alembert, the mathematician and Diderot's collaborator on the
Encyclopédie and one who would play an important part in Voltaire's later intellectual life. Most of the year 1748 was taken up
by Voltaire's two trips to the court of Stanislas Leszczinski, the
former king of Poland and father-in-law of Louis XV, at Lunéville,
a town in Lorraine not far from Nancy. After the death of Mme.
Du Châtelet, Voltaire decided to return to Paris in 1750 where he
set up residence with Mme. Denis. His Parisian stay was not long,
however, as he left in June 1750 for Berlin and the court of Frederick II who had named him his chamberlain. Voltaire would not
see Paris again for another twenty-eight years, until his brief return
there in 1778 to die.]*

63. *"I very much regret having a better knowledge of the English
language than of Italian. . . ."*

To Cardinal Domenico Passionei.[201] Versailles. January 9, 1746.

Your Eminence's pupil has the audacity to write in Italian
to one who is his master in French. Truly I am not astonished that
Your Eminence is one who belongs to all countries. He was appreciated and held in esteem by everyone in Holland at the time of
the peace of Utrecht; he later gained the affection of Louis XIV;
he obtained the friendship and admiration of the entire imperial

court in Vienna, and he is presently profiting from all of these favorable feelings in the world's capital where he has been its principal embellishment.

I will not conceal from Your Eminence that these letters, which are so humane and so appreciated, have aroused a very burning desire in me to see the august city of Rome, the seat of all the fine arts. We have very limited means of obtaining instruction in the Italian language. I have read some seventeenth-century writers, but I know Marchetti, Orsi, Filicaia, and many others only by name.[202] Moreover I have certainly become aware of the need to practice a language and to spend at least a few months in the country to acquire the fine points and the expressions proper to it. I very much regret knowing the English language better than Italian, but I spent an entire year in London and tried to gain an intimate acquaintance with the excessively vague language of that excessively uncertain people. Although it is rendered more agreeable by good English authors, the coarseness and barbarism of that language certainly would not allow one to compare it with Italian which is so pure and naturally elegant.

I cannot refrain from describing my fate as cruel when I reflect that a lengthy illness, eating away at my existence, deprives me of the consolation of going to Rome to pay you personally that tribute of sincere veneration which I can only offer by my letters.

I appreciate the value of your favors with all the strength in my soul, and I would be infinitely obliged if you would send me the works of the Marchese Orsi which Your Eminence mentioned in his last most cherished letter.

I think that our Boileau proved to be too aggressive with the great Tasso. I admit that certain ideas and nonsense are found in his works, but that is also true of Virgil:

Num capti potuere capi? num incensa cremavit Troja viros? [203] *Italiam metire jacens.* [204]

It is also true of Homer, and this defect frequently appears in Milton but

119

. . . ubi plura nitent in carmine, non ego paucis
Offendar maculis [205]

I am of the opinion that of all writers Crescimbeni [206] would provide me with the truest and deepest knowledge of your beautiful language. The *Biblioteca* of Fontanini [207] is not to be had here, and since Your Eminence deigned to be so humane as to promise me some books, I would be completely indebted to him for his favors because of the little Italian I may be able to learn. And while abandoning hope of being able to place myself under Your Eminence's protection in Rome, I will derive some advantage in Paris at least from such great kindness of yours. Would he give me pleasure by addressing these beautiful presents to me in care of the very eminent Cardinal de Tencin [208] or the Marquis d'Argenson, Minister of State for Foreign Affairs? In the meantime, I humbly kiss the border of Your Eminence's sacred purple robe. As I bow deeply before you, I remain Your Eminence's very humble, very devoted and very indebted servant.

V.

64. *The King's Historiographer Orders Some Repairs.*

To Charles-François Le Normant De Tournehem. June 14, 1746.

M. de Voltaire, the King's historiographer, prays the Director General of Buildings to please order the following repairs to be done to his apartment in the courtyard of the kitchens of monseigneur, the Prince de Condé, no. 14, formerly the apartment of Mme. Lebel, to wit:

A window and a shutter, a door and a partition, a drum for the smoking fireplace.

A coat of white on the walls.

A stone framework around the fireplace for fear of fire, and twelve square feet of parquet.

Requests also that a door be made for the public lavatories which are at the foot of the staircase, and that, if possible, the drain of the neighboring rain gutter be diverted to wash them.

65. *In Defense of Montaigne*

To Louis-Elisabeth de la Vergne, Count de Tressan.[209] Paris.
August 21, 1746.

In your mind, I must pass for an ingrate and a lazy fellow.
I am neither however. I am merely a sick man whose spirit is willing but whose flesh is very weak.[210] For a whole month, I have
been overcome by a violent malady and a tragedy they ordered
me to do for the churching of the dauphine. I was the one who
was expected to die naturally, but it turned out to be the dauphine
who died on the day I finished my play. That is how we err in all
our calculations!

Certainly you made no error with regard to Montaigne. I
thank you kindly for coming to his defense. You write more im-
peccably than he, and you think likewise. Your portrait, with which
you begin, seems to be his. You defend your brother; you defend
yourself. What a crying injustice to say that Montaigne only wrote
a commentary on the ancients! He cites them to the point, and this
commentators do not do. He is a thinker, but those gentlemen do
not think one iota! He buttresses his thoughts with those of the
great men of antiquity. He judges them, fights them, and converses
with them, with his reader and with himself. He is always original
in the way he presents things, always full of imagination, always
the painter, and, what I like, always capable of doubt. I should indeed like to know, moreover, whether he took from the ancients
everything he says about our fashions, our customs, the New
World which was discovered almost in his own time, the civil
wars that he witnessed, and the fanaticism of the two sects that
were laying France bare. I only forgive those who have opposed
this charming man because they obtained for us the apology you
were good enough to write.

I am quite edified to learn that the guardian of our coasts is
with Montaigne and Epictetus. Few of our officers are in similar
company. I imagine that you are also in the company of your
guardian angel whom you presented to me at Versailles. This
Michelle and that Michel Montaigne are good resources against
boredom. I wish you as much pleasure as you have given me.

I do not know whether the person to whom you sent your

equally instructive and urbane dissertation will dare publish his condemnation. As for me, I will dearly preserve the copy you did me the honor of sending. Forgive me once again, I implore you, for tarrying so long in thanking you affectionately for it. In truth, I would like to spend part of my life seeing you and writing to you, but who in this world does what he would like to? Mme. Du Châtelet sends you her sincerest regards; her mind is too fair not to be in total agreement with you. She is pleased with your little work as far as she understands it, and that is saying a great deal.

Farewell. Continue your acts of kindness to this poor sick man as they are his consolation, and you may believe that the hope of occasionally seeing you and of enjoying the charms of your company sustains me during my long infirmities.

66. *"I shall always love you. . . ."*

To Marie-Louise Denis. 1746(?) [211]

I have neither had time nor health. Anguish of the soul, sufferings of the body, loss of time, desiring much, working little, and doing nothing: this is my life. You are its only consolation. What are you doing? How is your health? How is your heart? I shall always love you, but always I regret our not spending the rest of my days together.

67. *"I kiss you a thousand times and will love you unto death."*

To Marie-Louis Denis. 1747.[212]

Dearest,

I am on holiday in Versailles, calm and peaceful amidst the agitations and storms of the court, and I would be happy if I were not far from you. But you are half of me and the better half, and my happiness is that of an exile. For pity's sake, tell me how you are, how music and the Italian language are fairing. A novel entitled *The Misfortunes of Love* is being circulated here. The greatest misfortune that one can experience in love is doubtless to live without you, my dear. This novel was composed by M. de Pont-de-Veyle,[213] and it is no better for that. It seems to me insipidly and boringly indifferent. Oh, what an enormous difference between an amiable, courteous and charming man and a man of wit and talent! Farewell, my dear. I kiss you a thousand times and will love you unto death.

V. Monday.

68. "*. . . as long as I live, I will admire and cherish in you the honor and example of the poor human race.*"

To Frederick II, King of Prussia. Paris. February 9, 1747.

Sire,

Well, you will have *Sémiramis*.[214] It is not in a rosewater style which is why I am not giving it to our sybaritic people but to a king who thinks the way people used to in the time of the great Corneille and the great Condé,[215] and who would like a tragedy to be tragic and a comedy comic.

May God preserve me, sire, from having the *History of the War of 1741* printed. These are fruits that time alone can ripen. I have certainly composed neither a panegyric nor a satire. But the fonder I am of truth, the less wasteful I ought to be with it. My work is based on memoirs and letters of generals and ministers. These are materials meant for posterity for on what foundations would history be constructed if contemporaries left nothing with which to build the structure? Caesar wrote his commentaries and you are writing yours. But where are the participants who can similarly give an account of the great role they have played? Was Marshal de Broglie [216] a man fit to write commentaries? Besides, sire, far be it from me to enter into the horrible and boring details of journals of sieges, of marches and countermarches, of trenches being taken over, and of all the things that make up the conversation of an old major and a lieutenant general in provincial retirement. War in itself must be something very ugly since its details are so tiresome. I have attempted to consider that human folly somewhat as a philosopher. I have portrayed Spain and England spending a hundred million waging war against each other over a matter of ninety-five thousand pounds; nations destroying the commerce over which they fight one another; war over the pragmatic sanction which has become like a sickness changing character three or four times, from a fever becoming paralysis, and from paralysis a convulsion; Rome which gives its blessing and opens its gates to the leaders of two enemy armies in the same day; a chaos of diverse interests intersecting at every moment; that which was true in the spring becoming false in the autumn; everyone crying peace, peace, and waging all-out war; finally, all the scourges that prey upon this poor human race; amidst all of that, a philosopher prince who always takes his time properly to make battles and operas, who knows how to make war and peace, poetry and music, who reforms the abuses of justice, and who is the greatest wit in Europe. This is how I amuse myself, sire, when I am not suffering, but I find myself very often close to death and suffer much more than those who have been seriously wounded in this deadly war.

I saw the Duc de Richelieu again who is desperate because he has been unable to pay his court to the great man of our times. He has no consolation, and I only ask nature for a month or two of health to see that great man again before going to the land where Achilles and Thersites,[217] and Corneille and Danchet [218] are equals. I will be devoted to Your Majesty until that beautiful moment when we discover just in time what the soul, the infinite, and the matter and essence of things are, and as long as I live, I will admire and cherish in you the honor and example of this poor human race.

V.

69. *"I am incapable of digesting, but I am capable of love."*

To Marie-Louise Denis.[219] September 1747.

I fell sick at Anet,[220] my dearest, but I hope to recover my health with you. As soon as I arrive, I will rush to you to restore my strength. So today is the day I will see you; today I will rediscover the only consolation that can sweeten the bitterness of my life. Nature, which granted me the tenderest of hearts, forgot to give me a stomach. I am incapable of digesting, but I am capable of love. I love you; I will love you until the day I die. I embrace you a thousand times, my dear virtuoso. You write Italian better than I do. You deserve to be admitted to the Academy della Crusca.[221] My heart and my phallus [222] send you the most affectionate compliments. Tonight I will see you for sure.

70. *A Love Note.*

To Marie-Louise Denis.[223] 1747-1748.

How is my dear friend? I have not seen her yet. But I burn with desire to see her every day at every hour. Wednesday.

V.

71. *"But how I would prefer your boudoir infinitely to all the courts!"*

To Marie-Louise Denis.[224] February 1, 1748.

My dear,

I have been to Cirey, and from Cirey your vagabond friend is now here in Lunéville [225] with a king who bears no resemblance to kings save in goodness and greatness of soul. But how I would prefer your boudoir infinitely to all the courts! Have you finished the second act of your comedy? What are you doing? Do you occasionally see the Prince de Beauvau? [226] I think he is in love with you. I passed through the city of Troyes but was unable to see your brother; we were travelling too rapidly, and one cannot delay a journey when accompanied by two ladies. I am very annoyed that I could not dine with his bishop and your preacher. But I imagine that I will see them on my return. Oh, when will that return be? I am here like the swans; I have a good nest, a gentle allowance of food (and a pleasant ambiance thanks to the good hearth). I am being put up at the palace, and my life would be happy if you were in Lunéville. But destiny always separates us. I have every appearance of happiness, yet I am unhappy.

It is often in simple inns and under humble roofs that hearts surrender themselves best to friendship. I am pining over the loss of your small roof, and each day I sense that I must devote the last days of my life to you and that after a springtime of folly, a stormy summer, and a languishing autumn, you alone will be able to soothe the severity of my winter. I flatter myself that I will see you again next month. But it is quite certain that I shall love you until death.

V.

72. *"You are the sole object of my eyes . . ."*

To Marie-Louise Denis.[227] May 22, 1748.

If there is something you ought to forgive me for, my dearest, pardon my shameful neglect to give you certain evidence of my affectionate and eternal friendship. You are the sole object of my eyes, and I flatter myself that soon I will be happier. You are my consolation, and I have no other desire than to make you happy during my lifetime and after my death. I shall always love you and tenderly until the day the law of nature separates what nature and love have joined. Let us love each other until that hour. I embrace you a thousand times.

Sunday, May 22.

73. *"My life is merely the journal of a sick man."*

To Marie-Louise Denis.[228] June 1748.

My very dear soul,

My life is merely the journal of a sick man. I have been attacked by seriously increased pain. Since I have been in Versailles, I have not enjoyed two hours of good health. I have never suffered so much, and if this cruel state worsens even slightly, you will lose your most affectionate and faithful friend. The desire to live with you makes me endure an existence which would seem a heavy burden to me were it not alleviated by your kindness. Love me. I flatter myself that I will see you on Thursday. If I am ill, I will kiss your beautiful hands, and if I am well your mouth. Farewell. I will love you unto death.

Sunday.

74. A Theatrical Premiere and an Expression of Physical Passion.

To Marie-Louise Denis. Commercy. July 27, 1748.

My dear child,

It is very difficult for me to return in spite of the strictest diet. I would even be all right if we were only punished for our faults. But to have nothing to reproach oneself for and to suffer, *questo e L'diavolo*.[229] Let us get down to your affair. That interests me more than my health. Must we not live together and can't I substitute for your major from Lille? I will make a violent sacrifice, I swear to you, when my heart will be forced to allow you to go to Flanders. I will be reduced to hoping that that major will soon give up his position. I will only be consoled if his marriage contract is soon followed by his testament. Moreover, I am relying on your prudence for the settlement. Do nothing without being very certain of its great advantage. Well, my dear child, I will come and visit you in your kingdom. But will your transplantation take place so soon? I flatter myself that my health will allow me to come and see you soon in Paris. You will be the only reason for my trip; *Sémiramis* will be its pretext should it have any success. The King is kind enough to give me a decoration that will cost fifteen thousand francs. As much as I am flattered by it, I fear that this distinction will sharpen the teeth of envy. I believe that the play will be well performed at least. You will have to see a rehearsal with your old major and suitor. Give me this pleasure, my dear child, and let me have your opinion on this decoration and on the actors's performance. You mention that small work I read to you in manuscript. Do you know that Crébillon [230] refused to approve it saying it was a dangerous work? That poor man has lost the little reason he had. I believe that M. Palu, the intendant in Lyons, has had it printed since, and there are perhaps some copies of it in Paris now. But the world is as lukewarm to panegyrics as

127

Crébillon is unreasonable, and probably that brochure, not being advertised, will not have a large circulation. Let us stick to *Sémiramis* and may it succeed. I recommend it to you. If it is well received at the premiere, you will probably see me at the fourth performance. Besides, I must thank the King. But I will come for you *e se il povero stato della mia salute me lo permesse mi gittarai alle vostre genochia e baccarei tutte le vostre Belta. In tanto io figo mile baccii alle tonde poppe, alle transportatrici natiche, a tutta la vostra persona che m'ha fatto tante volte rizzare e m'ha annegato in un fiume di delizie.*[231]

75. *A Request for Royal Protection.*

To Catherine-Sophie-Félicité-Marie Leszczynska, Queen of France. Commercy. October 10, 1748.

Madam,

I throw myself at the feet of Your Majesty. You attend the theater only out of condescension for your august rank, and this is one of your virtuous sacrifices to the proprieties of society. I implore that same virtue and, with the heaviest of hearts, beseech it not to permit these performances to be dishonored by an odious satire against me that is being planned before your eyes in Fontainebleau. The tragedy of *Sémiramis* is based throughout on the purest morality and, for that reason at least, it may hope for your protection.

Please consider, madam, that I am a member of the King's household and consequently of yours. My comrades, the Gentlemen Ordinary of the King, several of whom are employed in foreign courts and others in very honorable posts, will compel me to divest myself of my charge if I suffer such a cruel degradation before Your Majesty and before the entire royal family. I beseech Your Majesty out of the goodness and the greatness of her soul, out of her piety, not to deliver me in such a fashion to my declared and covert enemies who, after pursuing me with the most atrocious slander, want to ruin me by public stigma.

Please remember, madam, that these satiric parodies have been prohibited in Paris for several years. Must they then be revived for me alone within view of Your Majesty? She does not permit slander in her cabinet; would she allow it before her entire court? No, madam, your heart is too just not to allow itself to be moved by my prayer and by my anguish, and to cause an old servant, the first upon whom your kindness fell, to be put to death with anguish and shame. A word from you to the Duc de Fleury and to M. de Maurepas,[232] madam, will suffice to stop this scandal whose effects would ruin me. I hope that your humanity will be moved by my condition and that, after having depicted virtue, I will be protected by it.

I am with the deepest respect, madam, the very humble and very obedient servant and subject of Your Majesty.

De Voltaire

76. A Letter of Congratulations to a New Father.

To Sir Everard Fawkener.[233] Lunéville, at the court of Lorraine. November 5, 1748 (n.s.).

Dear s[r],

Y[r] letter has afforded me the most sensible satisfaction. For, when my friendship to you began, t'was a bargain for life. Time that alters all things, and chiefly my poor tattered body, has not altered my sentiments. You acquaint me you are a husband and a father, and i hope you are an happy one. It behoves a secretary to a great general, to marry a great officers's daughter and really i am transported with joy to see the blood of Marlborough mix'd with that of my dearest Fawkener.[234] I do present y[r] lady with my most humble respects, and i kiss y[r] child. You are a lusty husband; and i a weak batchelor as such unhealthy as you saw me, but some twenty years older. Yet i have a kind of conformity with you; for if you are attach'd to a hero, so i am in the retinue of another; tho not so intimately as you are; my King has appointed me one of the ordinary gentlemen of his chamber. Y[r] post is more profitable. Yet i am satisfied with mine, because if it gives not a great income, it leaves me at my full liberty, which i prefer to Kings. The King of Prussia would once give me one thousand pounds s[terl] per annum to live at his court; and i dit not accept of the bargain, because the court of a King is not comparable to the house of a friend. I live these twenty years since with the same friends, and you know what pouver friendship gets over a tender soul and over a philosophical one. I find a great delight in opening my heart to you, and in giving thus you an account of my conduct. I'll tell you that being appointed too historiografer of France i do write the history of the late fatal war wich did much harm to all the parties, and did good only to the King of Prussia. I wish i could shouv you what i have writ upon that subject. I hope i have done justice to the great duke of Cumberland. My history shall not be the work of a courtier, not that of a partial man; but that of a lover of mankind.

As to the tragedy of Semiramis i'll send it you within a month or two. I'll remember alluvais with great pleasure i dedicated to you the tender tragedy of Zaïre. This Semiramis is quite of an'other kind. I have try'd, tho it was a hard task, to change our french petitsmaitres into athenian hearers. The transformation is not quite perform'd; but the piece has met with great applause. It has the fate of moral books that please many, without mending any body.

I am now my dear friend at the court of king Stanislas, where i have pass'd some months with all the ease and cheerfulness that i enjoy'd once at Wandsworth; for you must know that king Stanislas is a kind of Fawkenear. He is indeed the best man living, but for fear you should take me for a wanderer of courts, and a vagabond courtier, i'll tell you i am here, with the very friend whom i never parted from for these twenty years past. The lady du Chastellet, who comments Newton, and is now about printing a french translation of it, is the friend i mean.

I have at Paris some ennemies such as Pope had at London, and i despise them as he did. In short, i live as happy as my condition can permit.

Nisi quod simul esses, caetera laetus! [235]

I return you a thousand thanks my dearest and worthy friend. I wish you all the happiness you deserve, and i'll be y^rs for ever.

Voltaire

77. *Taxes and Prosperity*

To Jean-Baptiste Machault d'Arnouville.[236] Paris. May 16, 1749.

Sir,

You remember the day I had the honor of spending with you on the occasion of the inspection of the guard. Among the brilliant carriages covering the plain, yours attracted attention and among the diamonds that adorned the ladies, those of your wife were looked upon with admiration. On our return, we stopped at your home and found ourselves in a group of fourteen or fifteen persons. For awhile we gambled in that magnificent salon which you decorated so tastefully. There were losses of approximately three hundred louis, but the jubilation of the company was not spoiled by this. As was the custom those who won paid for the cards at twenty times above their cost. Then we had supper. You know how everyone was struck by the beauty of your tableware; your double entrees won even greater approval. Your chef was highly praised, and we confessed that you were right to pay him a salary of fifteen hundred livres or five hundred francs more than you give your son's preceptor and almost a thousand francs above the appointments of your secretary. One of us reflected that in Paris there were five or six hundred tables where one could have a supper scarcely less worthy than yours. This thought did not displease you at all; you are not one who would reserve earthly happiness to himself alone.

An ill-humored man chose that occasion rather inopportunely to say that there were also many families eating meagrely in fifth-floor lodgings. We shut him up by proving to him that it is absolutely necessary to have poor people and that the magnificence of a house like yours was enough to provide at least two hundred workers with a livelihood from what they earned with you. It was further noted that what makes Paris the most prosperous city in the world is not so much the number of magnificent mansions displaying their opulence rather pompously as the phenomenal number of private houses where people live in a comfort unknown to our fathers and which other nations have not yet attained. Indeed let us compare Paris with London which is its rival in land area, but which is certainly very far from rivalling it in splendor, taste, sumptuousness, sought-after conveniences, commodiousness, the fine arts, and above all the art of society. I have no fear of error in assuring people that the middle class in Paris have five hundred times as much silverware as they do in London. Your notary, your attorney and your cloth merchant are much better housed, better furnished and better served than a magistrate in England's principal city.

More fowl and game are eaten in Paris in one evening than in London in a week. Perhaps a thousand times as many candles are burned here since in London, with the exception of the court area, one only sees tallow candles. I will not speak of the other capitals. Amsterdam, the most populous one of all after London, is a land of miserliness; Vienna and Madrid are merely mediocre cities; Rome is scarcely more populous than Lyons, and I strongly doubt that it is as wealthy. As we were making these reflections, we enjoyed the pleasure of being conscious of our felicity, and if Rome has more beautiful structures, London more numerous fleets, Amsterdam larger stores, we agreed that there is no city on earth where such a large number of citizens enjoys so much abundance, so many conveniences and such a delightful life.

Our rather lengthy inquiry into the wealth of Paris led us to speak of the other cities in the kingdom, and those guests who had not been out of the capital were astonished to learn how many beautiful houses had been built in the last forty years in the principal provincial cities and how many horses and carriages and how much splendid furniture were in evidence there. One man in the company assured us that there is no small city without at least one jeweller and that several in the lowest category have two or three. Whereupon another man who was very informed told us that the wrought silver in France was worth more than twelve hundred million. It seems that for nearly twenty-five years a like amount of specie has gone to the Mint. We know how favorable the balance of trade has been to us in years of peace, and certainly we earned more in these years than we lost in the war years. The war [237] was barely over when we suddenly saw an exchange rate with all the cities of Europe favorable to us. All negotiable instruments increased in their market value. Money, which had been at six per cent interest, fell back to five. You know that the value of public instruments, of money, and of currency exchange is the pulse of the body politic clearly indicating its health or unsoundness. You know with what phenomenal speed the immense trade of our merchant cities took on new vigor; you know that M. de Regio is now bringing the treasures of Havana back to Cadiz with more than eighty million for our account.

These are facts attested to by everyone present in your home and which could be contested by no one. The same rather annoying man who had already spoken of the poor in Paris then spoke of the poor in the provinces. "I admit," he said, "that the cities seem to be quite well off, but the countryside has entirely gone to ruin." A good citizen, a sensible man, spoke and said, "When you live affluently from the produce of your land in a castle, that is an infallible indication that this land is bringing in a return. Now cities certainly live only from the farming of the neighboring countryside for the plains of Magdeburg do not provide for the subsistence of Orleans and Dijon. Now if one lives affluently in Orleans and Dijon, this proves that the neighboring fields are not fallow. The countryside is always said to be desolate; there was no end to complaining about this in the time of the great Colbert, especially so in Paris. At dessert, while we were eating peas that cost a hundred écus a litron,[238] someone had the notion to amuse himself by bemoaning the fate of the peasants, and from the moment we witnessed that joyful display of pity the kingdom ought to have gone to ruin a hundred times. But I ask you when do you think those who live in the countryside enjoyed a happier fate, sold their goods more easily, were better fed and better clothed? Perhaps when the arbitrary headtax was imposed almost throughout the kingdom? Perhaps in 1709 when soldiers were short of loans and food, when an officer was obliged to discount bills given to him in payment at a seventy percent loss? Perhaps during the years when Louis XIV's ministers did extraordinary business valued at more than two hundred million or approximately four hundred million in our present currency? Would you like to go further back and see whether the provinces, the capital and the countryside were more prosperous when the enemy was at the shores of the Oise in Cardinal de Richelieu's time? When they took Amiens under Henry IV? Go back still further. Remember the civil wars, the English wars, the times when the peasants, oppressed by the lords of the castles, rose up against them and slew

133

those who fell into their hands; when the countryside was deserted, when the main roads were covered with bramble, when people were shouting in Paris: 'Abandoned land for sale!,' when people used to make their wills if they undertook a trip from one province to another. Compare those centuries to ours if you dare."

The contradictory man had nothing to reply, but after speaking vaguely like almost all critics, he said, "But admit that everything will be ruined if taxes are reduced from ten percent to five percent in order to discharge the debts of the state and if a sinking fund is formed from this five percent to pay off the principal on other taxes enacted during the war and to redeem government bonds."

The man who had already trounced our objector then took a piece of paper out of his pocket and asked all of us if we knew what taxes Louis XIV had imposed upon the nation during the seventy-two years of his reign.

You remember with what sincerity we all replied that we had no idea. "Well, I have this information," he said, "from a very enlightened and wise citizen who, after having served the king as an officer in his armies for a very long time, now serves him in finance. He went to the trouble of making the immense calculation of all imposts, sales of offices and rights of every kind established during that long and glorious reign. This is the result. It amounts to eighteen billion or two hundred million five hundred thousand livres in an ordinary year, the value of silver being calculated at twenty-seven to thirty francs a marc. Now, these two hundred million five hundred thousand livres which Louis XIV withdrew each year amount to three hundred thirty million in our money.

Now I ask whether Louis XIV, in spite of his mistake in handing everything over to the tax farmers, left his kingdom less rich, less extensive, less flourishing, less populous or less powerful than he had received it from Louis XIII. At his death, the debts of the state were found to add up to more than two billion. This is less than the current debt of England which does not have half the cash we possess. But to whom were these two billion that caused so much commotion owed? One part of the country owed this money to the other. Did this enormous debt rock the state more violently than the system of Law? [239] Did it overturn more fortunes? And is there a sensible man today who would not agree that it would have been preferable to continue the tithe in order to form a sinking fund like the English with some justified reductions, however, than to have recourse to the dangerous and fanciful schemes of Law? If a foreign system had to be adopted, it should have been the ministry's in London rather than that of a faro banker and fugitive from London. "Now," continued the same man, "do you gentlemen know what Great Britain pays in time of peace to eliminate its debts and maintain its sinking fund? Aside from other taxes, it still contributes a tenth of its land revenues. It just recently applied money from this fund to discharge the debts of the navy; it has just drawn a million pounds sterling from the fund for its king. In order to discharge our debts then, why would you not want us, who are twice as wealthy as the English, to provide half the amount they do?"

You then asked what debts we had contracted during the war. "What the king borrowed," you were told, "to pay for the blood shed on his behalf, to secure pensions for wounded officers, widows and the children of the dead, to help his allies, and to pay those who fed, clothed and armed our soldiers." Never were there more legitimate debts and never was there a wiser or easier way of disposing of them. It does not make the people prey to partisan plundering; it equally affects people of all stations who must all contribute to the common good without distinction, and each year brings relief with the elimination of a debt. What is a tax that is imposed fairly and does not in any way hinder trade? It is a part of one's wealth spent to make the other part productive. The entire nation, by making a contribution to itself, is exactly like the farmer who sows in order to reap. I am the owner of a piece of land on which I pay rights to the state; these rights have the function of making me pay for my income and my pensions punctually, of making me sell the commodities furnished me by land profitably. The simple farmer is in the same situation. If he pays a tenth of his harvest, he sells his harvest a tenth more dearly. The craftsman who is taxed sells his work in proportion to his tax. A state is as well governed as human weakness may allow when obligations are proportionately imposed, when one order of the state is not favored at the expense of another, when one contributes to public expenses not according to one's title but according to one's revenue, and that is what a tax like five per cent on all wealth accomplishes. If this arrangement is not permitted, an equivalent one will be necessary for we must begin by paying our debts.

Taxes do not weaken a nation; it is either the way they are levied or the poor use to which they are put that does. But if the king uses this money to satisfy debts, to establish a navy, to beautify the capital, to finish the Louvre, to improve those highways which are the admiration of foreigners, to support manufacturing and the fine arts, in a word, to encourage industry in every way, it must be admitted that such a tax, which seems like an evil to some, will have accomplished a great deal of good for all. The happiest people is the one that pays and works the most when it is paying and working for itself.

That more or less was the conversation that took place in your home. I submit these ideas to the judgment of all good citizens.

I will add that I have been assured that the King himself had proposed reducing the expenses of his own household. But what would such excessive kindness accomplish? An elimination of perhaps one million annually. Would England pay off its debts by reducing the civil list of its king by approximately fifty thousand guineas?

There would, I dare say, be very little justice and reason in asserting that the nation's debts could be paid for other than by the nation. What I have seen in foreign countries and in my studies since 1715 has convinced me of this truth. When I speak this way, I mean neither to displease nor to court any one. I speak as a good citizen who loves his country. To want it to be prosperous is doubtless to love it, and it seems clear to me that it can only prosper by helping itself.

78. *Mme. Du Châtelet Gives Birth.*

To René-Louis de Voyer de Paulmy, Marquis d'Argenson.
Lunéville. September 4, 1749.

Madame Du Châtelet informs you that while at her writing desk tonight scrawling some Newtonian chart, she felt a little need.

The little need was a daughter who appeared forthwith.[240] She was laid out on a quarto book of geometry. The mother went to bed as one must, and if she were not sleeping she would write you. As for myself, having given birth to a tragedy about Catilina,[241] I am a hundred times more fatigued than she. She has only brought into the world a silent little daughter, but I had to create a Cicero, a Caesar, and it is more difficult to make those people speak than to make children, especially when one does not wish to slight ancient Rome and the French theater a second time.[242] Continue being kind to me. Love Cicero with all your heart; he was a good citizen like you and not a pimp for his daughter as Crébillon has said. A thousand respects.

V.

79. *Mme. Du Châtelet is Dead.*

To Marie-Louise Denis. Lunéville. September 10, 1749.

My dear child,
    I have just lost a friend of twenty years standing. For a long time, I no longer looked upon Madame Du Châtelet as a woman, as you know, and I feel sure that you share my cruel anguish. To have seen her die and under what circumstances! And by what a cause! That is horrible. I am not abandoning M. Du Châtelet in the grief we both share. We must go to Cirey. There are important papers there. From Cirey, I will return to Paris to embrace you and to find in you again my only consolation and my life's only hope.

V.

80. *"I am coming back to Paris not knowing what will become of me. . . ."*

To Marie de Vichy de Chamrond, Marquise Du Deffand.
September 10, 1749.

I have just seen a friend of twenty years standing die, a friend who loved you truly and who, two days before this woeful death, spoke to me of the pleasure she would have seeing you in Paris on her first trip. I asked President Hénault [243] to inform you of a childbirth that had seemed so singular and so happy. There was a large passage for you in his letter. She had recommended my writing to you, and I thought I was fulfilling my duty by writing to President Hénault. The unfortunate little girl to whom she gave birth and who caused her death did not interest me sufficiently. Alas, we made sport of the event, and it was in that unfortunate tone that I wrote to her friends, following her orders. If something could have made my present state more horrible, it would have been my taking lightly an adventure whose consequences poison the rest of my miserable life. I did not write to you when she gave birth, and I announce her death to you. The sensitivity of your heart is my refuge in my despair. I am being dragged to Cirey with M. Du Châtelet. From there, I am coming back to Paris not knowing what will become of me and hoping that I will soon join her again. When I arrive, allow me the painful consolation of speaking to you about her, of weeping at your feet over a woman who, despite her weaknesses, had a respectable soul.

V.

Notes

1. Ovid, *Tristia,* Book I, 1, v. 41: "Poetry requires the writer to be in privacy and ease."
2. Horace, *Epistles,* Book II, 2, v. 57: "They are striving to wrest my poems from me."
3. The Abbé Michel Linant was a dramatic author and protégé of Voltaire. The *présidente* is Mme. de Bernières.

4. Alexandre-Jean-Joseph Le Riche de La Popelinière (1692-1762) was a poet, a wealthy farmer-general, and a patron of the arts.

5. A cordial flavored with orange and lemon peel.

6. See Chapter I, note 52.

7. Henri de La Tour d'Auvergne, Viscount and Prince of Turenne (1611-1675), the celebrated French warrior. The book in question is Andrew Michael Ramsay's *History of . . . Turenne* (London, 1735). A French edition under a Paris imprint also appeared that year.

8. The brilliant *Memoirs* of Cardinal de Retz (1613-1679), a prominent seventeenth-century French political and ecclesiastical figure, were published in 1717. François de Salignac de La Mothe Fénelon (1651-1715), a noted writer and Archbishop of Cambrai, published a series of *Eulogies,* including one on Turenne.

9. Jules de Mascaron (1634-1703) and Valentin-Esprit Fléchier (1632-1710) were two ecclesiastical orators.

10. The reference is to *Aben-Saïd* (1735), a tragedy by Jean-Bernard Le Blanc.

11. An anonymous and malicious character sketch of Voltaire which reveals contemporary opinion of him and established a critical image of him throughout the rest of the eighteenth century. It was inspired by the image of a *bel esprit* of the early Paris salons. See R. A. Leigh, "An Anonymous Eighteenth-Century Character-Sketch of Voltaire" in *Studies on Voltaire and the Eighteenth Century,* II, 241-272 (Geneva, 1956).

12. Louis-Gabriel, Chevalier de Froulay, was a diplomat and friend of Voltaire. On Des Alleurs, see chapter 1, n. 30. Antoine Feriol, Count de Pont-de-Veyle (1697-1774), elder brother of Count D'Argental, was a friend of Voltaire and a writer. On Du Deffand, see chapter 1, n. 29.

13. And all these most pleasant people.

14. Father Charles Porée (1675-1741) was one of Voltaire's Jesuit teachers at the Collège Louis-le-Grand.

15. Father Pierre Brumoy (1688-1742) was a Jesuit writer.

16. It is useless to have a greater number do what can be done by a lesser number.

17. Samuel Clarke (1675-1725), an English philosopher and

theologian, wrote *A Demonstration of the Being and Attributes of God* (1705) and *A Discourse Concerning the Unchangeable Obligations of Natural Religion* (1706).

18. This letter was written in English, except for the last paragraph.

19. Fawkener had been named English ambassador to Constantinople.

20. Voltaire's play, *Alzire or the Americans,* had its premiere on January 27.

21. Claude-Louis-Dominique de Chassé de Chinais (1698-1786) was an opera singer and actor.

22. Abraham-Alexis Quinault-Dufresne (1693-1767) performed the role of Zamore in *Alzire.*

23. Victor-Amédée de Savoie, Prince de Carignan, was director of the Opera.

24. On Desfontaines, see chapter 1, n. 43.

25. A French physicist and engineer (1695-1771). The memoir referred to in the first sentence is Mairan's *Dissertation sur les forces motrices des corps [Dissertation on the Driving Forces of Bodies].*

26. Wise and victorious throughout.

27. A work on optical theories.

28. Willebrord Snellius (1591-1626) was a Dutch physicist credited with the discovery of the laws of refraction.

29. Francesco Maria Grimaldi was a seventeenth-century Italian physicist who discovered diffraction (1665) around the same time as Newton.

30. Frederick II or Frederick the Great (1712-1786). He became King of Prussia in 1740.

31. Christina (1626-1689) was Queen of Sweden.

32. Mnemonics for classes of syllogisms.

33. Christian von Wolff (1679-1754), a German philosopher and mathematician and disciple of Leibniz. He is the author of the *Treatise on God, the Soul and the World* (1720) mentioned further on in the letter.

34. Roman emperor who lived from 331-363 A.D.

35. By Voltaire.

36. Michel Celse de Rabutin, Count de Bussy, named bishop of Luçon in 1723.

37. Pierre Du Puis, a president of the Great Council in Paris.

38. A church father of the third century.

39. Baron Jean Le Chambrier, Prussian minister to the French court.

40. Voltaire's *Prodigal Son.*

41. The last three titles refer to Voltaire's *Ode on Fanaticism,* his epistle to Mme. Du Châtelet which served as a preface to his *Elements of Newton's Philosophy,* and probably his letter of December 1735 to Father Tournemine.

42. In every genre.

43. Pierre-Claude Nivelle de La Chaussée (1692-1754), better known as a playwright.

44. Amiable couple of brothers with your permission.

45. Father Marin Mersenne (1588-1647) was a mathematician and a philosopher friend of Descartes. Voltaire uses Mersenne here as a nickname for Thieriot.

46. Virgil, *Aeneid,* Book VI, v. 129-130: "Few whom favoring Jove loved."

47. "Two hundred entire centuries beyond six thousand years," v. 68 of the *Newtonic.*

48. About fifty kilometers from Troyes.

49. Mme. Du Châtelet.

50. Jeanne-Françoise Quinault-Dufresne (1699-1783), an actress.

51. Cf. Virgil, *Eclogues,* I, v. 4: "lentus in umbra/formosam resonare doces Amaryllida silvas" ("at ease in the shade you teach the forests to re-echo the name of beautiful Amaryllis").

52. Jean-Baptiste Rousseau (1671-1741) was a prominent poet of the period whom Voltaire had admired early in his career and who later became his enemy.

53. Pierre Bayle (1647-1706), a seventeenth-century precursor of the *philosophes,* lived in exile in Holland.

54. Willem Jacob 'S-Gravesande (1688-1743), a Dutch mathematician and philosopher.

55. Baron Dietrich von Keyserlingk, Frederick's emissary to Voltaire.

56. Les vertus sont l'apanage
     Que vous reçûtes des cieux;
     Le trône de vos aïeux,

Près de ces dons précieux,
Est un bien faible avantage.
C'est l'homme en vous, c'est le sage
Qui m'asservit sous sa loi.
Ah! si vous n'étiez que roi,
Vous n'auriez point mon hommage.

57. According to Saint Luke, II, v. 26 "it was revealed unto him [Simeon] by the Holy Ghost, that he should not see death, before he had seen the Lord's Christ."

58. A reference to the Roman poet of the first century B.C. and his great literary patron, Maecenas.

59. The Abbé Dubos (1670-1742) was a historian, literary critic and diplomat. He was the author of *Critical Reflections on Poetry and Painting* (1719) and a *Critical History of the Establishment of the French Monarchy in Gaul* (1734).

60. The *régale* was a right of French kings to draw on the income of vacant bishoprics and to make ecclesiastical nominations to them. It was the subject of a dispute between Louis XIV and Pope Innocent XI.

61. Isaac de Larrey, Henri-Philippe de Limiers, and Guillaume de Lamberty all wrote lengthy histories of the period of Louis XIV. In the case of Rousset, Voltaire may be thinking of the contemporary historian Jean Rousset de Missy.

62. Philippe de Courcillon, Marquis de Dangeau (1638-1720) was the author of a *Journal* or diary kept from 1684 until his death. Although dull and insipid, it is a mine of information about the reign of Louis XIV.

63. Louis Le Tellier, Marquis de Barbézieux (1668-1701), was a statesman and son of Louvois, one of Louis XIV's principal ministers.

64. Paul Pellisson (1624-1693), a man of letters and historian.

65. Jacques Hardion (1686-1766) was curator of printed works in the Royal Library.

66. Pierre Jurieu (1637-1713), Pasquier Quesnel (1634-1719), and Louis Doucin (1652-1726) were all theologians of different persuasions. The first was a Protestant, the second a Jansenist, and the last a Jesuit.

67. Charles-Irénée Castel de Saint-Pierre (1658-1743) was the

author of some *Political Annals* published fourteen years after his death.

68. The Abbé Pierre Gassend, known as Gassendi (1592-1655), was a celebrated philosopher and physicist.

69. Virgil, *Aeneid,* Book IV, v. 88-89: "The works and huge threatening walls are suspended."

70. Virgil, *Aeneid*, Book IV, v. 89: "And the engines reaching the sky."

71. Yves-Joseph de la Mothe, also called La Hode (1688-1740), was an historian. He published *The Life of Philip of Orleans* in 1736.

72. Christian Huyghens (1629-1695), a Dutch physicist and astronomer.

73. James Bradley (1692-1862), an English astronomer.

74. See n. 68.

75. Jean-Dominique Cassini (1625-1712), a French astronomer and first director of the Paris Observatory.

76. John Flamsteed (1646-1719), a British astronomer.

77. Incorrectly quoted from Tasso's *Jerusalem Delivered,* Canto I, iii, v. 5-6: "Cosi all'egro fanciul porgiame aspersi/di soave licor gli orli del vaso" ("to sweeten the rim of the cup to make one swallow the bitter contents").

78. The thing itself refuses to be adorned; it is satisfied with being taught.

79. The reference is to *Conversations on the Plurality of Worlds* (1686), a work of scientific vulgarization by Bernard Le Bovier de Fontenelle (1657-1757).

80. Marguerite Heissein, Dame de La Sablière (1636-1693), a friend of La Fontaine. The quotation is from La Fontaine's *Fables,* Book XII, xv, v. 33. Jean-Pierre de Crousaz (1663-1750) was a Swiss mathematician and philosopher.

81. Probably Des Alleurs's brother.

82. If it pleases you, it is yours.

83. Horace, *Epistles,* Book I, v. 14: "Compelled by nothing to swear as my master dictates."

84. Antiochus Cantemirŭ Cantemir (1708-1744), a Russian statesman and poet, was an envoy to Paris at this time. His father, Demetrius (1673-1723), was a writer and hospodar of Moldavia.

85. A friend of Voltaire and Mme. Du Châtelet.

86. Marie-Elisabeth Sophie, Duchesse de Richelieu was the duke's second wife. She died in 1740.

87. This letter to Fawkener was written in English.

88. A part of the outskirts of Constantinople which, under the sultans, was reserved for foreigners and their embassies.

89. Constantinople is situated on the entrance of the Bosporus into the Sea of Marmara.

90. English statesman and man of letters (1696-1743). He wrote detailed and frank memoirs of the court of George II and, in 1740, became lord privy seal.

91. On October 23, 1739, Great Britain had declared war on Spain, and on November 21 succeeded in capturing the Spanish harbor of Portobello in Panama.

92. Giovanni de Medici, Pope Leo X (1475-1521).

93. Philippe Quinault (1635-1688), a French dramatic poet who composed libretti for Lully's operas. Eustache Le Sueur (1617-1655), a religious painter and decorator. Charles Lebrun (1619-1690), first painter to the King, oversaw the decoration of Versailles. Jean Jouvenet (1644-1717), a French portraitist and religious painter. François Mansard (1598-1666), the celebrated French architect. Claude Perrault (1613-1688), an architect; his brother Charles (1628-1703) was the author of *Tales of Mother Goose*. François Girardon (1628-1715), Pierre Puget (1620-1694), and Antoine Coysevox (1640-1720), three sculptors.

94. All seventeenth-century ecclesiastics.

95. In his *Age of Louis XIV*, Voltaire related the experimental voyage of French physicists to Cayenne in 1672 and maintained that man's first knowledge of the flattening of the earth was a result.

96. The Abbé Jean Picard (1620-1683) was an astronomer.

97. Michel Lambert (1610-1696) was a composer who had been music master in the King's Chamber. Lully became music master to the royal family in 1662.

98. D'Argens (1704-1771) was a writer and philosopher. The author of *Jewish Letters*, he became chamberlain to the King of Prussia.

99. His publisher, Paupie.

100. Charles-Jean-François Hénault (1685-1770), was a French

historian and magistrate and a friend of Voltaire and Mme. Du Deffand.

101. Voltaire had devoted considerable time and energy in getting Frederick's *Anti-Machiavelli* through the press.

102. René-Louis de Voyer de Paulmy, Marquis d'Argenson (1694-1757), a schoolmate of Voltaire at Louis-le-Grand, became Minister of Foreign Affairs in 1744.

103. Passart and Charrier were two police censors.

104. Mme. Du Châtelet.

105. These few gentlemen

106. Charles Dumolard-Bert, a librarian and printer.

107. Claude-Nicolas Le Cat (1700-1786), chief surgeon of the principal hospital of Rouen.

108. Edme Mariotte's *Treatise on the Movement of Waters and Other Fluid Bodies* appeared in Paris in 1686. The *Philosophical Transactions* are of the Royal Society of London.

109. Jean-Jacques Dortous de Mairan (1678-1771) was a physicist and geometer who served as Perpetual Secretary of the Académie des Sciences after Fontenelle. He was involved in a public dispute with Mme. Du Châtelet on the subject of physics.

110. A certificate signed by Mairan as Perpetual Secretary of the Académie des Sciences regarding the academy's examination of Voltaire's treatise entitled *Doubts Concerning the Measurement of Motor Forces and Their Nature*. The Académie had simply concluded that "Voltaire was informed about writings on Physics and had himself given considerable thought to that science."

111. See n. 33.

112. In a human and geometric way.

113. Samuel Koenig (1712-1757) was a German mathematician and a Leibnizian recommended by Maupertuis to Mme. Du Châtelet as a tutor.

114. Claude-Adrien Helvétius (1715-1771), French philosopher and farmer general.

115. A Dutch physicist and philosopher (1688-1742).

116. Sun stopper.

117. David-Renaud Boullier's *Lettres sur les vrais principes de la religion, ou l'on examine le livre de la Religion essentielle à l'homme, avec la défense des Pensées de Pascal, contre la critique de Voltaire [Letters on the true principles of religion in which are*

examined the book of Religion essential to man, with a defense of Pascal's Pensées against Voltaire's criticism] (Amsterdam, 1741).

118. Pierre-Nicolas Desmolets (1678-1760), a member of the Oratory, published some *pensées* of Pascal in the *Continuation des mémoires de littérature et d'histoire* (Paris, 1728).

119. Jean Hardouin (1686-1766), a Jesuit scholar.

120. François-Joseph de Beaupoil, Marquis de Sainte-Aulaire, a poet, died in 1742 at the age of ninety-eight.

121. This should probably read Lenclos for Ninon de Lenclos (1620-1705), a literary and social figure who died at the age of eighty-five.

122. Spurious selections from the *Philosophical Letters* were published in the *Lettres de M. de V °°°* (The Hague, 1738). The title of the volume suggested that it had been written by Voltaire.

123. I give it to consolidate the empire between its frontiers.

124. Vanity of vanities and metaphysical vanity. Cf. *Ecclesiastes*, I, 2: "Vanity of vanities! All is vanity."

125. Pieter Van Musschenbroek (1692-1761), a Dutch physicist.

126. Characters in Rabelais's *Pantagruel*.

127. Maupertuis led an expedition of academicians to Lapland (1736-1737) where he confirmed Newton's theory of the flattening of the earth at the poles. In 1740 he went to Berlin at the invitation of Frederick II and was later placed in charge of the new academy there. Maupertuis had been engaged in a controversy with the Cassini family, descendants of the French astronomer Jean Cassini, over the flattening of the earth at the poles.

128. The reference is to the following verses concerning Maupertuis written by Voltaire:

Ce globe mal connu, qu'il a su mesurer,
Devient un monument ou sa gloire se fonde.
Son sort est de fixer la figure du monde,
De lui plaire et de l'éclairer.
[This unfamiliar globe which he was able to measure becomes a monument on which his brilliant reputation is founded. His fate is to determine the shape of the world, to please it and to enlighten it.]

129. See n. 113.

130. Cf. *Matthew*, v, 15; *Mark*, iv, 21; *Luke*, xi, 33.

131. Leonhard Euler (1707-1783), the celebrated Swiss mathematician, was invited by Frederick to teach in Berlin in 1741 and did so until 1766.

132. Count Francesco Algarotti (1712-1764), an Italian philosopher and author of *Neutonianismo per le dame*. Frederick made him a Count of Prussia in 1740 and court chamberlain in 1747.

133. Baron Dietrich von Keyserlingk had been Frederick's envoy to Voltaire at Cirey.

134. The Abbé Joseph Privat de Molières (1676-1742), a scholar asociated with the Congregation of the Oratory.

135. The reference is to the deliberations regarding a successor to Charles VI.

136. Jean-Baptiste-Simon Sauvé, called La Noue (1701-1761) was an actor and playwright.

137. The daily fast that is rigidly prescribed from dawn until sunset during the ninth month of the Islamic calendar.

138. This letter was written in English by Voltaire.

139. Charles III.

140. Preceptor to the Dauphin.

141. In his play *Zaïre* (1732).

142. His play *Oedipe*, first performed in 1718.

143. *La Henriade*.

144. *The Age of Louis XIV*.

145. The son of Louis XV who was to become the father of Louis XVI, Louis XVIII and Charles X.

146. Luc de Clapiers, Marquis de Vauvenargues (1715-1747), a French moralist and soldier known for his *Maxims*.

147. Jean-Baptiste de Durfort, Duc de Duras (1684-1770), was a Maréchal de France.

148. In Corneille's *Horace*.

149. In Corneille's *Polyeucte*.

150. By Racine.

151. *John*, xiv, 2: "In my Father's house are many mansions."

152. Philippe Néricault, called Destouches (1680-1754), a playwright whose masterpiece was entitled *Le Glorieux*.

153. *Rhadamiste et Zénobie*, a tragedy by Prosper Jolyot de Crébillon (1674-1762).

154. Vincent Voiture (1598-1648), a man of letters noted for his preciosity and his role in the salon of the Hotel de Rambouillet.

155. Montesquieu.

156. Nicolas de Catinat (1637-1712), a Maréchal de France.

157. Amelot de Chaillou became foreign minister of France after the death of Cardinal de Fleury on January 29, 1743. This letter was transmitted in code.

158. The Abbé Jan-Ignace de La Ville, a secretary in the French embassy at The Hague at the time.

159. Robert Hampden-Trevor (1706-1783) represented Great Britain at The Hague from 1739 to 1746.

160. A one-act comedy whose author is unknown.

161. André-Hercule, Cardinal de Fleury (1653-1743), was prime minister of France (without the title) from 1726 to 1743.

162. At the Battle of Dettingen in 1743 the French were defeated by the Austrians and the English.

163. See n. 147.

164. *Matthew*, xii, 18: "in whom my soul is well pleased."

165. Voltaire wrote this letter in English to Ffolkes, the president of the Royal Society of which Voltaire had become an elected member on November 3, 1743.

166. With permission of the authorities.

167. Charles Lennox, second Duke of Richmond, was a London acquaintance of Voltaire; James Jurin (1684-1750) was an English physician and mathematician; Turner may have been an English physicist.

168. A German university professor and a Leibnizian.

169. Kahle's *Vergleichung der leibnitzischen und newtonischen Metaphysik [Comparison of Leibnizian and Newtonian Metaphysics]* published at Göttingen in 1740. The book was a defense of Leibniz in opposition to Voltaire and caused Voltaire to reply with his *Courte réponse aux longs discours d'un docteur allemand [Short Reply to the Lengthy Discourses of a German Doctor]*.

170. George Villiers, Duke of Buckingham; Jean Ogier de Gombauld (1570-1666), a French poet and one of the first members of the French Academy; Mathurin Régnier (1573-1613), a French satirical poet; Nicolas Rapin (1573-1608), a French poet

and one of the principal authors of the *Satyre Ménippée* (1594), a collective work directed against the Ligue.

171. Melchior, Cardinal de Polignac (1661-1741) was a diplomat and author of *Anti-Lucretius,* a Latin poem published in 1745.

172. Si monsieur le doyen peut jamais concevoir
Comment tout étant plein tout a pu se mouvoir.

173. Alexandre-Jean-Vincent Mignot Des Aunais was Mme Denis's brother.

174. The death of Mme. Denis's husband.

175. Charles-Gabriel de La Croix, Marquis de Castries (1727-1801), a Maréchal de France.

176. Louis-Jules Barlon Mancini-Mazarini, Duc de Nivernais (1716-1798), a soldier, diplomat and writer.

177. Nicolas-François Denis.

178. Jacob Vernet (1698-1789) was a Swiss Protestant minister.

179. François Jacquier (1711-1788), a mathematician and ecclesiastic.

180. A part of the *Essai sur les moeurs [Essay on Customs]* which appeared in 1756.

181. Adaloaldus (603-629) and Agilulf (590-615) were Kings of the Lombards.

182. Geneva.

183. Virgil, *Eclogues,* I, v. 30: "After Amaryllis began her sway."

184. *Réflexions critiques sur quelques poètes [Critical Thoughts on Some Poets.]*

185. Charles-Antoine Leclerc de La Bruère (1715-1754), a playwright.

186. Leclerc de La Bruère was the editor of the *Mercure de France,* an important periodical, from November 1744 to June 1748.

187. The brother of the French ambassador to Prussia and a resident of Lille.

188. Jean-François Boyer, Bishop of Mirepoix (1675-1755), had aroused Voltaire's enmity when, as a member of the French Academy, he opposed Voltaire's election to the august body.

189. A small town in Picardy.

190. A city on the Marne about 160 kilometers from Paris.

191. See n. 102.

192. Voltaire had been named royal historiographer on April 1.

193. Voltaire wrote this letter in Italian.

194. The Pope had consented to having Voltaire's *Mahomet* dedicated to him. The dedication was part of Voltaire's campaign to convince members of the French Academy of his "orthodoxy" and thereby gain entrance to that body.

195. One of a number of love letters to his niece written in Italian.

196. A tragedy by Quinault with music by Lully performed at Versailles on December 30, 1745.

197. The mother of Mme. de Pompadour, Madeleine de La Motte Poisson.

198. The original of this letter is in Italian.

199. A friend of Mme. Denis's family.

200. Jean-François Marmontel (1723-1799), a novelist and playwright. He wrote *The Incas* and *Bélisaire,* epic novels, and some *Memoirs.*

201. Cardinal Passionei was a librarian at the Vatican. Voltaire's letter to him was written in Italian.

202. Alessandro Marchetti (1663-1714) was an Italian translator of Lucretius and the author of *Exercitationes mechanicae* (1669) and *De resistentia solidorum* (1669). Giovanni-Gioseffo Orsi was the author of a preface to Maffei's *Merope* (1735). Vincenzo da Filicaia (1642-1707) was a poet and author of a series of sonnets entitled *All'Italia.* Apparently Voltaire's professed ignorance of Italian literature was exaggerated as he had quoted from the poetry of Filicaia in a letter to Frederick II in 1739.

203. Virgil, *Aeneid,* Book VII, v. 295-296: "Could they, captured, suffer captivity? Did the fires of Troy consume them?"

204. Based on Virgil, *Aeneid,* Book XII, v. 360: "Taking Italy's measure."

205. Horace, *Ars poetica,* v. 351-352: "When there are many brilliant points in a poem, I will not be offended by a few blemishes."

206. Giovanni Mario Crescimbeni (1663-1728) was a poet and critic who wrote *L'Istoria della volgar poesia* (1698).

207. Archbishop Giusto Fontanini (1666-1736) was a bibliographer known for his *Della eloquenza italiana* (1706) which was retitled *Biblioteca dell'eloquenza italiana.*

208. Cardinal Pierre Guérin de Tencin (1679-1758) was archbishop of Lyons and a minister of state.

209. Louis-Elisabeth de La Vergne, Count de Tressan (1705-1783), was a military figure, writer, and friend of Voltaire.

210. Cf. *Matthew,* xxxvi, 41 and *Mark,* xiv, 38.

211. The original of this letter is in Italian.

212. The original of this letter is in Italian.

213. Antoine Feriol, Count de Pont-de-Veyle (1697-1774), the elder brother of Count d'Argental, was a writer and a friend of Voltaire.

214. One of Voltaire's most popular plays first performed in Paris on August 29, 1748.

215. Louis II de Bourbon, Prince de Condé (1621-1686), one of Louis XIV's great generals.

216. François-Marie, Count and later Duc de Broglie (1671-1745) was a Maréchal de France.

217. In Greek legend, a member of the Greek army during the Trojan War. He was famous for his ugliness and unpleasant temper, and was killed by Achilles.

218. Antoine Danchet (1671-1748) was a minor playwright.

219. The original of this letter is in Italian.

220. A small town in the department of Eure-et-Loir, southwest of Paris.

221. One of the most famous Italian academies, founded in 1582, whose principal aim was the purification of the Italian language.

222. Mme. Denis crossed this word out and wrote above it "spirit."

223. The original of this letter is in Italian.

224. The original of this letter is in Italian.

225. A town in Lorraine, near Nancy and about fifty miles from Cirey, where Stanislas Leszczinski, the former king of Poland and father-in-law of Louis XV, held court.

226. Charles-Juste de Beauvau, Prince de Beauvau-Craon.

227. The original of this letter is in Italian.

228. The original of this letter is in Italian.

229. That is the devil.

230. Prosper-Jolyot, Sieur de Crais-Billon, called Crébillon (1674-1762), a playwright and rival of Voltaire at the Comédie Française, was the government censor.

231. And if the wretched state of my health permits I will throw myself at your knees and will kiss all your beauties. In the meantime, I apply a thousand kisses to the round breasts, to the exciting buttocks, to your entire body which has made me have erections so many times and plunged me into a river of delight.

232. André-Hercule de Rosset, Duc de Fleury, was the administrator of the Comédie Française. On Maurepas, see chapter 1, n. 36.

233. Voltaire wrote this letter in English.

234. Fawkener had married the daughter of General Charles Churchill, brother of the first Duke of Marlborough.

235. Cf. Horace, *Epistles*, Book I, 10, v. 50; "excepto quod non simul esses, cetera laetus" ("happy on all accounts except that you are not with me").

236. Jean-Baptiste Machault d'Arnouville (1701-1794) became controller-general of finance in December 1745. In 1749, he attempted a reform in the levying of direct taxes.

237. The War of the Austrian Succession was concluded in 1748 with the signing of the treaty of Aix-la-Chapelle.

238. An *écu* was generally worth three *livres*, the values of which varied widely in the eighteenth century. The *livre* was replaced by the *franc* with the coming of the French Revolution. The *litron* was a unit of measurement equivalent to about three quarters of a liter.

239. The system of John Law (1671-1729), the Scottish financier who was made controller-general of finance in France in 1720, led to a wave of speculation. With the bursting of the bubble and the collapse of his system, thousands of investors were ruined.

240. Mme. Du Châtelet had an affair with Jean-François, Marquis de Saint-Lambert (1716-1803), a soldier and poet, and died giving birth to his child on September 10.

241. His tragedy *Rome sauvée [Rome Preserved]* (first performed in Paris in 1752).

242. A reference to the failure of Crébillon's tragedy *Catilina*. Curiously, Crébillon, Voltaire's rival, was the government censor, and his permission had to be sought for the performance of a tragedy obviously written against him.

243. Charles-Jean-François Hénault (1685-1770) was an historian and president of the Parlement of Paris.

III

EXILE AND MILITANCY

(1750-1778)

EXILE AND MILITANCY

[*Shortly after his arrival at the court of Frederick II of Prussia, Voltaire wrote his friends, the D'Argentals, of his pleasure in finding a safe refuge at last after three decades of turbulence. He was indeed exuberant during his first stay in Prussia where he thought he saw "a renaissance of the brilliant age of Louis XIV on the shores of the Spree." But Voltaire was soon to have second thoughts about Frederick and his enlightened despotism.*

Mme. Denis had refused to leave Paris with him, and on his arrival in Berlin he took up with another woman, the unconventional Countess Bentinck. Although in exile, Voltaire lost no interest in cultural affairs at home. In anticipation of his future quarrels with Jean-Jacques Rousseau, he criticized the Dijon Academy for setting up a literary competition in which the moral beneficence of literature could be doubted. He expressed reservations about another fellow writer, Montesquieu, but concluded that fundamentally "his lofty boldness must please all who think freely." He noted the current preeminence of the English language and ascribed it to the boldness and intellectual independence of the English: "In England people ask no one for permission to think."

In 1751, some twenty years after he had first begun work on the project, Voltaire published his monumental Age of Louis XIV. *Although the history was intended to depict one of France's periods of greatness, the contrast with the state of affairs under Louis XIV was not very flattering for the regime in power and the work had to be published in Prussia. Another work that had a long period of gestation was the science-fiction* conte Micromégas *which was published in 1752 but reflects more deeply the intellectual pre-*

157

*occupations of Voltaire at Cirey between 1735 and 1740. The year
1752 was also eventful for the beginning of his critical* Philosophical
Dictionary *to be published only years later.*

*1752 was, moreover, the year of Voltaire's quarrel with the
scientist Maupertuis whom Frederick had appointed head of the
Berlin Academy. By the beginning of 1753, Voltaire had had
enough of Frederick and Prussia and informed the king he wanted
to leave. Permission was granted only on March 15. Voltaire then
visited the courts of Gotha and Kassel, and on May 29 he reached
the free city of Frankfurt where he was joined by Mme. Denis. The
two were promptly arrested as a result of Frederick's instructions.
No doubt Voltaire's dubious financial speculations in Prussia as
well as his publication of a pamphlet against Maupertuis, entitled*
Akakia, *in defiance of Frederick's order against it contributed to
the arrest. Voltaire fled Frankfurt on July 7, 1753, but the king
continued to vilify him in various writings, going so far as to call
him "the most treacherous rascal in the universe."*

*In October Voltaire settled in the Alsatian city of Colmar after
Louis XV forbade his coming back to Paris. During the year 1754,
he was at work on another great historical work, ths famous* Essay
on Customs, *in the library of the Benedictine Dom Calmet at the
abbey of Senones. In August, he went to the waters of Plombières
for another cure, and by the fall he was investigating the possibility
of buying property and settling in Switzerland, ready to begin, at
age sixty, another and more militant phase in his career.]*

81. *". . . perhaps the perfection of the Art should consist in a due
mixture of the french taste and english energy."*

To Sir George Lyttleton.[1] Paris. May 17, 1750 (n. st.).

You was beneficent to m[r] Thompson,[2] when he Liv'd, and
you is so to me in favouring me with his works. J was acquainted with the author when j stay'd in England. J discovered
in him a great genius and a great simplicity, j lik'd in him the poet
and the true philosofer, j mean the Lover of mankind. J think that
without a good stock of such a philosofy a poet is just above a
fidler, who amuses our ears and can not go to our soul.

J am not surpris'd y^r nation has done more justice to m^r Thompson's *Seasons* than to his dramatic performances. There is one kind of poetry of which the judicious readers and the men of taste are the proper judges. There is an other that depends upon the vulgar, great or small. Tragedy and comedy are of these last species. They must be suited to the turn of mind and to the ability of the multitude and proportion'd to their taste. Y^r nation, two hundred years since, is us'd to a wild scene, to a crowd of tumultuous events, to an emphatical poetry mix'd with low and comical expressions, to murthers, to a lively representation of bloody deeds to a kind of horrour which seems often barbarous and childish, all faults which never sullyd the greak, the roman or the french stage. And give me leave to say that the taste of y^r politest countrymen in point of tragedy differs not much in point of tragedy from the taste of the mob at bear garden. T'is true we have too much of words, if you have too much of action, and perhaps the perfection of the Art should consist in a due mixture of the french taste and english energy. Mr Adisson,[3] who would have reach'd to that pitch of perfection had he succeeded in the amourous part of his tragedy as well as in the part of Cato, warn'd often y^r nation against the corrupted taste of the stage and since he could not reform the genius of the country, j am affraid the contagious distemper is past curing.

Mr Thompson's tragedies [4] seems to me wisely intricated, and elegantly writ. They want perhaps some fire; and it may be that his heroes are neither moving nor busy enough. But taking him all in all, methinks he has the highest claim to the greatest esteem. Y^r friendship sir js a good wouschafer for his merit. J know what reputation you have acquir'd. If j am not mistaken, you have writ for y^r own sport many a thing that could raise a great fame to one who had in view that vain reward call'd glory. J have by me some verses that pass under y^r name and which you are suppos'd to have writ in a journey to Paris. They reflect very justly on our nation and they run thus:

A nation here j pity and admire
Whom noblest sentiments of glory fire,
Yet taught by custom's force and bigot fear

159

To serve with pride and boast the yoke they bear,
Whose noble, born to cringe and to command,
In courts a mean in camps a genrous band,
From priests and ta [?] jobbers content receive
Those laws their dreaded arms to Europe give;
Whose people vain in want, in bondage blest,
Tho plunder'd guai, industrious tho oppress'd.[5]

etc.

These verse deserve a good translator, and they should be learn'd by every french-man.

Give me leave to send you a little performance of mine. T'is but a pebble j do offer to you for y^r pretious stones.

J am with the highest respect

s^r

y^r most humble obed. servant

Voltaire

82. "My soul is divided between you and Frederick the Great."

To Charles-Augustin Feriol, Count d'Argental, and Jeanne-Grâce Bosc Du Bouchet, Countess d'Argental. Potsdam. August 7, 1750.

My divine angels,

So your Sans Souci[6] is at Neuilly! You have fewer marble columns, fewer balustrades made of gilded copper; however beautiful your salon may be, it has no magnificent cupola. The very Christian king has not sent you statues worthy of Athens, and you have not even been successful yet in ridding yourself of your busts.[7] Despite all that, I still maintain that Neuilly is the equal of Sans Souci. But I will detest Neuilly and your Bois de Boulogne if Mme. d'Argental's health is not restored there, if M. de Choiseul[8] does not have a full supper, and if the bishop's coadjutor has chest pains. I pass one indigestion on to you. Happy are those who are ill only when they want to be!

Everything I hear about the theater in Paris makes me regret

160

only Neuilly and my little theater. Poor taste has raised its head in Paris. You will have your fill of it for a few more years; it is an epidemic that must run its course, and you will only return to good things when you are tired of the bad. You have been ruined by affluence; too much wit has led talent and genius astray in almost every genre, and the protection given to Catilina [9] has finally brought total ruin. I confess that the Prussians do not compose better tragedies than we, but you will really have a hard time presenting as noble and gallant a spectacle as the one being prepared in Berlin for the lying in of the dauphine: a carrousel of four large Carthaginian, Persian, Greek and Roman quadrilles, led by four princes rivaling one another in magnificence, all illuminated by twenty thousand Chinese lanterns transforming night into day. There are prizes distributed by a beautiful princess and there is a host of foreigners rushing to this spectacle. Isn't all of this a renaissance of the brilliant age of Louis XIV on the shores of the Spree? Add the total freedom I enjoy here and the inexpressible consideration and kindness of the conqueror of Silesia who bears his entire royal burden from five in the morning until dinner time, who absolutely devotes the rest of his day to literature, who is willing to work with me three hours at a time, who submits his great genius to criticism, and who at supper is the most amiable of men, the bond and charm of society. After that, my angels, do me justice. What is there for me to regret except you alone? I also include Mme. Denis. As far as I am concerned, you alone are superior to what I observe here. I won't speak to you today about Aurélie and the editions of my works with which I am still threatened from every direction. I am learning from the king of Prussia to correct my faults. The time I do not spend with him is used working without respite, as far as my health will allow. O wise inhabitants of Neuilly, hold on to a friendship more precious to me than all the grandeur of a wholly worthy king. My soul is divided between you and Frederick the Great.

83. *"Here we are in the retreat of Potsdam."*

To Marie-Louise Denis. Potsdam. October 13, 1750.

Here we are in the retreat of Potsdam. The hubbub of festivities is over; my soul is more at its ease. I am not sorry to find myself beside the king without either court or council. It is true that Potsdam is inhabited by mustaches and grenadiers' caps, but, thank God, I do not see them one bit. I work peacefully in my apartment to the sound of drums. I have kept away from the king's dinners; there are too many generals and princes. I could not get used to constantly facing a king in state ceremony and to speaking in public. I dine with him in more intimate company; supper is shorter, gayer and healthier. I would die of grief and indigestion at the end of three months if I had to have dinner in public with a king every day.

I have been handed over, my dear child, to the king of Prussia in good form. So my marriage is made; will it be happy? I haven't the slightest idea. I could not keep from saying *yes*. I finally had to conclude this marriage after so many years of flirtation. My heart palpitated at the altar. I intend to come this next winter and give you a total account and perhaps take you away. My Italian trip is now out of the question; I have sacrificed the Holy Father and the underground city for you without remorse. Perhaps I ought to have sacrificed Potsdam for you. Who would have told me seven or eight months ago, when I was setting my house in order with you in Paris, that I would settle three hundred leagues away in someone else's house? And that someone else a master. He *swore* to me that I would not regret it. He has included you, my dear child, in a sort of contract he signed with me which I will send you. But will you come and earn your four thousand pound marriage settlement?

I am really afraid that you will do as Madame de Rothenburg who has always preferred the operas of Paris to those of Berlin. Oh destiny! how you arrange events and how you rule over poor human beings!

It is funny that the same literary men in Paris who would have *exterminated* me a year ago are now crying out against my absence, calling it desertion. It seems they are angry at having lost their victim. I did the wrong thing by leaving you; my heart tells me so every day more than you think. But I did very well to get away from those gentlemen.

I embrace you with tenderness and with sorrow.

84. *Montesquieu's "noble boldness must please all who think freely."*

To Charles-Emmanuel de Crussol, Duc d'Uzès.[10] Berlin.
September 14, 1751.

I owe the letter with which you honor me to your taste for literature. That taste further arouses my sensibility and provides me with a new cause for thanks. Surely you can do no better in the leisure which your glory, your wounds and peace have given you than to cultivate as vigorous a mind as yours. Everything in this world is almost completely vacuous but less so in study than in other things. That is a great resource at all times and nourishes the soul to the final moment. I am with a great king who, despite his royalty, would be vexed if he did not share your way of thinking, and I came to him after being attached to someone for sixteen years only because he joins a passionate love for the arts to all his great qualities. I resisted the temptation to live with him as long as Mme. Du Châtelet, whose memory, I am consoled to see, you have not forgotten, was alive. I believe that the Duchesse de La Vallière, your sister, and Mme. de Luxembourg have abandoned me somewhat since my desertion, but I will always be faithfully devoted to them. In the court of the King of Prussia, I can scarcely read compositions written by school children for prizes awarded by the Academy of Dijon,[11] but on the basis of the outline you give me, I quite agree with you. It even seems to me quite indecent that an academy appeared to have doubts as to whether literature has purified morals.

Would the gentlemen of Dijon have one think they were dishonest? Men of letters have sometimes abused their talents, but what is not abused? I would just as well have people say that we must not eat because we can get indigestion. Will I go tell these men of Dijon that all academies are ridiculous because they proposed an apparently ridiculous subject? All of this is only a misunderstanding and a false conclusion from the particular to the general.

Nor am I acquainted with the little pamphlets against M. de Montesquieu. I would have hoped his book had been as methodical and true as it is full of wit and great maxims, but such as it is, it has seemed useful to me. The author always thinks and causes others to think; "he is a formidable antagonist" as Montaigne put it; his imagination causes mine to rush forth. Mme. Du Deffand was right to call his book *De l'esprit sur les lois;* [12] it seems to me that it cannot be better defined. It must be confessed that few people have as much wit as he, and his lofty boldness must please all who think freely. It is said that he had only been attacked by slaves of prejudice; it is one of the merits of our century that these slaves are not dangerous. These wretches would like the rest of the world to be strangled by the same chains they are.

You do not seem suited to share those debasing chains of the human mind, and all your thoughts are those of a *magnanimous peer of France.* You announce a correspondence that flatters me considerably. I hope to be in Paris in a few months and receive the tokens of confidence with which you will honor me. I will make myself worthy of them by my discretion and the truth with which I will speak to you.

I am, with great respect, monseigneur, your very humble and very obedient servant.

Voltaire,
Chamberlain of the King of Prussia

85. "*. . . I have supper with the king and the conversation neither turns to private worries or general uselessness. . . .*"

To Marie de Vichy de Chamrond, Marquise Du Deffand. Potsdam. September 23, 1752.

The Swedish envoy tells me that you still remember me with unfailing kindness. We had an unceremonious supper with the wittiest king on earth at which only you were missing. He wishes to take on the burden of my regrets for having lost such company as yours and to send you my letter. You diminished my desire to take a trip to Paris when you deserted it. But I still hope to meet you there again someday. Retirement has its charms, but Paris also has its own. It perhaps seems astonishing to you that I boast of being in retirement when I am at the court of a great king. But you must not imagine that in the morning I go to a dressing room in a white powdered wig, that I then ceremoniously go to mass and then to a dinner, that I announce in the gazettes that I have access to the great, and that after dinner I compose hymns or romances. My life does not have that sparkle. I do not have the slightest court to pay, not even to the master of the house, and it is not on hymns that I am working. I am suitably lodged in a beautiful palace; I have two or three impious men with me with whom I dine regularly and more soberly than someone devout; when I feel well, I have supper with the king and the conversation neither turns to private worries or general uselessness, but to good taste, to all the arts, to true philosophy, to how one may be happy, to distinguishing truth from falsity, to freedom of thought, to the truths taught by Locke (and of which the Sorbonne is ignorant), to the secret of establishing peace in a kingdom by means of certificates of confession.[13] In fact, for the more than two years that I have been at what people believe to be a court and which is really only a philosopher's retreat, there has never been a day during which I have not found something with which to improve my mind. Never has one led a life more suitable for an invalid, for, having no visits to pay, no duties to perform, my time is all my own, and one cannot suffer in greater comfort. I enjoy the tranquility and freedom that you have where you are.

This is surely a match for the ridiculous turmoil I went through in Paris. President Hénault writes me occasionally but Count d'Argenson, as is reasonable, has completely forgotten me. If he had remembered me a little more when he headed the ministry in Paris, perhaps I would not have the kind of happiness that was finally procured for me. However, one always loves one's country in spite of all; one always speaks of the unfaithful with pleasure. I am giving you an exact account of my soul, and you can give me a certificate of confession when you wish. But you would also have to confess to me, tell me how you are, what you are doing for your health and happiness, when you intend to return to Paris and how you are taking the affairs of life. I intend to

165

send to you straight away a new edition of the *Age of Louis XIV* enlarged by a third and full of singular truths. I let myself go a little on the subject of writers; I have used all the freedom of Bayle; I have only tried to condense what he expatiated on too much. You will see two odd pieces in the hand of Louis XIV. With his defects, he was a great king and his century a very great century. But don't we have Mme. Duchapt [14] today?

Be well, madam, and remember the most devoted and most appreciative of your servants.

V.

86. *"I really see that they have squeezed the orange; we must think of saving the rind."*

To Marie-Louise Denis. Berlin. December 18, 1752.

My dear child,

I am sending you the two contracts of the Duke of Württemberg; [15] it is a small fortune guaranteed for your lifetime. I am adding my will to it. Not that I believe your old prophesy that the King of Prussia would cause me to die of grief. I do not feel in any humor to die such a silly death, but nature is doing me much more harm than he, and we must always have our bags ready and our feet in the stirrups to travel to that other world where, whatever happens, kings will not have much influence.

As I do not have a hundred fifty thousand mustaches at my disposal in this world, I have no intention of waging war. I am only thinking of honestly deserting, of tending to my health, of seeing you again, of forgetting this dream of three years.

I really see that *they have squeezed the orange;* [16] we must think of saving the rind. For my own edification, I am going to compose a small dictionary for the use of kings.

My friend means *my slave.*

My dear friend means *you are more than indifferent to me.*

Understand by *I will make you happy: I will put up with you as long as I need you.*

Have supper with me this evening means *I will make fun of you this evening.*

166

The dictionary may be long; it is an article that should be included in the *Encyclopédie*.

Seriously this makes my heart ache. Can everything I have seen be possible? To be amused by setting those who live with him against one another! To speak to a man in the most affectionate terms and write pamphlets attacking him! And what pamphlets! To wrest a man from his homeland with the most sacred promises and mistreat him with the most wicked malice! What contradictions! And this is the man who wrote me so many philosophical things and I thought was a philosopher! And I called him the Solomon of the North!

You remember that beautiful letter that never reassured you. "You are a philosopher," he said. "I am one also." In truth, sire, neither one of us is.

My dear child, I will only consider myself one when I am at home with you. The difficulty is getting out of here. You know what I informed you of in my letter of November 1. I can only ask for leave out of consideration for my health. There is no way of saying: I am going to Plombières in December.[17]

There is a sort of minister of the Holy Gospel here named Pérard who was born in France like me. He asked for permission to go to Paris on business; the king sent him a reply that he knew his business better than he did, and that he had no need to go to Paris.

My dear child, when I consider in some detail everything that is going on here, I finally come to the conclusion that it is not true, that it is impossible, that they are mistaken, that the thing happened in Syracuse some three thousand years ago. What is really true is that I love you with all my heart and that you are my consolation.

87. *". . . the city council today sent its secretary to our prison to interrogate us. . . ."*

Voltaire and Marie-Louise Denis to the Chevalier Charles-Nicolas de La Touche.[18] Frankfurt am Main. June 26, 1753. 5 p.m.

Since our last requests sent to His Majesty, the fate of which we are unaware of, the city council today sent its secretary to our prison to interrogate us and determine whether His Majesty has ordered our arrest. We replied that we had seen no order and that it seemed impossible for Messrs. Freytag and Schmidt, who are pursuing and ransoming us, to have received by June 17 an order to imprison us on the 20th.

The council believes, according to what its secretary has told us, that His Majesty will allow Mme. Denis her freedom. She is undergoing her sixth bout of fever and will hardly be able to enjoy that freedom, but she will owe His Majesty an eternal obligation. I am even in worse condition than she is. We both implore the goodness and mercy of the king, and we beseech the Chevalier de La Touche to send him this memorandum.

Voltaire. Denis.

88. *His Prussian Majesty Arrests M. de Voltaire.*

To Louis XV, King of France. June 28, 1753.

Sire,

M. de Voltaire is taking the liberty of informing His Majesty that, after working two and a half years with the King of Prussia to improve that prince's knowledge of French literature, he has respectfully returned to him his key, his decoration and his pensions, that he has cancelled in writing the contract which His Prussian Majesty had entered into with him, promising to return it as soon as he is in control of his papers and to make no use of it, and that he desires no other reward than to return to his homeland to die. He went to the waters at Plombières with Your Majesty's permission. Madame Denis met him at Frankfurt with a passport.

A man called Dorn, an agent for Mr. Freytag, who calls himself the resident of the King of Prussia in Frankfurt, on June 20 arrested Madame Denis, the widow of an officer of Your Majesty who had been provided with her passport. He personally dragged her into the streets with some soldiers without any order, without the slightest formality, without the slightest pretext, led her off to prison and had the insolence to spend the night with this lady in her room. For thirty-six hours she was near death and on June 28 has still not recovered.

In the meantime, a merchant named Schmidt, who calls himself an adviser to the King of Prussia, treated M. de Voltaire and his secretary in the same fashion, and without formality, seized all of their effects. The following day, Freytag and Schmidt came and informed their prisoners that their detention would cost them one hundred twenty-eight *écus* a day.

The pretext for this violence and depredation was an order, which Messrs. Freytag and Schmidt received from Berlin in the month of May, to ask M. de Voltaire for the return of the printed book of French poetry by His Prussian Majesty which His Prussian Majesty had given the aforesaid M. de Voltaire as a present.

Since this book was in Hamburg, M. de Voltaire surrendered himself as a prisoner on his honor and in writing in Frankfurt on June 1 until the return of the book, and Mr. Freytag signed these two notes for him, each complementing the other, in the name of the king, his master:

"Sir, as soon as the large package which you say is in Hamburg or Leipzig and which contains the poetical works of the King arrives here and the poetical works are returned to me, you may leave for whatever place you see fit."

M. de Voltaire gave him in addition two packages of literary and family business papers as a guarantee, and Mr. Freytag signed this third note for him:

"I promise to return to M. de Voltaire two packages of writings sealed with his arms as soon as the package containing the poetical works whose return the king is requesting has arrived."

The poetical works were returned with the box from Hamburg

169

on June 17 at Mr. Freytag's own address. M. de Voltaire was evidently within his rights to leave on June 20, but it was on June 20 that he, his niece, his secretary and his retinue were summoned to prison in the manner set forth above.

89. *Consolation to a Friend Going Blind.*

To Marie de Vichy de Chamrond, Marquise Du Deffand. Colmar.
March 3, 1754.

Your letter has moved me more than you think, and I assure you that there were a few tears in my eyes when I read about what has happened to your sight. I had judged from M. de Formont's letter that you were in a haze but not completely in the dark. I thought you were pretty much in the same state as Madame de Staal [19] but better off by the inestimable good fortune of being free, of living at home, of not being compelled, by living with a princess, to behave in an annoying and hypocritical manner, and finally of having friends who speak and think freely with you. Thus what I simply regretted about your eyes was the loss of their beauty, and I knew you were even philosophical enough to console yourself over this. But if you have lost your sight, I pity you infinitely. I shall not propose to you the example of M. de Senneterre [20] who was blind at twenty, and always gay, even too gay. I agree with you that life is not good for very much. We only put up with it by dint of an almost invincible instinct provided us by nature. Nature has added to that instinct the resource of Pandora's box: hope. When we are absolutely without that hope or when an unbearable melancholy comes over us, we muster that instinct which causes us to hold life's chains in affection and we have the courage to take leave of a residence that has been poorly put together and which we have no hope of repairing. That is what two persons recently decided in the region where I live. One of those two philosophers was an eighteen-year old girl whose head had been turned by the Jesuits and who departed for the next world to rid herself of them. This will not be my course of action, at least not soon, because I have arranged life annuities for myself with two sovereigns, and I would be inconsolable if my death were

170

to enrich two crowned heads. If you have life annuities with the King, take good care of yourself, eat little, go to sleep early, and live a hundred years.

It is true that Dionysius of Syracuse's [21] conduct is incomprehensible, like him. He is a rare man, and it is good to have been to Syracuse because I confess that it does not resemble the rest of the globe in any way. The Plato of Saint-Malo [22] with his flattened nose and mad visions is scarcely any less strange. He was born with considerable intelligence and talent, but excessive pride alone made a very ridiculous and wicked man of him in the end. Isn't it horrible that he persecuted his good doctor Akakia who had tried to cure him of his madness with his lenitives?

Now who could have told you that I was getting married? I'm an amusing one to be married off! For six months I haven't been out of my room, and out of twelve hours in a day I suffer ten. If some apothecary had a shapely daughter who could properly and agreeably give enemas, fatten chickens, and read aloud, I confess that I would be really tempted. But the truest and dearest of my desires would be to spend the evening of that stormy day called life with you. I have seen you in your brilliant morning, and it would be a great comfort for me if I could help console you and converse with you freely during those very brief moments that remain and which are followed by timelessness. I am not quite sure what will become of me, and I hardly care. But you may be sure that you are the person in this world for whom I have the most affectionate respect and unalterable friendship. Allow me to send M. de Formont a thousand regards. Does President Hénault still give the Queen preference over you? It is true that the Queen is very witty.

Farewell, madam. You may be sure that I feel your sad state acutely, and from the edge of my grave I should like to be able to contribute to the sweetness of your life. Will you remain in Paris? Are you spending the summer in the country? Are men and places indifferent to you? Your face will never be indifferent to me.

V.

90. *"The age of Louis XIV put the French language in vogue, and we are presently living on our credit."*

To Pierre-Joseph Thoulier d'Olivet. Colmar. March 26, 1754.

I thank you very sincerely, my dear and erudite abbé, for the very instructive little book you sent me.[23] It proves that the Academy is of greater use to the public than one thinks, and, at the same time, it shows how useful you are to the Academy. It seems to me that most of the difficulties in our grammar derive from those mute *e*'s which are peculiar to our language. One does not encounter that difficulty in Italian, Spanish or English.

I know all the modern languages of Europe a little, that is to say all those jargons that have been refined with time and which are as distant from Latin and Greek as a Gothic structure is from the architecture of Athens. Our jargon does not really merit preference in itself over that spoken by Spaniards which is much more sonorous and majestic, nor over that of the Italians which is much more graceful. It is the quantity of our agreeable books and of French refugees that has caused our language to be in style even in the far north. Italian was the language in general use in the time of Ariosto and Tasso. The age of Louis XIV put the French language in vogue, and we are presently living on our credit. English has begun to take on great favor since Addison, Swift and Pope. It will really be difficult for that language to become one of general intercourse like ours, but I see that everyone, even princes, wants to understand it because of all languages it is the one in which people have thought most boldly and forcefully. In England people ask no one for permission to think. It is that happy freedom which produced Pope's *Essay on Man*, and, to my way of thinking, this is the foremost of didactic poems.

Would you believe that in the city of Colmar, where I find myself, I discovered an old magistrate who took it into his head to learn English at the age of seventy and knows enough of it to read the good writers pleasurably? See if you can do as much. I warn you that there are no disputes in England over participles, but I think you will stay with our language which you purify and embellish.

172

Forgive me for not writing in my own hand. I am very ill. I will soon go and see La Chaussée.[24] I embrace you.

V.

91. *"I am no longer of this world, and I find that I am very well off for it."*

To Marie de Vichy de Chamrond, Marquise Du Deffand. Between Two Mountains. July 2, 1754.

I have been ill. I have been leading the existence of a monk. I have spent a month with St. Augustine, Tertullian, Origen, Alcuin and Raban. A relationship with the Church fathers and with the scholars of Charlemagne's time is no match for one with you. But what news can I send you from the mountains of the Vosges! And how can I write you when I have been occupied only with Priscillianites and Nestorians![25] Amid these fine works with which I have chastised my imagination, there were still orders from your friend M. D'Alembert to obey to do a few articles for his *Encyclopedia,* and I have done them very poorly. Historical research has dulled me. The more I delve into the seventh and eighth centuries, the less I am suited for ours and especially for you. M. D'Alembert has asked me for an article on mind. That is like a request to Father Mabillon or Father Montfaucon.[26] He will be sorry he asked for gavottes from a man who has broken his violin, and you will also be sorry for wanting me to write you. I am no longer of this world, and I find that I am very well off for it. However, I remain no less affectionately interested in you. But in the state we both find ourselves, what can we do for each other? We will confess that everything we have seen and everything we have done has passed like a dream, that our pleasures have taken flight, that we must not rely too heavily on men. Will we comfort ourselves this way, by telling each other of what little consolation the world is? One can only live in it with illusions, and as soon as one has had a little experience with life, all the illusions evaporate. I thought there was only one good and certain occupation for old age which would bring us to the end and still keep us from fret-

173

ting. I have spent a month with an eighty-four year old Benedictine who is still engaged in historical work. One can amuse oneself with that when the imagination falters. No wit is necessary to concern oneself with old events. That is the course I have taken. I waited for my health to recover a bit before going to Plombières for a cure. In the same way that I have read the fathers, I will take the waters although I do not believe in them. I will carry out your orders pertaining to M. D'Argental. I understand the strong reasons for the supposed separation of which you speak. But you have forgotten one: you moved from his neighborhood. So these are the great reasons on which the intercourse of life rolls along. Do you really know the most difficult thing in Paris? Snatching the day's end. May your days be tolerable, madam. This is still a fine lot since days that are constantly pleasant exist only in the *Thousand and One Nights* and in heavenly Jerusalem. Let us resign ourselves to the destiny that makes sport of us and carries us off. Let us live as long as we can and as we can. We will never be as happy as fools, but let us try to be happy in our own way. Let us try—what an expression! Nothing depends on us. We are clocks, machines. Farewell, madam. My clock would like to strike the hour that says it is time to be with you.

[*After being harassed in both France and Prussia, Voltaire decided to take up residence in Switzerland to buy some property in Calvinist Geneva. He had to overcome the fact that he was nominally a Catholic and did so by using a go-between in the real estate transaction by which he acquired, in 1755, an estate located in the open countryside about half a league outside of the boundaries of eighteenth-century Geneva (but within the present-day confines of the city). He expressed his feelings of joy and freedom by dubbing his new house Les Délices.*

Voltaire was disturbed at this time by the unauthorized publication of his poem La Pucelle [The Maid], *an irreverent satire of Joan of Arc which he had begun writing at least twenty-five years earlier but had refrained from publishing. The work was attacked many times and specifically condemned in a 1757 decree of the Inquisition. After more than twenty unauthorized editions had*

174

reached their way into print, Voltaire finally consented to the publication of a correct version in 1762.

1755 was also noteworthy for Voltaire's famous satirical letter to Jean-Jacques Rousseau in which he strongly objected to Rousseau's condemnation of civilization in his Discourse on the Origin of Inequality: "I have received your new book against the human race." The year was even more important for the great earthquake at Lisbon, an event which, like the Seven Years' War, aroused Voltaire's conscience in the face of human suffering, led him to criticize more virulently the philosophy of metaphysical optimism in vogue at the time, and inspired him to express his deeply felt philosophical reactions in his Poem on the Lisbon Earthquake [Poème sur le désastre de Lisbonne].

Among the subjects that engaged Voltaire in his correspondence for the next few years were his increasing dissatisfaction with the philosophy of optimism ("a cruel philosophy under a consoling name"), his concern for the success and continuing publication of Diderot's and D'Alembert's Encyclopédie in the face of powerful official opposition (especially after the appearance of D'Alembert's article Geneva in which he urged the toleration of a theater in Calvinist Geneva and praised the clerics of the city as proponents of Socinianism), his own personal contributions to that enterprise, and the importance of a united front for the philosophes in the face of harassment and persecution from established authority. Voltaire's work on the History of Peter the Great, his relationship with Diderot and his attitude toward the Seven Years' War including his own role as an intermediary in peace negotiations between Frederick and the French are additional concerns that find their way into his letters.

The book De l'Esprit by Claude-Adrien Helvétius, another philosophe and collaborator on the Encyclopédie, was published in 1758 and was promptly condemned by both the Royal Council and the Parlement of Paris. Voltaire wrote against the persecution of Helvétius, suspecting that it was part of a Jesuit attempt to get at Diderot: "I value these two men highly, and the indignities they are suffering make them infinitely dear to me." Voltaire also spent various parts of 1758 writing and editing his conte Candide, and the Geneva edition of the work was published under a pseudo-

175

nym on January 15, 1759. His attempts to deny the authorship of his greatest masterpiece provide entertaining reading.]

92. On Buying Some Property in Switzerland.

To Jacques-Abram-Elie-Daniel Clavel de Brenles.[27] Colmar. October 18, 1754.

I see that I will have to take a trip to Burgundy at the beginning of next month, and I would like to be informed in advance about the possibility of acquiring a pleasant retreat in your surroundings. I am not speaking about the conditions of this acquisition and of how to go about it. I am certainly aware that these are things that require a little time, but it is essential that I first be informed as to whether I can safely purchase a piece of land in your country without having the good fortune of belonging to the religion which is admitted there. I have an idea that the territory of Lausanne is like that of Attica. You have persuaded me to come and end my days there. I am persuaded that it would not be looked down upon at the court of France and that provided the purchase were made inconspicuously and under a name other than mine, I would enjoy the advantage of being your neighbor very peacefully. I suppose, for example, that if land bought under someone else's name were to be subsequently passed on by a secret contract in the name of my niece, one could then quietly settle there without this little trip being considered a transmigration.

We would still have to know whether my niece, once she had become the owner of the land, could subsequently dispose of it even though she had not been born in the country. I am putting you to considerable trouble. This is a strange abuse of your kindness, but forgive all of this since you have inspired me with the desire to come and end my career in the bosom of philosophy and freedom. M. de Gloire, who is soon to return to Lausanne, has given me the same picture of this country as you. The Alaman land would be very suitable for me, and if it were not possible to make this purchase, we could find another acquisition. I beg of you, while waiting until this settlement can be arranged, please inform me whether a Catholic can own landed property in your

176

country, whether he can enjoy the rights of a citizen in Lausanne, whether he can make a will in favor of his relatives living in Paris, and in case your laws do not permit these arrangements, what remedies your laws allow one to exercise.

With respect to the Alaman land, I still stand completely ready to give 225,000 livres in French money for it, even if that might not be equivalent to 9,000 livres in income, but that is all I can do. The disposition of my fortune does not allow me to go beyond this, and I will even find myself a bit hard put at first with respect to the furnishings. The manager of the estate you recommend will certainly please me greatly if he continues to manage it. He can be useful in getting it furnished and in procuring the necessary provisions, servants from the region, carriages, and horses. Perhaps there is furniture in the chateau which one might use.

I speak to you indiscreetly about all these arrangements when I ought only to speak to you about your health which concerns me much more. I earnestly beseech you, please send me news of it. Madame Goll and my niece send you and Madame de Brenles as well a thousand sincere regards. I beg you to reply as soon as possible so that I may make all my arrangements before my trip to Burgundy. Count on the friendship and inviolable gratitude of a man already devoted to you.

93. *Getting Settled.*

To Nicolas-Claude Thieriot. Les Délices, near Geneva. March 24, 1755.

I have not written you for a long time, my old friend. I have become a mason, a carpenter, and a gardener; my entire house is topsy-turvy and, in spite of all my efforts, I will not have the facilities with which to put up my friends as I would like. Nothing will be ready for the month of May; we must absolutely spend two months at Prangins [28] with Madame de Fontaine [29] before we can move into my Délices. [30] Les Délices is my torment at present. We are busy, Madame Denis and I, building enclosures for our friends and our hens. We are having carriages and wheelbarrows built; we are planting orange trees, onions, tulips and carrots. We are in need of everything; Carthage must be founded. My territory is scarcely larger than that of the oxen skin given to the fugitive Dido,[31] but I will not enlarge it in the same way. My house is in the territory of Geneva and my meadow in that of France. It is true that, at the other end of the lake, I have a house completely in Switzerland; it is also built somewhat in the Swiss style. I am putting it in order at the same time as my Délices; it will be my winter palace, and the hut I am presently in will be my summer palace. Prangins is a true palace, but the architect of Prangins forgot to plant a garden and the architect of Les Délices forgot to construct a house. No Englishman has lived in my Délices; it was the Prince of Saxe-Gotha. You will ask me how a prince was able to put up with this hovel; the answer is that this prince was a schoolboy at the time, and besides princes are scarcely required to provide guest rooms. I have only found some small salons, galleries, and attics here, and not one room for a wardrobe. It is as difficult to make something out of this house as it is out of the books and plays we are provided with these days. I hope, however, that with care, I will construct a rather nice grave for myself. I would like to fatten you in that tomb and have you be my vampire there. I imagine that the mania of building ruins princes as well as private individuals. It is sad that the Duc de Deux-Ponts [32] takes from his literary agent what he gives to his masons. I would advise you to spend a year on our lake to restore yourself; you would be fed, your thirst would be quenched, you would be shaven and conveyed from Prangins to Les Délices, from Les Délices to Geneva and to Morges which looks like the site of Constantinople and to Monrion which is my house near Lausanne. All around here you would find good wine and the greetings of a good host, and if I die within the year you will compose my epitaph. I still maintain that M. de Prangins would have to bring you along with Madame de Fontaine at the end of May. I would come and join you at Prangins on your arrival, and I would assume responsibility for you for all the time you would wish to philosophize with us. So do not resist your inspiration to see your old friend again.

I have been sent a few fragments of *The Maid* [33] which are making the rounds in Paris; they are as distorted as my *Universal History*. All my offspring are being crippled; that makes my heart bleed. I am waiting for Le Kain one of these days; we will find a bed for him in a gallery, and he will declaim verse to the children of Calvin. Their habits have become much more gentle. Today they would not burn Servet,[34] and they require no certificates of confession. I embrace you with all my heart and take much more interest in you than in all the nonsense of Paris with which half the world is so seriously concerned. I embrace you.

The sick V.

94. *"I have received your new book against the human race. . . ."*

To Jean-Jacques Rousseau. Les Délices, near Geneva. August 30, 1755.

I have received your new book against the human race.[35] I thank you for it. You will please mankind to whom you tell a few home truths but you will not correct it. You depict with very true colors the horrors of human society which out of ignorance and weakness sets its hopes on so many comforts. Never has so much wit been used in an attempt to make us like animals.

The desire to walk on all fours seizes one when one reads your work. However, as I lost that habit more than sixty years ago, I unfortunately sense the impossibility of going back to it, and I abandon that natural gait to those who are worthier of it than you and I. Nor can I embark on a search for the savages of Canada, first because the maladies to which I have been condemned make me require a European doctor; secondly because warfare has reached that country and the example of our nations has made the savages almost as wicked as we. I confine myself to being a peaceful savage in the solitude I have chosen near your homeland where you ought to be.

I agree with you that literature and the sciences have sometimes caused great harm.

The enemies of Tasso made his life a series of misfortunes; those of Galileo made him suffer in prisons at the age of seventy for recognizing the earth's motion and even more shameful was their compelling him to issue a retraction.

As soon as your friends began the *Encyclopedic Dictionary,* those who dared compete with them called them deists, atheists, and even Jansenists. If I ventured to include myself among those whose works have only been rewarded with persecution, I would show you a bunch of wretches eager to bring about my ruination from the day I first presented the tragedy of *Oedipus;* a library of ridiculous slander printed against me; a former Jesuit priest whom I had saved from capital punishment repaying me with slanderous satires for the service I had rendered him; a man even guiltier having my work on the *Age of Louis XIV* printed with notes in which the most shameless of deceptions are spouted in the crassest ignorance; another man selling a book dealer a so-called universal history under my name, and the book dealer greedy and stupid enough to print this shapeless tissue of blunders, false dates, facts, and mangled names; and finally, men cowardly and wicked enough to attribute that rhapsody to me. I would show you society infected by this new breed of men unknown to all of antiquity who, incapable of embracing an honest profession either as lackeys or as laborers but unfortunately able to read and write, become brokers of literature, steal manuscripts, and disfigure and sell them. I could complain that a jest written over thirty years ago on the same subject which Chapelain [36] was silly enough to treat seriously, is now being circulated because of the faithlessness and infamous avarice of those wretches who have disfigured it with as much stupidity as malice and who, after thirty years, are selling that work (which is certainly no longer my own and has become theirs) everywhere; I would add lastly that they have dared rummage through the most respectable archives and steal a part of the memoirs I had deposited when I was historiographer of France and that they sold the product of my work to a Paris book dealer. I would depict to you ingratitude, deception and pillage pursuing me to the foot of the Alps and even to the edge of my grave.

But also admit that these thorns attached to literature and to one's good name are but flowers compared to the other ills which have always flooded the earth. Admit that neither Cicero, Lucretius, Virgil, nor Horace were responsible for the banishment of Marius, of Scylla, of that libertine Anthony, of that imbecile Lepidus, of that uncourageous tyrant Octavius Cepias who has been nicknamed, in so cowardly a fashion, Augustus.

Admit that the bantering of Marot [37] did not bring about

180

St. Bartholomew's Day and that the tragedy of the *Cid* did not cause the wars of the Fronde. Great crimes have only been committed by celebrated ignoramuses. What makes and will always make of this world a valley of tears is the insatiable and indomitable pride of men, starting with Thamas Couli Can [38] who could not read and right up to the customs official capable of only making calculations. Literature nourishes the soul, rectifies it, consoles it, and it is even responsible for your glory as you write in opposition to it. You are like Achilles who flew into a passion against glory and like Father Malebranche whose brilliant imagination wrote against imagination.

M. Chapuis [39] informs me that your health is quite poor. You ought to come and restore it in the native air, enjoy freedom, drink with me the milk of our cows, and graze on our grass. I am, very philosophically and with the most affectionate esteem, your very humble and very obedient servant.

Voltaire

95. *Reflections on the Lisbon Earthquake.*

To Jean-Robert Tronchin.[40] Les Délices, November 24, 1755.

This is indeed a cruel sort of physics. People will really find it difficult to divine how the laws of motion bring about such frightful disasters in the "best of possible worlds." [41] A hundred thousand ants, our neighbors, suddenly crushed on our ant-hill and half of them probably perishing in inexpressible anguish amidst debris from which they cannot be extricated; families ruined at the ends of Europe, the fortunes of a hundred merchants from your homeland swallowed up in the ruins of Lisbon. What a sad game of chance the game of human life is! What will the preachers say, especially if the palace of the Inquisition remains standing? I flatter myself at least that the Reverend Fathers, the Inquisitors, will have been crushed like the others. That ought to teach men not to persecute men, for while some holy scoundrels burn a few fanatics the earth swallows up the whole lot of them.

I have already seen our friend Gauffecourt.[42] I will go to Monrion as late as possible. I think that our mountains are saving us from the earthquakes. Goodbye, my dear correspondent. Inform me, I pray you, of the results of this horrible adventure.

96. *"We need a God who speaks to the human race."*

To Elie Bertrand.[43] Monrion. February 18, 1756.

My dear philosopher,

My colic took a severe turn for the worse when I received your letter. My consolation now is that I will not be attacked by colic in the next world. Truly I hope so, and I say a small word on the subject in my sermon.[44] The question does not hang on that object of hope. It hinges solely on this axiom or rather joke: "All is well at present; everything is as it was supposed to be, and the present general happiness results from the present ills of each individual." Now, in truth, this is as ridiculous as that maxim of Posidonius who used to say to his gout: "You will not make me admit that you are a disease."

Men of all times and of all religions have felt the misfortune of human nature so sharply that they have all said that the work of God had been corrupted. Egyptians, Greeks, Persians and Romans have all imagined something approaching the fall of the first man. One must admit that the work of Pope destroys this truth and that my small discourse brings one back to it. For if *all is well,* if everything has been as it was supposed to be, then there is no fallen nature. But, on the contrary, if there is evil in the world, this evil indicates past corruption and the future remedy. That is the completely natural consequence. You will tell me that I do not draw that conclusion, that I leave the reader in sadness and in doubt. Well! one has only to add the word *to hope* to that of *to adore* and to write: *mortals, we must suffer, submit ourselves, adore, hope and die.*[45]

But the heart of the work unfortunately remains true beyond all question. Evil exists on the earth and to say that a thousand hapless persons make for happiness is to mock me. Yes, there is evil, and few men would wish to begin their career over again, perhaps not one in a thousand. And when people tell me that things could not be otherwise, they are committing an outrage to reason and to my grief. A worker who has poor materials and poor instruments is quite free to say: I could not do otherwise. But my poor Pope, my poor hunchback whom I knew, whom I loved, who told you that God could not shape you without a hunchback! You make sport of the story of the apple. It is still, humanly speaking and always excluding the sacred, more reasonable than the optimism of Leibniz; it gives a reasonable account of why you are hunchbacked, sick and a little crafty.

We need a God who speaks to the human race. Optimism is despairing. It is a cruel philosophy under a consoling name. Alas! If all is well when everything is in affliction, we will then be able to pass on to a thousand worlds where we will suffer and where all will be well. We will go from misfortune to misfortune to become better off. And if *all is well,* how do the Leibnizians allow for something better? Is this something better not a proof that all is not well? Ah! who is unaware that Leibniz was not waiting for something better? Between us, my dear sir, Leibniz, Shaftesbury, Bolingbroke and Pope all gave thought only to demonstrating their wit. As for me, I am suffering and I say so, and I also tell you just as truthfully that I am very anxious to go to Berne to thank you for your kindness and for that of M. de Freydenreik. You know all the news: all is well in France. Madame de Pompadour is pious and has taken a Jesuit for a confessor.

97. *". . . my way of thinking, which is neither that of a superstitious person nor of an atheist."*

To Pierre-Robert Le Cornier de Cideville. Les Délices, near Geneva. April 12, 1756.

My dear old friend,

I have composed so much verse that I am reduced to writing you in prose. I have put off giving you news of myself since I intended to send you at the same time the poems on the disaster of Lisbon, on *all is well,* and on natural law—works which have been published in Paris in completely distorted editions. Since I was forced to have these two poems printed myself, I had to correct them. I had to say what I think and say it in a way that would not shock minds that were either too philosophical or too credulous. I found it necessary to publicize my way of thinking which is neither that of a superstitious person nor of an atheist. And I venture to believe that all upright men will be of my opinion.

Geneva is no longer the Geneva of Calvin, far from it. It is a country filled with true philosophers. The reasonable Christianity of Locke is the religion of almost all the ministers, and the adoration of a supreme being linked with morality is the religion of almost all the magistrates. You see by the example of Tronchin [46] that the Genevese can contribute something useful to France. This year, from the shores of our lake, you have had smallpox innoculation, Idamé,[47] and natural religion.

My booksellers enjoyed assembling the heads of the Council and of the church in their city and reading my two poems to them. They received universal approbation in all respects. I do not know whether the Sorbonne would do the same. Since I do not agree with Pope on everything in spite of my friendship for him and the sincere esteem that I shall preserve for his works for the rest of my life, I felt obliged in my preface to do justice to him as well as to our illustrious friend, the Abbé du Resnel,[48] who did him the honor of translating him and often did him the service of softening the callousness of his opinions. Moreover notes were necessary. I have attemtped to fortify all of the avenues by which the enemy could penetrate. All this work required time. My dear old friend, you may judge whether a sick man burdened with this task as well as with a universal history now in press, and who is engaged in planting and construction and setting up a sort of small colony, has the time to write his friends. Forgive me then if I seem so idle at a time when I am most occupied. Let me know how I can address my poems on *all is not well* and natural religion to you. I do not know whether you are still in Paris; I do not know where the Abbé du Resnel is. I am writing you almost by chance not knowing whether you will receive my letter. Madame Denis sends you a thousand regards.

V.

I have not seen the old papers with which the Cramers [49] filled their edition for a long time. They considered a small letter in verse which was addressed to you worthy of publication. They

184

were mistaken, but the pleasure of seeing a small monument to our friendship prevented me from objecting to the printing.

98. "'Heavens, no bidet,' she said."

To Jean-Robert Tronchin. Les Délices. June 19, 1756.

On the one hand, the bets are open that Marshal de Richelieu will be brought to England by Admiral Byng; on the other hand, I have prophesied that Port Mahon will be captured.[50] I believe a fortune could be won by betting against the English. But what grieves me most is that Madame de Fontaine rightly finds my house poorly furnished. "Heavens, no bidet," she said. She is not yet accustomed to the severe and unclean habits of the city of Calvin. Madame Denis, in her capacity as a citizen of the territory, had disregarded that lack of modesty until the present moment, but luxury finally carries the day with the arrival of a delicate Parisian lady. By every rule we ought to address ourselves to a lady. Never has a great merchant been charged with such errands, but still you are gallant, you are our friend and you intend for us to be clean at Les Délices.

My dear correspondent, please do add to your shipments three bidets which, thanks to all your help, will be well furbished. It will cost you no more to order six medium-sized torches out of hammered silver to be attached to them.

What harassing requests! Hammered silver torches, coffee, sugar, candles, gilded nails, and, on top of everything, bidets! Still if there were reversals in Cadiz! Not at all. They are as behind in Cadiz as they are in Port Mahon. The English no longer understand reason. In London I am reproached for being too French and for not liking their poetry enough. Their heads are being turned. They will be beaten.

I forgot to tell you that you will get a case of paintings for our Délices. I hope that in a few days the doctor and Le Bat will be sleeping in Monrion. I will really be proud that I provided the doctor with lodgings.

I beg your forgiveness and embrace you.

V.

99. *"Our age is still quite barbaric."*

To Denis Diderot. Monrion (in the region of Vaud). February 28, 1757.

The work you sent me resembles its author.[51] It seems to me full of virtue, feeling, and philosophy. I believe as you do that there is much in the Parisian theatre that would have to be reformed but as long as fops interfere with actors on the stage there is nothing to hope for.[52] The most impertinent of all abuses is the excommunication and infamy attached to the talent of uttering virtuous feelings in public. This contradiction is irritating, but it is still one of our lesser follies. I am glad to forget, in my retreat, all those who work at making men unhappy or brutalizing them, and the more I forget these enemies of the human race, the more I think of you. I exhort you to spread the noble freedom of your soul as much as you can in the *Encyclopedia*. Cicero was not put in the turret of Vincennes for his book *De Natura Deorum*. Our age is still quite barbaric. Vale et scribe.

Tuus.

V. . . .

100. *The History of Peter the Great.*

To Ivan Ivanovich Shuvalov.[53] Les Délices, near Geneva. August 11, 1757.

This letter is to inform Your Excellency that I have sent him a sketch of the *History of the Empire under Peter the Great* from the time of Michael Romanov until the Battle of Narva.[54] There are errors that you will easily recognize. The name of the third ambassador who accompanied the emperor on his travels is erroneous. He was not chancellor as the memoirs of Le Fort, which are defective in this regard, state. I have only sent you this slight sketch so as to have instructions from you about the errors I have committed. You will probably not have time to bother, but it will be easy to get the necessary corrections to me. The manuscript I had the honor of addressing to you is only an attempt to be enlightened by your orders.

This package was sent to Paris on August 8 n.s. to M. de Bekteiew and in his absence to the Ambassador.

I have obtained everything that has been written on Peter the Great, and I confess that I have found nothing that could enlighten me, not a word on the establishment of manufacturing, nothing on river communications, public works, monies, jurisprudence, or land and naval forces. They are simply very faulty collections consisting of a few manifestoes, a few public writings that have nothing to do with everything great, new, and useful achieved by Peter I. In sum, what ought to be known most to all nations is really known to no one.

I venture to repeat that nothing will do you more honor, nothing will be worthier of the Empress's reign than to erect such a monument to the glory of her father throughout the world. I will merely arrange the stones of this great edifice. It is true that the story of this great man ought to be written in an interesting way. I will devote all my attention to this. Moreover, I will observe all the requisites of truth and propriety with the greatest exactitude. I will send you the entire manuscript as soon as it is completed. I flatter myself that my zeal and conduct will not displease your august sovereign under whose auspices I will work without interruption as soon as the necessary memoirs have reached me.

With respectful feelings of true devotion, I have the honor of being, sir, Your Excellency's very humble and obedient servant.

Voltaire

101. *"Only five or six philosophers who agree are needed to overturn the colossus."*

To Jean Le Rond D'Alembert.[55] Les Délices. December 6, 1757.

My very dear and very useful philosopher,

I have received your letter of December 1. I do not know whether I have thanked you sufficiently for the excellent work with which you honored the memory of Du Marsais [56] who, were it not for you, would have left no memorial. But I do know that I will never be able to thank you enough for having supported me with your eloquence and your reasons, as they say you have done, with regard to the infamous murder of Servet and the virtue of toleration in the article *Geneva*.[57] I am awaiting this volume impatiently. There were enough wretches in the sixteenth century for them to dare and justify the assassination of Servet in our own. These wretches are priests. I swear to you that I have read nothing they have written; to know that they were the shame of all upright people was enough for me. One of these rogues asked the Council of Twenty-Five of Geneva for a communication on that trial which will make Calvin forever execrable. The Council considered this request an outrage. Some magistrates detest the crime into which fanaticism lured their fathers, and some priests would canonize this crime! You may be sure that this last trait makes them as hateful as they deserve. I have received compliments from every righteous person in the region.

Who is that other young priest who would represent you to be a usurer? Could you have made a loan at a usurious rate during the battle of Kolin [58] when your Prussian looked as if he would be forced to pay poor pensions? But you will admit that during the battle on the fifth everyone had to advance you money. Here is another saddening piece of news concerning pensions that occurred on the 22nd outside of Breslau.

The Austrians avenge and humiliate us terribly. They made thirteen simultaneous attacks on Prussian defense positions, and these attacks lasted six hours. Never was a victory more bloody and more horribly beautiful. We funny Frenchmen are more expeditious; our business is over in five minutes.

The King of Prussia still writes me verse, sometimes as a desperate man, sometimes as a hero, and I attempt to be philosophical in my hermitage. He has obtained what he has always wanted—to beat the French, to please them and to mock them—but the Austrians are making genuine sport of him. Our shame on the fifth brought him glory, but he will have to be content with that passing glory which was too easily bought. He will lose his states along with those he conquered unless the French again find the secret of losing all their armies as they did in the War of 1741. You speak to me about writing his history. This is a concern with which he will charge no one; he is taking it upon himself. Yes, you are right; he is a rare man. I come back to you, a man as celebrated in your way as he is in his. I was absolutely unaware of the nonsense you spoke to me about. I will investigate, and you will get me to read the *Mercure*.

I do as Cato. I always finish my harangue by saying: *Deleatur Carthago*. You may be sure that there are aspects of the eulogy of Du Marsais that do considerable good. Only five or six philosophers who agree are needed to overturn the colossus. The issue is not one of preventing our lackeys from going to mass or a sermon. The matter is one of rescuing heads of families from the tyranny of impostors and of inspiring the spirit of toleration. That great mission already has had favorable success. The vineyard of truth is being well cultivated by the d'Alemberts, Diderots, Bolingbrokes, Humes, etc. If your King of Prussia had been willing to confine himself to that holy work, he would have lived happily and all the academies of Europe would have blessed him. The truth is winning out, so much so that in my retreat I have seen Spaniards and Portuguese detesting the Inquisition like Frenchmen. *Macte animo, generose puer; sic itur ad astra*.[59] In former times, they would have said: *Sic itur ad ignem*.[60]

I am sorry about Du Marsais's affectations at his death.[61] It was reported in print that that provincial Deslandes[62] who wrote the *Critical History of Philosophy* in such a provincial style recommended, as he was dying, that his book *Great Men Dying While Joking* be burned. And who the devil knew that he had written that book? Madame Denis sends you a thousand regards. The chatter-box embraces you with all his heart. Do you sometimes see the clairvoyant blind lady?[63] If you see her, tell her that I am still very much attached to her.

102. *"The King of Prussia can still wage a battle, utter witty words, be agreeable to the conquered, and tear sheets to make bandages for the wounded."*

To Jean-Robert Tronchin. Les Délices. December 7, 1757.

My dear correspondent,

You must know about that day when seventeen bridges were simultaneously laid across the Oder, when thirteen attacks were simultaneously waged against the Prussian entrenchments and blood was shed for six hours, when the Prussians were beaten and their artillery captured, and when they retreated into Breslau and Breslau was blockaded. I am awaiting more ample details from Vienna. This, more or less, is the information I was given on the arrival of the trumpeting postilions in Vienna announcing, on November 25, that great affair of the 22nd which avenges and humiliates us. I will really be amazed if they will listen to the King of Prussia's propositions in Versailles. What they fear most after the travelling madman is offending the empress in the slightest way. They can no longer separate what was joined in a moment. The King of Prussia can still wage a battle, utter witty words, be agreeable to the conquered, and tear sheets to make bandages for the wounded. That is what he did on the evening of November 5, but in the end he will have to give in unless they conduct themselves as they did in 1742. I still have no positive news about the loyalty of the Hanovrians and Hessians, but it is quite certain that without the Austrians we would be lost.

Anyone who had told Cardinal de Richelieu that one day the French would owe their salvation in Germany to Austrian armies would really have astonished him. Cosi va il mondo.

Fan' lega oggi Re, papi, imperadori,
Doman' saranno captiani 'nimici.[64]

Wheat is getting more expensive. So don't object if I place a small Andalusian banknote for 4,386 *tournois* in your wallet.

Let me place the enclosed in your package.

The trees will really come at the right time before I go to Lausanne and become completely Swiss.

190

I embrace you with all my soul. Madame Denis does likewise.

V.

By the way didn't I tell you that since I live in the country, I sometimes send my letters to the city too late and that you will receive them in the next regular mail?

103. *Encouragement to Continue with the* Encyclopédie.

To Jean Le Rond D'Alembert. Lausanne. January 8, 1758.

People in Geneva are boasting that you have to leave the *Encyclopédie* not only because of the article *Geneva*, but for other reasons which the priests do not explain to your advantage. If you feel somewhat disgusted, my dear philosopher, my dear friend, I beseech you to overcome this; do not become discouraged in so beautiful a career. I should like you and M. Diderot and all of your associates to protest that you will really abandon the work if you are not free, if you are not protected from calumny, if silence is not imposed, for example, on the new Garasses who call you *Cacouacs*.[65] But for you to give up this great work alone while the others continue, for you to provide this unfortunate triumph to your unworthy enemies, for you to let people think that you were compelled to leave, this is something I will never tolerate, and I earnestly beseech you to persist in your courage. This great work would have had to be composed and printed, I know, in a free country or under the eyes of a philosopher prince, but such as it is, there will always be aspects of it for which thinking people will owe you an eternal obligation.

What do those who admonish you for having betrayed the secret of Geneva mean? Was it in secret that Vernet,[66] who has just set up a commission of priests against you, printed that revelation is useful? Is it in secret that the word *trinity* is not found once in his catechism? Did the other impertinent priests of Holland want to condemn him in secret? You have only said what all Protestant communions know; your book is a public register of public opinions. Never retract and do not look as if you are giving in to these wretches by renouncing the *Encyclopédie*. You could not take a worse step, and of course you won't. They will write you a letter

191

sweet as honey; do not get trapped by it whatever its source. They will write to M. de Malesherbes; [67] it is up to him to support you, but you need no one's support.

Finally, in the name of letters and of your honor, be firm and work on the *Encyclopédie*.

Here are *Hemistiche* and *Happy*.[68] I have attempted to make the articles instructive; I detest declamation. Good night. Explain all of your intentions to me, I pray you, and rest assured that you have neither a greater admirer nor a more devoted friend than the old Swiss V.

104. *"I wrote to M. Diderot two months ago about a very serious matter which concerns him, and he has not given me any sign of life."*

To Charles-Augustin Feriol, Count d'Argental. Lausanne. February 26, 1758.

When I write to the King of Prussia and to the Abbé de Bernis [69] about insignificant things, they honor me with a reply within a week. I wrote to M. Diderot two months ago about a very serious matter which concerns him, and he has not given me any sign of life. I requested a reply in four or five letters sent in the regular mails, but I have received none. I asked for my letters to be returned. I properly considered this conduct outrageous. Of course, his offense was even more serious since I was the most outspoken supporter of the *Encyclopédie*. I even worked on some fifty articles which they were willing to confide to me. I did not become discouraged by the insignificance of the subjects that were relegated to me nor by the deadly aversion aroused in me by several articles of the sort that were handled with a similar ineptitude in the old *Mercure galant* and which disgrace a monument raised to the glory of the nation. No one has taken a keener interest than I in M. Diderot and his enterprise. The more ardent my interest, the more inevitable my outrage at his conduct.

I am no less distressed by the fact that he finally wrote me after two months. Commitments to publishers! A great man like him depending on publishers! The publishers ought to await his orders in his waiting-room. This immense enterprise will earn M. Diderot some thirty thousand livres! It ought to earn him two hundred thousand livres (I mean him and M. d'Alembert and one or two persons who are helping them), and if they had only been willing to honor the little out-of-the-way town of Lausanne with their work, I would have given them my note for two hundred thousand livres. And if they were persecuted and determined enough to take this course of action by arrangements with the publishers in Paris, we would still find a way of completing the work with suitable independence, tranquility, and safety for the Parisian publishers and the subscribers. But it is not a question of taking such an extreme course of action which is, nevertheless, not unfeasible and would do honor to philosophy.

The point is not to prostitute oneself with vile enemies, not to work like slaves for publishers and persecutors. The point is to draw rightful attention to one's work and to oneself. To achieve that essential goal, what must be done? Nothing. Yes, do nothing or look as if you are doing nothing for six months or a year. There are three thousand subscribers. These are three thousand voices that will cry out: "Let those who instruct us and do honor to the nation work with honor." The public outcry will make the persecutors loathsome. My dear and respectable friend, you inform me that the Attorney General was very pleased with the seventh volume. That is already good assurance. The work has been printed with the approval and authorization of the King. Therefore, we must not allow some scoundrel to dare preach against reason to the King once reason has been allowed to appear in print. Therefore, we must not allow the author of the gazette to say in provincial advertisements that the nation's preceptors seek to destroy religion and corrupt morals. Therefore, we must not allow a mercenary writer to distribute with impunity the defamatory pamphlet on the Cacouacs.

These two scoundrels depend on the government's offices, but surely neither the Abbé de Bernis nor Madame de Pompadour is giving them encouragement. I am convinced, on the contrary, that Madame de Pompadour would obtain a pension for M. Diderot. She would stake her pride on it, and I dare say that the matter would not be a very difficult one.

That is how they ought to spend their time for six months.

Let M. Diderot, M. d'Alembert, M. de Jaucourt and the author of the excellent article on procreation [70] declare that they will not work any longer if they are not given justice, if they are given censors with evil intentions, and it is evident to me that in three months public opinion, which is the most powerful of protections, will give those who educate the nation the authority over literature which they must have. Then M. d'Alembert will be obliged to work more than ever. Then he will work. But we must have both the wisdom to be completely united and the courage to persist for a few months in declaring that we do not want to work *sub gladio*. There is certainly no great harm in making the public wait. On the contrary, there is a very great benefit. In the meantime, we will gather materials; we will engrave plates; we will arrange patronage for ourselves, and then we will publish an eighth volume in which we will no longer insert the insipid declamations and trivialities with which the preceding ones were infected. At the beginning of this volume, we will include a preface that will crush the detractors with that nobility and air of superiority with which Hercules crushes a monster in a Lebrun painting.

In sum, I urgently ask that we unite, that we appear as if we are giving the whole thing up, that we assure ourselves protection and freedom, that we associate the entire public with us by making it afraid that it will witness the collapse of an indispensable work.

All of this unfortunate situation is due to M. Diderot's not first making the same declaration as M. d'Alembert. There is still time. We will be completely successful if we give the impression we want to do no further work. With time and friends, success is inevitable. I can write Madame de Pompadour letters in the strongest terms, and I will have persons of influence write if this device is found suitable.

But is a man who can let two months go by without making a reply on such essential matters able to bestir himself as he must in such an affair? I earnestly pray M. Diderot to burn, in M. d'Argental's presence, my note on the Cacouacs where I was in error concerning the author. I love M. Diderot, I respect him and I am angry.

V.

105. *Helping with the* Encyclopédie.

To Denis Diderot. Les Délices. June 26, 1758.

You do not suspect my honor and pleasure in occasionally placing one or two bricks on your great pyramid. It is really a shame that in everything concerning metaphysics and even history, we cannot tell the truth. The articles that ought to enlighten men the most are precisely those in which the mistaken opinions and ignorance of the public are increased. We are forced to lie, and still we are persecuted for not having lied enough. As for myself, I have told the truth so insolently in the articles *History, Idolatry,* and *Imagination* that I ask you not to submit them for censorship under my name. They may pass if the author is not named, and if they do pass so much the better for the small number of readers who are fond of the truth. I am going to take a little trip to the Palatine court. That diversion prevents me from adding new articles to those that M. D'Argental has kindly undertaken to deliver to you. I shall only send *Humor (moral)* and will address it to Briasson.[71]

I found two assistant bricklayers for you, one of whom is a scholar in Oriental languages and the other a lover of natural history who is acquainted with all the curiosities of the Alps and can provide good papers on fossils and on the changes that have befallen this globe or globule called the earth.[72] These two gentlemen are only asking for a copy of the work in order to guide themselves on the basis of what has already been printed. One of them has furnished a few articles, but it does not seem as if the publishers are willing to give them this little present. It seems very likely that we can do without their help. I hope that you will have as much profit as fame for your troubles. You may be sure that no one in this world expresses more good wishes for your success and is more imbued with esteem and devotion to you than the little Swiss V.

106. *"I know of no condition preferable to mine. It would be madness to want to change it."*

To Jean-Baptiste-Nicolas Formont.[73] c. October 3, 1758.

My dear philosopher,

I am charmed by your memento. You are a big fat epicurean in Paris and I a thin epicurean on the Lake of Geneva. It is good for brothers to give each other signs of life occasionally. Madame Du Deffand is more philosophical than the two of us since she endures the deprivation of sight so constantly and accepts life patiently. I take an affectionate interest not in her happiness because that phantom does not exist, but in all the consolations she enjoys, in all the amenities of her mind, in the charms of her delightful company. I would certainly want to take pleasure in that delightful company, I mean yours and hers, but to the devil with your Paris! I don't like it one bit and never have. I am a listless old man; I need gardens; I need a pleasant house I rarely leave and to which people will come. I have found all of that; I have found the pleasures of the city and the country together, and most importantly the greatest independence. I know of no condition preferable to mine. It would be madness to want to change it. I do not know whether I will be afflicted by that madness, but at least it is a disease from which I am not suffering at the moment in spite of all your favors. I neither regret Iphigenia in Crimea nor Hypermnestra.[74] I fear only even more for the loss of public funds than for that of talent. The India Company, trade and the maritime service seem to be in even greater decline than good taste. Never have so many books been written and never has our defense been in a more unfortunate state. I have thirty volumes about trade, and still it is in decline. Neither books on mind and matter nor decrees of the Council regarding these books will remedy so many ills.

What do you have to say about the defeat of my Russians? It is much worse than at Narva. Everyone has either died, been wounded or been taken prisoner. There were three consecutive battles. The Prussians had only three thousand men killed but at least ten thousand wounded. If Count Daun [75] were to meet them unexpectedly under these circumstances, perhaps he would

196

do to the Prussians what they did to the Russians. There is an English tragedy in which the prompter arrives at the end to announce that all the actors of the play have been killed. This cruel war may indeed end the same way. Not that it is not true that the Russians were beaten three times as is maintained; once is enough indeed.

I pray you, present my very affectionate respects to Madame Du Deffand and occasionally remember the old Swiss V. who will love you always.

107. *On the Persecution of Diderot and Helvétius.*

To Nicolas-Claude Thieriot. At the Chateau de Tournay, near Geneva. February 7, 1759.

My old friend,
I have received the geographical maps. My niece, de Fontaine, will pay you for all your little out of pocket expenses on her return and will present you with my thanks. I earnestly pray you to tell Messrs. Le Roy and Gravelot [76] how deeply I am moved by their consideration.

In an academic meeting, one could reproach the author of the book entitled *De L'Esprit* [77] that the work in no way corresponds to its title, that chapters on despotism are foreign to the subject, that on occasion commonplace truths are proved with ostentation, that what is new is not always true, that equating pride, ambition, avarice and friendship is an outrage to humanity, that there are many erroneous quotations, too many puerile stories, a mixture of poetic and bombastic style with the language of philosophy, little order, much confusion, a revolting affectation for praising inferior works, an even more revolting air of decisiveness, etc., etc. During the meeting, it should also be admitted that the book is full of excellent passages. But one cannot witness without indignation so relentless a persecution of a book that this harassment by itself may make the book dangerous, causing the reader to seek the secret poison it is supposed to contain. People are saying that this hateful persecution is the result of Jesuit intrigue to get at Diderot through Helvétius. I value these two men highly, and

197

the indignities that they are suffering make them infinitely dear to me. I pray you, tell me which councillor, president, geometer, metaphysician, mechanic, theologian, poet, grammarian, doctor, apothecary, musician, or actor is the principal judge of the *Encyclopédie*. It is like being a witness to the Inquisition's condemnation of Galileo. Certainly momentary insanity has taken hold of your poor city of Paris.

What a pity to inject a poem on *Natural Religion* amidst their cackling! People who are slightly informed know there is a poem on *Natural Law* in a collection of rather prominent works and that the abbreviated poem on *Natural Religion* is an inferior pamphlet in which the author is butchered. But the author is scarcely concerned and knows what he ought to think of fools and madmen. For a long time now I have kept more than a fathom's distance from them. When you get away from Montmorency, you would do well to come and philosophize in my retreats before I die. It is better to live with one's friends than to go from one resting place to another and from one patron to another to one's grave. I embrace you with all my heart.

V.

108. *Voltaire Denies His Authorship of* Candide.

To Gabriel and Philibert Cramer.[78] February 25, 1759.

What is this brochure entitled *Candide* [79] which people say is being scandalously circulated and is said to come from Lyons? I would like to see it. Could you get me a bound copy? It is claimed that there are people impertinent enough to impute this work, which I have never seen, to me! I pray you: tell me what the situation is.

109. *"Let us eat some Jesuit, let us eat some Jesuit."*

To Jacob Vernes.[80] February-March 1759.

All that is is right. Now two kings have been assassinated in
two years, half of Germany has been devastated, four hundred
thousand men have been massacred, etc., etc., etc. Some curious
people say that the Reverend Fathers of the Company of Jesus
Christ poisoned the King of Spain and claim to have proof, *ipsi
viderint*.[81] Everyone is shouting in the streets of Paris: "Let us
eat some Jesuit, let us eat some Jesuit." [82] It is a pity that these
words are drawn from a detestable book which seems to presume
original sin and the fall of man which are denied by you damned
Socinians who also deny the fall of Adam, the divinity of the Word,
the procession of the Holy Ghost and hell. We are a bit murky on
odes. However my rhapsody will await your orders. But you will
have to come and have dinner with us someday for however much
of a so-called priest you may be and however orthodox I may be,
I love you with all my heart. *Gratias ago* for the English journalist;
he is a *bon vivant*.

110. *"It is the eternity to come that makes for optimism and not
the present moment."*

To Jacob Vernes. c. March 15, 1759.

I have finally read *Candide*. They must have lost their senses
to attribute that filth to me. Thank God, I have better things to
do. If I could ever forgive the Inquisition, I would pardon the
Inquisitors of Portugal for hanging the reasoning Pangloss for de-
fending optimism. Indeed this optimism clearly destroys the foundations of our holy religion; it leads to fatalism; it makes one
consider the fall of man a fable and the curse pronounced by God
himself against the earth something vain. This is the opinion of all
religious and educated persons; they look upon optimism as a
horrible impiety.

As for my more moderate self, I would forgive this optimism

provided that those who uphold this system added that they believe God will give us in another life, according to his mercy, the good he deprives us of in this world according to his justice. It is the eternity to come that makes for optimism and not the present moment.

You are rather young to think about that eternity, but I am approaching it.

I wish you well-being in this life and in the next.

[By 1759, Voltaire had reached the age of sixty-five which in his case signified the beginning of a period of vigorous and meaningful activity on a variety of fronts. He had acquired the chateaux of Tournay and Ferney, the first piece of property located on the Swiss side of the Franco-Swiss border and the latter on the French side. He thus assured himself of a measure of protection against repression from either country. He spent considerable money and energy in building and reconstruction on these two properties, and in the case of Ferney devoted some twenty years of hard work helping the miserable and virtually enslaved population of the area to become liberated and prosperous.

Around this time, Voltaire also entered what he would repeatedly refer to as the war against the "infamous" by which he meant the repression brought about by religious superstition and fanaticism. The war against the "infamous" was waged by (1) publication, including such works as the satirical Account of the Malady, the Confession, and the Death and the Apparition of the Jesuit Berthier (1759), the Treatise on Toleration (1763), and most importantly the Philosophical Dictionary (1764); (2) by personal involvement and the marshalling of public opinion in cases of injustice and intolerance like the celebrated Calas affair where Voltaire was eventually successful in rehabilitating the name of a victim of the "infamous" through a decree of the King's Council nullifying the injustice perpetrated by the Parlement of Toulouse; and (3) by his encouragement and defense of the philosophes as a group that would bring France and Europe enlightenment and progress through reason. Thus he rose to the defense of his colleagues Diderot, d'Alembert and Helvétius when they were attacked by the *playwright Palissot in his satirical piece* The Philosophes *or by the maverick Jean-Jacques Rousseau who, in his* Letter to d'Alembert *criticized d'Alembert's (and inferentially Voltaire's) encouragement of the theater in Calvinist Geneva. Apart from the hostility created by a conflict in their personalities and life styles, Voltaire very much resented Rousseau's desires "to go it alone" and his refusal to support the cause of the* philosophes.

Another aspect of Voltaire's activity was his role as an intermediary in negotiations that attempted to bring about a peaceful conclusion to the Seven Years' War. He communicated various dispatches between the combatants and urged Frederick to end the hostilities. Although the war finally ended in February 1763 by the Treaties of Paris and Hubertusburg, Voltaire's own efforts were largely to no avail.

In 1759, Voltaire and Frederick resumed their friendship in a lengthy correspondence but were unable to purge themselves of the deep hostility caused by their relationship during Voltaire's Prussian sojourn earlier in the decade. Voltaire's open criticism of Frederick is more refreshing to the modern reader than his adulatory letters of the Cirey period. On the other hand, in 1762 Catherine II became Empress of Russia and she seemed to provide Voltaire with an adequate substitute for his illusory enlightened monarch.

Voltaire learned of the impoverished status of a young descendant of the great playwright Corneille and in 1760 decided to invite Marie-Françoise to stay with him and Mme. Denis at Ferney. He treated Mlle. Corneille like an adopted daughter, looking after her education and material needs. To provide the young lady with a dowry, Voltaire proceeded with an edition of Corneille's works in twelve volumes in which he included his own commentary. Not only did he oversee the whole publication, but he even obtained large subscriptions for the work from the sovereigns of France, Russia and the Empire and bought a hundred copies himself.

His letters of the early 1760s show his continued preoccupation with his integrity as an historian and his enduring concern with the problems of literary creation. The conflict between Voltaire's responsibilities as an historian and the desire of his Russian correspondents, on whom Voltaire relied for his documentation, to merely glorify the name of Peter I for posterity is made explicit in his correspondence on the second volume of his History of Russia under Peter the Great. *In the realm of literature, his views on such writers as Richardson, Rabelais, Corneille, Racine and Shakespeare find expression in his letters of this period.*

111. *Voltaire as a Secret Agent.*

To Charles-Augustin Feriol, Count d'Argental. To you alone. c. November 15, 1759.

> My divine angel,
> You are an angel of peace. Now that I have used the language of our bawdy house at Les Délices, let me speak to you in yours, Whatever the circumstances, you were born for my good fortune both in pleasure and in business. I am totally in your debt. You have been appointed my guardian angel for all time. Therefore listen to my devout supplication.
> 1. I should like to know generally whether the Duc de Choiseul is satisfied with me, and you can easily inquire about this on some Tuesday. All I can tell you is that I have a great desire to please him both as a person indebted to him and as a citizen.
> 2. If he were to go into any detail with you as he did with M. de Chauvelin,[83] could you not tell him on some other Tuesday the substance of the following?
> V. is in continuous correspondence with Luc.[84] But however bitter he may and ought to be toward Luc, since he was able to stifle his resentment in order to maintain this relationship, he will do the same much more effectively when it will be a matter of rendering service. He is on good terms with the Palatine Elector, the Duke of Württemberg, and the house of Gotha since he has had important business affairs with these three houses. They are pleased with him and write him in confidence. He has been the confidant of the apostate prince of Hesse;[85] he has friends in England. All of these connections enable him to travel everywhere without arousing the slightest suspicion and to be of service without causing any undue repercussions.
> He was sent to Luc secretly in 1743. He was fortunate enough to discover that Luc was then going to ally himself with France.

He gave his word; the treaty has been completed and signed by Cardinal de Tencin since. He could render some no less indispensable service today.

My dear angel, peace or total victories on land and sea are what is needed now. Such total victories are uncertain, and peace is preferable to so ruinous a war. Doubtlessly people are not closing their eyes to France's woeful state, a state worse financially and commercially than at the time of the Peace of Utrecht. Sometimes when one wishes to reach a desired goal without compromising the dignity of the crown, a Capuchin monk, an Abbé Gautier [86] or even an obscure man like myself is used just as a huntsman might be sent to divert a deer before the meet. I am not saying that I dare propose myself, that I look forward to this, that I anticipate the government's views or that I consider myself even worthy of executing them. I am only saying that you could try these ideas out and warm them in the Duc de Choiseul's heart. I would personally guarantee that he would never be compromised and that I would never go beyond anything he stipulated. I think it is not absolutely appropriate for him to ask for peace, but it is quite appropriate for him to create this desire in more than one power or rather enable these powers to indicate intentions that would subsequently allow one to act honorably.

Without a doubt his basic principle is as true as it is sorry: that we have nothing at all to gain in that bottomless pit that has swallowed up all of France's money. I have taken the liberty of predicting the capture of Quebec and Pondichéry [87] to him. One of these events has occurred, and I shudder over the other. There are citizens of Geneva who are in correspondence with the entire habitable universe. There are men from every nation around me: English ministers, Germans, Austrians, Prussians and even former Russian ministers. They see things more clearly than do people in Paris. They think that if the raid planned against one of the English provinces comes about, not a single Frenchman will return. The past, present and future make one shudder. I know that the government is courageous and has resources this year, but these resources are perhaps its last. And we are approaching that time when the statement that has been made that there is a power that would bring about peace and that that power is misery will be proven.

203

I fear they are determined to make some additional ruinous attempts after which they will be compelled to humbly request a disadvantageous peace which could be brought about today and which could be useful without being dishonorable.

Finally, my dear angel, you are used to setting my projects right. If this one does not meet with your pleasure, burn it and I will simply send you the knighthood.

You can at least determine whether the Duc de Choiseul is pleased with me. Not that I ought to fear his discontent, but it is pleasant to learn from your lips just how far he accepts my gratitude. Besides you may be certain that I am not anxious and that I am fine as I am, except for your absence. Farewell, I kiss the tips of your wings.

112. *"I believe Paris is only good for farmers-general, whores, and big wigs in the parlement. . . ."*

To Octavie Belot.[88] By Geneva at Les Délices. March 24, 1760.

I am no longer of this world, and my illnesses are carrying me slightly on to the edge of the next one. What can I do down in my valleys surrounded by mountains that reach to the heavens? I can but scarcely pray to them to send me some sunshine. I am even further from the graces of kings than from the graces of God. One must not rely on either in this world. They fall like the rain, by chance and often inopportunely.

I have no regular exchange of correspondence with Paris. M. Thieriot writes me once in six months. Intercourse with men of letters is dangerous and with the powerful very useless. Retirement in the utmost seclusion is the most suitable course for anyone cured of illusions and who wishes to live with himself. I am aware of all your merit, and the more I appreciate it the more I pity you for seeking its reward in Paris. It is not to be found there. Mlle. Du Chap may make her fortune by selling lace and other persons by selling their mines, but wit, knowledge, and true merit are not marketable. They are the ornaments of fortune but do not procure it. In this great city you will only find persons concerned with themselves and never with the sad situation of others, except perhaps to amuse themselves. I believe Paris is only good for farmers-general, whores, and big wigs in the *parlement* lording it. Literature at present is only a kind of depredation. If there are still some men of genius in Paris, they are persecuted. The others are crows quarrelling over a few swan's feathers from the past century that they stole and fit, as well as they can, on to their black tails. You cite the example of Madame de Graffigny. But she died of grief. In Paris you must either be a Mlle. Le Duc [89] or flee.

I have the honor of being, madam, with all the feelings due you, your etc.

113. *On Richardson and Rabelais.*

To Marie de Vichy de Chamrond, Marquise Du Deffand. Les Délices. April 12, 1760.

I have sent you none of those trifles with which you condescend to amuse yourself momentarily. I have cut my ties with humanity for more than six weeks. I have buried myself in my imagination. Then came the country work and after that the fever. Because of this whole beautiful regimen, you have received nothing and probably will receive nothing for sometime. You will simply have to send me word: "Madam wishes to be amused. She is fine, she is in good form; she is in good humor. She is ordering some inconsequential work to be sent to her." Then we will have some scientific or comical or philosophical or historical or poetical package sent off according to the kind of amusement Madam will desire provided she burns it as soon as she has had it read to her.

Madam was so enthusiastic about *Clarissa* [90] that I read it to relax from work during my fever. That reading set my senses afire. It is cruel for a man as alive as I am to read nine whole volumes containing absolutely nothing and whose only use is to give you a glimpse of Miss Clarissa in love with a libertine named Mr. Lovelace. I have said that if all those people were my relatives and friends, I could not become interested in them. I see in the author only a clever man who is aware of the curiosity of the human race and constantly promises something from volume to volume in order to sell them. I finally came across Clarissa in a place of ill repute in the tenth volume, and that really moved me. Pierre Corneille's Theodora,[91] who insists on entering the house kept by the Fillon woman [92] through Christian principle, does not approach Clarissa, her situation, and her feelings, but except for the place of ill repute in which that beautiful English lady finds herself, I confess that the rest gave me no pleasure and that I would not want to be condemned to reread that English novel. It seems to me that only those things that can be reread without repugnance are good. The only books of this kind are those that continually portray something to the imagination and flatter the ear with harmony. Men need music and painting with a few little philosophical precepts intermingled from time to time with honest discretion. That is why Horace, Virgil and Ovid will always please, except in translations that spoil them.

After *Clarissa* I reread a few chapters of Rabelais like the Battle of Brother Jean des Entommeures and the session of the Council of Picrochole.[93] But I know them almost by heart. Yet I reread them with very great pleasure because they contain the world's liveliest canvas. Not that I place Rabelais on an equal footing with Horace, but if Horace is the leading writer of good epistles, Rabelais, when he is good, is the best among good jesters. There need not be two men with this profession in a nation, but there must be one. I am sorry that in the past I spoke too disparagingly of him. There is one pleasure really to be preferred to all of that: seeing vast prairies turn green and beautiful crops grow. This is man's true life; all the rest is illusion. I beg your pardon for speaking to you of a pleasure that is enjoyed with one's eyes. The only pleasures still familiar to you are those of the soul. I find you admirable for bearing your state so well. At least you enjoy all the amenities of society. It is true that that is reduced almost to giving one's opinion of the news of the day. That, it seems to me, is quite dull in the long run. Only tastes and passions sustain us in this world. For these passions you substitute philosophy which is not their equal, and I substitute the tender and respectful devotion I shall always have for you. I wish your friend [94] good health, and I would like him to remember me a little.

114. *Voltaire Tells Frederick the Great A Few Home Truths.*

To Frederick II, King of Prussia. At the Chateau of Tournay, near Geneva. April 21, 1760.

Sire,

A little monk from Saint Just used to say to Charles V: "Holy Majesty, are you not tired of troubling the world? Must you still be the despair of a poor monk in his cell?" I am the monk, but you have not forsaken human grandeur and misery like Charles V. How cruel to tell me that I slander Maupertuis when I tell you that there was a rumor after his death that the works of the philosopher of Sans Souci [95] had been found in his money box? If indeed they had been found there, would that not prove, on the contrary, that he had guarded them faithfully, that he had communicated them to no one, and that a publisher might have abused them, which would have exonerated some persons who were perhaps unjustly accused? Besides, am I required to know that Maupertuis had sent them back? What advantage do I have to speak ill of him? Of what importance are his person and his memory to me? How could I have done him harm by telling Your Majesty that he had faithfully guarded what you had left in his custody until his death? I myself only think of death, and my hour is approaching. But do not trouble it with unjust reprimands and harsh words which have even greater effect since they come from you.

You have done enough harm. You have brought discord forever between me and the King of France; you have caused me to lose my posts and pensions; you mistreated both me and an innocent woman in Frankfurt,[96] an esteemed woman who was dragged into the mud and imprisoned, and later while honoring me with your letters you spoiled the sweetness of that consolation with bitter reproach. With reference to Dr. Tronchin,[97] you scolded me for receiving a pension from you. Could you possibly have treated me this way when my sole concern for three years was to try, however futilely, to be of service to you with no other plan than to pursue my own ideas?

The greatest harm caused by your actions was to inform the enemies of philosophy, spread over all of Europe, that the *philo-*

sophes cannot live in peace and cannot live together. Here is a king who does not believe in Jesus Christ; he summons an unbeliever to his court and mistreats him. There is no humanity among the would-be *philosophes,* and God is punishing them through each other. That is what people are saying; that is what is being printed everywhere. And while the fanatics are united, the *philosophes* are dispersed and wretched. And while at the court of Versailles and elsewhere I am accused of encouraging you to write against Christian religion, you censure me and add this triumph to the fanatics's insults. That makes me consider the world with horror and justly so. Happily I am far removed from it in my solitary domains. I will bless the day I die, when I no longer have to suffer, suffer especially because of you. But this will happen while I wish you happiness which your position does not allow and which philosophy alone could provide you with during life's tempests if fortune allowed you to merely cultivate that fund of wisdom within you, an admirable fund but one that has been impaired by passions that are inseparable from a strong imagination, by temperament to an extent, by difficult situations that fill your soul with malice, and finally by the unfortunate pleasure you have always taken in humiliating all other men, in telling and writing them biting remarks which are even more unworthy of you considering the superiority of your rank and your unique talents. Forgive these home truths told to you by an old man who has little time left to live, but he tells them to you with all the more confidence since he is convinced of his own wretchedness and weaknesses which are infinitely greater than yours but less dangerous because of his obscurity. You must not think that he considers himself without faults because he takes the privilege of complaining about some of yours. He laments some of the errors you may have committed as well as his own, and his only desire now is to think of remedying before he dies the fatal errors of a deceptive imagination by sincerely wishing that a great man like yourself might be as happy and great in all respects as he ought to be.

115. *The* Philosophes *Must Unite.*

To Jean Le Rond D'Alembert. April 25, 1760.

My dear and worthy philosopher,
I confess I am not dead, but I cannot say that I am alive. Berthier is in good health, but I am ill. Abraham Chaumeix has his digestion, but I do not have mine.[98] Therefore, I write you with my heart and not my hand. My heart tells you that it is obviously distressed to see the fanatics united to crush the *philosophes* while the divided *philosophes* calmly let themselves be slaughtered one after another. It is really too bad that Jean-Jacques got into Diogenes's tub completely nude.[99] That is a sure way to be eaten by the flies. Could they possibly allow a performance of that impudent farce we are threatened with?[100] That is how they did away with Socrates. I do not believe the comedy of *The Clouds*[101] holds a candle to the comic operas of the fair. I believe Favart and Vadé quite superior to the Athenian Gilles notwithstanding Madame Dacier.[102] But in the end that is how the priests began preparing for the destruction of the wise. Persecution is breaking out all over Paris. The Jansenists and Jesuits are joining hands in the slaughter of reason and are fighting among themselves for the spoils. I confess that I am as angry with the *philosophes* who offer no resistance as with the scoundrels oppressing them. Since I am already getting angry, I pass on to Luc. He is taking the plunge, disavowing his works, and having them printed abridged. That is really contemptible when there are a hundred thousand men at one's disposal, but that man will always be incomprehensible. Every week he sends me the most bumptious packets containing the most frightful verse and prose, things that would get the recipient locked up if he were in Paris, but he has not sent me the epistle he addressed to you which, people say, is his best work.[103] He is not sure of what he wants and even less of what will become of him. One would really wish he started being judicious. He would have been the happiest of men had he wished, and it would have been preferable a hundred times to be a patron of philosophy than to bring disorder to Europe. He missed a beautiful vocation. You really ought to speak to him about this a little, you who are capable of writing and dare to. It is quite

false to say that the Abbé de Prades betrayed him. He wrote the French minister only for permission to travel to France, and that at a time when we were not at war with Brandenburg. If he had indeed plotted a betrayal against his benefactor, you may be quite sure that they would not have just given him an apartment in the citadel of Magdeburg. You know that d'Arget preferred a small position as a subordinate in Paris to a salary of two thousand écus and the magnificent title of secretary. Algarotti preferred his freedom to a salary of three thousand écus (I mean three thousand imperial écus). You know that Chazot made the same choice. You know that in order to try to forget Maupertuis had started drinking brandy which led to his death. You know many other things. You know above all that your pension of fifty louis is only bait. Think about all of this. I rely on your integrity and seek your friendship. Send me news, I pray you, as to the course of the persecution being directed against the only men who can enlighten the human race. Do not imitate lazy Diderot. Spend a half hour of your time keeping me posted a little. People claim the cabal is saying: "Oportet Diderot mori pro populo." [104]

Is the *Encyclopedic Dictionary* continuing? Will it be disfigured and debased by cowardly accommodation of fanatics or will we be bold enough to tell dangerous truths? Is it true that for this immense work and for twelve years of labor Diderot will earn twenty-five thousand francs while those who provide our armies with bread earn twenty thousand francs a day? Do you see Helvétius? Do you know Saurin? [105] Who is the author of the farce against the *philosophes*? Which scoundrels among the great lords and which of the old religious whores at court are protecting him? Write me using the mails and indicate boldly: *To Voltaire, Gentleman Ordinary of the King, at the Chateau of Ferney by Geneva*, since I will be living at Ferney in a few weeks. We have Tournay for dramatic performances, and Les Délices is the third string on our bow. [106] The *philosophes* must always have two or three holes underground against the dogs chasing them. I advise you again that my letters are not being opened, and even if they were there is nothing to be feared from the Minister of Foreign Affairs who despises Molinist fanaticism, Jansenist fanaticism, and fanaticism of the *parlement* as much as we do. I unite with you in Socrates, Confucius, Lucretius, Cicero and all the other apostles, and

I embrace your brothers if there are any and if you are living with them.

116. *". . . I consider the enterprise of the* Encyclopédie *the most beautiful monument that could be erected in honor of science."*

To Charles Palissot de Montenoy.[107] Les Délices. June 4, 1760.

I thank you for your letter and your work. Please get ready for a long reply; old men like to babble a little.

I will begin by telling you that I consider your play well written. I even imagine that the philosopher Crispin walking on all fours must have created considerable merriment, and I believe that my friend Jean-Jacques will be the first to laugh.[108] This is gay, not at all malicious, and besides since the citizen of Geneva is guilty of treason against the theatre, it is quite natural for the theatre to give him his just desserts.

The same is not true for the citizens of Paris whom you have placed on the stage. Certainly there is nothing to laugh about here. I understand very well when we ridicule those who want to ridicule us; people ought to defend themselves. And I myself am aware that if I were not so old, Messrs. Fréron and de Pompignan [109] would have to deal with me, the former for vilifying me five or six years in a row according to what people who read pamphlets assure me, the latter for openly singling me out in the Academy as a dotard who has padded history with false anecdotes. I was very tempted to humiliate him with a good vindication and to show that the anecdote of the iron mask, the one about the will of Charles II, King of Spain, and the like are quite true, and that when I take it upon myself to be serious, I leave aside poetic fictions.

I am still vain enough to believe that I was singled out in the throng of those poor *philosophes* who never stop plotting against the state and who certainly are responsible for all our misfortunes. For, in fact, I was the first to write formally in favor of gravitation and in opposition to the great whirlwinds of Descartes and the little whirlwinds of Malebranche, and I defy the most ignorant persons, including M. Fréron himself, to prove that I misrepresented the philosophy of Newton in any way. The Society of London approved my little catechism on gravitation. I, therefore, consider myself philosophically very guilty.

If I were vain, I would believe I was even more culpable in the matter of a large book entitled *The Oracle of the Philosophers* which has even reached my retreat.[110] This oracle, may it not displease you, is myself. That would be enough to make one burst with excessive pride, but unfortunately my vanity was really humbled when I saw that the author of the oracle claims to have had dinner several times at my home near Lausanne in a chateau that I have never owned. He says that I received him very well, and as a reward for this good reception, he is informing the public of all the secret confessions he claims I made to him.

I confessed to him, for example, that I had gone to the king of Prussia to establish the Chinese religion there. So now I at least belong to the sect of Confucius. I would, therefore, quite rightfully share in the offensive remarks being made against the *philosophes*. Moreover, I confessed to the author of the oracle that the king of Prussia threw me out, a thing which is very possible but very false and about which this good man has lied. I further confessed to him that I am not at all devoted to France at a time when the king is showering me with his favors, retains the post of his gentleman ordinary for me, and deigns to favor my land holdings with the greatest privileges. In short, I confessed all these things to this worthy man in order to be included among the *philosophes*.

In addition, I had a hand in the infernal cabal of the *Encyclopédie*. There are at least a dozen articles by me printed in the last three volumes. I had prepared some for the following volumes, a dozen others that would have corrupted the nation and overturned every order of the state. Further, I am one of the first to have used with frequency that ugly word *humanity* against which you lashed out so gallantly in your comedy. If after this people refuse to bestow the name of *philosophe* on me, it will be the world's most flagrant injustice.

That, sir, is as far as I am concerned.

As for the persons you attack in your work, if they have offended you, you do very well to return the favor. The laws of society have always permitted us to ridicule those who have rendered us that small service. In the past, when I belonged to society,

I scarcely attended a supper party at which some laughing person would not make fun of some guest who in turn would try his best to enliven the gathering at the expense of the joker. Lawyers often use the same procedure at the bar; all writers with whom I am acquainted have ridiculed each other as much as possible. Boileau did so to Fontenelle and Fontenelle to Boileau. The other Rousseau, not Jean-Jacques, made great sport of *Zaïre* and *Alzire,* and I, your interlocutor, believe that I also made fun of his last *Epistles* even though I confessed at the same time that the *Ode on the Conquerors* was admirable and that most of his epigrams were very nice. For we must be just, that is the main point.[111]

You must examine your conscience and see whether you are fair in representing Messrs. d'Alembert, Duclos, Diderot, Helvétius, the Chevalier de Jaucourt, and *tutti quanti* as scoundrels who teach the art of pickpocketing.

Once again, if they tried to have fun at your expense in their books, I would think it very well for you to poke fun at theirs, but really your scoffing is too strong. If they were as you represent them to be, we would have to send them to the galleys which is no comic matter. I am speaking to you plainly; those whom you wish to dishonor are considered the most honorable people in the world, and I am not even sure whether their integrity is not still superior to their philosophy. I will tell you frankly that I know of no one more respectable than M. Helvétius who sacrificed two hundred thousand livres of income so that he could peacefully cultivate letters. If a half dozen bold and offensive propositions are expounded in a large book, he has repented sufficiently without your having to tear at his wounds on the stage.

M. Duclos, the secretary of the principal academy of the kingdom, seems to me to deserve much more consideration than you have for him.[112] His book on customs is not a bad book at all; it is, above all, the book of an upright man. In sum, have these gentlemen publicly offended you? It seems to me not. Why then do you offend them so cruelly?

I do not know M. Diderot at all. I have never seen him. I only know that he has been unfortunate and persecuted. That reason alone should have stopped you from writing.

Moreover, I consider the enterprise of the *Encyclopédie* the most beautiful monument that could be erected to the honor of science. There are admirable articles not only by M. d'Alembert, M. Diderot, and the Chevalier de Jaucourt, but by several other persons who have enjoyed working on these volumes with no incentive of glory or self-interest.

There are pitiful articles, no doubt, and mine could be included among that number, but the good outweighs the bad so stupendously that all of Europe desires the continuation of the *Encyclopédie*. The first volumes have already been translated into several languages. Why then make a performance on the stage out of a work that has become indispensable to the education of men and the glory of the nation?

I confess that I have not recovered from my astonishment over your news concerning M. Diderot. He has, you say, "printed two scurrilous satires against two ladies of the highest rank who are your benefactresses." You saw his confession signed in his own hand. If that is so, I have nothing further to say. I am stupefied; I forsake philosophy and all books, and henceforth will think only of my plough and sowing-machine.

But let me very earnestly ask you for proof. Let me write to the friends of these ladies. I absolutely want to know whether or not I ought to burn my library.

But if Diderot was so forsaken by God as to insult two respectable, and what is more, very beautiful ladies, did they instruct you to retaliate for them? Were the other persons whom you present on the stage so rude as to be disrespectful to these two ladies?

While I have never seen M. Diderot and do not find the *Père de Famille* amusing, I have always respected his deep knowledge. And at the beginning of the *Père de Famille*, there is an epistle to the Princess of Nassau which struck me as a masterpiece of eloquence and a triumph of *humanity*. Pardon the word. Twenty persons have assured me that he has a very beautiful soul. I would be distressed to find I am wrong, but I hope to be enlightened.

> Human frailty is to learn
> What one would not like to know.

I have spoken to you frankly. If you find deep in your heart that I am right, find out what you must do. If I am wrong, tell me so. Make me feel it. Correct me. I swear to you that I have no ties with any Encyclopedist except perhaps with M. d'Alembert who writes me Lacedaemonian letters once every three months. I value him infinitely. I flatter myself that he has not been disrespectful to Princesses de Robecq and de La Marck.[113] I ask you once again for permission to address M. d'Argental concerning this matter.

With a very real esteem for your talents and an extreme desire for peace which Messrs. Fréron, de Pompignan and a few others have been determined to deprive me of, I have the honor of being your very humble and very obedient servant.

Voltaire,
Gentleman in Ordinary
to the King

117. *Voltaire Is Horrified by Shakespeare.*

To Marie de Vichy de Chamrond, Marquise Du Deffand. December 9, 1760.

For more than six weeks I have been unable to enjoy one moment of leisure. This is ridiculous but true. As you do not agree to my writing you simply for the sake of writing, I have the honor of dispatching two small manuscripts that have fallen into my hands. One of them seems to me marvelously philosophical and moral. Therefore, few people will probably find it to their liking. The other one is an amusing discovery I made in my friend Ezekiel. Ezekiel is not read enough. I recommend reading him as much as I can; he is an inimitable man. I do not ask that these trifling works amuse you as much as me, but I would like them to amuse you for a few moments.

I have held fast against M. d'Alembert. He cannot demonstrate the beauty of a scaffold to me. I like entertainments, apparatus, and all of the demon's displays very much, but as for the gallows, I am his obedient servant. I refer him to Despréaux:

> But there are objects which judicious art
> Must offer the ear and withdraw from view.[114]

Besides I am angry with the English. Not only have they taken Pondichéry from me, I believe, but they have just expressed in print that their Shakespeare is infinitely superior to Corneille. Their Shakespeare is infinitely inferior to Gilles.[115] Imagine the tragedy of *Richard III*, which they compare to *Cinna,* has nine years for unity of time, a dozen cities and battlefields for unity of place, and thirty-seven principal events for unity of action. But that is nothing. In the first act, Richard says that he is a hunchback and smells, and to take his revenge against nature, he is going to be a hypocrite and a scoundrel. As he says these beautiful things, he sees a funeral procession—King Henry VI's. He stops the bier and the widow who is leading the procession. The widow cries out loudly; she reproaches him for killing her husband. Richard replies that he is delighted because he will be able to sleep with her more conveniently. The queen spits in his face; Richard thanks her and claims that nothing is as sweet as her spit. The queen calls him a toad, an ugly toad: "I wish my spit were poison." "Well, madam, kill me if you like; here is my sword." She takes it. "Hang it, I don't have the courage to kill you." "Well, then I am going to kill myself." "No, do not kill yourself since you found me pretty." She goes and buries her husband, and the two lovers do not speak of love any more for the remainder of the play. Isn't it true that if our water bearers wrote plays, they would make them more honest? I tell you all of this because I have had my fill. Isn't it sad that the same country that produced Newton has produced these monsters and admires them? Be well, madam. Try to have some pleasure. This is not an easy thing but not impossible.

V.

A thousand respects with all my heart.

118. *"The little church of Calvin, which makes virtue consist of usury and moral austerity, imagined that cuckolds only existed because of theatrical performances."*

To François-Achard-Joumard Tison, Marquis d'Argence.[116] At the Chateau of Ferney, in the territory of Gex, Burgundy, near Geneva. January 20, 1761.

You know my life. My occupations have increased considerably since I had the misfortune of losing you. I have not had a moment for myself. I wanted to write you every day but contented myself with thinking about you endlessly. I see from the letters with which you honor me that you are happy. There are only two types of happiness in this world: that of fools who become stupidly intoxicated with their fanatic illusions and that of philosophers. It is impossible for a thinking person to want to explore the first kind of happiness which is based on a state of stupidity. The more one is enlightened, the more one enjoys life. Nothing is sweeter than to laugh at the foolishness of men and to laugh with reason. If you deign to amuse yourself by discovering when certain people took it into their heads to say that two and two make five and when other doctors guaranteed that two and two make six, you will easily see that neither the opinion of Arius nor that of Athanasius [117] was new, and that ever since the third century, theologians, having become Platonists, have been fighting each other with blows of their inkstands to discover whether the egg was formed before the hen or the hen before the egg, and whether it is a mortal sin to eat soft boiled eggs on certain days of the year.

As for your partridge pie, fortunately it will reach us before Lent. Thus we will be able to eat some of it with a safe conscience because you know how irritated God is and how one risks eternal damnation if one is sufficiently perverse to eat partridge at the end of February or the beginning of March.

Since your departure, I have committed a terrible act of impiety. I forced the Jesuits to clear out of a piece of property they had seized from six gentlemen who are my neighbors—all brothers, all of them officers of the king, all of them serving in the Regiment of Two Bridges, all of them good people, and all of them clothed in rags.

I am bringing damnation on myself more and more. I am presently occupied in the criminal pursuit of a curé of our cantons who thought it was a divine right to beat his parishioners. He piously went at eleven o'clock in the evening with five or six peasants who were armed with iron rods to the home of a lady to prevent her from making love without his permission. His zeal went so far as to leave a young man in the family on the floor drenched in his blood, and if an impious person like myself had not been found, this poor boy would have been dead and the curé would have gone unpunished. The curé defends himself as best he can. He says that he has no wish to go to the galleys and that I will be damned. But unfortunately, a good priest just proved in Neuchâtel that hell is not eternal at all and that it is ridiculous to think that God has concerned himself for an infinity of centuries with the roasting of a poor devil. It is too bad this priest is a Huguenot. Otherwise my cause would have been a good one. I don't like these cursed Huguenots one bit. Recently we had a cuckold in Geneva. This cuckold, as you know, fired a pistol shot at his wife's lover. The little church of Calvin, which makes virtue consist of usury and moral austerity, imagined that cuckolds only existed because of theatrical performances. These scoundrels attacked the young people in their city who had performed in my theatre at Tournay, and they had the insolence to make them promise not to perform any more with Frenchmen who might corrupt the morals of Geneva.

You see that people are as foolish in Geneva as they are mad in Paris. But I forgive these barbarians because there are ten or twelve worthy persons among them. God did not discover five in Sodom. I am not powerful enough to cause fire to rain from the sky over Geneva. At least I can enjoy myself heartily at home under the noses of all these hypocrites. I would enjoy myself much more if you were still here. You would see the descendant of the great Corneille whom Madame Denis and I have adopted as a daughter.[118] Her character seems as agreeable as Corneille's genius is respectable.

Farewell, sir. We will miss you and love you forever. If there is someone in your country who thinks, send him my regards. Madame Denis sends you hers very affectionately.

V.

119. *"The* philosophes *are disunited."*

To Jean Le Rond D'Alembert. Ferney, Territory of Gex. March 19, 1761.

Don't write to me at Geneva any more or use the address *of the Academy.*

My very worthy and firm *philosophe,* true scholar, true wit and man indispensable to the century, I pray you, look at some of my answers to your energetic letter in my *Epistle* to Madame Denis.[119]

So my dear archdeacon and arch-bore Trublet is a member of the Academy! [120] He will compile a beautiful discourse with sentences from La Motte.[121] I should like you to answer him; that would be a fine contrast. I think you accuse Cicero d'Olivet wrongly; he is not a man who would lend his voice to the chaplain of Houdart and Fontenelle. Credit it all to the queen's steward.

The despairing thing for human nature is that this Trublet is an atheist like Cardinal Tencin and this wretch worked on the Christian journal in order to enter the Academy with the patronage of the Queen.[122]

The *philosophes* are disunited. The little flock is eating at one another while the wolves come and devour it. Your Jean-Jacques [123] is the one I am most angry with. This stark madman, who could have amounted to something if he had let you be his guide, has taken it into his head to go on his own. He writes against the theater after producing a bad comedy; he writes against the France that feeds him. He finds four or five rotten staves from Diogenes's tub and gets inside to bark. He abandons his friends; he writes me the most impertinent letters ever scribbled by a fanatic. He informs me in so many words: "You have corrupted Geneva as a reward for the asylum that it gave you." As if I were concerned with relaxing Geneva's morals; as if I needed asylum; as if I had taken asylum in this city of Socinian preachers; as if I had some obligation to this city. I have made no reply to his letter; M. de Chimène [124] gave my answer and annihilated his miserable novel. If Rousseau had been a reasonable man who could only be scolded for a bad book, he would not have been treated this way.

Let us come to pancratic Colardau; he is a courtier of Pompignan and Fréron.[125] It is not a bad thing to steep the snout of those people in the mire of their masters.

My worthy *philosophe!* What will become of truth? What will become of philosophy? If the sages will be firm, if they will be bold, if they will be bound to each other, I will be devoted to them. But if they are divided, if they abandon the common cause, I will only think of my plough, my oxen and sheep. But as I till the earth, I will pray God that you will still bring it enlightenment. And you will become my public. What do you say about Midas Omer's [126] square cap? I embrace you very affectionately.

V.

120. *"Have money and victories; then you do whatever you wish."*

To Etienne-François de Choiseul-Stainville, Duc de Choiseul.[127]
July 13, 1761(?).

Sire,

You know that at the conclusion of the session of the Great Council on the testament of the King of Spain, Louis XV met four of his daughters who were playing and told them: "Well, what would your decision be in my place?" The girls expressed their opinions at random, and the king replied: "Whatever opinion I hold, I will be criticized."

You deign to treat an ignorant old man as Louis XV did his children. You want me to chatter, chatter, and compile, compile. Your kindness and my manner of existence, which is of no consequence, thus give me the right of an ignoramus to apprise you of what you know infinitely better than I do.

First, I firmly believe that all men have been, are, and will be led by events. I respect Cardinal de Richelieu highly, but he only pledged himself to Gustavus Adolphus when Gustavus had landed in Pomerania without consulting him.[128] He took advantage of the circumstance. Cardinal Mazarin profited from the death of the Duke of Weimar; he obtained Alsace for France and the Duchy of Rethel for himself. As he concluded the Peace of Ryswick, Louis XIV had no idea, whatever people may say, that his grandson would be three years old after the succession of Charles V.[129] He suspected even less that his grandson's first war would be against his uncle. None of the things you have seen was predicted. You know it was chance that brought about the peace with England signed by that handsome Lord Bolingbroke on the beautiful buttocks of Mrs. Pultney. So you will proceed as all great men of your sort who have used the circumstances in which they found themselves to advantage.

You have had Prussia as an ally; you now have her as an enemy. Austria has changed systems and so have you. Russia did not exercise any influence in the balance of Europe twenty years ago and now exercises a very considerable one. Sweden used to play a great role and now exercises a very small one. Everything has changed, and everything will change in the future. But, as you have said, France will always remain a beautiful kingdom and formidable to its neighbors unless the classes in the *parlements* interfere.

You know that allies are like friends who used to be called to quadrille dances in my time; at each stroke of the music, we would change friends.

It seems to me, moreover, that the friendship of the house of Brandenburg has always been fatal to France. They abandoned you at Charles V's siege of Metz; they took a great amount of money from Louis XIV and waged war against him; they broke away from you twice in the War of 1741, and surely you will not put them in a position to betray you a third time. That power was only a matter of chance at the time based on the most extreme economy and Prussian-type training. The money that had been amassed disappeared. The Prussians, who had long been conquerors, were beaten despite their training. I do not believe that there are now forty families left in the kingdom of Prussia. Pomerania has been laid waste, Brandenburg is in a wretched state; no one eats white bread and only discredited currency is to be seen there, and even very little of that. The states of Cleves have been sequestered; the Austrians are victorious in Silesia. It would now be more difficult to support the king of Prussia than to crush him. The English are being ruined by giving him indirect help with Hesse, and you are making that help of no avail. Such is the state of things.

Now if one wished to wager, within the rule of probabilities one would have to wager three to one that Prussia's power will be destroyed.

But a stroke of desperation can also restore its affairs and ruin yours. If you prosper, you will have a beautiful congress where you will still be a guarantor of the Treaty of Westphalia. But I still come back to my statement that all the German princes will declare: "Brandenburg fell because it became embroiled with France. We must always have France as a protector." Certainly after the fall of the most powerful prince in the Empire, the Queen of Hungary will not come and ask you again for Strasbourg, Lille or Lorraine. She will wait at least ten years, and then you will set the Turk and Swede loose on her by giving them money if you have any.

The main point is to have plenty of money. Henry IV set about making himself the arbiter of Europe by having gold scales made by the Duc de Sully.[130] The English were only successful with guineas and a tenfold credit. The King of Prussia made Germany tremble for a time only because his father had more sacks than bottles in his cellars in Berlin. This is no longer the age of Fabricius.[131] The richest man carries the day, just as with us the richest man buys a magistrate's office in the Council of State and then governs the state. This is not noble, but it is true.

The Russians trouble me, but Austria will never have the means with which to hire them against you for two years.

Spain troubles me since it does not have much to gain from ridding you of the English, but at least it is sure that its hatred for England will always be greater than for you.

England troubles me since it will always want to chase you out of North America, and your naval expeditions will be of no avail. Your ships will always be captured after four or five years as we have seen in every war.

Ah! sire, sire, we must live from day to day when we have to deal with neighbors. We can follow a plan at home, and yet we scarcely do. But when we are playing against others, we play our cards according to our hand. A system, dear me! Descartes's has fallen; the Roman Empire no longer exists; even Pompignan is losing his influence. Everything is being destroyed; everything moves on. I am really afraid that in important affairs the situation is as in physics: we make experiments but have no system.

I admire people who say: "The house of Austria is going to be really powerful; France will not be able to resist." Well, gentlemen! An archduke has taken Amiens from you; Charles V has been to Compiègne, Henry V of England has been crowned in Paris. Come, come. We have been at death's door, and you do not have to fear the subversion of France whatever foolishness is committed. What! no system! I know of only one: to be in good form at home. Then everyone respects you.

Negotiations depend on the war and on finances. Have money and victories; then you do whatever you wish.

121. *"It is perhaps a perfection of military art to do almost nothing with the greatest armies. . . ."*

To Louise Dorothea of Meiningen, Duchess of Saxe-Gotha.[132] At the Castle of Ferney in Burgundy by Geneva. July 31, 1761.

Madam,

I resemble the greatest mistress of hearts in two ways, with my eyes and with my soul. My eyes can barely see any more but my soul still does, and in my imagination I am at the feet of Your Serene Highness. So she condescends to take an interest in the lineage of our great Corneille. I am not surprised since his works breathe grandeur and virtue, and his lineage is an unhappy one.

It seems to me that Corneille never depicted disasters greater than those being suffered from Kassel and into the heart of Silesia. This will end when it pleases God and not when it pleases men. They say that the philosopher Pangloss will leave Turkey and take a trip to Geneva. I will question him about the secondary causes and the primary cause, but I should especially like to bring him to Gotha. Then he would see the best of possible castles and certainly the best of possible princesses. But I would not want to mingle with those beautiful armies which suit me not at all. I have affection only for the heroes of history and tragedy.

I have still not finished the history of that Russian hero named Peter the Great since the Court of St. Petersburg treats me about the way Pharaoh treated the Jews. He asked them for bricks but did not give them any straw. They are asking me for a history but do not give me any of the materials.

It seems to me the Prince of Brunswick will keep his niche in history. He has covered himself with glory in all his campaigns. How will all that fracas end? Things on the continent will remain about as they were. Caesar's and Pompey's war was much less costly in blood but resulted in world domination. It is perhaps a perfection of military art to do almost nothing with the greatest armies since the forces are always balanced. The only result is the misery of the people. There are only five or six persons on either side who make immense fortunes by furnishing the necessary and the superfluous to the regimented murderers. I am sorry I have no more paper. I must leave my reflections to present my deep respect and inviolable devotion to Your Serene Highness.

The old Swiss V.

122. *Voltaire's Difficulties Writing* The History of Peter the Great.

To Ivan Ivanovich Shuvalov.[133] Ferney, near Geneva. November 7, 1761.

Although I promised you some new sections of *The History of Peter the Great* only for Easter, the desire to satisfy you made me accelerate rather considerably the time I planned to work on it. My devotion to Your Excellency and my preference for the work upon which I embarked under your auspices have taken precedence over some rather pressing duties with which I am occupied. I have conveyed to Your Excellency a copy of the material I have just risked writing solely on your behalf concerning so terrible and delicate a subject as the condemnation and death of the czarevitch.[134] I was very astonished by the statement that accompanied your last package. This statement is merely a copy, almost word for word, of the material found in the so-called Nestesuranoi.[135] It seems that that German from whom I had already received some memoirs sent this one. He must know that this is

224

not the way to write history, that we are accountable to all of Europe for the truth, that circumspection and a rather demanding art are indispensable if prejudices that have been widely disseminated are to be destroyed, that one does not believe a historian on his word alone, that public opinion cannot be attacked head-on except with authentic records, that everything that simply meets with the approval of a court that has a personal interest in the memory of Peter the Great would be suspect, and that, in sum, the history I am composing would only be a pale panegyric and a mere apology that would arouse people's indignation rather than persuade them. It is not enough to believe and flatter the country one inhabits; we must think of men of all countries. You know better than I everything I have the honor of pointing out to you, and deep in your heart your feelings have no doubt anticipated my reflections.

By a happy accident, I obtained some memoirs of accredited government ministers which compensated for the materials I lacked. Without this help, to what might I have been reduced? I have gathered manuscripts from all over Europe. I have been helped more than I dared hope.

I will not conceal from Your Excellency that among these manuscripts, among these ministers's letters, there are some that are more atrocious still than the anecdotes of Lamberty.[136] I believe I refute Lamberty rather successfully with the help of manuscripts favorable to us, and I leave aside those opposing us. Lamberty deserves very great consideration because of his reputation for being precise, for hazarding no opinions, and for reporting original documents, and as he is far from being the only one to report the horrible anecdotes that have been spread all over Europe, it seems to me that these hateful rumors require a complete refutation. I also thought that I ought not overburden the czarevitch and that I would be considered a cowardly, partial historian capable of any sacrifice to favor the branch of the family presently established on the throne taken from this unfortunate prince. It is clear that the term *parricide* used in judging this prince must have shocked every reader because in no European country is the term parricide used except for someone who has executed or actually prepared the murder of his father. We do not even classify a person as a rebel unless he has taken up arms against his sovereign. And the czarevitch's conduct is described as: a form of disobedience worthy of punishment, a type of scandalous obstinacy, a fanciful hope in some secret malcontents who might some day revolt, and a fatal desire to restore things to their former basis should he become sovereign. After four months of a criminal trial, this unfortunate prince was forced to declare and write that "if there had been powerful rebels who had revolted and called upon him, he would have become their leader."

Who has ever considered such a declaration valid and a true document in a trial? Who has ever judged a thought, an hypothesis, or a supposition of a case that never took place? Where are these rebels? Who took up arms? Who offered the prince leadership of the rebels some day? To whom did he speak about this and by whom was he confronted on this important point? This is what everyone is saying and what you cannot keep from saying to yourself. I am relying on your integrity and on your understanding. What I have the honor of writing you is between the two of us. I ask you alone how I ought to behave in such a delicate situation. Once again we labor under no illusions. By publishing this history, I am going to be judged by Europe. You may be quite convinced that there is not a single man in Europe who thinks the czarevitch died naturally. People shrug their shoulders when they hear that a twenty-three year old prince died of apoplexy as he read a decree that he must have expected would not be executed. This is why they have been so careful not to send me any statement from St. Petersburg about this fatal adventure. I am referred to the contemptible work of a so-called Nestesuranoi. Yet that writer, who is as mercenary as he is foolish and vulgar, cannot hide the fact that all of Europe thought Alexis had been poisoned. Therefore, with both your prudence and kindness to me and a sense of obligation to truth and propriety, you may judge whether my conduct in this very thorny situation has been surefooted.

What I have the honor of sending you is merely a request for advice and a statement of my doubts which I beg you to resolve. I am working for you and you must be the one to enlighten and guide me. A word in a margin will be enough or a simple letter with a few instructions about the passages causing me difficulty.

You will no doubt sympathize with my extreme quandary.

You may rely on all my efforts, on my extreme desire to satisfy you, and on the most respectful and affectionate feelings that you have inspired in me. You may take my frankness as a sign of my extreme devotion to Your Excellency, and you may be sure that from the bottom of my heart I will be Your Excellency's very humble and obedient servant for the rest of my days.

Voltaire

123. ". . . *I am striving to make peace between Corneille and Shake-speare.* . . ."

To George Keate.[137] Les Délices. February 10, 1762.

Forced labor and rather listless health have prevented me from writing you for a long time. But you have been present nonetheless both in my mind and heart. I have always been indignant with those who have not tolerated the honor you did them and which they did not deserve. One day, a great lord passing through a village with some excellent Tokay wine gave a few peasants some of it to drink; they found it bitter and thought they were being made fun of.

I have begun the edition of Corneille.[138] I am obliged to dictate almost everything since I can scarcely write in my own hand, and I am striving to make peace between Corneille and Shakespeare while waiting for our kings to condescend to restore peace to Europe.

Your Shakespeare was fortunate indeed. He could write tragedies half in prose, half in verse, and what verse at that! It is certainly not elegant and polished like that of Pope and Addison's *Cato*. He took the liberty of changing the place of almost every scene, of piling thirty to forty actions one upon another, of making a play go on for twenty-five years, and of mixing buffoonery with tragedy. His great merit, in my opinion, lies in strong and ingenuous paintings of human life.

Corneille certainly had a more difficult career to fulfill. There was the obstacle of rhyme that had to be continually mastered which is extraordinary work. He was forced to submit to the unity of time, place and action, to the rule of never making an actor enter or leave without a compelling reason, of always tying a plot artfully together and unravelling it with verisimilitude, of making all his heroes speak with noble eloquence, and of saying nothing which might offend the delicate ears of a very witty court and an academy composed of very learned and very difficult people.

You will admit that Shakespeare had a bit of a freer hand than Corneille. Besides you know in what esteem I hold your nation. I never lose an opportunity to do it justice in my commentary.

You would please me greatly if you would tell me who the author is of the small history of David entitled *The Man After God's Own Heart* and what diocese was given to that Warburton who proved that Moses was neither familiar with paradise, hell, nor the immortality of the soul and concludes therefore that he was inspired by God.[139] Apparently that bishop took Spinoza's son for his chaplain.

I will be for ever dear s^r y^r most faithfull and tender serv^t and friend.[140]

Voltaire

124. *"One must always have some crowned head in one's sleeve."*

To Marie de Vichy de Chamrond, Marquise Du Deffand. Les Délices. February 14, 1762.

Madam,

For a long time the pedantic commentator of Pierre Corneille [141] has not had the honor of writing you. I must tell you something of great consolation to women. In my neighborhood in Geneva, there is a little woman who has always been of weak temperament. Yesterday she was one hundred and four years old. Two years ago, her period returned quite regularly, and as you can imagine the wags proposed that she remarry. She loves her family too dearly to give brothers to her children. Her mental capacity has not weakened in any way. She walks, digests, writes, and governs the affairs of her house very well. I propose this example for you to follow one day.

As for men of such character, I know of none. Bernard de Fontenelle [142] was only a little boy compared to my woman in Geneva. I wish President Hénault at least reaches the age of a hundred like M. de Fontenelle, but I believe that Moncrif [143] will bury us all. They say his wig is tidier and better powdered than ever. The only thing that angers me is that he no longer composes small verse. That is a great pity. A propos of Moncrif, I have suffered a considerable loss in the Russian Empress, but I immediately acquired the Empress Queen,[144] and she has taken a subscription for Mlle. Corneille just like the King of France. One must always have some crowned head in one's sleeve. Besides Mlle. Corneille plays soubrettes very nicely. If I knew of any more important news I would tell you some in order to amuse you, but you have the best society of Paris there and no need for what transpires at the foot of the Alps. Live, digest, think, and even laugh at all of the follies of this world from the Lisbon Inquisition to the miseries of Paris, and receive my affectionate respect.

V.

125. *Voltaire's Niece Gets Married.*

To Marie-Elisabeth de Dompierre de Fontaine.[145] Ferney. March 19, 1762.

My dear niece,

I have but a moment to tell you how much I approve and congratulate you. There is nothing as sweet or as wise as marrying one's close friend. Your arrangements, of which you kindly inform me, seem very suitable for all of the interested parties. Hornoy [146] will gain from it; your castle will be embellished; life will become more animated there. The entire pity lies in the horrible distance separating your castle and mine.

I shall ask you to inform me of the day of your departure. An uncle must make arrangements for a little wedding present. I should like to be part of the ceremony and sign the contract. I am going to announce the news immediately to Madame Denis who is at present rehearsing her role as Statira,[147] and will soon perform it in a theater that is better laid out, better decorated, and better lighted than the one in Paris.

I am very sorry that I won't be marrying you off in my church in the presence of a big Jesus gilded like a chalice that looks like a Roman emperor and whose silly face I have removed. We would really give you a fine celebration because we are in good spirits and my head is swimming.

Madame Denis is coming. She shares my thoughts. We embrace you both affectionately, you and Cyrus's great armor bearer who has become my nephew.

126. Crush the Infamous.

To Jean Le Rond D'Alembert. June 17, 1762.

Excessive pride and envy have destroyed Jean-Jacques,[148] my illustrious philosopher. That monster dares speak of education! A man who refused to raise any of his sons and put them all in foundling homes! He abandoned his children and the tramp with whom he made them. He has only failed to write against his tramp as he has written against his friends. I will pity him if they hang him, but out of pure humanity, for personally I only consider him like Diogenes's dog [149] or rather like a dog descended from a bastard of that dog.

I do not know whether he is abhorred in Paris as he is by all the upright people of Geneva. You may be sure that whoever abandons the *philosophes* will come to an unhappy end.

Have you attended the gatherings where my impertinent remarks on *Rodogune* [150] were read? I tell the truth and shall continue to tell it, but always with a small compliment. I challenge all who long to disagree with me to provide one good reason against a single one of my remarks. I know a little bit about the theater, and unfortunately I have fifty years of experience. When you want to have a laugh, show up at the sessions at which Calderon's *Heraclius* and Shakespeare's *Julius Caesar* are read translated word for word in blank verse.

Brother Thieriot says that the Abbé Morellet [151] is composing an excellent work. All of you, crush the infamous without allowing it to prick you at the heels. If that monster Rousseau had wanted to, he would have given useful service in the light forces. Rather good officers are being trained everywhere, but I find the French generals a bit lukewarm.

I embrace you with the greatest warmth.

V.

127. *"Only he [Rousseau] is mad enough to say that all men are equal and that a state can survive without a hierarchy."*

To Louis-François-Armand du Plessis, Duc de Richelieu. Geneva. June 22, 1762.

Sire,

My miserable health presently confines me at Dr. Tronchin's side. I join the crowd of his devotees who go to the temple of Epidaurus. I assure you that although I am in the native land of Jean-Jacques Rousseau, I find that you are so right and I do not share his opinion at all. Only he is mad enough to say that all men are equal and that a state can survive without a hierarchy. He has carried the madness of his paradoxes so far as to say that if a prince were to find the hangman's daughter honest and pretty, he ought to marry her and his marriage ought to be universally approved.

I flatter myself that you make a distinction between Parisian men of letters and this madhouse philosopher. But you know that there is a bit of jealousy in literature as in the other estates. Corneille was accused of being in favor of dueling and of violating all of the proprieties in *The Cid*. Racine was reprimanded for incorporating the principles of Jansenism in the role of Phèdre. Descartes was accused of atheism and Gassendi of epicureanism. The fashion today is to claim that geometers and metaphysicians inspire the nation with an aversion to arms and that if we have been beaten on land and sea it was obviously the fault of the *philosophes*. But you know that the English are much more philosophical than we are and that has not prevented them from beating us.

231

Deep in your heart, you no doubt suspect other causes for our misfortunes which have nothing whatever to do with philosophy. You are too clearsighted and just to let yourself be led astray by the clamorings of a few envious individuals who, because they cannot attain the excellence of the few geniuses you still have left in France, attempt to discredit them and deprive the nation of its pride. You were made to be a patron of the worthy. That has always been the lot of superior men. Your own invariable kindness to me leads me to believe that you will be similarly disposed to those who are better than I. If works not authored by me are sometimes attributed to me by slander, those they have written are also infected by it. Look at how poor Helvétius was treated for a book which is merely a paraphrase of the thoughts of the Duc de La Rochefoucauld.

There is only good and bad fortune in this world. My good fortune is to be devoted to you with the deepest and most affectionate respect until the last moment of my life.

V.

128. *The Calas Affair.*[152]

To Dominique Audibert.[153] Les Délices. July 9, 1762.

Sir,
You were able to see the letters of the widow Calas and her son. I have looked into this affair for three months. I may be mistaken, but it seems clear as day to me that the rage of factionalism and the peculiarity of fate have coincided to cause the most innocent and unfortunate of men to be legally murdered on the rack, to disperse his family and reduce it to beggary. I am really afraid that in Paris little thought is being given to this horrible affair. You could put a hundred innocent men on the rack to no avail; in Paris people will only speak of a new play and think only of a good supper. However, by raising one's voice, one manages to be heard by the most hard of hearing, and sometimes even the outcries of the unfortunate reach the court. The widow Calas is in Paris with Messrs. Dufour and Mallet on the Rue Montmartre. Young Lavaysse is there also. I believe he has changed his name,

but the poor widow can manage for you to speak with him. I ask as a favor that you have the curiosity to see them both. This is a tragedy with a horrible and absurd ending, but the heart of the matter has not yet been really clarified.

I ask as a favor that you get these two principals to speak, that you draw every possible explanation out of them, and that you please apprise me of the main details you have learned.

Let me also know, I beg of you, whether the Calas woman is in need. If such is the case, I have no doubt that Messrs. Tourton and Baur will join me in providing her with relief. I have taken it upon myself to pay for the expenses of the suit which she must bring in the King's Council. I have recommended her to M. Mariette, a lawyer in the Council, who is asking for the extract of the proceedings at Toulouse in order to take action. The *parlement*, which seems ashamed of its judgment, has prohibited communication of the documents and even of the decree. Only the greatest support from the King can force this *parlement* to publish the truth. We are doing our utmost to obtain this support, and we believe that public outcry is the best means to success.

It seems to me that it is in the interest of all men to delve into this affair which, no matter how one looks at it, is the height of the most horrible fanaticism. To treat such an adventure with indifference is to forsake humanity. I am certain of your zeal; it will excite that of the others without compromising you.

I embrace you affectionately, my dear comrade, and am, with all the feeling that you merit, your very humble and obedient servant.

V.

129. *"Stay a Jew since you are one."*

To Isaac Pinto.[154] Les Délices, near Geneva. July 21, 1762.

Sir,
The lines about which you complain are violent and unjust. There are among you some very educated and very respectable men; your letter convinces me of this sufficiently. I will be careful to make an insertion in the new edition. When one is at fault, that

233

must be remedied, and I was at fault in attributing the vices of several individuals to an entire nation.

I will tell you just as frankly that many people can neither suffer your laws, your books, nor your superstitions. They say that your nation has always done considerable harm to itself and to the human race. If you are a philosopher, as you seem to be, you think as these gentlemen do but will not say so. Superstition is the most abominable scourge on earth. It has always been superstition that has caused the slaughter of so many Jews and so many Christians. It is superstition that causes people who are otherwise estimable to still send you to the stake. Human nature viewed from certain aspects is infernal nature. We would be consumed with horror if human nature were always considered in this light. But honorable persons, passing by the Place de la Grève where men are placed on the rack, order their coachmen to proceed quickly and go to the opera to divert themselves from the horrible spectacle they have seen on the way.

I could argue with you about the sciences you attribute to the ancient Jews and I could show you that they did not know any more about them than Frenchmen in the time of Chilperic. I could get you to admit that the jargon of a small province, mixed with Chaldean, Phoenician and Arabic, was a language as poor and as rough as our old Gaulish, but I would perhaps make you angry, and you seem to me too much of a gentleman for me to displease you. Stay a Jew since you are one. You will not slaughter forty-two thousand men for not pronouncing shibboleth correctly or twenty-four thousand for sleeping with Midianites.[155] But be a philosopher. That is the best that I can wish you in this short life.

I have the honor of being, sir, with all the feelings due you, your very humble and very obedient servant.

V.;
Christian, Gentleman
in Ordinary to the Chamber
of the Very Christian King

234

130. *The Jesuits are Suppressed in France and the Calases Obtain Justice.*

To Louise Dorothea of Meiningen, Duchess of Saxe-Gotha. Les Délices, near Geneva. March 7, 1763.

Madam,

I will soon be ready to take leave of this world which you embellish. I have scarcely any interest in it except if there are still a few souls left like yours. The King of Prussia plays a great role in it, and I believe that Your Serene Highness was not sorry that he resisted the house responsible for the loss of your Electorate. He acquired immortal glory. I know of one nation that cannot say as much for itself. But they say we have an Opéra Comique in Paris which is quite good, and that is enough. If we have not vanquished all our enemies, we have at least chased out the Jesuits.[156] That is quite a beautiful and reasonable beginning. We will end perhaps by separating ourselves from the Pope and by confining ourselves to Jesus Christ without passing through the hands of his vicar. But I shall be dead before that blessed day arrives.

The Calases, whose memoirs Your Serene Highness has seen, are finally obtaining justice, and the King's Council is ordering a review of their trial. It is a very rare thing in France for private individuals to be successful in getting the decree of a *parlement* quashed, and it is almost unbelievable that a Protestant family without influence or money, whose patriarch was broken on the rack in a far-off corner of the kingdom, has been successful in obtaining justice.

We must make a collection in favor of these unfortunate persons. The legal expenses are enormous. If Your Serene Highness wishes to include herself among the benefactors of the Calases, she will be in the front rank, and we will be more flattered by the good deed than by the sum which need not be considerable.

I am informed that while the entire world is at peace, your house is at war over the principality of Meiningen. I flatter myself that your war will not be long and that you will end it like the King of Prussia with the full enjoyment of your rights. I had the honor of seeing the late Prince of Meiningen in the past. I assure you that his court was not as brilliant as that of Gotha.

I do not know where the Countess of Bassevitz, who is so attached to you, is living. I must write her absolutely, and I do not know what to do without having recourse to Your Serene Highness. I beg her to let me take the liberty of placing the letter in this package. We have been led to hope that with peace we would have your children, the princes, nearby. I will at least have the consolation of paying my court to the mother in the person of her children.

I place myself at the feet of your entire family, and I am with the deepest respect and the most inviolable attachment, madam, the very humble and very obedient servant of Your Serene Highness.

Voltaire

As a blindman, I ask the great mistress of hearts for news through her eyes.

131. *Helping the Calases.*

To Jacob Vernes. Les Délices. Monday evening, March 14, 1763.

Since the Parlement of Toulouse has condemned Jean Calas, a merchant of Toulouse and a Protestant, on the basis of circumstantial evidence, to be broken and to die on the rack for strangling his elder son out of hatred for the Catholic religion, and since the widow Calas and her two daughters have come and prostrated themselves before the King, an extraordinary council, composed of all the Ministers of State, of all the Counselors of State and all the Magistrates of Petitions, was held on Monday, March 7, 1763. This council, allowing the petition on appeal, unanimously ordered the Parlement of Toulouse to submit the proceedings and grounds for its decree without delay.

This is indeed consoling news. I even imagined that I would soon have still more flattering things to report to M. Vernes, but I am quite fearful that everything will be ruined by the *Toulouse Letters,* composed, it is said, by M. De Court [157] and printed in

Lausanne under an Edinburgh imprint. If this book is circulated in France, it will doubtless supply the Parlement of Toulouse with ammunition. Count de St. Florentin,[158] who is already only too predisposed against the Calases and did not agree to the council of March 7, will be able to represent the Protestants to the King as seditious persons who imprudently attack the *parlements* and the King's Council at the very time the King is assembling at Versailles the largest council held in a hundred years in order to do justice to the Protestants in this affair of the greatest importance and concern.

The *Toulouse Letters* will especially do us great harm by confusing the Sirven affair [159] with the Calas affair. In less than three months people will behold two fathers accused of murdering their children for religious reasons. The Parlement of Toulouse will persuade the King that if the decree against the Calases is set aside, the Protestants will become more brazen and the King will perhaps leave this great case unsettled.

It is extremely important for the *Toulouse Letters* not to appear in France at all. The works that may be written on this delicate matter can be confided only to persons who are trustworthy and in a position to be useful. That is the course adopted by the author of the *Treatise on Toleration*.[160] People have written to Lausanne asking the author of the *Toulouse Letters* to suspend the sale of his book until the resolution of the Calas trial.

If M. Vernes can obtain so indispensable a suspension through his solicitations, he will be rendering a very great service. The author will have time to compose a very interesting second volume in which he can, with just reason, make the most of the king's kindness and the council's fairness. In this second volume, he will win over the minds he is frightening away in the first.

M. Vernes is aware of the necessity for the caution that is being requested. Each thing in its time, and certainly the author of the *Toulouse Letters* chose his badly.

We embrace M. Vernes affectionately and have the greatest desire to converse with him.

132. *Difficulties at Ferney.*

To César-Gabriel de Choiseul, Duc de Praslin.[161] Les Délices.
May 14, 1763.

Sire,
When the Duc de Choiseul was Minister for Foreign Affairs,
he was kind enough to have the royal warrant appended to the
petition I am now presenting granted to me.

The king's generosity would turn out to be useless if the rights
to the land at Ferney, confirmed by several kings and based on
their treaties with the neighboring authorities, were compromised
in the Parlement of Dijon which does not recognize these treaties
and makes judgments on the basis of common law.

I only bought the land at Ferney for my niece on the Duc
de Choiseul's kind assurance that the former privileges would be
preserved for me. Today I am being challenged on them by some
parish priests who wish to prosecute me in the Parlement of Dijon.
If such is the case, the land will become worthless. I am, therefore, resorting to your kindness, sire, and Madame Denis is presenting you with her petition. Both she and I beg you to grant us
your protection in an affair which is so essential to us. If our
request seems as just to you as it appears to us, we are certain
that you will deign to favor us. Our request is the natural result
of our warrant. Our case is unique and cannot be used as a prece-
dent.

We beg you to add this favor to the generosity with which
you have always honored us.

We are sending a copy of the petition and the warrant to the
Duc de Choiseul. We would indeed have to be very unfortunate
not to be successful with such patrons. We think that this favor
depends upon your offices, and we have every hope in the goodness
of your heart.

With the deepest respect, I have the honor of being, sire, your
very humble and very obedient servant.

Voltaire

133. *On Rousseau's* Emile.

To Louise Dorothea of Meiningen, Duchess of Saxe-Gotha. July 19, 1763.

Madam,
The people of Geneva are not as reasonable as Your Serene Highness. There are, in truth, many philosophers who deeply despise the infamous superstitions which the Savoyard vicar seems to have destroyed in poor Rousseau's *Emile.*[162] The section on this vicar is no doubt better than all of the remainder of the book. It is appreciated by large and small, and yet it is anathematized by the Council which is a bit servile to the priests. Everything is a contradiction in this world. It is no small one to condemn what one esteems and believes deep in one's heart. Two hundred citizens have protested the decree of the Small Council of Geneva, but much less out of friendship for Jean-Jacques than out of hatred for the magistrates. Their suit produced no results, and Jean-Jacques, having forsaken his handsome title of citizen, is left only with that of Diogenes. He is going to transport his tub to Scotland with Milord Maréchal.[163] That poor devil is dragging out a miserable existence, while the Pope remains a sovereign with an income of fifteen million. These are the ways of the world.

We French expel the Jesuits but remain prey to the Jansenist fanatics. To my knowledge, only the Protestant princes conduct themselves reasonably. They keep the priests in their rightful place and live in tranquillity (when the frenzy of war does not interfere).

I have the honor of sending you a little catechism which seemed reasonable to me.[164]

Accept my deep respect.

V.

134. *"The fatal dogma of toleration is today infecting every mind."*

To Claude-Adrien Helvétius. August 25, 1763.

Sir,

Pax Christi. I see with saintly joy how moved your heart is by the sublime truths of our sacred religion and that you wish to devote your works and great talents to remedying the scandal you may have created by including in your famous book a few truths of a different order which seemed dangerous to persons of a delicate and timid conscience like Messrs. Omer Joly de Fleury, Gauchat, Chaumeix [165] and several of our fathers.

The small tribulations which our fathers are enduring today harden them in their faith, and the more we are dispersed, the more spiritual good we do. I am able to see this progress as the chaplain of the Resident of France in Geneva. I cannot bless God sufficiently for the resolution you have taken to fight personally for the Christian religion at a time when it is being openly attacked and made sport of by the whole world. The fatal philosophy of the English was at the root of all this evil. Under the pretext of being the best mathematicians and physicists in Europe, those people have abused their minds and dared even to investigate the mysteries. This contagion has spread everywhere. The fatal dogma of toleration is today infecting every mind. Three fourths of France, at least, is beginning to ask for freedom of conscience; it is being preached in Geneva.

Well, imagine that when the magistrate of Geneva was unable to refrain from condemning M. Jean-Jacques Rousseau's romance entitled *Emile,* six hundred citizens came to the Council of Geneva three times to protest that, unless there were a hearing, they would not suffer the condemnation of a citizen who had indeed written against the Christian religion but who might have had his reasons which had to be heard, and that a citizen of Geneva may write what he wishes provided he gives proper explanations.

Well, the attacks against our sacred truths made by Emperor Julian and the philosophers Celsus and Porphyry from the earliest times are being renewed each day.[166] Everyone thinks like Bayle, Descartes, Fontenelle, Shaftesbury, Bolingbroke, Collins and Woolston. Everyone boldly states that there is only one God, that the holy virgin Mary is not the mother of God, and that the Holy Ghost is nothing other than the light given to us by God. They preach some indefinable virtue which, since it merely consists of doing good to man, is completely worldly and of no value. To the *Christian Pedagogue* and to the *Admonition of Careful Considera-tion*,[167] books that used to bring about so many conversions, they oppose little books of philosophy which they carefully and skill-fully circulate everywhere. These little pamphlets quickly follow upon each other. They are not sold; they are given to confederates who distribute them to young persons and to women. Sometimes it is the *Sermon of the Fifty* [168] which they attribute to the King of Prussia; sometimes it is an extract from the will of that unfor-tunate curé, Jean Meslier,[169] who, at his death, asked God forgiveness for having taught Christianity; sometimes it is a non-descript *Catechism of the Upright Man* written by a certain Abbé Durand. What a title, *The Catechism of the Upright Man!* As if there could be virtue outside the Catholic religion!

Fight this torrent since God has given you the grace of en-lightenment. You must care for reason and virtue which have been shamefully outraged. Fight the wicked as they fight, without compromising yourself, without their suspecting you. Be satisfied with doing justice to our sacred religion in a clear and perceptible way, seeking only the glory of being engaged in good works. Imi-tate our great King Stanislas, father of our illustrious queen,[170] who occasionally deigned to have little Christian books printed entirely at his expense. He was always modest enough to conceal his name, and it was only discovered through his worthy secre-tary, M. de Solignac. I am out of paper. I embrace you in Jesus Christ.

Jean Patourel, one-time Jesuit

135. *"What difference does it make whether one is burned by the councils of Leo X or by the orders of Calvin?"*

To Elie Bertrand. Ferney. December 26, 1763.

I agree with you that Jews and Christians have talked a great deal about brotherly love. Judging by the results, their love rather resembles hatred. They have only considered and treated as brothers those dressed in their colors. Any adherent was considered a saint. Anyone who was not was slaughtered in a saintly fashion in this world and damned for the next. My dear friend, you believe it the very essence of Christianity that one must thoroughly prove the need for toleration. Yet it is on the precepts and interests of this religion that the charitable persecutors base their cruel rights. Jesus Christ seems to me gentle and tolerant as he does to you, but the members of his sect have always been inhuman and barbaric. The strongest faction has always plagued the weakest in the name of Jesus Christ and for the glory of God. When we papists persecute you, we are consistent with our principles because you must submit yourselves to the decisions of our Holy Mother Church. Outside of the church there is no salvation. Therefore, you are impudent rebels. When you persecute, you are inconsistent since you grant every man the right of inquiry. Thus your reformers have only overturned the authority of the Pope to place themselves on his throne. For the council's decisions you have proudly substituted those of your synods, and Barneveldt has perished like John Huss.[171] Is the synod of Dordrecht better than that of Trent? What difference does it make whether one is burned by the councils of Leo X or by the orders of Calvin?

What remedy is there for so many follies and evils which distress the best of all worlds? Cling to morality, scorn theology, leave the quarreling to the obscurity of schools where it was begotten by pride, persecute only those unruly minds who disrupt society over matters of words. Amen! Amen!

The sick man of Ferney, who would persecute no one but muddleheads, tenderly embraces the charitable and beneficent heretic.

V.

[By 1764, Voltaire had reached his seventh decade, and during the next five years, bad health and personal distress notwithstanding, his literary production was nothing less than phenomenal.

In 1764, Voltaire finally published his Philosophical Dictionary, the subversive work that he had begun twelve years previously dur-

242

*ing his Prussian sojourn. A popular work that was reprinted in nu-
merous editions, the* Dictionary *was repeatedly disavowed by its
author who was convinced that those engaged in "crushing the infamous" should speak out but be protected by anonymity. The character and purpose of the* Dictionary *are suggested by his remark
about the great* Encyclopédie *in his letter of April 5, 1766 to
d'Alembert:* "Twenty folio volumes will never create a revolution;
the little thirty penny portable books are the ones to be feared. If
the Gospel had cost twelve hundred sesterces, the Christian religion
would never have been established."

In 1764, Voltaire also published his Treatise on Toleration
*written two years previously in connection with the Calas affair but
which also dealt more generally with the problem of intolerance
over the course of history. The following years saw the publication
of the* Philosophy of History *which Theodore Besterman has described as "a handbook of history for the use of freethinkers." 1767
brought forth a rash of works including his celebrated pseudo-
primitive* conte, The Ingénu, *his allegorical play on Geneva,* The
Scythians, *and critical works in various genres like the* Questions
of Zapata, *the* Literary Honesties, *the vigorously anti-Christian* Important Scrutiny of Milord Bolingbroke, *the* Letters to Monseigneur
the Prince *which discusses a group of authors accused of writing
in defiance of Christianity, the* Homilies Delivered in London *on
atheism, and the* Defense of My Uncle, *another polemic in the field
of history.*

*1768 saw the issuance of two works in the field of natural sci-
ence: a long essay entitled* On the Singularities of Nature *in which
Voltaire was especially concerned with geology and with the oddi-
ties and mysteries of nature, and a work called* The Snails of Reverend Father L'Escarbotier *concerned with theories of reproduc-
tion and spontaneous generation, including his own experiments in
cutting off the heads of snails. In the same year, he published his*
conte, The Princess of Babylon, *his burlesque poem on* The Civil
War of Geneva, *another important story called* The Man With
Forty Crowns [L'Homme aux quarante écus] *which was really an
essay on political economy, some dialogues on the subject of religion gathered together under the title of* The Dinner of Count
Boulainvilliers, *and another important dialogue developing Voltaire's ideas on government and called simply* ABC. *His essay on*

243

historical skepticism, The Pyrrhonism of History, *was written in 1768 and published early in 1769.*

Voltaire's letters in this period reflect some important personal concerns: his grief over the death of Mme. de Pompadour in 1764; his assistance to some Huguenot galley slaves and his proposal to establish a colony of French Protestants in Guyana; his involvement in cases of injustice and intolerance, including that of the Chevalier de La Barre who was condemned, by the tribunal of Abbeville, to torture and burning at the stake because of his neglect to remove his hat before a passing religious procession; his deep distress at the conduct of his niece and mistress, Mme. Denis, whom he was forced to dismiss from Ferney under rather painful circumstances.

These letters continue to demonstrate the breadth of his intellectual and humanistic interests as they range over a variety of subjects including historical skepticism, his notions on the requirements of modern taste, his criticism of the theory of spontaneous generation, his convictions about contemporary progress, and his views on opera and the theater. Thus, the aging Voltaire impresses the reader of his correspondence with a continuing remarkable vigor and with the breadth of his intellect and commitments.]

136. *"Rarely is the final period of life very pleasant."*

To Marie de Vichy de Chamrond, Marquise Du Deffand. Ferney. January 6, 1764.

Madam,

It does not astonish me any more that you have not received the copy of *Jeanne* [172] I sent you by post and countersigned by one of the administrators. No book can enter France by mail without being seized by the clerks who have been putting together a rather nice library for themselves for some period of time and will become men of letters in every sense. One dare not even send books addressed to government ministers. Indeed, you may be certain that the postal service is infinitely curious, and unless President Hénault uses the name of the queen in order to get you a copy of the *Maiden,* I do not see how you will be successful in obtaining one from abroad.

Since I am unable to read at all anymore, I amused myself

by composing some Mother Goose stories. I am not exactly like you, but do you remember the eyes of the Abbé de Chaulieu [173] during the last two years of his life? Imagine an intermediate state between yours and his. This is precisely my situation.

I share your belief that if one will be blind, it ought to be in Paris. It is ridiculous to be in that state in a countryside that has one of the most beautiful views in Europe. In such a state one absolutely requires the consolation of society. You enjoy that advantage. The best society comes to see you, and you have the pleasure of expressing your opinions about all the silly things people do and print. I am quite aware that this is feeble consolation. Rarely is the final period of life very pleasant. We have always hoped rather vainly that we would enjoy life, and in the end all we can do is endure it. Bear this burden as long as you can. Only great suffering makes it intolerable. In growing old, we still have one great pleasure not to be neglected, that is to count the number of impertinent men and women we have seen die, the government ministers we have seen dismissed and the throng of ridiculous persons who have passed before our eyes.

If out of fifty new works appearing each month there is one that is tolerable, we have it read to us and that constitutes another little amusement. All of this does not make for infinite joy, but in the end we have nothing better, and the choice is a compulsory one.

As for President Hénault, that is a completely different matter. He grows younger; he is a gadabout; he is gay and will be gay at eighty while Moncrif and I are probably quite solemn. God distributes his favors as he pleases. Do you sometimes have the pleasure of seeing M. d'Alembert? Not only is he a man of great intellect but of a very decisive kind of intellect, and that is something considerable for the world is full of intelligent men who do not know how they ought to think.

Farewell. Remember, I pray you, that you owe me some respect for if in the kingdom of the blind the one-eyed are kings, I am assuredly more than one-eyed. But let this respect not diminish any of your kindness. I have been deprived of the good fortune of seeing and hearing you for a long time. I shall probably die without that delight. In the meantime, let us try to play with life. But the game is only one of blindman's buff.

V.

245

137. *On the Subject of Polygamy.*

To Arthur Hill-Trevor.[174] March 8, 1764.

This is my answer to the *anonime* letter j have receiv'd.

If it is reported in a pamphlet impos'd upon me, that a minister of state under Charles the second, was a candid and good husband to two wives at once, and that he wrote a pretty book on those patriarcal good manners, j know neither that pamphlet nor that statesman, but j should be very glad to peruse the pretended book writ on the plurality of wives, tho j am no way concern'd in the business of poligamy or bigamy or even monogamy.

Voltaire
gentleman ord[r] of
the Kings chamber

at the castle of Ferney
8 March n. st. 1764

138. *Helping Some Victims of Persecution.*

To Louis Necker.[175] March 19, 1764.

Sir,
First I must tell you that the government minister whom I addressed in order to obtain the release of that poor galley-slave required great skill to succeed as quickly as he did in a matter outside the jurisdiction of his office. It would be impossible to obtain the same favor for twenty-four persons most of whom were condemned by *parlements*. You know our situation. But here are the proposals I have made and they may be successful if you are supported by the relatives and friends of those who have been condemned for religious reasons.

The government ministry is very favorably disposed to the new colony of Guyana. We are assured that the soil is excellent and that persons who are industrious and active can become rich there in a few years. Besides it has nature's most beautiful climate, and the inhabitants of the southern coasts of France will not find

246

the air very different considering the vast forests that temper the heat of the sun in that region more than elsewhere. It seems to me that it is better to grow rich in Cayenne than to be in chains in Marseilles.

You have told me that they might provide a sum of between fifteen and twenty thousand livres to obtain their freedom. I can assure you there is no government minister in France who would give his favor for money. But if you can have this sum made ready for goods to be taken aboard ship and to buy things necessary for their settlement and for the kind of farming they will want to undertake, and if they make up their minds to leave with their families or even enlist several of their friends to leave with them, all you would have to do then is to send me a little memorandum concerning their proposals. I already have word that everything humanly possible will be done to encourage their settlement, their freedom and their success in Guyana.

They should not, in my opinion, request permission to build a house of worship and to bring clergymen with them. They must present themselves as growers either of indigo, cochineal, cotton, silk, tobacco or sugar and not as the people of God passing over the seas to go and sing the psalms of Marot. They can secretly put a minister or two on board if they find that suitable, and once they are in Guyana they will be dealing with a governor who is a worthy man, who knows better than anyone else the value of toleration, and who is leaving only with a firm resolution to grant everyone freedom of conscience.

See if you can support this enterprise and if we might be assured of a few families who would join those presently detained in Marseilles. This entire affair can be arranged with a slip of paper. I already have the names of the galley-slaves I will send to the government minister. It is merely a matter of finding someone who will stand for them and for the families who will want to sail. They must merely promise to come to the port indicated by the minister, within three months time at the latest, with all the tools necessary for the kind of farming each family will undertake.

They would also have to promise, I believe, to take along provisions at their expense to make up for anything that might be lacking during the trip. The government ministry would have to commit itself to furnishing them with a part of these food stores and the emigrants would have to concern themselves with the other part.

I am only proposing this arrangement in order to facilitate the whole thing, for I think once the government has had them set sail, it would certainly have to feed them. But they will be much better off if each person arrives with his small provision, and the money you spoke of can easily serve that use. So make your proposal as soon as you can. It will find favor with a worthy minister of state, and he will have it passed in the Council unless he finds some insurmountable obstacles to it. We must never guarantee anything, but I have high hopes. There is not a moment to lose. You will have the glory of rendering humanity a very great service, and I will be your head clerk on the relief committee. I am yours unceremoniously.

V.

139. *Madame de Pompadour is Dead.*

To Jean Le Rond D'Alembert. Les Délices. May 8, 1764.

My dear philosopher,

Some people tell me there will be a *lit de justice*,[176] others that there will not, and this is all leaves me quite indifferent. Some add that the expulsion of the Jesuits will be enacted into the basic law of the kingdom, and that is quite amusing. They speak of public borrowings, but I will not lend one penny. However, I will speak to you about yourself and Corneille. People find me a little insolent, but I think you consider me rather discreet since, between the two of us, I have not pointed out a fifth of his errors. One must not reveal the turpitude committed by one's father. I think I have said enough about it to be useful. If I had said more, I would have been considered an evil man. Be that as it may, I have married off two daughters by doing verse criticism. Scaliger and Saumaise [177] have not equalled that.

Were you sorry about Madame de Pompadour? [178] Yes, doubtlessly, for deep in her heart she was one of us. She was a patroness of literature to the extent possible for her. That's a beautiful dream over with. They say she died with a steadfastness

248

worthy of your praise. All peasant women die that way, but at court the thing is rarer. There life is regretted more, and I am not too sure why.

I am informed that an inquisition against literature is being instituted. They noticed Frenchmen were beginning to develop their wings, and they are clipping them. It is not good for a nation to take it into its head to think. This is a dangerous vice that must be left to the English. I am afraid certain statesmen will do as Madame de Bouillon who used to say: "How will we edify the public on Holy Friday? Let us make our people fast." They will say: "What good will we do the state? Let us persecute the *philosophes*." You may be sure that Madame de Pompadour would never have persecuted anyone. I am very grieved at her death.

If there is anything new, I ask you as a favor to inform me. Your letters instruct me, console me and amuse me; you surely know that. I cannot reciprocate for what can one say from the foot of the Alps and Mt. Jura?

Do you sometimes come across brother Thieriot? I would really like to know why I cannot draw a word out of that lazy fellow.

People have told me that you are at work on a great book. If you put your name to it, you will not dare tell the truth. I should like you to be a bit of a scoundrel. Try to weaken your virile and concise style if you can. Write dully. Certainly no one will suspect you. Some very good things can be said ponderously. You will have the pleasure of enlightening the world without compromising yourself. That would be a fine act. You would be steeling yourself against everything for the good cause, and you would be an apostle without becoming a martyr. Ah! My God, if three or four persons like you had been able to get together, the world would be wise. And I shall die perhaps with the grief of leaving it as idiotic as I found it.

Do you still plan to go to Italy? Would to heaven you do! I imagine that I would then see you in the course of your journey, and I would bless the Lord. I embrace you from too great a distance, and for this I am really sorry.

140. *On the Writing of Ancient History.*

To the *Gazette littéraire de l'Europe*. May 1764.

Gentlemen,

In reviewing the work of Mr. Hooke,[179] you said that we have yet to write the history of Rome, and nothing is truer. One could forgive Roman historians for illustrating the first period of the republic with fables which may no longer be transcribed except for purposes of refutation. Anything contrary to probability must at least inspire doubt, but that which is impossible must never be recorded.

To start with we are told that after assembling 3,300 bandits Romulus built the town of Rome a thousand feet square. Now a thousand feet square would scarcely be adequate for two small farms. How could 3,300 men have lived in that town? Who were the ostensible kings of that small pack of thieves? Weren't they obviously gang leaders sharing a government in upheaval with a small, ferocious, and undisciplined horde? When we compose ancient history should we not make people aware of the enormous difference between these bandit chiefs and true kings of a mighty nation?

By the admission of Roman writers, it has been established that for nearly four hundred years the Roman state was no more than ten leagues long or wide. The state of Genoa is much larger today than the Roman republic was at that time.

Veii was captured only in the year 560 after a sort of siege or blockade that had lasted ten years. Veii was near the site of present-day Civitavecchia, five or six leagues from Rome, and the land around Rome, the capital of Europe, has always been so sterile that the people wanted to leave their native city to settle in Veii.

None of its wars, until that of Pyrrhus, would deserve space in history had they not been a prelude to its great conquests. All of these events until the time of Pyrrhus are, in the main, so insignificant and obscure that they had to be highlighted through incredible miracles or totally improbable facts, starting with the adventure of the she-wolf that fed Romulus and Remus and the adventures of Lucretius, Clelia and Curtius, including the ostensible letter of Pyrrhus's doctor in which he proposed the poisoning of his master to the Romans, it is said, in exchange for a suitable reward for this service. What reward could the Romans, who at that time had neither gold nor silver, give him? And how can one suspect a Greek doctor of being so imbecilic as to write such a letter?

All our compilers collect these tales without the slightest scrutiny; they are copyists, and not one of them is a philosopher. We see them all paying homage to men who basically were nothing more than daring bandits by calling them virtuous. They repeat that Roman virtue was corrupted in the end by wealth and luxury as if there were virtue in pillaging nations and vice only consisted of enjoying the stolen fruits. If they wanted to compose a moral treatise instead of a history, they ought to have inspired even greater revulsion for the Roman depredations than for their use of the treasures which they stole from so many nations whom they sacked one after another.

Modern historians of those distant times ought to have at least clearly recognized the period of which they speak. The rather unlikely battle of the Horaces and Curiaces, the romantic adventures of Lucretius, Clelia, and Curtius ought not to be treated like the battles of Pharsalia and Actium. It is essential to differentiate between the century of Cicero and those during which the Romans could neither read nor write and kept track of the years by nails driven into the Capitol. In sum, no Roman history in a modern language has yet proved satisfactory to the reading public.

No one has yet successfully investigated the nature of a people that was meticulous in its devotion to superstition, that could never regulate the period of its holidays, that did not even know what a sun dial was for nearly five hundred years; of a people whose Senate sometimes prided itself on humanity and which very Senate would sacrifice two Greeks and two women of Gaul to the Gods in order to atone for the love affair of one of its vestal virgins; of a people constantly exposed to injury and which, after five centuries, had only a single doctor who served as both surgeon and apothecary.

The only art practiced by this people for six hundred years was warfare, and as it was always armed, it conquered nations that were not continually under arms, one after another.

The author [180] of the small volume on the greatness and

decadence of the Romans teaches us more than the enormous books of modern historians. He alone would have been worthy of writing that history if he had especially been able to resist over-systematization and the pleasure of frequently providing ingenious thoughts instead of reasons.

One of the defects which makes the reading of new Roman histories not very tolerable is their authors's desire to go into details in the manner of Livy. They do not remember that Livy was writing for his nation for whom these details were precious. One has a poor knowledge of men indeed if one imagines that Frenchmen will be interested in the marches and counter marches of a consul waging war against the Samnites and Volsci in the same way that we are interested in the battle of Ivry and the swimming across the Rhine.

All of ancient history must be written differently from our own, and to these proprieties the authors of ancient histories have been unfaithful. More concerned with displaying a misplaced eloquence than with discussing truths that could be of some use, they repeat and expatiate on harangues that were never delivered. The frequently puerile exaggerations and erroneous evaluations of ancient monies and of the wealth of states lead the ignorant into error and distress the educated. Today people affirm in print that Archimedes threw arrows infinite distances, that he lifted a galley in the middle of the water and transported it to shore by moving the tip of his finger, that the cost to clean the sewers of Rome was six hundred thousand écus, etc.

Histories that are more ancient are written with even less care. There is a greater neglect of sound criticism; the miraculous and the incredible prevail in them. They would appear to have been written more for children than for men. The enlightened age we live in demands of writers a greater cultivation of reason.

141. *On the Requirements of Modern Taste.*

To Michel-Paul Gui de Chabanon.[181] At the Chateau of Ferney. September 2, 1764.

Sir,

I owe you esteem and gratitude, and I acquit myself of these two debts by thanking you with a feeling of appreciation equal to the pleasure with which I read you. You think like a philosopher and compose verse like a true poet. The decline of the fine arts must not be laid at the door of philosophy. The best English poets flourished in the time of Newton; Corneille was a contemporary of Descartes and Molière a student of Gassendi. Our decadence derives from the orators and poets of the age of Louis XIV telling us what we were ignorant of whereas today's best writers might only be able to state what people already know. Our discontent had its source in our abundance. You have understood Homer's merit perfectly but you are quite aware that today we must no longer write according to his taste, that we must not fight in the manner of Achilles and Sarpedon. Racine was a clever man; he praised Euripides considerably, imitated him slightly (at the very most he took a dozen verses from him), and surpassed him infinitely. This was because he knew how to accommodate himself to the taste, to the genius of the somewhat ungrateful nation for which he was working. This is the only way to success in all of the arts. I am willing to believe that Orpheus was a great musician, but if he were to return among us to create an opera, I would advise him to attend the school of Rameau.

I certainly realize that today the Welches [182] only have their comic opera, but I am persuaded that geniuses like you can bring the age of Louis XIV back to them. You are the one to rekindle the remains of the sacred fire that has not yet been completely extinguished. Now I am merely an old soldier retired to his cottage. I passionately hope you will wage the struggle against poor taste more successfully than we have resisted our other enemies. With these very sincere feelings, I have the honor of being, sir, your very humble and very obedient servant.

Voltaire

142. *"The* philosophes *must make the truth public but hide themselves."*

To Etienne-Noël Damilaville.[183] September 19, 1764.

My dear brother,
I received your letter of the thirteenth in which you ask me for a *Philosophical Dictionary.*[184] This dictionary is a cruel fright to the devout. I would never wish to be its author. I am writing in this tone to M. Marin [185] who spoke to me about it in his last letter, and I imagine that the true brothers will support me. This work must be looked upon as a compilation by several authors put together by a Dutch publisher. It is really cruel to name me. That strips me of my freedom to be of any future service. The *philosophes* must make the truth public but hide themselves. I fear above all that some starving book dealer will print the work under my name. We must hope that M. Marin will prevent that thievery.
You have probably received the package I sent you a few days ago for M. Blin de Sainmore.[186] He is devoting himself courageously to the defense of truth in the matter of commentaries.
Good evening, my dear philosopher. There are many people who detest the infamous as we do, but there are very few true brothers. Crush the infamous.
Would you have this letter passed on to brother Protagoras? [187]

143. *Voltaire Professes His Philosophical Orthodoxy.*

To the Magnificent Council of Geneva. The Chateau of Ferney. January 12, 1765.

I am obliged to advise the Magnificent Council of Geneva that among the pernicious and scurrilous satires with which this city hase been flooded for sometime, all of them printed in Amsterdam by Marc-Michel Rey, next Monday a package is coming to a man named Chirol, a book dealer in Geneva, containing *Philosophical Dictionaries, Gospels of Reason* and other nonsense which people are insolent enough to attribute to me and which I despise almost as much as the *Letters from the Mountain*.[188] I believe I am fulfilling my duty by giving this notice, and I rely completely on the wisdom of the Council which will certainly know how to repress every breach of public peace and good order.

I must only confine myself to assuring it of my deep respect.

Voltaire

144. *Voltaire Knows Nothing About the Soul.*

To James Boswell. At the Chateau of Ferney, near Geneva. February 11, 1765.[189]

My distempers and my bad eyes do not permit me to ansuver with that celerity and exactness that my duty and my heart require. You seem sollicitous about that pretty thing call'd soul. J do protest you j know nothing of it. Nor wether it is, nor what it is, nor what it shall be. Young scolars, and priests know all that perfectly. For my part j am but a very ignorant fellow.

Let it be what it will, j assure you my soul has a great regard for your own when you will make a turn into our deserts, you shall find me (if alive) ready to show you my respect and obsequiousness.

V.

145. *"One day there will surely be a great intellectual revolution."*

To Elie Betrand. March 26, 1765.

My dear philosopher,

My heart is deeply moved by your efforts filled with friendship, and I shall never forget them. The Calases are not the only persons to have been sacrificed to fanaticism. There is an entire family in Languedoc that has been condemned for the very abomination the Calases had been accused of. They are fugitives in this country. The Council of Berne has even given them a small pension. It will be difficult to obtain for these new unfortunate persons

255

the justice finally extracted for the Calases after three years of concern and diligence. I do not know when the spirit of persecution will be turned back to the depths of hell whence it came, but I do know that only by despising the mother can we overcome the son, and the mother here, as you certainly understand, is superstition. One day there will surely be a great intellectual revolution. A man my age will not see it, but he will die in the hope that men will be more enlightened and gentle. No one could make a better contribution to that than you, but in every country, good hearts and good minds are enslaved by those possessing neither.

My respects, I pray you, to M. and Mme. de Freudenreich. I embrace you with all my heart.

V.

146. *Encouragement to a Leading Actress.*

To Claire-Josèphe-Hippolyte Léris de Latude Clairon.[190] Ferney. July 23, 1765.

Mademoiselle,

If I could have received your reply before writing my epistle, that epistle would have been far better since I overlooked the acclaim you deserve for having taught the French on the subject of costumes. I was very wrong to omit that item from the list of your talents. I do beg your pardon and promise that this sin of omission will be remedied. Look after your health which is even more precious than the perfection of your art. I should really have liked it to have been possible for you to spend a few months with Aesculapius Tronchin.[191] I fancy he would have enabled you to embellish the French stage, to which you are so indispensable, for a long time. When someone develops an art as profoundly as you do, it becomes respectable even for those who are so uncouth and barbarous as to condemn it. I do not utter your name, I do not read a passage from Corneille or from a play of Racine without becoming vehemently indignant with those scoundrels and fanatics who insolently proscribe an art which they ought to study at least if they are to deserve a hearing (if that is possible) when they

256

dare speak. This infamous superstition has been making me angry for nigh on sixty years. Those animals have precious little understanding of their interests when they rebel against persons who are able to think, speak, and write and force them to treat them like the lowest of men. The hateful inconsistency of the French, who denounce what people admire, must displease you as much as it does me and cause you violent disgust. Would God grant you to be wealthy enough to leave the Parisian stage and perform with your friends at home as we do in a retreat where we make terrible sport of nonsense and of fools! I have firmly resolved not to leave this place. My only hope is that Tronchin is the one man in the world who can cure you, and that you will have to come here.

Farewell, mademoiselle. Enjoy the happiness you deserve. You must believe that I admire you as much as I despise the enemies of reason and the arts, and that my affection for you is as great as my hatred for them. Continue your kindness to me. I appreciate your full worth. That is saying very much.

V.

147. *In Defense of the Theater.*

To Claire-Josèphe-Hippolyte Léris de Latude Clairon. August 1765 (?).

Mademoiselle,

It is true that beautiful Oldfield,[192] England's leading actress, enjoys a handsome mausoleum in the Church of Westminster like the country's kings and heroes and even the great Newton. It is also true that Mademoiselle Lecouvreur,[193] the leading actress of France in her time, was brought to the corner of the then unpaved Rue de Bourgogne in a cab, that she was buried there by a street porter and has no mausoleum. Everything has its example in this world. The English have established an annual holiday in honor of the famous actor and poet Shakespeare. We still do not have a holiday for Molière. Louis XIV, at the peak of his greatness, danced with dancers from the opera house within view of all Paris when he returned from the celebrated campaign of 1672. If the Archbishop of Paris had been willing to do the same, he would not have been as well received even if he had been Europe's leading performer of the minuet.

At the beginning of the sixteenth century, Italy saw the rebirth of tragedy and comedy thanks to the taste of Pope Leo X and the genius of the prelates Bibiena, La Casa, and Trissino. Cardinal de Richelieu had the hall of the Palais Royal built for the presentation of his plays and those of his five boy poets. Two bishops did the honors of the hall at his behest and presented refreshments to the ladies during intermissions.

We are indebted to Cardinal Mazarin for the opera house, but notice how everything changes. Cardinals Du Bois and Fleury, both prime ministers, have not even brought us one farce for our fairs. We have become more regular; our manners are probably more severe. The Jansenists have been suspected of providing the ecclesiastical power with weapons against theatrical presentations so that they might have the pleasure of attacking the Jesuits who put on performances of tragedies and comedies using their students and included these exercises among the first duties of a good education. People even maintain that the intimidated Jesuits suspended their theatrical entertainments sometime before their society was abolished in France.

You have probably heard from the great scholars who visit with you that the contrary was the case among our masters, the Greeks and Romans. The money intended for theatrical expenses in Athens was sacred money. It was not even permissible to tamper with it during the most pressing circumstances and the greatest dangers of war.

The ancient Romans went even further. Rome was devastated by the plague around the year 390 of its founding. The gods had to be appeased by the most sacred of ceremonies. What did the Senate do? It ordered a play to be performed, and the plague ended. Any good doctor should not be surprised by this. He knows that honest pleasure is very good for one's health.

Unfortunately we are neither like the Greeks nor the ancient Romans. It is true that there are many amiable Frenchmen in France but there are also Welches, and they would not consider the theater as a specific if they were attacked by the plague. As for myself, I should like to spend my life listening to you; otherwise may the plague stifle me. I confess that the contradictions that divide those who have thought about your art are innumerable, but you know that society lives on contradictions. There are no contradictions among those who live with you. They all join together with the feelings of esteem and friendship which they owe you.

148. *Against the Theory of Spontaneous Generation.*

To Lazzaro Spallanzani.[194] At the Chateau of Ferney, near Geneva. February 17, 1766.

A few weeks ago, I received by way of Geneva two dissertations on physics without any author's name. There was no letter in the package. I have just learned that these two works, which demonstrate great sagacity and very thorough knowledge, are by you and are worthy of being so. I should like to be able to thank you in your beautiful Italian language which you speak with such polish, but my present condition does not permit me to write. My old age and my illnesses reduce me to dictation.

You are quite right to attack the so-called experiments of Mr. Needham. He has recently been attacked in Geneva on the subject of miracles. He could indeed boast that he had performed miracles if he had been able to produce eels without a germ. One must be wary of all of these foolhardy experiments which contradict the laws of nature. You seem to be as accurate in your experiments as you are precise in your reasoning. After reading you, one cannot deny you the highest esteem.

With these feelings and with considerable gratitude, I have the honor of being, sir, your very humble and very obedient servant.

Voltaire,
Gentleman Ordinary
of the King's Chamber.

149. *"Twenty folio volumes will never create a revolution; the little thirty penny portable books are the ones to be feared."*

To Jean Le Rond D'Alembert. April 5, 1766.

My dear and great philosopher,

In a hodgepodge of letters that I received by way of Geneva, I inadvertently opened the one I am sending you. I only noticed that it was addressed to you after stupidly unsealing it. I very humbly beg your pardon and swear to you, on my word as a philosopher, that I have not read one word of it. In general I had ordered the removal of any letters addressed to you from Italy. This is the only one I found in my package. I imagine that it is not from the reigning Pope; I presume that it is from some thinking person since it is intended for you.

There are few such thinking persons. My old crowned disciple [195] informs me that there is scarcely one in a thousand. That is about the number in cultivated society, and if there are at present about a thousand reasonable men, there will be a tenfold increase in ten years. The world is losing its innocence at a furious pace. A great intellectual revolution is everywhere in the offing. You would not believe the progress reason has made in part of Germany. I am not speaking of the impious who openly embrace the system of Spinoza. I am speaking of honorable people who have no fixed principles on the nature of things, who do not know what exists but know very well what does not. These are my true philosophers. I can assure you that of all those who have come to see me, I have only found two who are fools. It seems to me that never have intelligent men been feared in Paris as much as they are today. The inquisition against books is severe; I am informed that the subscribers do not yet have the *Encyclopedic Dictionary*. That is not only being severe; it is being very unjust. If the circulation of this book is stopped, the subscribers will be robbed and the book dealers ruined. I should really like to know what harm a book costing a hundred écus can do. Twenty folio volumes will never create a revolution; the little thirty penny portable books are the ones to be feared. If the Gospel had cost twelve hundred sesterces, the Christian religion would never have been established.

As for me, I have my copy of the *Encyclopédie* due to my status as a foreigner and as a Swiss. The Swiss are allowed to incur damnation, but from what I see the salvation of Parisians is being closely looked after. If you could send me something to end my damnation, you would give me a diabolical pleasure for which I would be very obliged to you. I can no longer work, but I like to amuse myself and want something rousing.

I have to tell you that I have just read Grotius's *De Veritate, etc.*[196] I am quite astonished at the reputation of this man. I scarcely know of a sillier book than his except for the bombastic Houteville.[197] In his time, people acquired reputations cheaply. There is a good article on Hobbes in the *Encyclopédie*. Would to God that this entire work were written like your *Preliminary Discourse*.[198]

Farewell, my very dear philosopher. Will it be said that I shall die without seeing you again?

150. *"France is arriving late, but it is arriving."*

To Joseph-Michel-Antoine Servan.[199] At the Chateau of Ferney. April 13, 1766.

Sir,

The letter with which you honor me is precious for more than one reason. I see the progress which the mind, eloquence and philosophy have made in this century. People did not write this way in the past, and at present the provincial Advocates General are leaving those in the capital very far behind. I have noticed in the Jesuit affair that only in the provinces has anything eloquent been written. In addition, by developing their right judgment people have divested themselves of their prejudices. I am not speaking about Toulouse where fanaticism still prevails and where right judgment is unknown despite literary competitions. But the spirit of youth is beginning to be more receptive even in Toulouse. France is arriving late, but it is arriving. First it fought against the circulation of blood, gravitation, the refraction of light and inoculation. It is finally acknowledging them. We are not ordinarily either profound or bold enough. Our magistrature has certainly dared to combat some papal pretensions, but it has never had the courage to attack them at their source. It is opposed to a few irregularities, but allows an Italian priest to be paid eighty thousand francs so that someone might marry his niece. It tolerates annates. Without complaining, it witnesses subjects of the King assume the title of bishop by permission of the Holy See. Finally, it has accepted a papal bull which is nothing but a monument of insolence and absurdity. It was courageous and fortunate enough to seize the opportunity to expel the Jesuits, but not to prevent monks from receiving novices before the age of thirty. It allows Capuchins and Recollect friars to depopulate the countryside and recruit our young farm laborers.

We are quite inferior to the English on land as on sea, but we must confess that we are learning. Philosophy is bringing about a bright new day. It seems to have filled you with its light. You may be sure that it is doing mankind considerable good. Orpheus, you say, did not soften the stones he made dance. No, but he pacified the tigers: *mulcentem tigris et agentem carmine quercus.*[200] Philosophy causes virtue to be loved by making fanaticism detested, and if I dare say so, it is avenging God for the insults of superstition.

I impatiently await your present of Moses for which I give you my very humble thanks. I suspect that it is a small plagiarism, a theft from the book by Gaulmin printed in Germany a hundred years ago, but surely there will be useful things.[201] The more we delve into antiquity, the more we rediscover the materials with which a strange edifice has been built. Starting with the scapegoat and the red cow and including confession and holy water, you know that everything is pagan. *Sursum corda ite missa est* [202] are the phrases of the mysteries of Ceres. The entire history of Moses was taken word for word from that of Bacchus. We have only been old clothes dealers turning the garments of the ancients inside out.

The small book on preaching is by the Abbé Coyer who wanted to put the Montmorencys and the Chatillons into the shops and who now wants us to have censors instead of preachers or who rather only wants to amuse himself.[203]

I am sending you a little message from the King of Prussia which will not please the ecclesiastical jurisdiction. If you do not have the *Philosophy of History,* I will be honored to get it as well as any little works that may appear into your hands.[204]

I am as much imbued with your memory as I am with your excellence. I do not know whether Grenoble will continue to be the seat of your activities, but you will always ennoble whatever place you go to. I ask you to continue your kindness.

I have the honor of being respectfully, sir, your very humble and very obedient servant.

V.

Forgive a poor sick man if he has been unable to write you in his own hand.

151. *"One is astonished by the progress which human reason has made in so few years."*

To Jean Le Rond D'Alembert. June 26, 1766.

My kind and worthy philosopher,

I have seen good Mords-les [205] who bit them so well. He is by nature one of the truly good who are as gentle as they are courageous. He evidently has the calling of an apostle. By what fate could so many imbecilic fanatics have founded sects of madmen and so many superior minds can scarcely succeed in establishing a small school of reason? Perhaps because they are wise; they lack enthusiasm, activity. All philosophers are too lukewarm; they are content with laughing at the errors of men instead of crushing them. Missionaries run about the earth and over the seas; philosophers must at least run about the streets. They must go and sow the good seed from house to house. One is even more successful with preaching than with the writings of the fathers. Discharge yourself of these two great duties, my dear brother. Preach and write, fight, convert, make the fanatics so hateful and so contemptible that the government will be ashamed to support them.

In the end, those who have earned honor and wealth through a fanatical and persecuting sect will have to content themselves with their advantages, confine themselves to a peaceful enjoyment of life, and rid themselves of the idea of making their errors respectable. They will tell philosophers: "Leave us to our enjoyment and we will leave you to your reasoning." One day people will think in France as they do in England where religion is only looked upon by the parliament as a political affair, but to reach that point, my dear brother, work and time are necessary.

The church of wisdom is beginning to spread in our wards where a dozen years ago the darkest fanaticism prevailed. The provinces are becoming enlightened; young magistrates are thinking loftily; there are Advocates General playing the role of anti-Omers.[206] The book attributed to Fréret and which is perhaps by Fréret is doing a prodigious amount of good.[207] There are many confessors, but I hope there will be no martyrs. There is much ill-natured political interference in Geneva, but I know of no city where there are fewer Calvinists than in this city of Calvin. One is astonished by the progress which human reason has made in so few years. That small professor of nonsense named Vernet is the object of public scorn. His book against you and against the *philosophes* is completely unknown in spite of the alleged third edition. You are certainly aware that the curious letter by Robert Covelle [208] which I sent you is only intended for the meridian of Geneva and to mortify that pedant. He has a brother who is the owner of a small farm on my land at Tournay. He sometimes comes there. I am looking forward to the pleasure of having him pilloried as soon as I recover my health a bit. This is an amusement that philosophers can allow themselves with such priests without being persecutors like them.

It seems to me that all who have written against the *philosophes* get their punishment in this world. The Jesuits have been chased out; Abraham Chaumeix has fled to Moscow; Berthier died of a cold poison; Fréron has been put to shame in every area and Vernet will inevitably be pilloried.[209]

In truth, you ought to punish all those scoundrels with one of those half serious, half amusing books which you are able to write so well. Ridicule overcomes anything. It is the most powerful of weapons, and no one handles it better than you. To laugh while taking vengeance is a great pleasure. If you do not crush the infamous, you have missed your vocation. I can do nothing more. I have little time left to live. I will die laughing, if I can, and loving you for sure.

152. *Voltaire is Incensed by the La Barre Affair.*

To Jean Le Rond D'Alembert. July 18, 1766.

My dear philosopher,

Brother Damilaville has no doubt communicated to you the account from Abbeville.[210] I cannot conceive how thinking human beings can remain in a country of apes who turn so frequently into tigers. For my part, I am even ashamed to be at the frontier. In truth, now is the time to break one's ties and carry the revulsions with which one is filled elsewhere. I have not been successful in obtaining a copy of the lawyer's legal opinion; you have seen it no doubt and shuddered. This is no longer a time for joking; witty words are not what is called for in massacres. What! in Abbeville, Busirises[211] dressed in robes send sixteen year old children to their deaths suffering the most horrible torture! And their sentence is confirmed despite the opinion of ten humane and upright judges! And the nation tolerates it! People barely speak of these things for a moment and then rush on to the Opéra-Comique. Barbarity, grown more insolent by our silence, tomorrow will lawfully slaughter whomever it will, and especially you who will have raised your voice momentarily in opposition. Here Calas is broken on the rack; there Sirven is hanged; elsewhere a lieutenant general is gagged; two weeks later five youngsters are condemned to the stake for some tomfoolery that should have been punished by a stay at the Saint-Lazare house of correction. What matter the *Foreword* of the King of Prussia?[212] Does it bring the slightest remedy to these loathsome crimes? Is this the country of philosophy and refined living? It is the country of the Saint Bartholomew's Day massacre.[213] The Inquisition would not have dared commit what Jansenist judges have just executed. At least send me word, I pray you, as to what people are saying since nothing is being done. It is sorry consolation to learn that monsters are held in abhorrence, but it is the only consolation left to our feeble being and I ask you for it. The Prince of Brunswick[214] is outraged with indignation, anger, and pity. Intensify all these feelings in my heart by two words written in your own hand and sent through the local post to brother Damilaville. Your friendship and that of a few thinking individuals is the only pleasure I can still appreciate.

The mistake of the *Foreword* consists in supposing that these words, *in principio erat,* etc., were tampered with. These are the two passages on the trinity interpolated in the Epistle of John. What a pity all of that! People waste time unearthing errors which might be spent discovering truths.

N.B. The theologian Vernet complained to the Geneva Council that he was being made sport of; the Council offered him an affidavit on his life and morals as to how he had never been a highwayman or even a pickpocket. This last part of the affidavit seemed rather risky.

153. *Further on the La Barre Case.*

To Louise Dorothea of Meiningen, Duchess of Saxe-Gotha. Ferney. August 25, 1766.

Madam,
Allow the family to prostrate itself at your feet and thank Your Serene Highness's beautiful soul with tears of joy and all the emotion of gratitude. Providence rightfully brings hearts like yours into existence while those apes prancing about in Paris are being transformed into wild animals.

Some silly newsletters may have informed you that the Parlement of Paris has condemned five young gentlemen to perish at the stake, but these gazettes have not stated that the only crime perpetrated by these gentlemen was the singing of two eighty-year old songs and not removing their hats before a procession of Capuchin monks. The King of Prussia has informed me that he would have sentenced them to speak to the Capuchins with hats off and to sing some psalms. They were, however, condemned to be burned alive by a majority of fifteen votes to ten in spite of an excellent statement composed on their behalf by eight celebrated Parisian lawyers. There is nothing exaggerated about anything I have the honor of telling you. These unfortunate men were only reprimanded and presented with an allegation of words and indecencies for which two days in jail would have been proper punishment. The eldest of these young men was twenty-one years old. He was the Chevalier de La Barre, who was from an old family, the grandson of a general, and who would have become one himself. He died calmly and courageously like Socrates. Such an abomination is worthy of the twelfth century. The Portuguese inquisition would not be as cruel. When it is a matter of men's lives, fifteen fanatical votes ought not to suffice against ten wise men. It has been alleged that the Parlement of Paris, which is accused daily of sacrificing religion to its hatred of the bishops, wanted to provide a terrible example that would show what good Catholics they were. What a proof of religion! It is no proof of reason and humanity. Only the Chevalier de La Barre was executed; the others fled rather than steep their hands in the blood of their judges. This affair has soon been forgotten in keeping with the spirit of the nation and of most men. People have been to the Opéra-Comique; they have gone to supper with girls from the opera house; they have preached; they have written novels, and so goes the world while at Gotha goodness, equity, and generosity reign.

I place myself at the feet of Your Serene Highness along with Sirven.

V.

154. *On Opera and the Theater.*

To Michel-Paul Gui de Chabanon.[215] December 18, 1767.

My dear child, my dear friend, my dear colleague,

I am not too much of an expert in C G C and F C F. I am hard of hearing, a bit deaf. However, I confess to you that there are tunes in *Pandora*[216] that have given me considerable pleasure. In spite of myself, I remember for example:

Ah! You have grandeur and glory for yourself.

Other tunes have made a great impression on me and still leave a confused noise in my eardrum.

Why do we know Racine's verses by heart? Because they are good. Therefore the music remembered by the ignorant must also be good. People will tell me that everyone knows by heart:

> I call a cat a cat and Rolet a rogue.
> Do you like nutmeg? They've put some everywhere, etc.[217]

These are trivial verses, and yet everyone knows them by heart. I agree that most of Lully's ariettas are trivial tunes and Venetian barcaroles. Therefore, they are not remembered as being good but as being facile. But if one only has taste, one can fix all of poetic art and all four acts of *Armide* in one's memory.[218] Lully's declamation is so perfect a recitative that I recite it entirely by following his notes and by only softening its intentions. Then I have a very great effect on the audience, and no one remains unmoved. Lully's declamation then is in nature. It is adapted to language; it is the expression of feeling.

If this admirable recitative no longer produces the same effect today as in the beautiful age of Louis XIV, it is because we no longer have any actors. They are in short supply in every genre, and besides Lully's ariettas have done his recitative harm and people penalize his recitative for the weaknesses of his symphonies. One must admit that there is considerable arbitrariness in music. All I know is that there are things in M. de La Borde's *Pandora* that have given me extreme pleasure.

I have strong reasons in addition to be attached to *Pandora*. Above all I ask you to do some work behind the scenes, to organize a strong cabal so that they do not eliminate:

> Oh Jupiter, oh inhuman furies!
> Eternal persecutor
> Of misfortune creator, etc.

and not *of the unfortunate* as has been printed. This is very Jansenist, therefore very orthodox at the present time. Those fellows make God the cause of sin, I mean at the opera. This little blasphemy, moreover, is marvelously appropriate in the mouth of Prometheus who, after all, was a very great lord, very much within his rights to tell Jupiter off.

If you receive Jansenists in your academy, everything will be ruined. They will inundate the face of France. I know of no sect that is more dangerous and barbaric. They are worse than Scottish Presbyterians. Commend them to M. d'Alembert so that he may treat these monstrous enemies of reason, the state, and pleasure as they deserve.

I very much pity Mlle. Durancy if it is true that she has a hard voice and soft buttocks. They say that Mlle. Dubois has a very fine arse; [219] she ought to have been satisfied with that advantage and not tamper with my letter so as to make that poor child abandon that bawdy house they call the Comédie Française. This is no scheme for an honorable woman; it's a trick a priest would play. But if she is beautiful, if she is a good actress, we must forgive her for everything. The Duc de Duras [220] has taken note of that little artifice, but he is very indulgent toward beautiful women as one ought to be. He has set up a little school for oratory at Versailles.

May you have actors for your Roman Empire! [221] My concern for your glory is like that of an affectionate father. I will love both you and the fine arts until my dying day. Mama shares my feelings.

V.

155. *Madame Denis Leaves Voltaire.*

To Marie-Louise Denis.[222] Tuesday, March 1, 1768 at 2 o'clock in the afternoon.

Fate doubtlessly exists, and it is often quite cruel. I came to your door three times; you knocked on mine. I tried to take my grief to the garden. It was ten o'clock; I set the needle on the sundial to ten; I waited for you to awaken. I met M. Mallet. He told me that he was distressed by your departure. I thought he was leaving your apartment. I thought you would have dinner at the chateau as you had said. No servant informed me of anything; they all thought I knew. I sent for Christin and Father Adam. We talked until noon. Finally I returned to your apartment; I asked where you were. Wagnière told me: "What! You don't know that she left at ten o'clock!" I turned toward Father Adam more dead than alive. He replied as Wagnière had: "I thought you knew!" I immediately sent to the stable for a horse. No one was there. So in the same house with twenty servants we looked for each other to no avail. I am desperate, and the persistence of my misfortune augurs a rather sinister future for me. I know that the moment of separation would have been horrible, but your leaving without seeing me while we searched for one another is even more horrible. I quickly sent for Mme. Racle to weep with her. She was having dinner with Christin, Adam and her husband, but dinner was rather far from my thoughts. I am tormented and write you. I hope that my letters and the packages for M. de Choiseul and Marmontel will be delivered to you Friday morning by M. Tabareau. I was keeping them all ready. I had still other papers to communicate to you when you left!

Here is another proof, indeed, of the persecutions of my destiny. La Harpe is the cause of my unhappiness.[223] Anyone who would have told me that La Harpe would be the death of me while you were a hundred leagues away would not have been believed. In the end, it has all been proven to be true. Damilaville went to Antoine [224] who resides on the Rue Hautefeuille, that Antoine to whom La Harpe said that he had given a copy of the trifle in question, that Antoine who "had only given him an inaccurate copy on the basis of which he corrected those that La Harpe circulated" (because apparently La Harpe had an accurate copy). Take good note of all this. Antoine replied that La Harpe had lied and did not add very honorable epithets to his name. La Harpe scarcely conducted himself better during his fuss with Dorat. That, in short, is the source of my misfortune. That is what is carrying me to the grave I ordered prepared in Ferney. I will not complain about La Harpe; I will only accuse that destiny which is responsible for everything, and I forgive La Harpe entirely.

You will see Messrs. de Choiseul, de Richelieu, and d'Argental. You will soothe my misfortunes; that is still your destiny. You will be successful with your business and mine in Paris; you will see your brother and nephew again. If I die, I die completely yours; if I live, my life is yours. I embrace M. and Mme. Du Puits affectionately.[225] I love them; I miss them; my heart is broken.

156. *"You have deluded your country into believing that I hold Shakespeare in contempt."*

To the Hon. Horace Walpole.[226] From the Chateau of Ferney in the territory of Gex via Versoix and Lyons. July 15, 1768.

Sir,

I have not dared speak English for forty years, and you speak our language very well. I have seen letters of yours that speak your mind. Besides, my age and maladies do not allow me to write in my own hand. So you will have my thanks in my language.

I have just read the preface to your *History of Richard III;* it seems too short to me. When one is so obviously in the right and adds to one's knowledge so steadfast a philosophy and so virile a style, I should like to be spoken to at greater length. Your father was a great statesman and a good orator, but I doubt if he could have written as you do. You must not say: *Quia pater major me est.*[227]

I have always shared your opinion that we must be wary of all ancient histories. Fontenelle, the only man in the age of Louis XIV who was, at once, a poet, a philosopher and a scholar, used to say that they were admittedly fables, and it must be confessed that Rollin compiled too many visionary tales and contradictions.

After reading the preface to your history, I read the one to your novel.[228] There you make sport of me a little. The French can take a joke, but I am going to answer you seriously.

You have deluded your country into believing that I hold Shakespeare in contempt. I was the first to acquaint the French with Shakespeare; I translated passages from his works forty years ago as well as from Milton, Waller, Rochester, Dryden and Pope. I can assure you that almost no one in France before me was acquainted with English poetry; they had scarcely even heard of

Locke. I was persecuted for thirty years by a host of fanatics for saying that Locke is the Hercules of metaphysics who set the bounds of the human mind.

It was my lot also to be the first to explain to my fellow citizens the discoveries of the great Newton which some fools among us still call systems. I have been your apostle and your martyr. In truth, it is unjust for the English to complain of me.

I said a very long‧time ago that if Shakespeare had come along in the age of Addison, he would have added to his genius the elegance and purity that make Addison estimable. I said "that his genius was his own and that his faults were those of his age." He is, in my opinion, precisely like the Spaniards's Lope de Vega and Calderon. His is a beautiful nature, but savage; no regularity, no propriety, no art, baseness with grandeur, and buffoonery with the terrifying. It is the chaos of tragedy with a hundred flashes of light.

The Italians, who brought about the restoration of tragedy a century before the English and the Spanish, did not fall into the same error. They imitated the Greeks better. There are no clowns in Sophocles's *Oedipus* and *Electra*. I strongly suspect that this vulgarity had its origin with our court fools. We were all a little barbaric as long as we were on this side of the Alps. Every prince had his official jester. Ignorant kings, raised by ignoramuses, could not be aware of the noble pleasures of the mind. They degraded human nature to the extent of paying people for reciting nonsense to them. That is the origin of our *Mère sotte*,[229] and before Molière there was always a court fool in nearly every comedy. That vogue is abominable.

I did say, it is true just as you report, that serious comedies that are masterpieces like the *Misanthrope* do exist, that there are funny ones like *George Dandin*,[230] that the humorous, the serious, and the pitiful can go together very well in the same comedy. I have said that all genres are good except that which bores. Yes, but vulgarity is no genre. "There are many lodgings in my father's house," [231] but I never claimed that it was right to give lodgings in the same room to Charles V and Don Japheth of Armenia, to August and a drunken sailor, to Marcus Aurelius and a street clown. It seems to me that Horace shared the same opinion in the finest of centuries. Look at his *Ars Poetica*. All of

enlightened Europe is of like mind today, and the Spanish are beginning to rid themselves of both poor taste and the Inquisition
at the same moment since intelligence equally proscribes the one
and the other.

You know so well to what extent the trivial and the base
disfigure tragedy that you reproach Racine for making Antiochus
say in *Bérénice:*

> This door is next to her apartment
> And the other leads to the Queen's.[232]

These are certainly not heroic lines, but please observe that they
are in an expository scene which must be simple. This is not poetic
beauty, but a beauty of precision which determines the setting,
suddenly informs the spectator of what has happened, and notifies
him that all the characters will appear in the study adjacent to
the other apartments. Otherwise it would be completely improbable for Titus, Bérénice and Antiochus to be constantly speaking
in the same room.

"Let the setting of the scene be fixed and marked," said the
wise Despréaux, the oracle of good taste, in his *Poetic Art* which
is at least the equal of Horace's. Our excellent Racine almost never
violated that rule, and it is a thing worthy of admiration that
Athalie appears in the temple of the Jews and in the same place
that the high priest was seen with no offense to verisimilitude
whatsoever.

You will be even more forgiving of the famous Racine when
you recall that the play *Bérénice* was in a way the story of Louis
XIV and your English princess, the sister of Charles II.[233] They
were both living on the same floor in Saint-Germain with a salon
separating their apartments.

You unrestrained Britons neither observe unity of place, unity
of time, nor unity of action. In truth your results are no better for
that. Verisimilitude must have some value. Because of it art becomes more difficult, and obstacles that have been mastered provide
pleasure and pride in every genre.

However much of an Englishman you may be, let me side

somewhat with my country. I try to set her right so often that it is really fair if I caress her when I think she is right. Yes, I believed in the past, I now believe, and I will believe in the future that Paris is much superior to Athens in the matter of tragedies and comedies. Molière and even Regnard [234] seem to me to prevail over Aristophanes, just as Demosthenes prevails over our lawyers. I will tell you unhesitatingly that all Greek tragedies seem to me like the works of schoolboys in comparison with the sublime scenes of Corneille and the perfect tragedies of Racine. That was Boileau's way of thinking, however much of an admirer he may have been of the Ancients. He had no difficulty writing beneath Racine's portrait that this great man had surpassed Euripides and served as a corrective to Corneille.

Yes, I think it has been demonstrated that there are many more men of good taste in Paris than there were in Athens because there are more than thirty thousand persons in Paris whose sole concern is with the fine arts, and in Athens there were not ten thousand; because the lower classes of Athenians attended spectacles, but such is not the case with us; because those of us who are judges of the fine arts are scarcely concerned with anything else; because our continual relationships with women have added much more refinement to our feelings, more propriety to our manners, and more finesse to our taste. Leave us be with our theater; let the Italians have their *favole boscarecie;* [235] you are wealthy enough in other respects.

It is true that some very bad plays, barbarously written and with ridiculous plots, have been supported by cliques, partisan attitudes, fashion, or the temporary backing of persons of repute, and do achieve phenomenal success in Paris for a time. But in a very few years, the illusion disappears, the cliques pass, and the truth survives.

Let me add another word on the subject of rhyme for which you chide us. Almost all of Dryden's plays are in rhyme; it is an added obstacle to be mastered. Those lines of his that are remembered and quoted by everyone are rhymed, and I further maintain that since *Cinna, Athalie, Phèdre* and *Iphigénie* are in rhyme, anyone who would try to remove this yoke in France would be considered a feeble artist without the strength to bear it.

As an old man, I must tell you an anecdote. One day, I

asked Pope why Milton had not put his poem into rhyme while other poets were rhyming theirs in imitation of the Italians. He answered: "Because he could not."

I have told you everything on my mind. I admit that I erred grossly when I did not notice that the Earl of Leicester was first named Dudley, but if the fancy takes you to go to the House of Lords and change your name, I will always remember the name of Walpole with the most respectful esteem.

Before my letter was sent off, I had time to read your *Richard III*. You would be an excellent attorney general. You weigh all the probabilities, but it seems you have a secret inclination for that hunchback. You wish he were a handsome fellow and even a ladies' man. The Benedictine Calmet [236] wrote a dissertation to prove that Jesus Christ had a very handsome face. I would like to share your belief that Richard III was neither as ugly nor as wicked as people say, but I would not like to have had any dealings with him. Your white rose and your red rose had terrible thorns for the country:

Those gratious kings are all a pak of rogues.[237]

In truth, when you read the history of the Yorks, the Lancasters and many others, you think you are reading a history of highwaymen. As for your Henry VII, he was only a pickpocket.

Be a minister or an anti-minister, a lord or a philosopher, I will be with an equal respect

S^r y^r most humb. ob^t serv^t

Voltaire

Be so kind as to tell me frankely if Jumonville was assassinated near the river called Oyo.[238]

157. *Against Atheism.*

To Jean-François Dufour, Seigneur de Villevieille. Ferney. August 26, 1768.

My dear marquis,

I am expecting you in the month of September. You are enough of a philosopher to come and share my solitude. Ferney is right on the road to Nancy. In the meantime, I must compliment you for not being an atheist. Your predecessor,[239] the Marquis de Vauvenargues, was not one, and whatever some present-day scholars may say, one can be a very good philosopher and still believe in God. Atheists have never responded to the objection that a clock proves the existence of a clockmaker, and Spinoza himself admits an intelligence presiding over the universe. He is in agreement with Virgil:

Mens agitat molem et magno se corpore miscet.[240]

When the poets are on your side, your position is really strong. Consider La Fontaine when he speaks about the child given birth to by a nun. He says: "But after all he did not produce himself." [241]

I have just read a new book on the *Existence of God* by a certain Bullet, Dean of the University of Besançon. This dean is a scholar and treads in the footsteps of the Swammerdams, Nieuwentijdts and Derhams.[242] But he is an old soldier subject to panic and fear. He is completely put to fright by the atheists's great argument that if one casts the letters of the alphabet from a dice box, chance can produce the *Aeneid* within a given number of throws. To produce the first word *arma,* only twenty-four throws are necessary, and to produce *arma virumque* only one hundred twenty million are required. This is a trifle, and in an infinite number of billions of centuries one could finally achieve what one sought in an infinite number of chances. Thus, in an infinite number of centuries, the odds are one against an infinity of ciphers that the world could have been created completely by itself.

I do not see how M. Bullet could have been overwhelmed by this argument. All he had to do was reply, without taking fright, that the probability of the existence of a creative God is infinite and that the odds favoring you gentlemen are only one at the very most. Now decide whether chance does not favor my position.

Besides the mechanism of the world is something much more complicated than the *Aeneid*. Two *Aeneids* together will not produce a third, whereas two creatures endowed with life produce a third creature which in turn produces others, which stupendously increases the advantage of the wager.

Would you really believe that an Irish Jesuit has furnished weapons lately to atheistic philosophy by claiming that animals were produced all by themselves? That Jesuit Needham, in the guise of a layman who thought he was a chemist and an observer, fancied that he had produced eels with flour and mutton juice.[243] He even carried the illusion so far that he thought these eels immediately produced others like the children of Punchinello and Madame Gigogne.[244] Now another madman named Maupertuis immediately adopted this system and added it to his other methods which include digging a hole to the center of the earth to determine its weight, dissecting heads of giants to gain familiarity with the soul, waxing sick people with resin to cure them, and bringing his soul to a state of exaltation so that he might see the future as he does the present. May God preserve us from such atheists. This last gentleman was inflated with a ferocious, persecuting and vilifying pride. He caused me considerable harm. I pray God to forgive him, assuming God might intervene in disputes between Maupertuis and myself.

What is worse I have just seen a very good translation of Lucretius with very scholarly remarks in which the author cites the alleged experiments of the Jesuit Needham in order to prove that animals can be produced from decay. If these gentlemen had known Needham was a Jesuit, they would have been wary of his eels and would have said:

Latet anguis in herba.[245]

In the end, Mr. Spallanzani, Europe's best observer, had to demonstrate the evident falsehood of that imbecile Needham's experiments. I have compared him with Malacrais de la Vigne, the fat, nasty customs official in Croisic, Brittany who deluded the wits of Paris into believing that he was a pretty girl prettily composing verse.

My dear marquis, there is nothing good in atheism. That is a very bad system both physically and morally. An upright man may very well rebel against superstition and fanaticism; he may detest superstition; he does mankind a service if he spreads the humane principles of toleration. But what service can he render if he spreads atheism? Will men be any more virtuous for not recognizing a God who prescribes virtue? Doubtlessly not. I want princes and their ministers to recognize a God, even one who punishes and forgives. Without that restraint, I consider them like ferocious animals who, indeed, will not devour me after they have had a big meal and are gently digesting it on a sofa with their mistresses, but who certainly would devour me if they found me by chance beneath their claws when they were hungry. And they would not even think they had done something wrong. They will not even remember in the slightest that they had had me between their jaws when they have other victims. Atheism was very common in Italy in the fifteenth and sixteenth centuries. And what horrible crimes at the court of Alexander VI, Julius II and Leo X! The pontifical throne and the church were beset with pillage, assassinations and poisonings. Only fanaticism produced more crimes.

The most fruitful sources of atheism are, in my opinion, theological disputes. Most men only reason half-way, and the number of those who are in error is infinite. A theologian says: "All I have ever heard and said in school is nonsense. Therefore my religion is ridiculous. Now my religion is without contradiction the best of them all. The best is worthless; therefore there is no God." This is an abominable way of reasoning. I would say rather: "Therefore there is a God who will punish theologians and especially theologians who persecute."

I know full well that I would not have convinced Le Tellier, the Norman from Vire, that there is a God who punishes tyrants, vilifiers and forgers who serve as confessors to kings.[246] As a

278

reply to my arguments, the rascal would have had me put in a dungeon. I will not persuade a judge who is a scoundrel, a barbarian who is avid for human blood and who deserves the punishment of death at the hands of the hangmen he employs, of the existence of a rewarding and avenging God. But I will persuade righteous persons, and if that is an error it is the most beautiful of errors.

Come to my convent. Come and reoccupy your old cell. I will tell you the adventure of a priest upon whom high position had been conferred and whom I regard, practically speaking, as an atheist since he did the opposite of what he teaches and dared to use the most cowardly and foul slander against me with the King. The King made sport of him, and the monster is worse off for his infamy. I will tell you other anecdotes. We will reason, and above all I will tell you how dearly I hold you in affection.

V.

158. *"Society has become so well perfected that nothing more can be read without permission of the syndical chamber of booksellers."*

To Chevalier Jacques de Rochefort d'Ally.[247] November 2, 1768.

Sir,

The dead man has come to life again for a moment to tell you that if he were to live for an eternity, he would hold you in affection for all that time. He is gratified by your generosity. Two additional large cheeses have arrived for him through your munificence. If he were healthy, he would find his fate much preferable to that of the rat who retired from the world into a Dutch cheese.[248] But when one is old and sick, all one can do is put up with life and hide.

I sent you four volumes of *The Age of Louis XIV and Louis XV*. But in France cheese arrives by coach with much greater certainty than do books. I think all of your influence will be required for the clerks at the customs house of thoughts to deliver the account of the battle of Fontenoy and the capture of Minorca to you. Society has become so well perfected that nothing more can be read without permission of the syndical chamber of booksellers.

They say a famous Jansenist has proposed an edict by which all the *philosophes* will be prohibited from speaking except in the presence of two deputies from the Sorbonne who will provide an account at the *prima mensis* of everything uttered in Paris in the course of the month.

As for myself, I think it would be much more useful and suitable *to cut off their right hands* to prevent them from writing and *to tear out their tongues* lest they speak. It is an excellent precaution that has already been used and which has done considerable honor to our nation. That little preventive has even been tried with success in Abbeville on the grandson of a lieutenant general. But these are only palliatives. My judgment would be to have a St. Bartholomew's massacre of all the *philosophes* and slaughter in their beds anyone possessing Locke, Montaigne or Bayle in their libraries. I should even want them to burn all books except the *Ecclesiastical Gazette* and the *Christian Journal.*

I will not give up my solitude until I see those happy days when thought is banished from the world and men have reached the noble state of brutes. As long as I have thoughts and feelings, however, you may be sure that I will be affectionately devoted to you. If there were a St. Bartholomew's massacre of those with just and noble ideas, you would surely be one of the first to be slaughtered. In the meantime, continue your kindnesses to me. I place myself at the feet of Madame de Rochefort.

[The final years of Voltaire's life repeat what had become a persistent pattern for the feverishly energetic octogenarian; almost ceaseless literary activity, a humane commitment to bettering the lot of his fellow man by personal engagement, and a refusal to become complacent about human existence. His final writings—varied and plentiful as always—are not much read today, but they reflect the concerns of his day. Among these were the History of the Parlement of Paris *(1769) in which he demonstrated the urgent need for reforming this basic judicial institution of the ancien régime; various editions of the* Reason by Alphabet *(1769-1776) and the* Questions on the Encyclopédie *(1769-1772) which were augmented versions of the* Philosophical Dictionary; *a commentary on the seventeenth-century philosopher Malebranche called* All in God

[Tout en Dieu] *(1769) whose purpose was to demonstrate the fallacies and unsoundness of Christianity; a verse satire on metaphysical systems,* Les Systèmes *(1772); an interesting autobiographical work, the* Historical Commentary on the Works of the Author of the Henriade *(1776); a critical work on the Bible,* The Bible Finally Explained *(1776); an extensive commentary on Montesquieu, the* Commentary on the Spirit of the Laws *(1777), and a metaphysical essay,* The Dialogues of Euhemerus *[Dialogues d'Evhémère] (1777). In his eighty-fourth and final year, Voltaire was even involved in the casting and rehearsal of his last play* Irène *(1777).*

Despite this obvious energy, the letters of his last years do convey the pathos of an aging man whose body was given over progressively to greater suffering. The letters of these years repeatedly bear the signature: The Sick Old Man of Ferney. *And yet despite his desire, often expressed, to die in tranquillity, he remained involved. He wrote to Catherine the Great offering advice on the conduct of her war with the Turks; he gave his assistance to the watchmakers of Geneva; he received countless visitors at Ferney; he encouraged and helped, in a practical way, craftsmen and laborers to settle at Ferney. He was ebullient at the naming of Turgot to the post of comptroller-general in 1774 and expressed his approval of Turgot's plans for reform (which corresponded to some of Voltaire's own economic ideas). When Turgot's efforts were defeated by a powerful establishment, some of whose special privileges were at stake, and he was dismissed from office in May 1776, Voltaire wrote expressing his anguish and his fears for the future of France. He also remained involved in another notorious case of injustice, that of the Comte de Lally, an officer in charge of a French expeditionary force in India who had been obliged to surrender to the English at Pondichéry in 1761, was held responsible for the French defeat there and finally put to death by the French in 1766 after imprisonment in the Bastille. Voltaire's campaign to rehabilitate the name of Lally was pursued to the end of his life, and his very last letter dated May 26, 1778, just four days before his death, expresses his joy at the news that this act of injustice had been remedied at last.*

After the long years of exile from the city of his birth, Voltaire returned to Paris on February 19, 1778 and stayed in a house on the corner of the Rue de Beaune and the Quai des Théatins (now the Quai Voltaire) that was owned by the Marquis Duplessis-Villette. He, of course, became the object of tremendous public attention and was honored by both the Académie Française and the Théâtre Français, two Parisian institutions with which he had long been associated. Among the many visitors to the house on the Rue de Beaune during the final three months of Voltaire's life were Diderot, Gluck and the American diplomat Benjamin Franklin. In poor health and overcome by physical suffering, Voltaire became bedridden on May 11, 1778 and died on May 30 between eleven o'clock and midnight in his eighty-fourth year.]

159. *"I consider Racine unquestionably the best of our tragic poets, the only one who has spoken both to the heart and to reason. . . ."*

To Aleksandr Petrovich Sumarokov.[249] At the Chateau of Ferney. February 26, 1769.

Sir,

Your letter and your works are great proof that genius and taste belong to all countries. Those who have said that Poetry and Music were limited to the temperate climates were quite mistaken. If climate exercised such a powerful effect, Greece would still be producings Platos and Anacreons as it produces the same fruits and flowers; Italy would have Horaces, Virgils, Ariostos and Tassos. But Rome now only has processions and Greece only bastinadoes. Sovereigns who care for the arts, who are familiar with them, and who encourage them are therefore absolutely essential. They change the climate; they breed roses in the midst of snow.

Such are the accomplishments of your incomparable sovereign. I might think the letters with which she honors me come from Versailles and that yours is from a colleague in the Académie Française. Prince Kozlovsky [250] who delivered her letters and yours to me expresses himself as you do, and that is what I have admired about all the Russian lords who have come to see me in my retreat. You have a stupendous advantage over me; I do not know one word of your language but you possess mine perfectly.

282

I am going to answer all your questions which, though couched in a pretense of doubt, reveal your point of view rather well. I take pride in saying that I agree with you in every respect.

Yes, I consider Racine unquestionably the best of our tragic poets, the only one who has spoken both to the heart and to reason, the only one who has been truly sublime without pomposity, and who has provided diction with a charm previously unknown. He is still the only one who has treated love in a tragic manner because prior to him Corneille had only really expressed that passion in the *Cid* and the *Cid* is not by him. Love is either ridiculous or insipid in almost all his other plays.

Moreover, I share your opinion of Quinault.[251] He is a great man in his genre. He could not have written the *Poetic Art,* but then Boileau could not have written *Armide.*

I subscribe entirely to everything you say about Molière and the *comédie larmoyante* [252] which, to our national disgrace, has become the successor to the only truly comic genre that had been perfected by the inimitable Molière.

Since the time of Regnard, who was born with a truly comic genius and who alone has come near Molière, we have only had sorts of monsters. Authors incapable of even writing a good joke tried to produce comedies merely to earn money. They lacked the intellectual strength to write tragedy; they lacked the gaiety to write comedy; they could not even create a valet on the stage with the proper speech. They presented tragic adventures under bourgeois titles. It is said that these plays have some interest and hold one's attention sufficiently when they are performed well. That may be. I have never been able to read them, but they claim comedies do create illusions. These bastard plays are neither tragedies nor comedies. When you have no horses, you are only too happy to be dragged by mules.

I have not seen Paris for twenty years. People have informed me that Molière's plays were no longer being performed there. The reason, in my opinion, is that everyone knows them by heart; almost all the sallies in his plays have become proverbs. Besides there are tedious passages; the plots are sometimes weak and the dénouements rarely ingenious. His only aim was to portray nature, and without a doubt he was the greatest painter of nature.

283

This is my profession of faith which you requested. I am sorry that poor health is what we both have in common. Happily you are younger and will honor your nation longer. As for myself, I am already dead for my country.

I have the honor of being with the infinite esteem that I owe you, sir, your very humble and very obedient servant.

Voltaire

160. *"Farewell to beautiful verse; farewell to feelings of the heart; farewell to everything."*

To Charles-Augustin Feriol, Count d'Argental. October 13, 1769.

My dear angel,

I should have sent you condolences sooner on your sad trip to Orangis.[253] I would have asked you what Orangis is, to whom it belongs, whether there is a beautiful theatre there, but I have been in a state sadder than yours. Imagine snow falling around here on the first of October. Suddenly I had travelled from Naples to Siberia. This has not repaired my old and listless machine. People will tell me that I must be used to these changes after fifteen years, but it is precisely because I have experienced them for fifteen years that I can no longer tolerate them. People will tell me still: "It serves you right, George."[254] George has the same answer others do: "I was beguiled; I made a mistake; I was dazzled by the most beautiful view in the world. I am suffering. I am sorry. That is the way the human race is."

If men were wise, they would always place themselves in the sun and flee the north wind like their worst enemy. Look at dogs. They always get into the corner of the hearth, and when there is a ray of sunshine they rush to it. La Motte,[255] who lived on your quay, used to be transported in a chair along the carriage road adjacent to the gallery of the Louvre from ten in the morning until midday, and there he was gently baked by a reflector.

I am afraid Madame d'Argental's maladies come in part from your exposure to the north. Haven't you ever noticed that all the inhabitants of the Quai des Orfèvres have ruddy faces and the plumpness of a canon, and those who live two dozen feet behind on the Quai des Morfondus almost all look like the excommuni-cated.[256]

Enough talk about the north wind which I detest and is the death of me.

You have doubtlessly seen *Hamlet*. Ghosts are going to become fashionable. I started them on their career in a modest way.[257] Now people are going to rush toward them full speed: *domandavo aqua non tempesta*.[258] I tried to bring a little life to the theatre by introducing more action, and now everything is action and pantomime. Nothing is so sacred that it is not abused. We are going to lapse into the extravagant and the gigantic in all things. Farewell to beautiful verse; farewell to feelings of the heart; fare-well to everything. Music will soon be nothing more than an Italian din, and theatrical plays nothing more than conjurers's tricks. They wanted to improve everything, but everything has degenerated. I am also degenerating like everyone else. However, I have dis-patched to my friend La Borde the little modification I had sent you for *Pandora*, slightly embellished. I confess that I hold *Pandora* in great affection because Jupiter is absolutely in the wrong, and I find incorporating philosophy into opera extremely amusing. If *Pandora* is performed, you could carry me in a litter to that spec-tacle. But *sic vos non vobis mellificatis apes*.[259]

I have sometimes given pleasures to Paris that I have not ex-perienced myself. I have worked for others and not for myself. In truth nothing is more noble.

I believe I sent you two petitions for the Duc de Praslin. Again it is not for me. I am no sailor which really annoys me. On a ship, I am a dying man. Otherwise wouldn't I have gone to China more than thirty years ago to forget all the persecution I have suffered in Paris and because of which I still grieve?

A thousand affectionate respects to Madame d'Argental.

By the way, if everything about me has fallen into decay, my affectionate devotion to you has not.

161. *Voltaire's Body and Soul in Disrepair.*

To Suzanne Necker.[260] Ferney. May 21, 1770.

Proper modesty and reason made me think, at first, that the idea of a statue was a good joke, but since the thing is serious, let me also speak to you seriously.

I am seventy-six years old and have scarcely recovered from a serious illness that treated my body and soul rather poorly for six weeks. M. Pigalle [261] is to come, people say, and take a mold of my face. But someone would have to supply me with a face; you would scarcely guess where mine is. My eyes are set in three inches; my cheeks consist of some old parchment badly pasted to bones clinging to nothing. The few teeth I had are gone. I am not being coy when I tell you this; it is the unadulterated truth. Never has a poor man been sculpted in this state. M. Pigalle would think people had made sport of him, and as for myself, I am so proud that I would never dare appear in his presence. If he wishes to conclude this strange adventure, I would advise him to take his model more or less from the little Sèvres porcelain figure. What difference does it make for posterity, after all, whether a block of marble resembles one man or another? I remain very philosophical about this business. But since I am even more grateful than philosophical, I give you the same power over the remains of my body as you have over those of my soul. Both are in great disorder, but my heart is yours, madam, as though I were a man of twenty-five, and all of this with very sincere respect.

V.

My obeisance, I pray you, to M. Necker.

162. *Voltaire Helps the Watchmakers of Geneva.*

To the French Ambassadors. At the Chateau of Ferney, the Territory of Gex in Burgundy by Versoix. June 5, 1770.

Sir,
I beg to inform Your Excellency that since the bourgeois of Geneva have unfortunately murdered some of their compatriots,

286

several families of good watchmakers have taken refuge on a small piece of land that I own in the territory of Gex,[262] and since the Duc de Choiseul has placed them under the protection of the King, I have been fortunate in enabling them to exercise their talents. They are the best artisans in Geneva. They work in every style and at a price more moderate than that of any other manufacturing establishment. They create in enamel any portrait with which one may wish to adorn a watchcase and with great promptness. They deserve the protection of Your Excellency all the more since they have great respect for the Catholic religion. I pray Your Excellency, under the patronage of the Duc de Choiseul, to favor them either by giving them your orders or by condescending to have them recommended to the most accredited merchants.

I beg you to forgive the liberty I am taking out of consideration for the advantage that will result for the kingdom.

I have the honor of being very respectfully, sir, the very humble and obedient servant of Your Excellency.

Voltaire, Gentleman
Ordinary of the
King's Chamber

163. *"The worst of French Poets and Philosophers is almost dying."*

To William Jones.[263] 1770.

The worst of French Poets and Philosophers is almost dying: Age and Sickness have brought him to his last day: he can see and converse with no body: he desires Mr Jones to excuse and to pity him; he makes him his most humble respect.

164. *Some Advice to Catherine the Great.*

To Catherine II, Empress of Russia. Ferney. July 20, 1770.

Madam,

Your letter of June 6, which I suspect is in the new style,[264] shows me that Your Imperial Majesty is taking pity on my passion for her. You provide me with consolations, but you also inspire me with fear so as to keep your worshipper in suspense. My consolations are your victories, and my fear is that Your Majesty will make peace next winter.

I believe the news from Greece occasionally comes to us by way of Marseilles a bit sooner than it reaches Your Majesty through couriers. According to this news, the Turks have been beaten four times and all of the Peloponnesus is yours.[265]

If Ali-Bey [266] has indeed seized Egypt, as people say, that means two large horns snatched away from the Turkish crescent. And the star of the north is certainly much more powerful than their moon. Why then make peace when you can extend your conquests so far?

Your Majesty will tell me that my thinking is not sufficiently philosophical and that peace is the greatest good. No one is more convinced than I of this truth, but let me ardently hope that this peace will be signed by you in Constantinople. I am persuaded that if you win one rather decent battle on either side of the Danube, your troops will be able to march straight to the capital.

The Venetians must certainly use the occasion to their advantage; they have vessels and some troops. When they took Morea,[267] they were only aided by the diversion of the Emperor in Hungary. Today they have much more powerful support. It seems to me this is no time to hesitate. Mustafa must ask for your forgiveness and the Venetians must ask you for laws.

My fear is still that the Christian princes or so-called are jealous of the star of the north. These are secrets which I am not permitted to fathom. I fear, in addition, that your finances will be put in disarray by your very victories, but I believe those of Mustafa are in greater disorder because of his defeats. It is said that Your Majesty is floating a loan with the Dutch. The Padishah Turk [268] will not be able to borrow from anyone, and this is another advantage Your Majesty has over him.

I pass from my fears to my consolations. If you make peace, I am very sure that it will be a very glorious one, that you will hold on to Moldavia, Walachia, Azov and the navigation on the Black Sea, at least until Trebizond. But what will become of my poor Greeks? What will become of the new legions of Sparta? You will doubtless renew the Isthmian games during which the

288

Romans assured the Greeks of their freedom by public decree, and this will be the most glorious act of your life. But how can the strength of this decree be preserved if no troops remain in Greece? I should like, moreover, for the course of the Danube and navigation on this river along Walachia, Moldavia and even Bessarabia to be under your control. I do not know whether I am asking for too much or not enough. This decision and whether to have a medal stamped eternalizing your successes and good deeds will be up to you. Then Thomyris [269] will be transformed into Solon and will make her laws complete wholly at her leisure. These laws will be the finest monument in Europe and Asia, for in every other state they are created after the event like ships being calked after they spring leaks. The laws are innumerable because they are created according to needs that constantly rearise. They are contradictory since these needs have always changed. They are very poorly drafted because they have almost always been written by pedants under barbaric governments. They are like our cities which are built haphazardly and irregularly and jumbled with palaces and huts in narrow and tortuous streets.

Finally, may Your Majesty provide laws to countries within a distance of two thousand leagues after you have boxed Mustafa's ears.

These are the consolations of the old hermit who will be filled, until his dying day, with the deepest respect, the most legitimate admiration, and limitless devotion for Your Imperial Majesty.

165. *Voltaire at Seventy-Seven.*

To Marc-René de Voyer de Paulmy, Marquis d'Argenson. Ferney. December 14, 1770.

Sir,

I think I have informed you that I am seventy-seven years old; that I suffer eleven out of twelve hours a day or thereabouts; that I go blind as soon as the wilderness I live in is covered with snow; that since I have set up establishments for manufacturing watches all around my tomb in my little village where the people are hungry for bread despite the *Ephémérides du citoyen*,[270] I find I am overcome by the ills of others even more than by my own; that I very rarely have the strength and the time to write, even less to be able to philosophize. I will tell you what Saint-Evremond replied to Waller as he was dying and Waller asked him what he thought about eternal truths and eternal lies: "Mr. Waller, you take too great advantage of me." [271]

I am about in the same situation with you. You are as intelligent as Waller; I am almost as old as Saint-Evremond and do not know as much about these things as he.

Amuse yourself looking for everything I have sought in vain for sixty years. It is a great pleasure to put one's thoughts down on paper, to understand them very clearly, and to illuminate others while illuminating oneself.

I flatter myself that I am not like those old people who are afraid to be taught by men just out of their youth. I welcome a truth today with great joy since I am condemned to die tomorrow.

Continue making your vassals happy and instructing your old servants. But to discuss with you by correspondence things over which Aristotle, Plato, Saint Thomas, and Saint Bonaventura came a cropper is certainly something I will not do. I prefer to tell you that I am a lazy old man who is devoted to you with the most affectionate respect and with all his heart.

V.

166. *"I have been persecuted enough. I want to die in peace."*

To Louis-François Armand du Plessis, Duc de Richelieu. Ferney. February 18, 1771.

Yes, my hero, I confess. I laughed a little when you sent me news that you had the gout. But do you really know why I laughed? Because I have it too. I thought it quite amusing that after sharing your way of thinking on almost all matters and having the same ideas, I would also have the same sensations. God made me so that I might be reformed after your example. It is really a shame that I am always so far from you, that I am a planet so distant from the center of my orbit.

D'Argens has just died in Toulon. Now I am the only one of your old servants left who has been scoffed at either by you or by kings. I am also very much scoffed at by nature now. My blood-shot eyes are absolutely blinded by the snow at the very moment I write you.

I am passing through my seventy-eighth year now, and you are a young man close to seventy-five. Now, unless I am mistaken, is the time to reflect on the vanities of this world. The few days I have left to live and the twenty some odd years that remain for you are not that much of a difference.

I laugh at the follies of this world even more than at the gout. But I do not laugh one bit when my hero berates me, in accordance with his praiseworthy habit, for not sending him some books or others printed in Holland that he spoke to me about. Did he want me to send them by post so that the package would be opened, seized and carried off somewhere else? Did he provide me with an address? Did he furnish me with the wherewithal? Is he unaware that I am neither in Prussia, Russia, Sweden, Denmark, England, Holland nor in the north of Germany where men enjoy the right of being able to read and write?

Has he forgotten the poor apothecary boy who was whipped two years ago, branded with a scalding *fleur de lis*, and condemned to the galleys for life by *Messieurs* and who died of grief the following day, with his wife and daughter, for selling a mediocre comedy in Paris called *The Vestal* which had been printed with tacit approval? [272]

Have you forgotten that one of the most horrible crimes mentioned in the trial of the Chevalier de La Barre was that he had some so-called prohibited books in his study, which, together with the detestable act of not removing his hat in the rain before a procession of Capuchin friars, impelled the king's guardians to have his wrist cut off, to cut out his tongue, and to have his head thrown into the flames on one side and his body on the other?

Didn't you know, my hero, that among these Welches for whom you fought under Louis XIV and Louis XV for sixty years there are wild animals bent on devouring mankind as well as apes busying themselves turning somersaults?

I have been persecuted enough. I want to die in peace. Thank God I am not writing any books since that is such a dangerous occupation. I am finishing out my years at the foot of the Jura, and I would go to the foot of the Caucasus to die if I were persecuted again. I would have preferred making merry with you at Richelieu, but my hero cannot transport philosophy that far. He will be in the bustle of things until the age of ninety like the Duc d'Epernon[273] who was not his equal. Every individual must fulfill his destiny.

I thank you very affectionately for favoring M. Gaillard[274] who deserves it.

I believe your gout to be as unburdensome as your brilliant imagination. It isn't possible, with your bathing almost every day, for your attack to be very violent and painful. Mine is also a trifle, but my eyes, my eyes, that is what crushes me. I do not conceive how Mme. Du Deffand can be so gay and so sprightly after losing her sight. May God preserve those two eyes of yours that have done so much ogling and been ogled at so much! May God preserve all the rest for you! Do not chide your old servant, who certainly does not deserve it, any more.

Do you remember Couratin who was always in the wrong with you whatever he might do?

Allow me to place myself at the feet of the Countess of Egmont.[275]

The Old Hermit

167. *The Trials and Consolations of Old Age.*

To Philip Dormer Stanhope, 4th Earl of Chesterfield.[276] At the Chateau of Ferney, near Geneva. September 24, 1771.

The Earl of Huntingdon[277] did me the honor of coming to my hermitage. I did not write you; I was too occupied listening to him. I seek my consolation for his departure by writing to thank you for commending him to me. He pleased me by speaking about you at length. I asked him especially for news about you rather than for information about your aldermen and sheriffs and all such annoyances.

Enjoy an honorable and happy old age after having been

subjected to life's trials. Enjoy your intellectual faculties and keep healthy physically. Of the five senses which are our lot, only one of yours has become enfeebled, and Milord Huntingdon assures me your stomach is good which is certainly as valuable as a pair of ears. I might be the right person to decide which is saddest: to be deaf, to be blind, or to have no digestion. I can be a judge of these three conditions with full knowledge. But for a long time, I have not ventured to make decisions about trivia and with greater reason about things that are so important. I simply believe that if there is sunshine in the beautiful house you built, you will have some tolerable moments. That is all one can hope for at our age. Cicero wrote a beautiful treatise on old age, but he did not substantiate his book with the facts; his last years were very unhappy. You have lived longer and more happily than he. You have not had to deal with either perpetual dictators or triumvirs. Your lot has been and still is one of the most desirable in this great lottery where winning tickets are so rare and where the first prize of continual happiness has not yet been drawn by anybody. Your philosophy has never been disordered by fantasies that have occasionally set rather good minds into confusion. You were never a charlatan nor a charlatan's dupe in any respect, and I consider this a very unusual merit that contributes to the shadow of bliss which we are able to enjoy in this short life.

Receive my sincere and useless wishes with kindness and my regrets for being unable to spend a few of my days beside you with affectionate and respectful devotion.

The sick old man of Ferney, V.

168. *Voltaire Sends Wishes of Prosperity to Goldoni.*

To Carlo Goldoni.[278] Ferney. April 4, 1772.

A sick old man of seventy-eight, almost blind, has just received by way of Geneva the charming phenomenon of a very gay, very purely written, very moral French comedy composed by an Italian. This Italian was made to provide models of good taste for every country. The sick old man had already read this pleasant work. He thanks the author with the greatest feeling, and not knowing his abode he addresses his letter in care of his publisher. He wishes Mr. Goldoni all the prosperity he deserves.

V.

169. *". . . there is nothing so extraordinary in the entire world as Your Majesty. . . ."*

To Catherine II, Empress of Russia. Ferney. August 28, 1772.

Madam,

Forgive me. Your Imperial Majesty is not only my patroness, but she instructs me. She was kind enough to disabuse me of some French errors concerning Siberia. She allows me to question.

I therefore take the liberty of asking her whether it is true that there exists in Siberia a species of completely white heron with wings and a tail of a fire-like color and particularly whether it is true that by the Peace of Prut [279] Peter the Great was obliged to send one of these birds with a diamond necklace every year to the Porte. Our books say that you call this bird *kratsshot* and the Turks *chungar*.

I strongly doubt whether Your Imperial Majesty will pay a tribute of chungar and diamonds to Lord Mustafa in the future. The gazettes say that she has bought a diamond valued at approximately three million in Amsterdam. I hope that Mustafa will pay for this gem by signing the treaty of peace, if he knows how to write.

Your extreme indulgence has accustomed me to the boldness of questioning an empress. That is not usual, but, in truth, there is nothing so extraordinary in the entire world as Your Majesty at whose feet the sick old man of Ferney places himself with the deepest respect.

170. *"I am overwhelmed by suffering. Pity me."*

To Gabriel Cramer. 1772-1773.

My dear friend,

I am in despair. I was so horribly sick all night that I will not be able to leave my bed all day. I am incapable of pleasure. I really beg Madame Cramer's forgiveness. Today I am deprived of both wit and music. I am overwhelmed by suffering. Pity me.

I am very pleased with friend Panckoucke.[280] It was a misunderstanding.

Monday morning.

171. *On Corneille and Racine.*

To Jean-François de La Harpe. Ferney. January 22, 1773.

My dear friend, my dear successor,

Your eulogy of Racine is almost as beautiful as that of Fénelon, and your notes are superior to both. Your very eloquent discourse on the author of *Télémaque* [281] earned you a few enemies. Your notes on Racine are so judicious, so consummate in taste, finesse, strength and warmth that they may very well bring you further reproach. But your critics (if there are any who dare show themselves) will be obliged to hold you in esteem and, I dare say, respect you.

I am sorry I did not tell you sooner what I had often heard from the late Maréchal de Noailles [282] forty years ago: Corneille would suffer a gradual decline and Racine's star would rise. His prediction has been fulfilled with the evolution of taste. The reason for this is that Racine is always within the bounds of nature and Corneille almost never.

When I undertook the commentary on Corneille, my purpose was only to increase the dowry I was giving to his little niece whom you have met, and, as a matter fact, Mlle. Corneille and the publishers have shared a hundred thousand francs earned from this first edition. My reward was to be increasingly hated and slandered by those whom my feeble successes turned into everlasting enemies. They said that the admirer of the sublime scenes of *Cinna*, *Polyeucte*, the *Cid*, *Pompée*, and the fifth act of *Rodogune* [283] had only written his commentary to disparage that great man. What I did out of respect for his memory and much more out of friendship for his niece was interpreted as a form of mean jealousy and vile self-interest by those who are familiar with that feeling alone, and their number is not small.

I sent almost all my notes to the Academy; they were discussed and approved. It is true that I was aghast at the enormous number of errors I found in the text. I did not have the courage to point out half of them, and M. Duclos [284] informed me that were he called upon to do the commentary, he would find many others. I finally have the courage. The ridiculous outcries of my ridiculous enemies, but even more the voice of truth that orders one to speak his thoughts, have emboldened me. A very beautiful quarto edition of Corneille and of my commentary is presently under way. It is as correct as that of my feeble works is faulty. In it I tell the truth as boldly as you:

> He who has but a moment left to live
> Has nothing further to conceal.[285]

Do you know that the niece of the father of our theater becomes angry when people speak ill of Corneille to her? But she is incapable of reading him; she only reads Racine. Her feminine feelings are stronger than the duties of a niece. All the same, we men who compose tragedies owe our father the deepest respect. I remember that when I presented *Oedipe* (I do not know how) and as I was quite young and very thoughtless, a few ladies told me that my play (which is of no great worth) was superior to Corneille's (which is of no worth at all). I replied with these two admirable verses from *Pompée:*

> Traces of a demi-God whose great name I can never equal
> However victorious over him I may be.[286]

Let us admire, let us love that which is beautiful, my dear friend, wherever it is. Let us detest the Visigothic verses with which we have been bored for so long, and let us make sport of the rest. Little cabals must not frighten us. They always exist at court, in the cafés and among Capuchin monks. Racine died of grief because the Jesuits told the King he was a Jansenist. They could have told the King I was an atheist because I had Henry IV say:

I make no decision between Geneva and Rome.[287]

but I would not have died because of that.

I agree with your judgment that we must admire and cherish the perfect plays of Jean and the scattered inimitable selections of Pierre. Being neither Pierre nor Jean, I should have wanted to send you these *Laws of Minos* [288] that will either be performed or not on your Parisian stage. But people have tried to find allusions, allegories in it. I was compelled to remove the most biting passages and spoil my work in order to get it passed through. My only aim in having it printed is to do some notes like you; they will not have the value of yours but will be curious. You will hear about that soon.

Farewell. The sick old man of Ferney hugs you very tightly.

172. *The Sick Old Man of Ferney.*

To Jean-François Marmontel.[289] March 13, 1773.

The sick old man of Ferney who is dying prays M. de Marmontel to read and judge this printed piece.

If he dies, M. de Marmontel may be sure of losing a true friend.

173. *A Letter of Praise to Diderot.*

To Denis Diderot. Ferney. April 20, 1773.

I was very pleasantly surprised to receive a letter bearing the signature of Diderot as I was returning from one shore of the Styx to the other. Imagine the joy of an old soldier covered with wounds if M. de Turenne [290] had written to him. Nature has allowed me to spend some additional time in this world, that is to say a second between what they call two eternities, as if there could be two.

So I will vegetate another instant at the foot of the Alps in the passage of time that engulfs all. My intellectual faculty will vanish like a dream, but with the regret of having lived without seeing you.

You send me the *Fables* of one of your friends.[291] If he is young, I reply that he will go very far. If he is not, it will be said of him that he wrote with wit that which he invented with genius. That is what was said of La Motte. Who would believe there could be even higher praise? It is that accorded to La Fontaine: "He wrote artlessly." There is in all of the arts a *je ne sais quoi* that is quite difficult to grasp. All of the world's philosophers combined could not have produced Quinault's *Armide* or *The Animals Sick With the Plague* which La Fontaine wrote without even realizing what he was doing. It must be confessed that in the arts having genius as their basis, everything is the product of instinct. Corneille composed the scene of Horace and Curiace the way a bird builds its nest, except that a bird always succeeds and the same is not true of us wretches. M. Boisard seems like a very pretty bird of Parnassus to whom nature has given, instead of instinct, much reason, exactness and finesse. I am sending you my letter of thanks meant for him. My illness, whose after effects are still harassing me, scarcely allows me to become prolix. You may be sure that I shall die thinking of you as a man who had the courage to be of use to ingrates and who deserves the praise of all wise men. I love you, I hold you in esteem as might a wise man.

The sick old man of Ferney. V.

174. *"Sometimes we must really fight with our neighbors, but we must not burn our compatriots over arguments."*

To Prince Dmitry Alekseevich Gallitzin.[292] Ferney. June 19, 1773.

Prince,

You do reason a great service by having the book of the late M. Helvétius reprinted.[293] This book will encounter persons taking exception to it, even among the *philosophes*. No one will agree that all minds are equally suited to the sciences and differ merely by education. Nothing is more false; nothing has been shown to be more erroneous by experience. Sensitive souls will always regret what he says on the subject of friendship, and he himself would have condemned his statements or toned them down considerably if a systematic turn of mind had not carried him away.

Perhaps people will wish for more method in that work and for fewer little anecdotes, most of which are false. But it seems to me that everything he says about papism, the abominations of intolerance, freedom, arbitrary power, and the misfortune of mankind will be well received by anyone who is not a fool or a Jesuit. Some philosopher could have corrected his first book *De L'Esprit*, but to condemn it as people have done and to persecute the author is as barbaric as it is absurd and an act worthy of the fourteenth century. Everything fanatics have denounced in Helvétius, who was so estimable a man, was, at bottom, in the little book by the Duc de la Rochefoucauld and even in Locke's first chapters. One may write against a philosopher while seeking the truth, like him, by different roads, but one dishonors oneself, one makes oneself execrable to posterity by persecuting him. Some Meletuses and Anytuses,[294] assassins of the Chevalier de La Barre, almost steeped their hands in the blood of the author of the book *De L'Esprit*.

I thank Your Excellency for your kindness in sending me the posthumous work which, with its defects, is very precious to me. The notes especially will be a success. The typographical errors are almost no drawback because this book will be read principally by those whom these errors will not hinder and who will correct them as they read.

If it is dedicated to the Empress, every upright person will owe you the greatest obligation. People will see that the leading sovereigns of Europe and the best are horrified by superstition and persecution. They will remember that there was never a single philosopher persecuted in the Roman Empire, which is what Tertullian [295] complains about in his fiery apology.

I owe further thanks to Your Excellency for that history of the civil war of the sublime Catherine against the Sublime Porte of the not very sublime Mustafa. You know my interest in that war is almost as great as in the universal toleration that condemns all wars. Sometimes we must really fight with our neighbors, but we must not burn our compatriots over arguments. It is said that the Pope is as tolerant as a Pope may be. I hope so for the love of humanity. I hope as much for the Muphti, the sherif of Mecca, the Dalai Lama, and the Dairi.

I am the owner of a heap of mud as large as a mite's paw on this miserable globe. We have papists, Calvinists, Pietists, some Socinians and even a Jesuit. All these people have been living together in the greatest harmony, at least until now. The same is true of your vast empire under the auspices of Catherine. For a long time people have enjoyed this good fortune in England, Holland, Brandenburg, Prussia, and in several cities of Germany. Why then not all over the world? Why that abominable maxim attributed to God and dictated by the devil (assuming one to exist): "Let him who does not listen to the assembly be as a farmer general and as a heathen"? [296] Why cast into outer darkness the man who did not have a wedding garment for supper with the architri . . . ? [297] Why tell us that they caused Ananias and his wife to die of a stroke because they gave almost all of their wealth to their leaders but kept a few florins to have dinner? [298] Why . . . ? Why . . . ? Why . . . ?

If I am asked why I am so devoted to you, I reply: "Because you are tolerant, just and charitable." Therefore, prince, accept my very appreciative and respectful gratitude

V.

175. *Some Predictions about Louis XVI.*

To Louise-Florence Pétronille de Tardieu d'Esclavelles d'Epinay. July 8, 1774.

What! My philosopher was at the frontier of death like me, and we did not meet! I had no idea she was ill. I have no doubt that during this fatal period her old friend Aesculapius Tronchin gave her proofs of his friendship and of his power over nature. If such is the case, I shall revere him all the more although he has treated me a bit severely.

My miserable eighty-four years are the very humble servants of your suffocations and swellings, and were it not for these eighty-four years, I could certainly come and seat myself beside your lounge chair.

A long time ago, I had news from one of your philosophers dated at the arctic pole, but nothing from the other one who is still in Holland. I do not know where M. Grimm [299] is presently. They say he is travelling with Messrs. Rumyantsev.[300] He really ought to make them take the road to Geneva. It is good for those who are born to be the mainstays of absolute power to visit republics.

I admire the King for giving himself over to reason and for braving the outcries of prejudice and nonsense. That gives me a high opinion of the age of Louis XVI.[301] If he continues, people will not be talking about the age of Louis XIV any more. I hold him in too high esteem to believe that he could make all the changes with which we are threatened. It seems to me that he was born prudent and firm. Therefore he will be a great and good king. Happy are those who are twenty like him and who will long relish the sweet pleasures of his reign! No less happy are those beside your lounge chair! I have settled at the lakeshore, and from Charon's bark I wish you the most ample and the happiest of lives from the bottom of my heart. Please receive, madam, my very affectionate respects.

V.

176. *Voltaire Expresses His Views on Some Economic Issues.*

To Nicolas Baudeau.[302] March-April 1775.

I cannot thank you enough for your kindness in forwarding your *Ephémérides.* Truths that may be put to use are so clearly expounded in it that I always learn something although, at my age, one is usually incapable of learning. The freedom of trade in grains is discussed in proper fashion, and this inestimable advantage would be even greater if the state had been able to spend on interprovincial canals one twentieth of our expenditures in two wars, the first of which was completely useless and the other fatal. If anything has ever been demonstrated, it is the necessity of forever abolishing forced labor. These are two essential services that M. Turgot wishes to render France, and in this respect his administration will be far superior to that of the great Colbert. I have always admired that artful minister of Louis XIV much less for what he did than for what he wished to do because you know that his plan was to do away with the tax farmers forever. The war of 1672, which was more brilliant than wise, destroyed his entire economy. The glory of Louis XIV had to be served instead of France. Recourse had to be made to burdensome loans instead of the imposition of an equal and proportionate tax like the tithe. Let France be administered like the feeble province of Limoges was, and then, extricating itself from its ruins, France will become a model of the most fortunate of governments.

I am really delighted with everything you say about the obstacles being put in the way of craftsmen, about superintendencies, and about guild masterships. I have before me a great example of what honest and moderate freedom can achieve in matters of commerce as well as in agriculture. At a site possessing the most beautiful view in Europe after Constantinople but the most ungrateful and unhealthy soil, there was a small hamlet inhabited by forty miserable wretches consumed with scrofula and poverty. A man with moderate wealth bought this horrible territory specifically in order to change it. He began by getting some of the foul marshes dried out. He brought the land into cultivation. He brought in foreign craftsmen of every kind, especially clockmakers who knew nothing about superintendencies, guild masterships or trade guilds but who worked with marvelous industry and could provide finished products at a third under what they sold for in Paris.

The Duc de Choiseul granted them his patronage with the nobility and grandeur that have imparted such luster to his whole conduct. M. Dogni supported them with generosity without which they would have been lost. M. Turgot, considering that they were foreigners who had become Frenchmen and good people who had become useful, gave them every facility consistent with the law. In short, within a few years, a lair of forty savages was turned into a small opulent city inhabited by twelve hundred useful people, practical physicists, and wise men whose minds provide employment for their hands. If they had been subjected to the ridiculous laws invented to oppress the crafts, that place would still be a filthy wasteland peopled by the bears of the Alps and the Jura.

Continue to enlighten us, to encourage us, to prepare the materials with which our government ministers will erect the temple of public felicity.

I have the honor of being with respectful gratitude your very humble and very obedient servant.

Voltaire

177. *On Turgot and Necker.*

To Jean de Vaines.[303] May 8, 1775.

You sent me word that M. de Condorcet had not yet left when you received the package in which you are kind enough to take interest. I did not know that he had gone on a trip. He has apparently gone to his country property.

In my present uncertainty, let me still take the liberty of addressing to you this little letter meant for him with a few copies of a small work on wheat which he entrusted to me. These copies are for you. He is requesting only one for himself.

It is worthy of the Welches to oppose M. Turgot's great projects. And you who are a true Frenchman are as indignant as I am about the stupidity of the people. The citizens of Paris are like those of Dijon who, as they cried that they were short of bread, threw two hundred *setiers*[304] of wheat into the river. These

same citizens of Dijon wrote that the style of the Burgundian Crébillon was more flowing than Racine's and that Alexis Piron was
superior to Molière.[305] All of this is worthy of the age.

We do not yet have in Geneva the Genevese Necker's hodgepodge against the best government minister France has ever
had.[306] Necker will be very careful not to send me *his little quip*.
He knows well enough that I do not agree with him. Seventeen
years ago I had the good fortune of having M. Turgot in my den
for a few days. His heart won my affection and his mind my admiration. I see that he has fulfilled every one of my desires and
hopes. The edict of September 13 seems to me a masterpiece of
true wisdom and eloquence.[307] If Necker thinks and writes better, I immediately declare Necker to be the world's greatest
eminence. But as of now, I share your opinion.

I am imbued with your kindness and with your way of thinking, feeling, and expressing yourself.

V.

If you could be kind enough to forward a Necker to me, I
would be very obliged.

178. *Voltaire and Frederick the Great Help a Victim of French
Persecution.*

To Frederick II, King of Prussia. Ferney. July 29, 1775.

Sire,
There is no virtue, be it tranquil, active, gentle, proud, human
or heroic, which you do not practice. Here you are, after having
engaged in some fifty battles, busily concerning yourself with your
family's amusement. You have Le Kain and Aufresne perform for
you.[308] Aemilius Paulus used to say that the same mind could
be used to order a feast and beat King Perseus.[309] You are superior
to all in both war and peace.

I thank you for your willingness to employ a small part of
your infinite greatness in protecting d'Etallonde Morival and in
remedying the crime of his assassins.[310] That is worthy of
Your Majesty. The great Julian, the most eminent of men after

304

Marcus Aurelius, conducted himself more or less in the same manner, and what is more he was not your equal.

Your kindness to Morival is a great example you give to our nation. Our nation is beginning to cleanse itself; almost all our government offices are composed of philosophers. The Abbé Galiani [311] has maintained that Rome could only recapture a bit of its splendor if there were an atheistic Pope. At least, it is quite certain that an atheist as successor to St. Peter would be much preferable to a superstitious Pope.

In France, we hope that philosophy, which is close to the throne, will soon be within. But it is only a hope. Hope is often deceptive. There are so many people with a self-interest to support error and stupidity; there are so many high positions and so much wealth attached to that profession that one must fear the hypocrites will always have the upper hand over the wise. Hasn't Germany itself turned your principal ecclesiastics into sovereigns? Which elector and bishop among you will champion reason against a sect that provides him with an income of four or five million? We would have to turn the whole world topsy-turvy to put it under the rule of philosophy. The only expedient left to the wise, then, is to prevent the fanatics from becoming too dangerous. You are doing just that through the strength of your genius and your knowledge of men.

May you live a long time, sire, and provide the world with new examples.

Some gazettes have stated that Pöllnitz has died.[312] That is too bad. It makes me fear for Milord Maréchal who is worthier and not far apart in age. As for myself, I am sustained by the consolations which you deign to provide me, and my greatest consolation when I die will be to remember that I leave you on earth full of life and glory.

I beseech Your Majesty to please inform me whether I am to send Morival back to Wesel or direct him to Potsdam.

May he condescend to receive my thanks, my admiration and my respect.

179. *Voltaire an Admirer of Turgot.*

To Jean de Vaines. January 11, 1776.

Sir,

I must interrupt you for a moment. I must tell you absolutely, speaking for some ten or twelve thousand men, how indebted we are to M. Turgot, how dear his name is to us, and how supremely overjoyed our little province is. I have no doubt that this little essay on liberty and territorial tax anticipates greater future events. The smallest province in the kingdom will certainly not be the only fortunate one. I know full well there are notorious thieves afraid of enlightened virtue. I know there are scoundrels who murmur against the public welfare and that they are listened to by their parasites. They shout that everything will be lost if the people's burden is ever lightened and if the king becomes wealthier. But I have high hopes in the tenacity of the king who will support his minister against a despicable clique. He already dumfounded them by replying to their scurrilous and satirical pamphlet and designating you as his reader. It will be impossible for you to get him to read a work better than those you are working on under M. Turgot's supervision.

Stay kindly disposed a little to your very humble and obedient servant.

The sick old V.

180. *Voltaire Speaks for the Local Community.*

To the Farmers-General. Ferney. May 3, 1776.

Gentlemen,

The nobility of your conduct toward me emboldens me to make some proposals on some subjects of greater importance. The matter is your interest in the inhabitants living at the edge of the territory of Gex toward the Jura Mountains along the small river called La Valserine. The inhabitants of this land, from the small canton of Lelex to the Rhone, are offering to pay you such indemnity as you may judge suitable if you will include that small spit of land in the territory of Gex. It does seem that keeping the Bellegarde bridge would protect us from all contraband. It is for you gentlemen who doubtlessly know the locale perfectly to decide whether this arrangement is suitable or not.

The other request our States have to make is to please tell us how much salt you can order us to be supplied with.

If you will confide your intentions to me, I shall communicate them to our States who will share my gratitude.

I beg to remain with every feeling due you, gentlemen, your very. . . .

181. *Turgot is Dismissed.*

To Anne-Robert-Jacques Turgot. May 17, 1776.

An old man of about eighty-three is really at death's door when he hears such news.[313] But he will consume his few remaining moments respecting you, loving you, and very sincerely pitying France.

V.

182. *"If you ever return to Russia, please do pass by my grave."*

To Denis Diderot. Ferney. August 14, 1776.

Sir,
Not having been fortunate enough to see you and listen to you on your return from St. Petersburg, I could not have had greater consolation than the appearance of your friend M. de Limon. It is true that my hateful old age, worn out by continual sickness, did not permit me to enjoy his company as much as he inspired an eagerness within me to do so. I merely caught a glimpse of his immense talent, and I hoped that Denis might have many similar Platos at his side. Sound philosophy has been gaining ground from Archangel to Cadiz, but our enemies still have the heavenly dew, the fat of the earth, the bishop's mitre, wealth, the sword and the riffraff on their side. We have been limited com-

pletely to informing decent people throughout Europe that we are in the right and perhaps to making general conduct a little more pleasant and civil. The blood of the Chevalier de La Barre, however, still rages. The King of Prussia, it is true, has given the post of engineer and captain to the Chevalier de La Barre's unfortunate friend who was included in the execrable decree issued by the cannibals, but the edict still stands and the judges live. The horhible thing is that the *philosophes* are not united and the persecutors will always be. There are two wise men at court. The secret was found by which to deprive us of them. They were not in their element. Ours is retirement. I have been taking shelter here for twenty-five years. I hear that in Paris you only communicate with minds worthy of your acquaintance. That is the only way to escape the rage of fanatics and rogues. May you live long and strike mortal blows against the monster whose ears I have merely bitten. If you ever return to Russia, please do pass by my grave.

V.

183. *The Rumor Spreads that Rousseau is Dead.*

To Philippe-Antoine de Claris, Marquis de Florian.[314] Ferney. December 26, 1776.

The ridiculous trial being instigated against you will probably do you no more harm than to make you wait awhile for your old clothes. I have more embarrassing and more disagreeable business here. The colony is going very poorly. The longer we live, the more we suffer. Jean-Jacques really did the right thing by dying.[315] People claim it is not true that a dog killed him; he recovered from the wounds that his friend the dog had inflicted on him, but it is said that on December 12 he took it into his head to do some climbing in Paris with an old Genevese named Romilly. He ate like a devil and, getting indigestion, he died like a dog. A philosopher is a trifling thing.

The sick old man, still astonished he is alive, embraces you with all his heart and dares not do the same to Mme. de Florian.

V.

184. *Voltaire Plagued by Illness and Fortune.*

To Jean Le Rond D'Alembert. May 9, 1777.

My dear friend and dear philosopher,
Your stomach and your ass cannot be in a worse state than my head. My little stroke at the age of eighty-three is certainly comparable to your evacuations at age sixty. Let us put them both on the same plate, your bowels and my brain, and serve them up to philosophy. I am dying, worn out by nature which attacks me from above as it plagues you from below. I am dying persecuted by fortune which made sport of me when I set up my colony. I am dying pursued by a deluge of bad books. I am dying barked at by the dogs tearing away at Delisle.[316] I know that as part of the quarry they want to devour me also. But they won't fare well. I am an old stag with more than ten horns, and I will give them some good blows with my tines before I die in their jaws. There is such a stupendous ringing in my brain as I write you that my amanuensis and I cannot hear each other any more. My heart is still sound. It will be yours until the final moment.
Farewell, sage, farewell. My regards to Pascal-Condorcet.[317] He will play a great role. Farewell, dear Bertrand. Remember Raton.[318]

185. *"I am an old Swiss who is dead and forgotten in France. . . ."*

To Louis-François-Armand Du Plessis, Duc de Richelieu.
September 22, 1777.

Monseigneur,
I do not know what has happened to me since you flattered me by saying that I would pay you my court at age one hundred and fifty and be a witness to your love affair with the Abbess of Rennes. But I was just about to go down below and ask Lucifer for my leave. He occasionally sends some of his guards to summon me before him, and he makes me aware that a poor fellow like me is not one to dare follow in your footsteps.

I saw a man in my retreat who, I believe, used to be your nephew. It was the Prince de Beauvau [319] who did me that honor. I wished his uncle had done the same even without the company of the Abbess of Rennes. You may be sure that I have been tempted to go to Paris a hundred times. But as my legs, my head and my stomach have denied me their service, I have decided to await my destiny very calmly. I believe you are governing yours very well and have made yourself absolutely superior to it. Most other men have not. You have been a great actor on the stage of this world; you are the most clairvoyant of spectators. The scenery has changed; the new spectacle is catching everyone's eye. I catch a glimpse of all that from the depths of my cavern but only through very poor glasses. I am an old Swiss who is dead and forgotten in France, but I cannot refrain from telling you that by an unusual affinity the King of Prussia is the only correspondent I have left. This word affinity must seem out of place to you. I do not believe I have anything in common with the conqueror of Rossbach, any more than I do with the conqueror of Minorca. [320] There is, however, a certain way of thinking that has brought that hero of the north close to my wretched self just as there has been a certain kindness, a certain indulgence in you that has always prevented you from forgetting me completely. I will tell you that recently the King of Prussia gave me solid signs of support during a period when my affairs were in horrible disrepair. I would not have expected such generosity when I quarrelled with him so imprudently thirty years ago. Doesn't that show we must never abandon hope about anything?

I remember writing you several times about the catastrophe of that unfortunate Lally. [321] I asked for your opinion; discreetly you never replied. But, at last, Lally has found an avenger in his son who seems to me to have his father's courage and character. He is pursuing the reconsideration of the trial with a zeal and tenacity that appear to deserve universal commendation. He has great intelligence; his style is vigorous as is his soul; the *parlement* is not gagging him. I fancy that you will not be gagged and that you will condescend to tell me whether it is true that the request for appeal has been granted. I am really persuaded that it ought to be. The horrible adventure of the Chevalier de La Barre and of d'Etallonde also merited a petition to an appeals court. One of these two martyrs is alive and is a very good and very brave officer. I secured a position for him with the King of Prussia; he is his military engineer. Who knows whether someday he won't come and lay siege to Abbeville while you are commanding an army in Picardy? I am expecting this to occur in fifty years. In the meantime, I am dying despite all your pleasantries. I do not get out of bed at all, and I ask you for a requiem.

V.

186. *Voltaire Returns to Paris from His Long Exile.*

To Marie de Vichy de Chamrond, Marquise Du Deffand. Paris. February 11, 1778.

I have arrived dead and want to be restored to life only to throw myself at the knees of the Marquise Du Deffand.

187. *"A bit of swelling . . . seems to be announcing the impending destruction of this frail machine."*

To Théodore Tronchin. February 17, 1778.

The old Swiss whom M. Tronchin was kind enough to visit at M. de Villette's [322] points out to him that the continual alternation of strangury and diabetes with a complete cessation of the peristaltic movement of the bowels is a quite disagreeable and somewhat dangerous thing, that a machine so thrown out of gear can only survive another few days with the same kindness of M. Tronchin.

Madame Denis's pills have recently done him a great deal of good but have not reduced any of his pain. A bit of swelling in his legs, a swelling difficult to discern in a body so dry, seems to be announcing the impending destruction of this frail machine.

The sick old man will be very glad if he can converse with M. Tronchin for a moment before taking leave of society.

He saw Mr. Franklin [323] who brought along his grandson whom he instructed to ask for the old man's blessing. The old man gave it in the presence of twenty persons and pronounced these words as a blessing: GOD AND LIBERTY.

188. *Voltaire's Final Agony.*

To Théodore Tronchin. This Friday. April-May 1778.

The sick old man of the Quai des Théatins throws himself into M. Tronchin's arms. He is suffering unbearable pain. He may not have a fever but there is an agitation in his pulse and blood that is increasing all his torment. He has not slept at all for fifteen nights. His state is a horrible one. Nothing brings him relief. His only hope is in M. Tronchin; he hopes he will have pity on him.

V.

189. *The Patient on the Rue de Beaune.*

To Théodore Tronchin. c. May 20, 1778.

The patient on the Rue de Beaune had convulsions from a violent coughing all night and is still having them. He vomited blood three times. He asks forgiveness for taking so much trouble over a cadaver.

190. *"Man does not live by bread alone."*

To Théodore Tronchin. c. May 20, 1778.

Non cecidit.
Panem mitto. Non in solo pane vivit homo, sed in omni verbo quod oritur ex ore Tronchin.[324]

V.

191. *A Final Injustice Remedied.*

To the Chevalier Trophime Gérard de Lally-Tolendal.[325]
May 26, 1778.

The dying man was restored to life when he learned this great piece of news. He embraces M. de Lally very affectionately. He sees that the king is the defender of justice. He will die content.[326]

Notes

1. An English statesman and man of letters (1709-1773) who edited the works of James Thomson (1750).

2. James Thomson (1700-1748), the English poet and author of *The Seasons* (1726-1730).

3. Joseph Addison (1672-1719), the English essayist, poet and statesman. His neoclassic tragedy *Cato*(1713) was a great success in its time but has since been judged to be artificial.

4. Thomson was one of the most celebrated dramatists of his time. His tragedies, written in a classical mode with a strong political flavor, include *Sophonisba* (1730), *Edward and Eleanora* (1739), and *Tancred and Sigismunda* (1745).

5. From Lyttleton's "To the reverend dr. Ayscough, at Oxford, written from Paris, in the year 1728." Voltaire is quoting from memory with remarkable accuracy.

6. The palace built (1745-1747) at Potsdam by Frederick II who lived there for forty years. Voltaire resided at Sans Souci during his Prussian sojourn.

7. In 1740 Voltaire had promised to ask Frederick to buy some busts, representing the first twelve emperors, attributed to Bernini and which had been found in the family chateau of Mme. d'Argental.

8. Etienne-François, Duc de Choiseul (1719-1785), a French statesman. He supported the publication of the *Encyclopédie* and became Minister of Foreign Affairs (1758-1770) and Minister of War and the Navy (1761-1770).

9. A reference to Crébillon's play, *Catilina.*

10. Charles-Emmanuel de Crussol, eighth Duc d'Uzès (1707-1762).

11. In October 1749, the Academy of Sciences and Belles-Lettres of Dijon announced the subject of its competition for the award in ethics for the year 1750 in the *Mercure de France*: "Whether the re-establishment of the Sciences and Arts has contributed to a purification of morals." The award was won by Jean-Jacques Rousseau who answered paradoxically in the negative in his landmark *Discourse on the Sciences and Arts.*

12. A play on words on the title of Montesquieu's *Spirit of the Laws.* The French word *esprit* may mean spirit or wit, and Mme. Du Deffand used the word in the latter sense, parodying the title of Montesquieu's work.

13. In the middle of the eighteenth century, bishops ordered their clergy to deny the sacraments to those not presenting a certificate of confession signed by a priest who had accepted the papal bull Unigenitus condemning the Jansenists.

14. A fashionable Parisian couturière.

15. Charles Eugene, Duke of Württemberg (1728-1793). Voltaire had bought a substantial annuity secured on properties owned by Württemberg.

16. The philosopher La Mettrie reported a conversation concerning Voltaire he had had in the summer of 1751 with Frederick in which the latter was quoted as having said: "I will need him another year at most. We squeeze the orange and throw away the rind."

17. A famous watering place in the Vosges. In addition to Voltaire, Montaigne, Beaumarchais, King Stanislas of Poland, and Napoleon III have taken the cure there.

18. La Touche was the French envoy to Potsdam.

19. Marguerite-Jeanne Cordier, Baronne de Staal de Launay (1684-1750), a French writer. Her *Memoirs* and *Letters* present a portrait of the Regency period.

20. Henri-Charles, Count de Senneterre, a playwright.

21. Dionysius the Elder, tyrant of Syracuse (c. 432-367 B.C.).

22. A nickname for Maupertuis.

23. *Opuscles sur la langue française [Treatises on the French Language]* by "various Academicians" and edited by d'Olivet.

24. Pierre-Claude Nivelle de la Chaussée (1692-1754), the playwright, died on March 14.

25. Two sects of Christian heresy of the fourth and fifth centuries.

26. Jean Mabillon (1632-1707) and Bernard de Montfaucon (1655-1741), two erudite historians.

27. Clavel de Brenles (1717-1771), an assiduous correspondent of Voltaire and Mme. Necker, was a member of a Swiss noble family that exercised manorial rights in Brenles, a village in the outskirts of Lausanne.

28. A Swiss village on the Lake of Geneva.

29. Marie-Elisabeth de Dompierre de Fontaine, Mme. Denis's sister.

30. Voltaire's new residence which was then about half a league outside of Geneva. Called "Sur Saint Jean" by its previous owners, Voltaire renamed the house which was located in the open countryside Les Délices to express his delight with his feeling of freedom and independence there. The house still stands today in the city of Geneva.

31. According to the *Aeneid*, the Tyrian princess Dido fled her brother Pygmalion, landed on the coast of Africa, and asked the local inhabitants for land as large as an oxskin. When her claim was granted, she cut the skin into strips, thus encompassing enough space to build her city of Carthage.

32. Christian IV, Duke of Zweibrücken.

3. Voltaire's satiric poem on Joan of Arc, *La Pucelle [The Maid]*. Pirated and incorrect manuscripts of the work, on which Voltaire had started work at least twenty-five years earlier, found their way into print in 1755. An approved edition first appeared in 1762.

34. Michael Servetus (1511-1553), a Spanish physician and theologian, was burned for heresy in Geneva at the instigation of Calvin.

35. Rousseau's *Discourse on the Origin of Inequality* (1755).

36. Jean Chapelain (1595-1674) was a French critic and poet who contributed to the formation of the doctrine of French classicism. His poem on Joan of Arc, *La Pucelle ou la France délivrée [The Maid or France Delivered]*, dates from 1656.

37. Clément Marot (c. 1496-1544) was a French poet with a bantering style committed to the Reformation.

38. Nadir Shah (1668-1747), shah of Persia from 1736 to 1747.

39. Marc Chapuis, a minor official of Geneva.

40. A banker and merchant at Lyons and a general factotum of Voltaire.

41. This phrase, from Leibniz's *Theodicy* (1710), became a catchword of the philosophy of optimism which Voltaire was to satirize mercilessly in *Candide* (1759).

42. A French official in Geneva and the owner of a private press at his summer house in Montbrillant, near Geneva.

43. Elie Bertrand (1717-1797) was a liberal Protestant minister from Berne who later furnished Voltaire with documents for his *Philosophical Dictionary*. Bertrand delivered four sermons in Berne on the occasion of the Lisbon earthquake of November 1, 1755 and preached that the disaster should be considered as a lesson in humility before God and as part of the divine moral plan for the world.

44. The reference is to Voltaire's *Poem on the Lisbon Earthquake* (1755) which questioned the doctrine of metaphysical optimism and divine Providence in light of the recent disaster.

45. The original edition of Voltaire's *Poem on the Lisbon Earthquake* ended with these lines except for the word *hope*.

46. Théodore Tronchin (1709-1781), a Swiss physician and collaborator on Diderot's *Encyclopedia*, introduced smallpox innoculation to Versailles.

47. A character in Voltaire's play *L'Orphelin de la Chine [The Chinese Orphan]* (1754).

48. The Abbé Jean-François Du Resnel (1692-1761) adapted Pope's *Essay on Criticism* and *Essay on Man* into French verse.

49. Philippe and Gabriel Cramer, publishers in Geneva, produced three major editions of Voltaire's collected works in 1756, 1768 and 1775.

50. Admiral John Byng (1704-1757) was sent to save the British Mediterranean base at Minorca, but when he arrived in May 1756 a force under the Duc de Richelieu had landed. Byng decided his forces were inadequate and returned to Gibraltar, leaving Minorca and its capital, Mahon, to their fate. Byng was executed in 1757 for neglect of duty.

51. Diderot's play *Le Fils naturel [The Natural Son]*.

52. It was only in 1759 on Voltaire's urging that spectators were finally removed from the stage and restricted to seating in the auditorium.

53. Shuvalov (1727-1789), chamberlain of Empress Elizabeth Petrovna of Russia, provided Voltaire with information for his *History of Russia*.

54. The Romanov dynasty was founded by Michael in 1613. Charles XII defeated the Russians at Narva in 1700.

55. Jean Le Rond d'Alembert (1717-1783), the French mathematician and philosopher, was Diderot's principal collaborator on the *Encyclopédie* and the author of its *Preliminary Discourse*. He withdrew from the *Encyclopédie* in 1759.

56. César Chesneau du Marsais (1676-1756), a French grammarian and collaborator on the *Encyclopédie*.

57. D'Alembert's article *Geneva* in the *Encyclopédie* urged the establishment and toleration of a theater in the stronghold of Calvinism, a project favored by Voltaire. The article aroused a storm of protest including a reaction from Rousseau in his *Letter to d'Alembert on Spectacles* (1758). On Servet, see n. 34.

58. A city in Czechoslovakia on the Elbe near which Frederick II was defeated by Field Marshal Daun (1757) during the Seven Years' War.

59. Inaccurately quoted from Virgil, *Aeneid*, IX, 641: "A blessing, child, on thy noble soul; so man scales the stars."

60. "So man scales the fire."

61. According to volume VII of the *Encyclopédie*, Du Marsais "fell sick last year. He soon realized the danger he was in and requested the Sacraments which he received with great presence of mind and tranquillity."

62. André-François Boureau Deslandes, the author of a *Critical History of Philosophy* (1737) and *Reflections on Great Men Dying While Joking* (1755). Both works were published anonymously.

63. Mme. Du Deffand.

64. Adapted from Ariosto, *Orlando Furioso*, XLIV, ii, 3-4;

"Today Kings, Popes and Emperors become allies;
Tomorrow they will be leaders in opposition."

65. In his *History of the Cacouacs* published in December 1757, Jacob Moreau used this term, signifying evil spirits, to attack the *philosophes*. François Garasse (1585-1631) was a Jesuit preacher noted for the violence and vulgarity of his polemics.

66. Jacob Vernet (1698-1789) was a Protestant minister and professor of theology in Geneva. He reacted very unfavorably to d'Alembert's article *Geneva* and urged the Protestant ministers of the city to protest. In his *Christian Instruction,* Vernet had written that revelation was *useful* in persuading the simple-minded and gave it priority over rational conviction.

67. Guillaume de Lamoignon de Malesherbes (1721-1794) was the government official charged with overseeing the book-trade from 1750 to 1763 and was of great help to the *philosophes* and Encyclopedists.

68. Two articles that appeared in the eighth volume of the *Encyclopédie* in 1765.

69. The Abbé and later Cardinal François-Joachim de Bernis (1715-1794) was Minister of Foreign Affairs from 1756 to 1758.

70. The Chevalier Louis de Jaucourt (1704-1779) was a collaborator on the *Encyclopédie* and after the prohibition of the work became Diderot's principal assistant for the final volumes. The author of the article on procreation was Albrecht von Haller (1708-1777), a Swiss physiologist and botanist.

71. Briasson was one of the publishers of the *Encyclopédie*.

72. The Oriental scholar was Antoine-Noé Polier de Bottens (1713-1783), a liberal Protestant who had become the leading minister of the churches of Lausanne in 1754. The lover of natural history was Elie Bertrand. On Bertrand, see n. 43.

73. Jean-Baptiste-Nicolas Formont, a longstanding friend of Voltaire, was a counsellor in the Parlement of Rouen. Formont was also a musician and poet. Literature is frequently the subject of Voltaire's letters to him.

74. Voltaire is referring to two tragedies, *Iphigénie en Tauride* by Claude Guymond de La Touche produced on June 4, 1757 and *Hypermnestre* by Antoine Marin Le Mierre produced on August 31, 1758.

75. Count Leopold Joseph Daun (1705-1766) was the Austrian fieldmarshal who defeated Frederick II at Kolin.

76. Charles-Georges Le Roy was a friend of the philosopher

Helvétius and a contributor to the *Encyclopedia;* Hubert-François-Bourguignon Gravelot was an illustrator of Voltaire's works.

77. Claude Helvétius's book *De L'Esprit [On Mind]* dates from 1758.

78. See n. 49.

79. It is likely that Voltaire sketched *Candide* in January 1758, edited it in July, finished it in October, and went over it again. The Geneva edition was published pseudonymously on January 15, 1759, and Voltaire denied authorship of the work.

80. Jacob Vernes (1728-1791), a young Protestant minister, was one of Voltaire's more ardent supporters as he settled in Switzerland.

81. An attempt on the life of Joseph, King of Portugal, was made in 1758. It was used as a pretext for the persecution of the nobility and resulted in the expulsion of the Jesuits in 1759. The other attempted regicide was that of Robert-François Damiens on Louis XV. His fanatical behavior may have been excited by the polemics between Jesuits and Jansenists. He was publicly tortured and torn to pieces by horses in Paris on March 28, 1757. Ferdinand VI of Spain died on August 10, 1759.

82. In chapter 16 of *Candide,* Candide and Cacambo come across a group of South American natives who mistake them for Jesuits and prepare to roast them alive shouting: "Let us eat some Jesuit, let us eat some Jesuit."

83. Bernard-Louis, Marquis de Chauvelin (1716-1773) was a French diplomat and general.

84. A nickname for Frederick II, King of Prussia.

85. Frederick II of Hesse-Cassel had been converted to Protestantism.

86. The Abbé Gautier, who had lived in London, brought secret English peace proposals to Versailles in 1711.

87. The British took the city of Quebec in September 1759. Pondichéry, a city on the Bay of Bengal about ninety miles southwest of Madras and controlled by French merchants since 1683, was surrendered to the British on January 16, 1761.

88. Octavie Guichard, Dame Belot (1719-1804), the widow of a lawyer in the Parlement of Paris. She was the author of works on Rousseau and English literature, and was an intimate of Palissot.

89. A courtesan.

90. Samuel Richardson's epistolary novel dates from 1747-1748.

91. One of Corneille's flops, *Theodora Virgin and Martyr* (1646) is the story of a young princess condemned as a Christian to prostitution.

92. A famous procuress of the Regency period.

93. Chapters 27 and 33 of *Gargantua*.

94. Charles-Jean-François Hénault (1685-1770), a French magistrate, poet and historian.

95. Frederick.

96. Mme. Denis.

97. See n. 46.

98. Guillaume-François Berthier (1704-1782), a Jesuit priest, was for many years the editor of the Jesuit *Journal de Trévoux*. Abraham Chaumeix (1730-1790) was the author of eight volumes of *Préjugés légitimes contre l'Encyclopédie [Legitimate Prejudices Against the Encyclopédie]* (1758) which were instrumental in the suspension of the *Encyclopédie* in 1759. Both men were frequent butts of Voltaire's satire.

99. Voltaire was angry that Rousseau went his own way and refused to ally himself with the *philosophes*. To live in greater conformity with nature, the Greek cynic philosopher Diogenes, who scorned wealth and social convention, lived in a tub.

100. Charles Palissot de Montenoy's comedy *Les Philosophes* was produced at the Comédie Française on May 2, 1760.

101. Aristophanes's comedy (423 B.C.) against Socrates.

102. Charles-Simon Favart (1710-1792) and Jean-Joseph Vadé (1720-1757) were authors of comic operas and vaudevilles. Gilles was a silly and fearful comic character in the contemporary theater of the fair. Anne Lefebvre Dacier (1654-1720), a French translator of Homer, was famous for her defense of the Ancients in the celebrated Quarrel of the Ancients and Moderns.

103. Frederick's *Epître à d'Alembert*.

104. "Diderot must die for the people." A parody of the gospel, *John*, XVIII.

105. Bernard Saurin (1706-1781), a dramatist, was the secretary of the Duke of Orleans and later the protégé of Helvétius.

106. In 1758, Voltaire bought the chateaux of Tournay and Ferney, the first just inside the French frontier and the second

just inside the Swiss frontier. He built a theater at Tournay which soon came under the interdiction of the ecclesiastical and civil authorities of Geneva. On Les Délices, see n. 30.

107. Charles Palissot de Montenoy (1730-1814) was a writer noted for his attacks on the Encyclopedists in his comedy *The Circle* (1755), his *Little Letters on Great Philosophers* (1757), and especially his comedy *Les Philosophes* (1760). He had, however, been on good terms with Voltaire. Voltaire's letter indicates his method of attempting to defend his philosophical colleagues without categorically rebuking Palissot so as not to incur the anger of the playwright's protectors in the Duc de Choiseul's entourage. D'Alembert and Diderot were not happy with Voltaire's cautious handling of Palissot and considered him to be dragging his feet.

108. The Parisian theater-going public rushed to the performance of Palissot's *Les Philosophes* to see the actor Préville coming on stage on all fours satirizing the person and philosophy of Rousseau.

109. Elie Fréron (1719-1776), a critic and founder of the journal *L'Année littéraire,* was an adversary of the Encyclopedists and Voltaire. Jean-Jacques Lefranc, Marquis de Pompignan (1709-1784) was another unfriendly critic of the Encyclopedists.

110. Published in 1759 at Berne by Claude-Marie Guyon.

111. The reference is to the French poet Jean-Baptiste Rousseau (1671-1741).

112. Charles Pinot Duclos was Voltaire's successor as official historiographer of France.

113. Princess de Robecq, the former mistress of the Duc de Choiseul, was instrumental in getting Palissot's play accepted by the Comédie Française. The second lady is Marie-Anne-Françoise de Noailles, Countess de La Marck.

114. From Despréaux's *Art poétique,* III, 53-54.

115. On Gilles, see n. 102.

116. An enthusiastic supporter of Voltaire.

117. Arius (c. 256-336) was the Libyan theologian who advanced the fourth-century heresy known as Arianism. Saint Athanasius (c. 297-373), patriarch of Alexandria, was an orthodox opponent of Arianism.

118. Voltaire invited Marie-Françoise Corneille, an impover-

ished descendant of the playwright, to Ferney in 1760 where he and Mme. Denis treated her as a daughter. He undertook the publication of a standard edition of Corneille's theater in twelve volumes with commentary to provide a dowry for the girl.

119. D'Alembert had written Voltaire ten days previously complaining of what d'Alembert took to be his excessive praise of persons frequenting the Court and disparaging some of his fellow liberal writers. In his *Epistle to Mme. Denis on Agriculture*, dated March 14, 1761, Voltaire specifically lauded both d'Alembert and Diderot.

120. Nicolas-Charles-Joseph Trublet (1697-1770) was a French writer who aroused Voltaire's ire by his criticism of Helvétius's *De L'Esprit*.

121. Antoine Houdar de La Motte (1672-1731) was a French poet, critic and playwright.

122. Pierre Guérin de Tencin (1680-1758) became cardinal in 1739, archbishop of Lyons in 1740, and minister of state in 1742.

123. Rousseau.

124. Augustin-Louis, marquis de Ximénès (1726-1817) was a frequent guest of Voltaire's at Ferney and a lover of Mme. Denis. Voltaire used his name when he published his *Letters on the Nouvelle Héloïse* which appeared in 1761, a few months after Rousseau's novel, and severely criticized the work for lack of taste and obscenity.

125. Charles-Pierre Colardeau (1732-1776) was a poet and member of the French Academy. On Pompignan and Fréron, see n. 109.

126. A nickname for Omer Joly de Fleury (1715-1810), a magistrate who was named president of the Parlement of Paris in 1768. His *Réquisitoires* were sharply attacked by Voltaire.

127. The Minister for Foreign Affairs from 1758 to 1770.

128. Gustavus Adolphus, King of Sweden (1611-1632), landed in Pomerania in 1630.

129. The Treaty of Ryswick was signed in 1697 and Philip V, grandson of Louis XIV, became King of Spain in 1700 succeeding Charles II, the last king from the house of Charles V.

130. Maximilien de Béthune, Duc de Sully (1560-1641), Henry IV's closest adviser, became superintendent of finances in 1598.

131. Fabricius was a Roman general and statesman of the third century B.C. noted for the simplicity of his habits and his honesty in public life.

132. The Duchess of Saxe-Gotha (1710-1767) had received Voltaire at her court in 1753 during the period of his Prussian difficulties and the two subsequently maintained an active correspondence.

133. See n. 53.

134. Alexis (1690-1718) was the son of Peter the Great and Russian czarevitch who was arrested and tried for treason on his father's orders. Alexis was sentenced to death but died from the torture he endured prior to his execution.

135. Ivan Nestesuranoi was a pseudonym under which the French writer Jean Rousset de Missy (1686-1762) published his *Memoirs on the Reign of Peter the Great of Russia* in four volumes at The Hague in 1725-1726.

136. Guillaume de Lamberty (1660-1742) was a Swiss historian and author of the fourteen-volume *Memoirs Useful to the History of the Eighteenth Century* published at The Hague from 1724 to 1740.

137. George Keate (1729-1797) was a British poet and author of *A Short Account of the Ancient History, Present Government, and Laws of the Republic of Geneva* (London, 1761) to which Voltaire alludes in the third sentence of the letter.

138. See n. 118.

139. Peter Annet (1693-1769), an English deist, was the author of *The Life of David* which was translated into French by D'Holbach as *David ou l'histoire de l'homme selon Dieu* (London, 1768), and William Warburton was bishop of Gloucester.

140. This last sentence was written by Voltaire in English.

141. See n. 118.

142. The French writer Bernard Le Bovier de Fontenelle lived to the age of one hundred (1657-1757).

143. François-Auguste Paradis de Moncrif, a French writer and secretary to both Count d'Argenson and the Duke of Orleans, died at the age of eighty-three (1687-1770). Voltaire survived him by eight years.

144. Maria Theresa.

145. Voltaire's niece and Mme. Denis's sister. Her marriage to

the Marquis de Florian was to be her second; she had married M. de Fontaine in 1738.

146. The site of her chateau in central Picardy.

147. A character in Voltaire's tragedy *Olympie* (1763).

148. Rousseau.

149. See n. 99.

150. Corneille's tragedy (1644-1645).

151. André Morellet, a French writer and philosopher and contributor to the *Encyclopédie*.

152. Jean Calas (1698-1762) was a merchant in Toulouse. On October 13, 1761, his oldest son Marc-Antoine, age thirty, hanged himself in his store. To avoid improper burial, Marc-Antoine's parents claimed he had not committed suicide. A Protestant, Calas was accused of killing his son because the latter had expressed his intention of converting to Catholicism. By decree of the Parlement of Toulouse, Calas was broken on the rack in March 1762. Voltaire was successful in rehabilitating the name of Calas by 1765 after obtaining an edict of the King's Council nullifying the official decree of Toulouse. Voltaire's *Treatise on Toleration* (1763) resulted from his experience with the Calas affair.

153. A Protestant merchant in Marseilles, Audibert had been in Toulouse shortly after Calas's execution. He had recently come to Geneva and was the first person to tell Voltaire about the Calas affair. Others mentioned in the letter include the bankers Dufour & Mallet and Tourton & Baur, and Lavaysse, a young lawyer from Toulouse and a friend of the Calas who had been accused of complicity in the ostensible murder.

154. Voltaire had published an essay on the Jews (*Des Juifs*) in 1756 which is now included in his *Philosophical Dictionary*. Pinto (1715-1787), a Jewish moralist, publicly replied to Voltaire in a forty-page book published in Amsterdam in 1762 and entitled *Apology for the Jewish Nation or Critical Reflections on the First Chapter of Volume VII of the Works of M. de Voltaire [Réflexions critiques sur le 1er chapitre du tome VIIe des Oeuvres de M. de Voltaire]*.

155. The Biblical references are to *Judges*, XII, 6 and *Numbers*, XXV, 6.

156. The French *parlements* condemned the Constitutions

and doctrine of the Society of Jesus and closed its colleges (1761-1763). In 1764, the government approved these acts and suppressed the Jesuits in France and its possessions.

157. Antoine Court de Gébelin (1728-1784) renounced the ministry in Lausanne and became a representative of the Protestants in Paris where he fought for the rehabilitation of Calas and Sirven. His *Toulouse Letters* in favor of Protestantism were dated 1763.

158. Louis Phélypeaux, Count de Saint-Florentin and later Duc de La Vrillière (1705-1777) was the queen's chancellor (1743), secretary of state in the royal household (1749), and minister of foreign affairs (1770-1771).

159. The daughter of a French Protestant named Pierre-Paul Sirven (1709-1777) was brought up in a convent. To escape conversion to Catholicism she jumped into a well. Her father was accused of murdering her and fled to Switzerland. Both he and his wife were condemned to death in absentia. Through Voltaire's efforts Sirven was rehabilitated in 1771 by the Parlement of Toulouse.

160. Voltaire himself.

161. César-Gabriel de Choiseul, Duc de Praslin (1712-1785) was a political figure and cousin of the Duc de Choiseul. At the time of Voltaire's letter, he was Secretary of State for Foreign Affairs after having served as ambassador to Vienna.

162. *Emile* had been published in 1762.

163. George Keith (c. 1694-1778), tenth Earl Marshal, was a zealous Jacobite befriended by Frederick the Great.

164. *The Catechism of the Upright Man [Le Catéchisme de l'honnête homme]* written by Voltaire but published anonymously as early as 1758. In his letter of August 25, 1763 to Helvétius (no. 134 in this collection), he attributes the work to "a certain Abbé Durand."

165. On Omer Joly de Fleury and Chaumeix, see n. 125 and n. 98. Gabriel Gauchat (1709-1774) was another French writer hostile to Voltaire and a critic of Helvétius's *De L'Esprit*.

166. Julian the Apostate was Roman emperor from 361 to 363. He forsook Christianity, unsuccessfully attempted to restore paganism, and issued an edict of toleration. Celsus was a Roman philosopher of the second century noted for his hostility to Chris-

tianity. The neoplatonic philosopher Porphyry (233-c. 304) wrote fifteen books in opposition to Christianity which were destroyed in 448.

167. Two orthodox Christian guides written in French, the first by Philippe d'Outreman (Rouen, c. 1630) and the second by André Colinot (Paris, 1721).

168. A fiercely anti-Christian tract by Voltaire (1749) whose authorship he never admitted since it would have placed his life in jeopardy.

169. Jean Meslier (1664-1729) was a country priest who composed a violently anti-Christian tract called *My Will [Mon Testament]*. Fragments of it were published by Voltaire and D'Holbach.

170. Marie Leszczynska, wife of Louis XV.

171. Johan van Oldenbarneveldt (1547-1619) was a Dutch statesman sentenced to death by the specially convened Synod of Dort for his opposition to orthodox Calvinism and his republican attitudes. Although executed for treason in The Hague, Oldenbarneveldt had a highly irregular trial and no incriminating evidence has ever been found against him. John Huss (1369?-1415) was tried as a heretic in Prague and was burned at the stake.

172. Voltaire's *La Pucelle [The Maid]*. On Voltaire's difficulties with this irreverent work see pp. 43 and 174-75.

173. The epicurean Abbé Guillaume Armfrye de Chaulieu (1639-1720) was a poet whom Voltaire frequented in the early years of his career.

174. Voltaire wrote this letter in English. Arthur Hill-Trevor was the first Viscount Dungannon (d. 1771).

175. The elder brother of Jacques Necker, the future director general of French finances. A Swiss mathematician and a former student of d'Alembert, Louis Necker (1730-1804) entered the banking business in Paris in 1762.

176. A procedure by which the king could order the registration of an edict by the *parlement* with or without its consent. Literally the *lit de justice* referred to the throne on which the king sat during a session of the *parlement*.

177. Giulio Cesare Scaligero or Jules-César Scaliger (1484-1558) was an Italian philologist and physician noted for his *Poetics* (1561). Claude de Saumaise (1588-1653) was a French humanist

and philologist who succeeded Scaliger at the University of Leiden.

178. Mme. de Pompadour, the mistress of Louis XV and a patroness of writers and artists of the period, including Voltaire for a time, died on April 15, 1764 at the age of forty-two.

179. The review is of a book of Nathaniel Hooke, *The Roman History from the Building of Rome to the Ruin of the Commonwealth* which appeared in the issue of the *Gazette* for March 28, 1764.

180. Montesquieu.

181. A playwright, scholar and translator of Pindar and Theocritus (1730-1792).

182. A nickname of Voltaire for the French or Parisians, particularly those who were repressive or reactionary.

183. Etienne-Noël Damilaville (1723-1768) was an anonymous contributor to the *Encyclopédie*. As an important government tax official, he was able to provide his friend Voltaire with publications that had been proscribed.

184. Voltaire began work on his *Philosophical Dictionary* in 1752, but the first edition of this important publication appeared only in 1764. It was condemned by the authorities, but characteristically Voltaire denied any responsibility for the work.

185. François-Louis-Claude Marin (1721-1809) was the royal censor and secretary general of the booktrade.

186. Adrien-Michel Blin de Sainmore (1733-1807) was a man of letters who wrote in defense of Voltaire's critique of Corneille in his *Letter on the New Edition of Corneille [Lettre sur la nouvelle édition de Corneille]* (1764).

187. The nickname for d'Alembert.

188. *The Gospel of Reason [L'Evangile de la raison]*, published in 1764, probably by Voltaire, contained a number of heretical works including Meslier's *Will* and Voltaire's tragedy *Saul and David*. Voltaire, of course, denied any knowledge of the work. *The Letters from the Mountain*, attacking both Calvinism and Catholicism, are by Jean-Jacques Rousseau.

189. The original of this letter is in English.

190. Mademoiselle Clairon (1723-1803) was a celebrated actress of the eighteenth century. She appeared with the Comédie Française and starred in Voltaire's tragedies.

191. Dr. Tronchin, Voltaire's physician.

192. Anne Oldfield (1683-1730), a celebrated actress at Drury Lane, was buried in Westminster Abbey.

193. Adrienne Lecouvreur (1692-1730), a famous actress of the Comédie Française, was denied a religious burial.

194. Spallanzani (1729-1799) was an Italian priest, biologist and experimenter in physiology. In a dispute with Needham, he refuted (1765) the theory of the spontaneous generation of Infusoria and other microscopic organisms.

195. Frederick II.

196. A theological work of the Dutch jurist and humanist Hugo Grotius (1583-1645), the full title of which is *De veritate religionis christianae* (1627).

197. Alexandre-Claude-François Houteville (1688-1742), an Oratorian and member of the French Academy, published *The Christian Religion Proven by the Facts [La Religion chrétienne prouvée par les faits]* in Paris (1722).

198. The article on Hobbes was written by Diderot. The *Preliminary Discourse* is d'Alembert's celebrated preface to the *Encyclopédie*.

199. Servan (1737-1807) was a famous magistrate and Advocate General of the Parlement of Grenoble sympathetic to the *Encyclopédie* and the liberal ideas of the *philosophes*.

200. Virgil, *Georgics*, IV, 510: "soothing the rage of the tigers and moving the oaks with his singing."

201. Gilbert Gaulmin translated and edited an anonymous *De vita et morte Mosis* (1629).

202. Words taken from the Mass.

203. Gabriel-François Coyer (1707-1782) was a Jesuit prelate among whose works are *The Merchant Nobility [La Noblesse commerçante]* (1756) and a 176 page volume *On Preaching [De La Prédication]* (1766). The Montmorencys and the Chatillons or Colignys were two celebrated French noble families.

204. *The Philosophy of History* is Voltaire's most complete work on ancient history and a condemnation of the Judaeo-Christian religion. It was later used as an introduction to his universal history, *The Essay on Customs [L'Essai sur les moeurs]*.

205. A pun referring to the Encyclopedist Morellet (see n. 151) whose name is a homonym of the French words *mords-les*:

bite them. Voltaire suggests thereby Morellet's function in the war against fanatics.

206. i.e., against Omer Joly de Fleury (see n. 126).

207. Nicolas Fréret (1688-1749) was a French philologist and Orientalist. The book attributed to him was the *Critical Examination of the Apologists of the Christian Religion [Examen critique des apologistes de la religion chrétienne]* (1766).

208. Robert Covelle's immortality stems from his having been accused of illegitimately siring the child of a woman of Geneva. He admitted intercourse with the woman in question but maintained he could not be sure he was truly the father of the child. The Consistory of Geneva censured Covelle and ordered him to ask divine forgiveness by kneeling. Covelle refused and the case was brought to the Magnificent Council of Geneva. Voltaire was much amused by the affair and satirized it in his *Guerre de Genève ou les Amours de Robert Covelle [The Geneva War or The Loves of Robert Covelle].*

209. Berthier's death referred to here was only literary and occurred in a satirical piece by Voltaire. He actually died in 1782.

210. Jean-François Lefebvre, Chevalier de La Barre (1747-1766) was charged with blasphemy and mutilating a crucifix. He was arrested with three young persons accused of not uncovering their heads before a passing holy procession. His sentence by the tribunal at Abbeville, a city near Amiens, included cutting off his wrist, removing his tongue and burning him at the stake. He appealed to the Parlement of Paris which, in its mercy, ordered him decapitated before being sent to the stake. Voltaire fought in vain for his rehabilitation which was finally decreed only during the Revolution (1793).

211. In Greco-Egyptian mythology, Busiris was a cruel monarch who sacrificed all foreigners entering Egypt.

212. Frederick wrote a foreword to an abridged edition of the Abbé Claude Fleury's *Ecclesiastical History [Abrégé de l'Histoire ecclésiastique]* published in 1766.

213. The massacre of French Protestant leaders in Paris which began on August 24, 1572.

214. Karl Wilhelm Ferdinand, Duke of Brunswick (1735-1806), the German general noted for his exploits in the Seven Years' War.

215. Michel-Paul Gui de Chabanon (1730-1792) was a dramatist and writer on musical subjects. He visited Voltaire at Ferney and corresponded with him on the contemporary literary and musical scene.

216. By Jean-Benjamin de La Borde (d. 1794), a composer and writer who was a favorite of Louis XV.

217. From Boileau's *Satires*, I, 52: "J'appelle un chat un chat et Rolet un fripon" and *Satires*, III, 119: "Aimez-vous la muscade? On en a mis partout."

218. Jean-Baptiste Lully's opera in five acts with libretto by Quinault was presented at the Paris Opera in 1686.

219. Magdelaine-Céleste Fienzal de Frossac, called Mlle. Durancy and Marie-Magdeleine Blouin, called Mlle. Dubois were two actresses of the period.

220. Emmanuel-Félicité de Durfort, Duc de Duras (1715-1789) was a noted courtier of the period with considerable influence at Versailles. As first gentleman of the King's Chamber, he was charged with the superintendency of the royal theaters.

221. A reference to Chabanon's tragedy *Eudoxie*.

222. Voltaire had wanted to keep his satirical poem on the *Guerre de Genève* out of print for fear of arousing strong negative reactions from Geneva. He kept the manuscript under lock and key, but part of the poem was published despite his precautions. It developed that the young critic and writer La Harpe, with encouragement from his niece Mme. Denis, had stolen the work. Voltaire decided it was time for her to leave Ferney which she did at ten o'clock in the morning of March 1, 1768.

Among the persons mentioned in this letter are Jean Mallet, a Marseilles merchant who owned property near Ferney; Charles-Frédéric-Gabriel Christin, a liberal jurist and habitué of Ferney; Antoine Adam, a former Jesuit who served as Voltaire's almoner and chess companion at Ferney; Jean-Louis Wagnière, Voltaire's secretary from 1756 until his death; Mme. Racle, the wife of Voltaire's architect; and Jean-François-René Tabereau, the director of the Lyons post office.

223. Jean-François de La Harpe (1739-1803), the French critic and future author of the monumental *Course on Ancient and Modern Literature [Cours de littérature ancienne et moderne]*.

224. The sculptor Antoine had accused La Harpe of possess-

ing a canto of the *Guerre de Genève,* Voltaire's mock-heroic poem on the religious disputes of Geneva. Joseph-Claude Dorat (1730-1780) was a French poet and imitator of Voltaire satirized in verses of La Harpe that were making the rounds.

225. The former Mlle. Corneille and her husband (see n. 118).

226. Walpole (1717-1797), the English author and son of Sir Robert Walpole, wrote his *Historic Doubts on Richard III* (1768) in an attempt to rehabilitate the character of Richard.

227. *John,* XIV, 28: "because the father is greater than I."

228. *The Castle of Otranto* (1765).

229. A reference to Pierre Gringoire's dramatic trilogy, *The Play of the Prince of Fools [Le Jeu du prince des sots],* staged in Les Halles in 1511.

230. Both plays by Molière.

231. *John,* XIV, 2.

232. Act I, scene 1:

"De son appartement cette porte est prochaine,
Et cette autre conduit dans celui de la Reine."

233. Henrietta of England, called Madame (1644-1670), wife of Philippe of Orleans and sister-in-law of Louis XIV.

234. Jean-François Regnard (1655-1709) was a French comic playwright.

235. Pastoral tales.

236. Augustin Calmet (1672-1757) was a French Biblical scholar.

237. This quotation has not been identified.

238. The final two sentences of this letter were written in English. Coulon de Jumonville (1725-1753) was a French officer killed by the English near the shores of the Ohio River as he was carrying a white flag of truce. His death was considered in France a violation of the law of nations.

239. i.e., in the king's regiment.

240. Virgil, *Aeneid,* VI, 727: "a mind, pervading its limbs, stirs the whole mass and mingles with the vast frame."

241. In his tale *The Spectacles [Les Lunettes].*

242. Jan Swammerdam (1637-1680), was a Dutch naturalist and author of *The Book of Nature* (1737-1738), Bernard Nieuwentijdt (1654-1718), a Dutch mathematician and author of *The Existence of God Demonstrated by the Wonders of Nature,* and Wil-

liam Derham (1657-1735), a British philosopher and theologian and author of *The Artificial Clockmaker* (1696).

243. John Needham (1713-1781) was a British biologist and ecclesiastic whose experiments favored the theory of spontaneous generation.

244. Madame or Mère Gigogne was a stock character in tales and farces of the theater of the fair, representing inexhaustible fertility forever renewing the human species.

245. Virgil, *Eclogues*, III, 93: "a cold snake lurks in the grass."

246. Michel Le Tellier (1643-1719) was a Jesuit born near Vire, a town in Normandy. As court confessor, he urged the decree of the papal bull Unigenitus against the Jansenists and the repression of Protestants. Le Tellier attended Louis XIV at his death.

247. The Chevalier Jacques de Rochefort d'Ally was an habitué of Ferney and a correspondent of Voltaire on contemporary events and thought.

248. In La Fontaine's fable *Le Rat qui s'est retiré du monde* [*The Rat Who Retired from the World*].

249. Aleksandr Petrovich Sumarokov (1718-1777), a Russian dramatist and poet, was director of the first imperial Russian theater from 1756 to 1761.

250. Prince Fedor Alekseevich Kozlovsky (d. 1770), a Russian general and writer, had been charged by Catherine with delivering certain papers to Voltaire at Ferney in 1769.

251. Philippe Quinault (1635-1688) was a French dramatist and author of fourteen opera librettos, including his masterpiece *Armide*, for Lully.

252. A theatrical genre that made its appearance in France in the first half of the eighteenth century and was developed particularly by Nivelle de La Chaussée. The characters in the *comédie larmoyante* were bourgeois and the plays were intended to arouse emotion and pity. Although Voltaire was critical of it, the genre was innovative in France at the time. He himself went along with the new fashion, despite his attacks, by writing *Nanine*.

253. D'Argental had gone to Orangis, in the environs of Paris, to see a performance of Voltaire's tragedy *Les Guèbres* (1769).

254. An expression from Molière's play *George Dandin* (Act I, scene 7) that has become proverbial in French.

255. Antoine Houdar de La Motte (1672-1731) was a French writer, critic and translator of Homer.

256. The Quai des Orfèvres and the Quai des Morfondus: two Parisian quays.

257. In his play *Sémiramis* (1748).

258. "I asked for water, not a storm."

259. Attributed to Virgil: "Thus you bees make honey, but not for yourselves."

260. Suzanne Necker (1739-1794), a French writer, was the wife of Jacques Necker and mother of Mme. de Staël. She conducted a celebrated salon.

261. Jean-Baptiste Pigalle (1714-1785), the French sculptor.

262. Until the Revolution, Gex was an independent jurisdiction in France, near Geneva, and situated between the Alps and the Jura.

263. Sir William Jones (1746-1794) was an English philologist and jurist. This letter was written in English.

264. i.e., the new style calendar.

265. Events of the Russo-Turkish War (1768-1774) which ended with the Treaty of Kuchuk Kainarji making Russia the dominant power in the Middle East.

266. Ali-Bey (1728-1773) was a famous Mameluke and one of the beys who governed Egypt. He succeeded in making himself virtual ruler of Egypt.

267. The name used for the Peloponnesus from the Middle Ages until relatively recently. During the Turko-Venetian Wars, which lasted from the fifteenth century until 1718, Venice held parts of Morea at various times and the entire peninsula from 1687 to 1715.

268. i.e., the Sultan of Turkey.

269. Thomyris was queen of the Massagetes, a Scythian people that inhabited the eastern shores of the Caspian Sea. Voltaire used the name in referring to Catherine.

270. A physiocratic journal.

271. Edmund Waller (1606-1687) was an English poet and Saint-Evremond (1616?-1703) a French writer and critic. But the anecdote does not seem to make much sense since Waller died before Saint-Evremond.

272. Jean-Baptiste Josserand, Jean Lécuyer and his wife were sentenced on September 24, 1768, the two males to branding and the woman to five years of detention for selling three works: Joseph Gaspard Dubois-Fontenelle's *Ericie ou la vestale*, D'Holbach's *Christianity Unmasked [Le Christianisme dévoilé]*, and Voltaire's *The Man of Forty Crowns [L'Homme aux quarante écus]*. Messieurs were the Jansenists.

273. Jean-Louis de Nogaret de La Valette, Duc d'Epernon (1554-1642), an unpopular French general who served under Henry III and Henry IV and ended his career in disgrace.

274. Henri Gaillard (1726-1806), an historian, had just been elected to the French Academy.

275. Richelieu's daughter.

276. Chesterfield (1694-1773) was an English statesman and author whose literary reputation is based on his letters to his illegitimate son, Philip Stanhope, and those to his grandson.

277. i.e., Francis Hastings, the tenth Earl of Huntingdon whom Chesterfield had introduced to Voltaire.

278. The Italian dramatist (1707-1793). The play referred to in this letter is Goldoni's *Le Bourru bienfaisant [The Beneficent Bear]* which he wrote in French for the wedding of Louis XVI and Marie-Antoinette.

279. By the Peace of Prut (1711), Peter I restored Azov to the Turks.

280. Charles-Joseph Panckoucke (1736-1798), a Parisian publisher and an owner of the *Mercure de France*, planned to issue an edition of Voltaire's complete works. The project was finalized after Voltaire's death, however, by a group led by Beaumarchais with the publication of the so-called Kehl edition of Voltaire's works in seventy octavo volumes.

281. Fénelon.

282. Adrien-Maurice de Noailles (1678-1766), a commander in chief of the French army.

283. All plays by Corneille.

284. Charles Pinot Duclos (1704-1772), a moralist, novelist, and member of the French Academy.

285. From Quinault's *Atys* (Act I, scene 6): "Qui n'a plus qu'un moment à vivre/ N'a plus rien à dissimuler."

286. Slightly altered from Corneille's *Pompée* (Act V, scene

1).

287. In his *Henriade*, II, 5.

288. A tragedy by Voltaire (1773).

289. A dramatist, novelist, and member of the French Academy (1723-1799).

290. Henri de La Tour D'Auvergne, Vicomte de Turenne (1611-1675), the great French general.

291. Jean-Jacques-François-Marin Boisard (1744-1833), the author of light verse and of several collections of fables.

292. Dmitry Alekseevich Gallitzin (1738-1803) was Russian ambassador to The Hague and later to Paris where he became acquainted with Voltaire and Diderot.

293. *The Treatise on Man [De L'Homme]*.

294. Meletus and Anytus were among the accusers of Socrates.

295. A Christian apologist of the second century.

296. Cf. *Matthew*, XVIII, 17: "And if he shall neglect to hear them, tell it unto the church but if he neglect to hear the church, let him be unto thee as an heathen man and a publican."

297. Cf. *Matthew*, XXII, 11-13. In ancient Rome, an architricline directed the slaves who served meals and generally presided over the arrangement of repasts.

298. The reference is to *Acts*, V, 1-10.

299. Baron Friedrich Melchior Grimm (1723-1807) was a German writer and critic who had a well-known liaison with Mme. d'Epinay. He was editor of the *Correspondance littéraire*, a periodical important for the understanding of French thought in the Enlightenment.

300. Piotr Alexandrovitch Rumyantsev (1725-1796) was a Russian general who distinguished himself in the Seven Years' War. His son Nicolai Petrovitch (1754-1826) was a Russian statesman imbued with Western liberal ideas.

301. Louis XVI became King of France on May 10, 1774 at the age of twenty.

302. Abbé Nicolas Baudeau (1730-1792) was the founder of the *Ephémérides du citoyen*, a periodical which at first opposed Quesnay's physiocratic ideas and then adopted them. Baudeau was a strong supporter of Turgot when the latter came into office in 1774.

303. A financial official in Turgot's ministry.

304. A variable measure of capacity in the *ancien régime*. A *setier* in Paris was equivalent to 156 liters of wheat.

305. On Crébillon, see chapter II, n. 230. Alexis Piron (1689-1773) was a minor poet and playwright from Dijon.

306. Necker's *On the Legislation and Commerce of Grains [Sur la législation et le commerce des grains]*.

307. The edict decreed free trade in grains.

308. Henri Louis Cain, called Lekain (1729-1778) and Jean Rival, called Aufresne (1720-1806) were two celebrated Parisian actors. Both men also performed for Voltaire at Ferney.

309. Plutarch, *Aemilius Paulus*, xviii.

310. Dominique Gaillard d'Etallonde (1749-1788) was a French officer sought as an accomplice of the Chevalier de La Barre. He fled France but was sentenced in absentia to have his right hand cut off, his tongue torn out, and to be burned alive. He joined the Prussian army under the name Morival and Voltaire prevailed upon Frederick to make him an officer. He subsequently became Frederick's aide de camp.

311. The Abbé Ferdinando Galiani (1728-1787) was an Italian diplomat and economist associated with the French Encyclopedists. He was a familiar figure in Parisian salons while he was secretary of the embassy of the King of Naples.

312. Freiherr Karl Ludwig von Pöllnitz (1692-1775) was a German adventurer and writer, and a favorite of Frederick the Great. Pöllnitz died in Berlin on June 23, 1775.

313. Turgot had been relieved of his duties on May 12.

314. Philippe-Antoine de Claris, Marquis de Florian was the second husband of Voltaire's younger niece Marie Elisabeth. She died in 1771 and Florian remarried three years later.

315. Rumors of Rousseau's death circulated in Paris after he had been knocked down by a dog and fainted in October. He actually died in Paris on July 3, 1778, a few weeks after Voltaire.

316. Jean-Baptiste-Claude Isoard Delisle de Sales (1743-1816) was a *philosophe* and author of the *Philosophy of Nature [La Philosophie de la nature]*. Delisle was condemned for an edition of the work published in 1774. Following an appeal to the *parlement*, the sentence was overturned in 1777.

317. The philosopher and mathematician Condorcet (1743-

1794) published an edition of Pascal's *Pensées* in 1776 which was reprinted in 1778 with a commentary by Voltaire.

318. Voltaire used the nickname of Bertrand for d'Alembert and that of Raton for himself.

319. i.e., Charles-Juste de Beauvau, Prince de Beauvau-Craon, a tolerant former governor of Languedoc.

320. The conqueror of Minorca was Richelieu.

321. Thomas, Baron de Tollendal, Comte de Lally (1702-1766) was a French officer who capitulated at Pondichéry in 1761. He was considered responsible for the French defeat there and was condemned to death. Voltaire initiated a campaign for the rehabilitation of Lally in 1773, but this was only finally possible in 1778.

322. Charles-Michel, Marquis Duplessis-Villette (1736-1793) lodged Voltaire during his final stay in Paris in his house on the Rue de Beaune.

323. i.e., Benjamin Franklin.

323. Based on *Deuteronomy*, VIII, 3 and *Matthew*, IV, 4. "*He has not perished.* I forego bread. Man does not live by bread alone, but by every word that proceedeth out of the mouth of Tronchin doth man live."

325. Lally's son. See n. 321. The news referred to in this letter is the repeal of Lally's condemnation.

326. This is the last extant letter of Voltaire. He died in Paris, the city of his birth, four days later on May 30, 1778.

INDEX

Lebrun, Charles, 82, 83, 194
Le Cat, Claude-Nicolas, 87
Le Chambrier, baron Jean, 60
Lecouvreur, Adrienne, 8, 257
Le Fort, François, 186
Lefranc de Pompignan, Jean-Jacques, marquis, 211, 215, 220, 222
Le Grand, Marc-Antoine, 16
Leibniz, Gottfried Wilhelm, 54, 57, 71, 75, 89, 92, 94, 183
Leipzig, 169
Lekain, Henri Louis Cain, *called*, 179, 304
Lelex, 306
Le Normant de Tournehem, Charles-François, 120
Leo X, pope, 81, 241, 242, 258, 278
Leonardo da Vinci, 103
Lepidus, Marcus Aemilius, 180
Leseau, Mme de, 16, 17
Le Sueur, Eustache, 82
Le Tellier, Michel, 278
Lettres philosophiques, 24, 34, 46
Leucippus, 72
Lille, 104, 111, 115, 127, 222
Limiers, Henri-Philippe de, 69
Limoges, 302
Linant, abbé Michel, 45
Lisbon, 175, 181
Livry, Suzanne de, 6
Livy, 252
Locke, John, 29, 33, 51, 57, 60, 62, 75, 92, 94, 96, 103, 165, 184, 272, 280, 299
London, 20, 23, 25, 26, 27, 29, 81, 108, 119, 130, 131, 132, 135
Lorraine, 43, 106, 118, 129, 222
Louis XIII, king of France, 134
Louis XIV, king of France, 44, 46, 68, 69, 81, 82, 83, 118, 133, 134, 157, 161, 166, 172, 253, 257, 268, 271, 273, 291, 301, 302
Louis XV, king of France, 18, 69, 118, 158, 168, 220, 291
Louis XVI, king of France, 301
Louisiana, 66
Louis-Le-Grand, collège, 3, 62
Louvre, 136
Lovelace, 205
Luçon, bishop of. *See* Bussy, comte de
Lucretius, 180, 210, 250, 251, 277
Luis I, king of Spain, 15
Luke, saint, 34

Lully, Jean-Baptiste, 53, 82, 83
Lunéville, 43, 45, 118, 125, 129, 136, 137
Lutrin, Le, 25
Luxembourg, Mme de, 163
Lyons, 132, 198, 271
Lyttleton, sir George, 158

Mabillon, Jean, 173
Machault d'Arnouville, Jean-Baptiste, 131
Machaut, Louis-Charles de, 7
Machiavelli, Niccolò, 85, 98, 99
Madrid, 132
Maecenas, 68
Magdeburg, 210
Mahomet, 77, 100, 115
Mairan, Jean-Jacques Dortous de, 33, 54, 55, 60, 77, 89
Maisons, Jean-René de Longueil, marquis de, 11, 14, 15
Malebranche, Nicolas de, 71, 75, 96, 181
Malesherbes, Guillaume de Lamoignon de, 192
Mansard, François, 82
Marchetti, Alessandro, 119
Marcus Aurelius, 84, 86, 272, 305
Mariamne, 8, 11, 16, 17, 19, 21
Marie Leszczynska, queen of France, 18, 128
Marin, François-Louis-Claude, 254
Mariotte, Edme, 88
Marius, Caius, 180
Marivaux, Pierre de Chamblain de, 52, 53
Mark, saint, 34
Marlborough, John Churchill, first duke of, 129
Marmara, Sea of, 80
Marmontel, Jean-François, 117, 270, 297
Marot, Clément, 180, 247
Marseilles, 27, 247, 288
Mascaron, Jules de, 46, 82
Massillon, Jean-Baptiste, 82
Maupertuis, Pierre-Louis Moreau de, 33, 77, 84, 95, 158, 171, 207, 277
Maurepas, Jean-Frédéric Phélypeaux, comte de, 22, 129
Maximilian II, elector of Bavaria, 97
Mazarin, Giulio Mazarini, *called*, cardinal, 220, 258
Médecin malgré lui, Le, 19
Memnon, 118

345

347

Tahmasp Quli Khan, 181
Tasso, Torquato, 31, 119, 172, 179, 282
Templars, 3
Tencin, Pierre Guérin, cardinal de, 120, 203, 219
Tertullian, 173, 300
Théodore, vierge et martyre, 206
Thieriot, Nicolas-Claude, 8, 10, 14, 18, 20, 22, 23, 25, 26, 45, 59, 177, 197, 204, 230, 249
Thomson, James, 158, 159
Thomyris, 289
Titian, Tiziano Vecelli, *called*, 103
Titus, 86
Toulon, 291
Toulouse, 117, 200, 233, 236, 237, 261
Tournay, 197, 200, 207, 210, 218, 264
Tournemine, René-Joseph, 4, 5, 47, 62, 74
Traité de Dieu, de l'âme et du monde, 58
Trajan, 86
Trebizond, 288
Trent, Council of, 242
Tressan, Louis-Elisabeth de la Vergne, comte de, 121
Trissino, Gian Giorgio, 258
Tronchin, Jean-Robert, 181, 185, 190
Tronchin, Théodore, 184, 207, 231, 256, 257, 311, 312
Troyes, 125
Trublet, Nicolas-Charles-Joseph, 219
Turenne, Henri de la Tour d'Auvergne, vicomte de, 46, 290
Turgot, Anne-Robert-Jacques, 302, 303, 304, 306, 307
Turkey, 27, 80, 223

Ukraine, 78
Ussé, 8, 10
Utrecht, Peace of, 203
Uzès, Charles-Emmanuel de Crussol, duc d', 163

Vadé, Jean-Joseph, 209
Vaines, Jean de, 303, 306
Valory, abbé Paul-Frédéric-Charles de, 115
Van Robais, Josse, 83

Vassy, 52, 54, 61
Vaud, 186
Vauvenargues, Luc de Clapiers, marquis de, 102, 113, 276
Vega Carpio, Felix de, 272
Veii, 250
Vergil. *See* Virgil
Vernes, Jacob, 199, 236, 237
Vernet, Jacob, 30, 100, 111, 191, 264, 266
Veronese, Paolo, 103
Versailles, 16, 22, 43, 113, 117, 118, 121, 190, 208, 269, 282
Versoix, 271, 286
Vienna, 119, 132, 190
Villars, Claude-Louis-Hector, duc de, 27, 47
Villette, Mme de. *See* Bolingbroke, viscountess
Villevieille, Jean-François Dufour, seigneur de, 232, 276
Vincennes, 186
Vire, 278
Virgil, 10, 31, 180, 206, 276, 282
Voiture, Vincent, 103
Vosges, 173

Wade, Ira, 43
Wagnière, Jean-Louis, 270
Walachia, 289
Waller, Edmund, 271, 290
Walpole, Horace, 271, 275
Wandsworth, 80, 98, 130
Warburton, William, 228
Wesel, 305
Westminster, 257
Westphalia, Treaty of, 222
Whitehall, 23
Willars. *See* Villars
Wolff, Johann Christian, 57, 58, 75, 84, 89, 92, 95, 96
Woolston, Thomas, 240
Württemberg, Charles Eugene, duke of, 166, 202

Yuste, San Jerónimo de, 207

Zadig, 118
Zaïre, 24, 28